"*The Bonus Army* is a terrific book. Exhaustively researched but simply written, it holds the reader's attention from beginning to end. I personally remember the momentous events of the July day in 1932, but before reading this account I had no idea of the drama, the pathos, the confusion, and the lasting importance of the event. Highly recommended for any reader who seeks a rounded knowledge of America of the twentieth century."—John S. D. Eisenhower

"A model of clear-eyed history. The book never flinches, though you will. And, here and there, readers may speculate as to today's military, its eventual return from the Middle East, and its response to the riches that some U.S. civilians have meanwhile amassed."—James H. Bready, *Baltimore Sun*

"So well researched and historically accurate that this reader was only left with a sense of disgust in my gut and a renewed resolve to fight for the just respect the American veteran has earned . . . Read this book."—*Veterans Journal*

"A tragic yet enormously important chapter in the making of 20th-century America, beautifully and brilliantly told by Dickson and Allen. The GI Bill lifted ten million veterans into the middle class through vocational rehabilitation, low-cost home mortgages, college tuition, and living expenses. Without the Bonus Army tragedy, there never would have been a GI Bill. You cannot fully understand contemporary America unless you understand the Bonus Army."—Mark Shields

"In *The Bonus Army*, authors Paul Dickson and Thomas B. Allen provide an astonishing, and largely forgotten, account of how our veterans, fueled by desperation and determination, anger and honor, overcame political obstacles and tactics as formidable as those they had faced on the battlefield. This is must reading, not only for today's political leaders, but for all Americans who understand the need to fight for the fair treatment of those we ask to carry the fight for freedom."—William S. Cohen, former Secretary of Defense

"Meticulously researched and engagingly written, *The Bonus Army* captures the pathos and high emotion that this under-appreciated episode in American history generated in 1932. As the nation prepares to welcome home another generation of wartime veterans, it offers a cautionary and instructional tale about the permanent bond that modern military service creates between veterans and the state."—Jennifer D. Keene, author of *Doughboys, the Great War, and the Remaking of America*

"In the current era of rights and entitlements, the back story to the saga of the Bonus Army—the federal government refusing to pay its citizens what it owes them—is hard to fathom . . . In *The Bonus Army*, Paul Dickson and Thomas B. Allen tell the whole story, all the way to its legacy, the GI bill enacted for veterans of World War II."—*Washington Post*

"This thoroughly researched and eminently readable book is one that every veteran, indeed, every American should read . . . Mr. Dickson and Mr. Allen have done a fine job of reminding Americans of the almost forgotten fight a relatively few of them made to finally shame the Congress into paying what in effect was a mere pittance in return for the sacrifices they had made during the Great War."—Lyn Nofziger, *Washington Times*

"A timely reminder of society's obligations to returned soldiers."—Roger K. Miller, *Denver Post*

"The authors argue that this is one of the pivotal events of 20th-century U.S. history, and they make a good case . . . The benefits veterans have today express a stronger appreciation of service. This book is a reminder that they also have another purpose, which is to ensure nothing like this ever happens again."—Bruce Ramsey, *Seattle Times*

"Extensively researched and documented, *The Bonus Army* provides a valuable historical record as well as a timely look at how this nation has treated its veterans." —Jewel Lansing, *Portland Oregonian*

"By a far stretch the best-written account of the Bonus Expeditionary Force and the first scholarly attempt in nearly two decades. The authors, both experienced history writers, debunk many of the old myths and shine new light on this astonishing episode . . . In telling the story of *The Bonus Army*, in a gripping style packed with facts, Dickson and Allen do great honor to all veterans—and remind us that one of our most important battles was fought with blood and fire at the steps of our own government."—Joel Turnipseed, *Minneapolis Star Tribune*

"Dramatic . . . *The Bonus Army* is more than a story of a group of strong and determined veterans. It is also a history of World War I and the economic depression that led thousands of men and women to march on the nation's capital."—*Daily Oklahoman*

"The Bonus Army has long been a topic of scholarly interest, but this is the most complete story we have of the movement and its aftermath . . . An excellent book." —*American Scholar*

"An impressive, important, and extremely well researched account of what happened when the U.S. reneged on its pledge."—Murray Polner, *History News Network*

"Dickson and Allen have done some great research and are superb storytellers. They expand beyond the dimensions of a conventional history, telling the stories of veterans in the camps, the leaders of government and the local resident . . . This highly readable book covers the event in fine detail. It serves as a great civics lesson on how countries should and should not treat those who serve in uniform."—Kevin M. Hymel, *Army Magazine*

"Dickson and Allen have written a thoroughly researched and spirited narrative. They have done yeoman work in mining the relevant archives, and their interviews with many of the surviving witnesses add new testimony to the record of the March . . . The Bonus Army has received much less attention than it deserves. But, with their readable and exhaustive account, Dickson and Allen have gone a long way toward remedying that situation."—Tom Miller, Military.com

"In describing the use of tanks, bayonets and tear gas to expel the unarmed vets and their families from Washington—as well as the deadly mistreatment of BEF members in government work camps after the march—Dickson and Allen highlight the sacrifices these women and men made on our own soil to win fair treatment for veterans of future wars. Their important and moving work will appeal to both professional historians and casual readers interested in the history of America's changing attitudes towards its soldiers."—*Publishers Weekly*

"Dickson and Allen, who have written numerous books of American history, assert that the long-range importance of the Bonus Army has been grossly underestimated. In this agreeably written and often moving account, they describe a unique gathering of whites, blacks, and urban and rural poor united by a vision of social justice. This is an important reexamination of a still controversial event."—*Booklist*

"Here a demonstrator is clubbed and tear-gassed, but there real reforms are won: thus unfolds this memorable story of a now-forgotten episode in 20th-century history . . . The lesson the New Deal government took home: avoid ticking off discontented veterans, whence the GI Bill. A lively, engaging work of history."—*Kirkus Reviews*

Selected Books by Paul Dickson

Think Tanks

The Future of the Workplace

The Electronic Battlefield

The Future File: A Guide for People with One Foot in the Twenty-first Century

The Official Rules

The Library in America

On This Spot: Pinpointing the Past in Washington, D.C.
    (with Douglas E. Evelyn)

Baseball: The President's Game (with William B. Mead)

The Congress Dictionary: The Ways and Meanings of Capitol Hill
    (with Paul Clancy)

War Slang

Sputnik: The Shock of the Century

The Hidden Language of Baseball

Selected Books by Thomas B. Allen

George Washington, Spymaster

Why Truman Dropped the Atomic Bomb on Japan (with Norman Polmar)

Remember Pearl Harbor

World War II: America at War, 1941–1945 (with Norman Polmar)

Spy Book: The Encyclopedia of Espionage (with Norman Polmar)

The Blue and the Gray

Merchants of Treason (with Norman Polmar)

War Games

Rickover: Controversy and Genius (with Norman Polmar)

America from Space

Paul Dickson and
Thomas B. Allen

Walker & Company, New York

The Bonus Army

An American Epic

*To Nancy Dickson and Scottie Allen for
their total support and belief in this book.*

All papers used by Walker & Company are natural, recyclable products made from
wood grown in well-managed forests. The manufacturing processes conform to the
environmental regulations of the country of origin.

Library of Congress Cataloging-in-Publication Data available on request

Paperback ISBN-10: 0-8027-7738-4
ISBN-13: 978-0-8027-7738-6

First published in 2004 by Walker & Company
This paperback edition published by Walker in 2006

Book design by Ralph L. Fowler

The large photograph appearing on page vi is courtesy of Underwood & Underwood/
Library of Congress; the highlighted photograph on page vii is from the authors' collection.

Visit Walker & Company's Web site at www.walkerbooks.com

Printed in the United States of America by Quad/Graphics Fairfield

4 6 8 10 9 7 5

History is littered with governments destabilized by masses of veterans who believed that they had been taken for fools by a society that grew rich and fat at the expense of their hardship and suffering.

—Anthony J. Principi, U.S. Secretary of Veterans Affairs,
   alluding to the Bonus Army in a March 14, 2001,
   speech to the Smithsonian's Wilson Library on
   "Veterans as Revolutionaries"

Contents

The Bonus Army

Prologue

O NE NIGHT toward the end of May 1932, Pelham Glassford, the police chief of Washington, D.C., was driving south from New York City through New Jersey when suddenly in his headlights appeared what he later described as "a bedraggled group of seventy-five or one hundred men marching cheerily along, singing and waving at the passing traffic." One man carried an American flag and another a banner that read, "Bonus or a Job." Atop a pushcart, an infant girl lay sleeping, nestled amid one family's clothes. Glassford pulled over.

He later wrote that the group cheered upon seeing his District of Columbia license tags. "And when I stopped, they gathered around with many questions on their possible reception, on the road they should take." They asked him to join them. He declined and they handed him a leaflet entitled *Don't Let the Bankers Fool You*. A marcher urged him to give a copy to President Herbert Hoover.

For the previous several days, newspapers across the nation had been carrying accounts of marchers bound for the nation's capital. The demonstrators were part of a growing army of veterans and their families heading to Washington from across the country to collect payment of the "bonus," promised in 1924 to soldiers who had served in the Great War, but deferred until 1945 because of wrangling over the federal budget. Now, deep in the Depression, the vets had dubbed the delayed payment the Tombstone Bonus, for the only way to get the cash before 1945 was to die, in which case the payment would be made to the next of kin as a death benefit.

In 1932, a year in which unemployment had soared to almost 25 percent, leaving roughly one family out of every four without a breadwinner, two million people wandered the country in a futile quest for work. But unlike most of the men, women, and children on the move, the veterans knew where they were going and why they were going there. Washington was a goal, a place to stay while they lobbied Congress for immediate payment of their bonus.[1]

Glassford, who had become the U.S. Army's youngest field grade brigadier general in 1918 during the Great War, had been police chief for only six months. Hired to put a professional shine on a police force tarnished by corruption and the lawlessness fostered by Prohibition, he had already twice dealt with angry demonstrators—in the Communist-led Hunger March in December 1931 and, a month later, during a march against unemployment by about ten thousand jobless men and women led by a Pittsburgh priest.[2] But the veterans' march was different. They were going to Washington to lobby for what they—and many in Congress—felt was their due.

Victorious war veterans have vexed politicians since the days of Caesar's legions. Returning warriors were both a potential power bloc and a threat—men who marched off to serve the state in war and then straggled back in peacetime, brewing discontent and looking for rewards. The Romans established the *Aerarium Militare,* the first veterans' bureau, to deal with the ex-soldiers who demanded pensions and balm for their wounds.

In Elizabethan times, discharged soldiers and sailors became beggars and highwaymen. London ironically invoked martial law to cope with the warrior mobs. A royal proclamation threatened summary executions for "mariners, soldiers, and masterless men" who did not leave London immediately.[3]

In colonial America's earliest days, recognition was given to wounded soldiers. In a proclamation of 1636, the leaders of the Plymouth Colony of Massachusetts declared, "If any person shall be sent forth as a soldier and shall return maimed he shall be maintained competently by the Colony during his life." Early in the Revolutionary War, the Continental Congress provided pensions for both disabled veterans and the dependents of soldiers killed in battle. The last surviving dependent of the Revolutionary War continued to receive benefits until 1911.

But what of the men who return whole? Even as noble a cause as the American Revolution ended with a disgruntled army, menacing the politicians.

After the British surrendered at Yorktown in 1781, rumors spread throughout the ranks that the Continental Army would be demobilized without being paid. In June 1783, a small band of soldiers from the unit known as the Pennsylvania Line marched on the capital of the new nation in Philadelphia, demanding the back pay owed to them. They surrounded the State House and poked their bayonet-tipped muskets through the windows at the assembled Congress, which included such members as James Madison and Alexander Hamilton. When the governor of Pennsylvania, who was in attendance, was asked to call for his militia, he said he would not be able to protect Congress because he could not count on his militia to follow his orders. Fearing a coup d'état, Congress "quit the building," pushed through the jeering armed mob, and headed to Princeton, New Jersey.

For weeks the soldiers held their ground. They grew into a mutinous mob of four hundred, making daily demands on the government and terrorizing the citizens of Philadelphia. Finally, after weeks of the renegade soldiers' daily demonstrations and threats, George Washington sent a force of fifteen hundred Continental soldiers to compel the men to return to their homes. Two of the leaders of the mutiny were sentenced to be shot, led out to be executed, and faced a line of soldiers with loaded guns. At the last minute they were pardoned by Congress. Other leaders were whipped before being released.

The Revolutionary War mutinies were not about power or ideology but simply about being paid for services rendered. They would establish what became a social contract between the nation and those who fight its battles: when a war ends, members of the military must be paid in full for their service. Although most Revolutionary War veterans were not paid for years, most eventually got back pay and pensions.[4]

The mutiny had another consequence. During the Revolutionary War, Congress had retreated three times from Philadelphia—first to Baltimore, then to Lancaster, and then to York—to avoid capture by the British. But Congress had always returned to Philadelphia. After the 1783 mutiny and the humiliating departure, the members vowed never to return. They stayed at Princeton until the end of the year, then moved to Annapolis, followed by Trenton, and finally to New York.

When the Constitutional Convention met in 1787, memories of 1783 were still so fresh in the delegates' minds that they wrote a provision into the Constitution, providing for a new kind of capital—a federal enclave, which would become Washington, D.C., by the turn of the century.

Just as mutinous veterans of the Revolution had had enough power to move the capital, veterans of the Great War, by marching on that capital in

1932, were able to move the nation to a new social contract that is still valid today.

From the end of the Revolution to the return of the first American troops from Europe in 1918, the issue of compensation for veterans had frequently confronted Congress. When the Civil War began in 1861, there were about eighty thousand pensioners whose service dated back as far as the War of 1812. By the end of the Civil War in 1865, nearly 2 million veterans were collecting pensions.[5] Veterans, who made up about 5 percent of the population, became a powerful voting bloc. They showed that power by forming America's first veterans' organization, the Grand Army of the Republic. Five presidents were GAR members, as were most northern governors. Membership in the GAR was practically a requirement for election to any public office in the North. Thanks primarily to the GAR, at the height of its power in the 1870s more than one-fifth of the national budget went toward veteran pensions. America evaded the problem of disgruntled veterans by paying relatively generous pensions—and by expanding westward, creating jobs for homecoming veterans of North and South.

When World War I began in 1914, there were still more than four hundred thousand Civil War veterans collecting pensions, along with tens of thousands of men who had fought in the Spanish-American War. Although the original intention of pension legislation was to provide for the wounded and their survivors, by 1914 the overwhelming majority of pensioned veterans had left the Army, Marines, or Navy intact in mind and body. But as the power of the GAR waned, so did congressional sympathy toward able-bodied veterans. The war in Europe inspired interest in another kind of benefit: insurance. In 1914 Congress passed the War Risk Insurance Act, which provided government insurance to American ships running the German submarine gauntlet to carry war supplies to Europe. American politicians and corporate executives believed that this would be the extent of America's participation in a strictly European war.

In 1917, however, America was drawn into the war, and President Woodrow Wilson endorsed war-risk life insurance for American soldiers and sailors who voluntarily signed up and paid the premiums through deductions from their pay. Congress authorized the plan with a unanimous vote. Wilson and the Congress wrongly believed that there would be no demand for postwar compensation to those who were not injured during their service.

The Doughboys who came home carried a palpable sense that they had been left behind and deserved some kind of financial compensation for their service beyond the mere dollar-a-day base pay they had received. Their demands reached Congress through successors to the GAR: the American Legion and Veterans of Foreign Wars. Year after year, Congress debated, always holding out the promise of reward. Finally, in 1924, six years after the Armistice that ended the Great War, Congress enacted a law that granted Great War veterans "adjusted universal compensation," which became known as the bonus. The legislation was passed over the veto of President Calvin Coolidge, who declared, "We owe no bonus to able-bodied veterans of the World War." The law would give any veteran who served during the war compensation at the rate of a dollar a day for domestic service, and an extra twenty-five cents for each day spent overseas. Those entitled to fifty dollars or less were paid immediately; the rest were to receive certificates that could not be redeemed until 1945.

Although there were periodic calls for speeding up payments, nothing happened until May 1929, five months before the stock market's Black Tuesday, when the Dow Jones Industrial Average plunged by 12.9 percent, beginning the great stock market crash and foreshadowing the Great Depression. Freshman representative Wright Patman, a Texas Democrat and a veteran, cosponsored a bill calling for immediate cash payment of the bonus, which Patman called "an honest debt." The bill never made it out of committee.

Under Patman's leadership, further attempts to get the bonus paid failed; the nation slipped deeper and deeper into economic and spiritual despair as many of the millions of the homeless settled in communities of makeshift shacks called "Hoovervilles" after the president they blamed for their plight.

The bonus impasse went on until March 15, 1932, when a jobless ex-sergeant, Walter W. Waters, stood up at a veterans' meeting in Portland, Oregon. He proposed that every man present hop a freight and head for Washington to get the money that was rightfully theirs. He got no takers that night, but pressed on with his idea for a march, bending the ear of every veteran he could find. Finally, on May 11, when a new version of the Patman bill was shelved in the House, some 250 veterans, with only thirty dollars among them, rallied behind a banner reading "Portland Bonus March—On to Washington" and trekked to Portland's Union Pacific freight yards. A few hours later, a freight train emptied of livestock but still reeking of cow manure stopped to board some three hundred men. They called themselves the Bonus Expeditionary Force (BEF), a play on American Expeditionary Force, the collective name for the troops sent to France. They became known as the Bonus Army.

Some people saw them simply as men of the Great Depression, homeless, hopeless, and looking for cash. But for many who had fought in the war, these were their comrades, the Yanks of France, the Doughboys who had been "Over There." These were men who had lived in the trenches and, when the order came, had gone over the top.

Waters became a symbol for the individual who, in seeking redress for a grievance, changes the course of history. Among those he inspired was a thin, battered man named Joe Angelo of Camden, New Jersey. As he made his way to Washington, Angelo carried his Distinguished Service Cross, won for valor in the trenches of France. Another was Sewilla LaMar, a black woman who had lost both her first husband and her brother in the war; she walked and rode boxcars from Los Angeles to Washington to fight for the bonus.

The events in Washington in the summer of 1932 involved men who would become three of the most famous American generals of the twentieth century, acting in roles largely forgotten today. On Douglas A. MacArthur, George S. Patton, and Dwight D. Eisenhower would fall the duty of obeying commander in chief Herbert Hoover, who ordered the expulsion of the Bonus Army from Washington. At the foot of Capitol Hill were tanks, bayonets, and tear gas. Two veterans were killed by a policeman who was murdered less than a month later. Soldiers put to the torch the sprawling main Bonus Army camp. The veterans and their families began a forced exodus.

Most accounts of the Bonus Army end with newsreel coverage of veterans marching off into obscurity. But this is not how it played out in real life. What lay ahead for many of the veterans were futile returns to New Deal Washington, dollar-a-day labor in remote federal work camps, and a hurricane unlike any ever recorded in the United States. Wind gusts estimated at two hundred miles an hour slammed into work camps in Florida's upper Keys, turning granules of sand into tiny missiles that blasted flesh from human faces. The storm brought death to at least 259 veterans. The final indignity was mass cremation.

In many ways the legacy of the Bonus Army is still being felt. Harry Specter, who had been wounded in the Argonne, had too little money to leave Wichita, Kansas, and march to Washington. He also had a wife and four children to provide for. The youngest child was two-year-old Arlen, who as a U.S. senator from Pennsylvania said much later, "In a figurative sense I have been on my way to Washington ever since to collect my father's bonus—to push the government to treat its citizens, the millions of hardworking Harry Specters, justly."[6]

How could this all be forgotten? This question dogged us at the outset of this project. Early in our research we obtained a copy of a thesis written in.1994 by Cielo Marie Dorado Lutino, a young scholar who examined the Bonus Army in the context of the American memory and in the pages of textbooks and twentieth-century histories. "Why," she asked, "had historians seen the Bonus March as an insignificant event?" Why had they ignored the impact of the largest and most sustained public demonstration of the Great Depression? Her conclusion was that the Bonus Army had been looked upon narrowly as an incident leading to the defeat of Herbert Hoover, rather than as a major historic event and a catalyst for social change.[7]

Following her lead, we tracked that change and discovered an odyssey that began in Portland in 1932, wove through the Great Depression and into World War II, and returned finally to Washington, where in June 1944 President Franklin D. Roosevelt signed into law the GI Bill.

We concluded that a combination of factors conspired to keep the Bonus Army from America's collective consciousness. Racism was one. The American Expeditionary Force had been segregated—America's 404,000 black soldiers, barred from all-white units, had fought under a French flag. But the Bonus Expeditionary Force was integrated. Veterans of both races marched together in the Bonus Army and lived together in Washington in integrated camps. Roy Wilkins, a young writer for the NAACP magazine, the *Crisis,* saw the BEF as a model for an integrated America.

Another reason for marginalizing the Bonus Army is that so many, even today, have been willing to dismiss the whole movement as a radical one, a function of Communist organizers. This erroneous belief was supported by covert work of a federal national intelligence apparatus that kept the Bonus Army under constant surveillance for dangerous radicals. Informants, sometimes using coded radio messages, passed along the names of suspected subversives to military leaders who feared armed rebellion. Undercover operatives ferreted out "plots" from both the left and the right. The key subversive hunter was General MacArthur's "most trusted subordinate," Brigadier General George Van Horn Moseley, who, from his post in the U.S. Army's Military Intelligence Division, saw in the integration of black and white veterans living proof that "Negro and Jewish" Communists were planning a revolution. Working with Moseley were the U.S. Secret Service, the "Red Squads" in big-city police departments from Portland, Oregon, to New York City, and the Justice Department's Bureau of Investigation under a young J. Edgar Hoover. Evidence of this widespread domestic spying remained secret for decades; many surveillance files were not declassified until 2000.

There were, in fact, radicals and Communists among the bonus seekers, but they were an ineffective minority disdained and dismissed by the main body of the BEF.

The march of the Bonus Army was not a mere Depression-era incident—it was a great American epic lost in the margins of history. Those who recall it are prone to slant events to advance their own political beliefs. Just as there are those who feel that it was a tale of government turning on its people, there are those who believe the veterans were hapless victims of Communist manipulation. There are even some that deny it ever happened, perceiving it as a fairy tale concocted to discredit Hoover and MacArthur.

The need for a social contract between nation and soldiers, first perceived by the angry veterans of the Revolutionary War and then peacefully sought by the Bonus Army, became a reality with the GI Bill in 1944. And the contract endures, for veterans of war and peace, into the twenty-first century. That great change, that guarantee of a just reward and the resulting creation of a vast productive and creative middle class, is the magnificent legacy of the Bonus Army.

Over There

EX-SERVICE MEN DEMAND JOBS
No one knows
No one cares if I'm weary
Oh how soon they forgot Château-Thierry

—From Newsreel XLVI,
   The Big Money, a volume in the USA Trilogy
   by John Dos Passos

PRESIDENT WOODROW WILSON and his wife rode in an open carriage from the White House to the Capitol for his second inaugural on the morning of Monday, March 5, 1917. For the first time since the Civil War, a president was given special protection on Inauguration Day. Letters threatening the president's life had alarmed the Secret Service. Agents had inspected every building on Pennsylvania Avenue along the mile-long route. Soldiers were stationed eight feet apart on both sides of the broad avenue.[1]

Wilson, running on the campaign slogan "He kept us out of war," had been reelected by a slim margin. Now he had to speak of the nearness of war. In the inaugural address he said, "We are provincials no longer. The tragic events of the thirty months of vital turmoil through which we have just passed have made us citizens of the world. There can be no turning back."[2]

Those months of turmoil traced back to June 1914, when an assassin killed a man few Americans had ever heard of—Archduke Franz Ferdinand, heir to the Austro-Hungarian throne, slain in Sarajevo, Serbia. The murder reverberated through Europe and erupted in a war whose causes bewildered Americans; in Wilson's words, the events "run deep into all the obscure soils of Europe."[3] Austria-Hungary declared war on Serbia, and Russia declared war on Austria-Hungary. Germany declared war on Russia and France and invaded Belgium. Britain declared war on Germany. Bulgaria and Turkey allied with Germany. German troops advanced into France and threatened Paris. By the end of the year, both sides were fighting from trenches along the 350-mile Western Front that extended from Switzerland to the English Channel.[4]

Wilson kept America officially neutral while U.S. factories shipped arms to Britain and France, defying German U-boats. The war seemed far away to most Americans until May 7, 1915, when a U-boat torpedoed, without warning, the British passenger liner *Lusitania.* Some 1,200 men, women, and children—including 128 Americans—were killed. A few days before the sinking, Americans had read about a horrible new weapon—poison gas, used by Germany for the first time on the Western Front. The sinking and the gas intensified anti-German sentiment while simultaneously producing a plea for continued neutrality from German-Americans, one of the nation's largest and oldest immigrant groups.[5]

Between the time of the election and his inauguration in March 1917, German submarines shattered Wilson's hope of ending the war through mediation, a noble idea he called "peace without victory."[6] No country was interested. Germany declared a U-boat blockade of Great Britain and in a note to the United States warned that any ship entering the embargo zone would be sunk without warning. Wilson broke off diplomatic relations with Germany. Then Wilson obtained from British sources a copy of a telegram sent by German foreign minister Arthur Zimmermann to the German ambassador in Mexico, instructing him to offer Mexico an alliance with Germany with the promise of "an understanding" that Mexico would reconquer and keep Texas, New Mexico, and Arizona. British code breakers had decrypted the telegram. Wilson arranged for the telegram to be released on March 1 by the Associated Press. The German plan to ally with Mexico stunned and infuriated Americans.[7]

On the evening of Monday, April 2, Wilson again traveled up Pennsylvania Avenue to address a joint session of Congress, this time in a car escorted by a squad of cavalry, sabers drawn. The cavalrymen, ceremonial troops from Fort Myer, across the Potomac, routinely rode out for funerals and occasions of state. As the car turned onto Pennsylvania Avenue, the dome of the Capitol could be seen ahead, glowing, illuminated for the first time by a new system of indirect lighting.[8]

At eight-thirty, in a light spring rain, cavalrymen eased their horses into the silent crowd on the Capitol Plaza, opening a path for Wilson's car. He got out and, alone, walked up broad stairs that had been cleared of picketing pacifists. The building and grounds were guarded by cavalry troopers, U.S. Marines, Secret Service agents, postal inspectors, and uniformed police.

Senators marched into the House carrying little American flags. The galleries were packed with people who had been issued special passes by jittery security men. Justices of the Supreme Court sat before the Speaker's platform. Foreign diplomats, in formal evening attire, sat to the side, invited to a joint session for the first time in memory.[9]

As Wilson walked down the aisle, the justices rose and led the Senators and representatives in applause, cheering and yelling for two minutes and giving Wilson the kind of reception he had never received before. Holding the speech he had typed himself, at first not looking up, Wilson began describing Germany's "warfare against mankind." He spoke to silence until he said, "There is one choice we cannot make, we are incapable of making; we will not choose the path of submission."

Chief Justice Edward White, who had fought for the Confederacy in the Civil War, suddenly rose, dropped his hat, raised his hands above his head, and clapped them once. Then from the Congress, a reporter wrote, came "a cheer so deep and so intense and so much from the heart that it sounded like a shouted prayer." More cheers came when Wilson said, "Neutrality is no longer feasible. . . . The world must be made safe for democracy."[10]

When Wilson finished his thirty-six-minute speech, he slowly walked out of the chamber to more cheers, more flag-waving. Back in the White House, he said to his secretary, "Think of what it was they were applauding. My message of today was a message of death for our young men." Then, by one account, he put his head down on a table and sobbed.[11]

Early in the morning of April 6, following an 82 to 6 vote in the Senate, the House voted 373 to 50 to declare war.[12] Wilson received a similarly overwhelming response in letters and telegrams, including a congratulatory message from London signed by forty-year-old Herbert C. Hoover, chairman of the American Commission for Relief in Belgium. Hoover, a millionaire mining engineer, had taken over the task of feeding the Belgians, whose food supplies had been sharply curtailed after German troops invaded the small kingdom in 1914. He directed a mammoth effort that saved Belgium from starvation. When America entered the war, Hoover returned home, and Wilson immediately made him U.S. food administrator, increasing his reputation and bringing his name into everyday use: housewives who aided the war effort by serving nonwasteful meals said they were "Hooverizing."[13]

When a song-and-dance man named George M. Cohan read the "war declared" headlines, he was on a train heading for New York City from suburban New Rochelle—only "forty-five minutes from Broadway," according to one of his songs. He began humming a tune, and by the time his trip ended, he had written a song that would echo the cocky patriotism of the nation. That night Cohan telephoned Nora Baye, a star of vaudeville, and on May 12 she sang the song for the first time to a cheering audience.[14] Most Americans heard it on their Victrolas or gathered around their pianos, reading the words from a song sheet with a cover by Norman Rockwell, then twenty-four years old. He would soon be in the U.S. Navy.

> *Over there, over there*
> *Send the word,*
> *Send the word over there*
> *That the Yanks are coming,*
> *The Yanks are coming,*
> *The drums rum-tumming Ev'rywhere. . . .*

When Congress declared war, the Regular Army had 127,588 officers and men to send into a war of attrition, where in a single month 300,000 British soldiers had been killed, wounded, or gassed.[15]

At first, people believed that the army sent off to fight the Germans, like the army raised for the Spanish-American War, would be made up of volunteers. Teddy Roosevelt offered to lead a volunteer force, as he had done in that "splendid little war."[16] But this war needed men by the millions, and the only way to get them was by a draft. Pacifists, radicals, and patriots found themselves on the same side in opposition to the draft. Anarchist Emma Goldman, later jailed and deported for her opposition to conscription, predicted the draft would bring civil war. Speaker of the House Champ Clark, advocate of an all-volunteer army, declared that in his state of Missouri there was "precious little difference between a conscript and a convict."[17] Conscription was given a soothing label—Selective Service—and the act passed. President Wilson signed it on May 18, and it would be the basis for conscription in World War II, Korea, and Vietnam.

The act outlawed the Civil War practice of buying one's way out of the draft. During the Civil War, wealthy men could legally duck the draft for three hundred dollars—this at a time when a typical laborer was making less than five hundred dollars a year. That inequity had touched off the New York City draft riots of 1863, in which as many as two thousand may have died, and similar, less deadly riots in other cities.

More than nine million men between the ages of twenty-one and thirty-one registered on June 5, 1917, and placed their fate in the hands of local, governor-appointed "boards of responsible citizens." Each draft board had a set of numbers to bestow on the selectees (a term that vied with *draftee*). On July 20, Secretary of War Newton D. Baker, himself a pacifist,[18] was blindfolded as he stood next to a large glass bowl. He pulled from it a small piece of paper bearing the number 258. The drawing kept up throughout the day until more than 10,000 numbers had been drawn. For American young men, a life of chance had begun. "Your number came up" entered the language.

They began their military lives in hastily built training camps that sprouted in twenty-three states—white men and black men who had never been on a train before, college boys, farmers' sons, and slum dwellers. About 18 percent of them were immigrants of forty-six nationalities, many of them unable to speak English.[19] By the beginning of October, more than 500,000 men were in the camps, which were mostly in the South. Regulations said that the men, about 70 percent of them draftees, were to be turned into soldiers in four months of seventeen-hour days.[20] Many of the recruits had only wooden guns, and many would go to the front without ever having aimed or fired a rifle.[21]

Most of the junior officers were either National Guardsmen or recent college graduates given a few weeks of training in officer candidate schools. The senior officers were of a different type—Regular Army officers who had learned their soldiering on the parade grounds of West Point, men who had gone to war against Spain in Cuba in 1898, or chased Pancho Villa across the Mexican border, or fought guerrillas in the Philippines.

The Regular Army had four Negro regiments, which traced their lineage to the freed slaves of the Civil War. They boasted a legacy that included the Indian-fighting "Buffalo Soldiers" of the Old West and the 10,000 black troops who fought in the Spanish-American War, some under Captain John J. Pershing, giving him his nickname Black Jack. Some African-American leaders believed that service in the Great War would do nothing to advance black civil rights. But in 1918 William E. B. DuBois, editor of the *Crisis*, official organ of the National Association for the Advancement of Colored People (NAACP), wrote, "*first* your Country, *then* your Rights!" His belief was that

During World War I, Major George S. Patton Jr. commanded the Ist U.S. Tank Brigade in France. He stands before one of his French-built tanks, predecessor to those he would lead in World War II. (U.S. Army Military History Institute)

loyalty and courage in wartime France would inevitably produce equal rights and opportunity in peacetime America.[22]

Men of the American Expeditionary Force, the AEF, first reached France in May 1917, a short time after the triumphant arrival of General Pershing and his stirring salutation to France. Standing at the tomb of the Marquis de Lafayette, who fought for the United States in the Revolutionary War, a spokesman for Pershing exclaimed, "Lafayette, we are here!" On his staff was Captain George S. Patton Jr., whose sister Anne was secretly engaged to Pershing, a widower.[23] Patton, bristling at the implication of favoritism, was trying to get off Pershing's staff and into action. A cavalryman with a love for horses, Patton was transferred to a new kind of cavalry unit called the tank corps.[24]

As Americans continued to pour into France and made their way to the front, they fought alongside French forces at Belleau Wood and on the river Marne. Among them were the black American regiments not attached to U.S. forces but assigned to French divisions made up of Africans from French colonies. They wore French helmets and fired French rifles. One such unit was the 369th Infantry Regiment of the New York National Guard, dubbed by the French the Harlem Hellfighters.[25]

In August Pershing set up an American front along what the battle maps called the Saint-Mihiel salient, a sharp angle in the German line. The salient looked like a dagger aimed at Paris, with the town of Saint-Mihiel, on the river Meuse, as its point. General Pershing decided to hurl three hundred thousand American troops against the salient, which the Germans had controlled since the hell of trench warfare had begun in 1914. Then he would shift those troops, along with hundreds of thousands more, to the battle line known as Meuse-Argonne. There, in 1918, he would open what he hoped would be the decisive campaign of the war. As he later wrote, he had launched with practically the same army and within twenty-four days "two great attacks" on battlefields only sixty miles apart.[26]

During this campaign, individuals who would play key roles in the events of 1932 first revealed themselves. Among the units at Saint-Mihiel was the Yankee Division, formed by National Guardsmen from all six New England states. Like other divisions, the Yankee had Regular Army officers in key commands, including Colonel Pelham D. Glassford. Because his men had no cannon of their own, they had to learn to fire French 75-millimeter guns and the heavier 155 guns. Glassford's men could not match the French on accuracy, but he could speed up the firing by teaching his Yankees the dangerous feat of loading on the recoil. They learned to fire forty shells a minute—so fast that some German officers insisted the Americans were armed with machine-gun cannons. One of Glassford's guns became famous as Betsy the Sniper, aimed by a man who had been a star pitcher for Yale. He treated the gun like a rifle, picking off targets at seven thousand yards. His men could fire and load so fast that they could have four of Betsy's shells in the air at one time.[27]

Joining the Yankee Division in the Saint-Mihiel battle was the 42nd Division, formed by National Guard units from twenty-six states and the District of Columbia. Brigadier General Douglas MacArthur, a 1903 West Point graduate and the son of a Union general who had won the Medal of Honor, said it "stretches like a rainbow from one end of America to the other," and Rainbow became its nickname.[28] He commanded an infantry brigade within the Rainbow Division.

One of the Rainbow's units was the 327th Tank Battalion, whose light Renault tanks—new, untried weapons—were under the command of now-Major George Patton. Tanks led the way at Saint-Mihiel, cutting barbed wire and taking out machine-gun nests. "We passed through several towns under shell fire but none did more than throw dust at us," Patton wrote his wife, Beatrice. "I admit that I wanted to duck and probably did at first but soon saw the futility of dodging fate, besides I was the only officer around who had left on his shoulder straps"—a target for German snipers—"and I had to live up to them."[29]

Patton went on toward Essey, where he met MacArthur. "I joined him and the creeping barrage came along toward us. . . . I think each one wanted to leave, but each hated to say so, so we let it come over us. . . . I asked him if I could go on and attack the next town, Pannes. He said to move, so I started." In Pannes, "I saw the paint fly off the side of the tank, and heard machine guns, so I jumped off and got into a shell hole. It was small and the bullets knocked all of the front edges in on me."[30]

The American attack shattered the Saint-Mihiel salient, and the surviving troops trudged down muddy roads for the next assault, the Meuse-Argonne offensive, aimed at cracking the German Second Army and ending the war. At 2:30 A.M on September 26, 3,800 guns—from French 75s to 14-inch railroad guns—fired along a forty-mile front. This preparatory barrage fired more shells than were fired by both sides during the U.S. Civil War.[31] Patton enthusiastically predicted this would be the biggest battle in the history of the world.[32]

A mist engulfed Patton's tanks as they clanked to the front. Unable to see as far as he wanted, Patton headed forward on foot with two other officers and several enlisted men. Enemy artillery and machine guns pinned them down in the little village of Cheppy. When Patton spotted several tanks stopped before two trenches, he ran down a hill and supervised a spate of frantic digging—hitting one soldier on the head with a shovel to speed him up. With the tanks rolling again, Patton led about a hundred men up the hill, waving his walking stick and shouting, "Let's go get them! Who is with me?"

At the top of the hill, German machine guns opened fire. "I was trembling with fear," Patton later wrote, "when I thought of my progenitors and seemed to see them in a cloud over the German lines, looking at me. I became calm at once and saying aloud, 'Is it time for another Patton to die?' called for volunteers and went forward to what I honestly believed to be certain death."

He shouted, "Let's go!" and charged ahead through a torrent of machine-gun bullets. Looking around, he saw his orderly, Private Joe Angelo, and five other men. In moments, only he and Angelo still stood.

"We are alone," Angelo said, looking at the dead and dying.

"Come on anyway," Patton calmly replied. A moment later a bullet struck him, entering his left thigh and tearing through his buttock. He stumbled along for a few feet and fell.

Angelo pulled Patton into a shell hole. "He was spouting blood," Angelo later said. He knelt over Patton, cut open his trousers, and bandaged the wound with dressing from his first-aid kit. They could hear the German machine gunners, forty yards away, talking between bursts of fire.[33]

After an hour or so, Patton's tanks appeared. Patton ordered Angelo to sprint to the tanks and tell them where the guns were. The tanks rumbled off toward the guns. But there were about twenty-five other machine-gun nests, and as the tanks went off, some guns kept firing, pinning down Angelo and Patton.

A little while later, a sergeant found Patton, who ordered him to look for the next in command and tell him not to try to tend to Patton until the German guns were wiped out. More tanks came along, and again Angelo ran out to point them toward the guns, which had stopped firing to hide themselves. Finally, the tanks finished off all the guns, and Patton was carried on a stretcher to an ambulance about two miles away. Angelo stayed with him in the ambulance, which Patton commandeered, ordering the driver to take him to division headquarters, where he could make a report, before bearing him to a field hospital.

Pounding the German artillery that threatened Patton's tanks were the guns of Battery B, 129th Field Artillery, of the 35th Division, made up of 27,000 National Guardsmen from Missouri and Kansas. The commander of the battery was a bespectacled captain named Harry S. Truman. He had been in the Missouri National Guard until 1911, when he was discharged as a corporal. In 1917, at the age of thirty-three and the sole male in his family, he would not be called up in the draft. But he rejoined the National Guard. In a custom dating to the Civil War, troops voted for their officers, and in this first election of his life, he was voted in as a first lieutenant.[34]

By the time Patton lay wounded, Truman's guns, hauled across no-man's-land, were about 150 yards in front of Patton, in the midst of what an artilleryman called "a cemetery of unburied dead."[35]

Artillery batteries had strictly defined areas of fire. But when Truman saw German artillery just beyond his boundary line, he fired and destroyed it. Fuming at this technical disregard of orders, a colonel threatened Truman with court-martial. Next day, Truman did just what he had done the day before. He was defending the division's infantrymen, and no sputtering, second-guessing colonel was going to stop him. Harry Truman was not court-martialed. He had used his head and gone beyond orders. And his men knew it.

"I was censoring letters today," he wrote his wife Bess on November 5, "when I ran across this sentence by one of my best sergeants. He said that he and the Battery had been in some very tight places and came out all right but that they had a captain that could take them to h——— and bring them all back."

In the four days of fighting, 1,126 men of the 35th were killed or died of wounds, and 4,877 were carried away as severely wounded. The "lightly wounded" stood and fought. The Allied offensive went on for three weeks, at the cost of 100,000 casualties, finally driving back the Germans, whose defeat led to negotiations for an armistice that took effect on November 11.

The Great War was over, at the cost of 116,708 American lives.

When the first waves of soldiers came back from Europe, the nation turned out to honor them with parades—New York City alone had six of them—but the bands stopped playing and the banners began to fade as they kept coming home. The men in the army of occupation, discharged long after the Armistice, returned to an indifferent society eager to forget the war. Those veterans were like Ernest Hemingway's hero in the short story *Soldier's Home:* "By the time Krebs returned to his home town in Oklahoma the greeting of heroes was over. He came back much too late."

The cold reality of the homecoming went deeper than indifference. The veterans found their jobs filled by others or their farms lost to creditors and back taxes. The new members of the growing middle class did not come from the legions of veterans but from those who had provided support for the war. "The Keys to the City had turned out only to be a pass to the flophouse," wrote one historian.[36]

The 204,002 men wounded in the war came home to some help, doled out through a federal program to train disabled vets for jobs. A veteran might learn a skill at an institution for vocational education, but many among them would never lose the blankness and the shakes of shell shock, that dreaded new word for the madness born in the trenches and no-man's-land of France. Some men were placed in colleges and vocational schools, but only a few thousand attended.[37]

Many who survived—and more than 4 million did—found happy postwar lives. Some states and municipalities provided aid to veterans through special employment bureaus and job programs, which put a million men back into the workforce. Seventeen states granted bonuses to vets, and Oregon and New York provided educational aid. California and several other states gave reclaimed land to veterans.

But countless vets still strongly resented the fact that civilian war workers had prospered in safety, their pay increasing by an average 200 to 300 percent, while soldiers and sailors barely subsisted on military pay. The Senate Finance Committee determined that the average soldier was paid "very much less" than the lowest class of labor at home, even when two dollars a day was factored in for the soldier's free room, board, and clothing. When they returned, many did not get their prewar jobs back, and the men without savings could not take part in the great orgy of spending that followed the war.[38]

If this treatment recalled earlier wars, there was a new element to the homecoming—it was dry. On November 1, 1917, in Washington, D.C., a prohibition against the sale of all alcoholic beverages was imposed. Under the provisions of the Sheppard Act, the last of 269 legal retail liquor stores and bars within the confines of the city were shut down at the stroke of midnight. The first phase of the "Great Experiment" was under way, and began to falter within minutes as several of the just-shuttered gin mills quickly reopened with slightly inflated prohibition prices in effect.[39]

Among those who felt most singled out and punished by the nation's decision to ban alcohol were the veterans, still returning from France in great numbers as national Prohibition was passed by Congress, overriding the veto of President Woodrow Wilson, on October 28, 1919, and, after being ratified by forty-six of the forty-eight states, going into effect as the Eighteenth Amendment on January 16, 1920.

One man who felt punished by Prohibition was an outgoing twenty-five-year-old veteran named George L. Cassiday, born in West Virginia of a teetotaling father and a mother who was a member of the Women's Christian Temperance Union. Cassiday had his first taste of liquor in France. He was still overseas when Congress passed the bill. "I believe my attitude toward Prohibition was no different than that of most of the American boys who went overseas," he later wrote. "We saw liquor being used in all the allied countries and when we were at the front, detailed with French troops, I received rations of cognac along with the other men."

Cassiday served with the 321st Light Tanks, a heavily decorated unit, which returned in late 1919 on a transport ship carrying 2,200 American troops. "We took a straw vote on Prohibition just before the ship docked in New York," Cassiday wrote. "All but 98 of the men aboard voted against it."[40]

George Cassiday soon had larger worries than Prohibition. When he returned to his home in Washington, he tried to regain a railroad job he had held before going overseas. But he was turned down because of a disability he had incurred in France. He got married and entered the new decade without steady work. By the summer of 1920 he had become desperate in his search for a livelihood.

Sometime during the summer of 1920 George Cassiday heard from a friend that good brand-name liquor brought top dollar from members of Congress who were no longer content with the novelty of the corn liquor or "white lightning" easily trucked in from backcountry stills of Maryland and Virginia. Cassiday's friend insisted that somebody could make a decent living slaking the thirst of Capitol Hill. Two days later, that friend met him in a hotel lobby and introduced him to two members of the House of Representatives—both of whom had voted for Prohibition in 1919. They placed an order with him. He obtained good liquor and was soon filling many congressional orders, launching his illegal career. At the suggestion of a member of the House of Representatives, Cassiday set up a bootlegging operation inside the House Office Building. He had an office, storeroom, and lavatory—all supplied at taxpayer expense—and was soon serving scores of congressmen and their constituents, spending, as he would later brag, "more time there than most of the Congressmen."[41]

His first major source of high-quality bonded liquor was an operation on Seventh Avenue near Thirty-fourth Street in Manhattan, a source he was led to by a former agent of the Treasury Department, the agency in charge of enforcing Prohibition. Cassiday's solution was not the norm (though it was not that uncommon, either). But his experience underscored the dilemma of the many jobless, damaged vets who were trying to feed their families in the years following the war.

W. Bruce Shafer Jr., a wealthy Virginia farmer, had worked to prevent wartime food shortages by promoting the use of potatoes as a substitute for wheat and other grains, which gave a much lower yield per acre. Thanks to his efforts, there was a nationwide doubling of the planting of potatoes, preventing the expected shortages. As the war was winding down, Shafer's father held a dinner for local boys in the Army and Navy. The younger Shafer found that many were making a dollar a day. "I thought it was a darn shame that these fellows didn't have enough money to take a girl to the moving pictures," he later recalled. A few days later, Shafer went to Washington to lobby for a doubling of the servicemen's daily pay rate. But while he was in Washington, the Armistice was declared. Shafer then started pushing for one year's extra pay: a bonus. As he put it, "They won the war that everyone thought was going to take twice as long."[42]

Shafer recruited congressional support and began printing and mailing twenty thousand circulars a day to promote the bonus. In a few months more than a million appeals had been mailed, and more than a hundred bills introduced in Congress and state legislatures. The bonus idea soon evolved into a plan to readjust the pay of the men who had served in the military. The American Legion, from the day it was founded in 1919, lobbied the Congress for passage of a bill that would correct the low pay the servicemen had received during the war. Congress took up the question, and after weeks of debate passed a stopgap measure in which the government granted an extra $60—two months' base pay—to any serviceman mustering out, regardless of grade. The name given to the stipend appeared in the page-one headline over a story in the March 7, 1919, Paris edition of *Stars and Stripes*: "Sixty Dollar Bonus for A.E.F. on Discharge." The term and concept were thereby implanted in the mind and vocabulary of the soldier and the new veteran.[43]

The $60 was an acknowledgment of the problem rather than a solution to it, and the process started all over again after the payment was authorized.[44] The Veterans of Foreign Wars lobbied Congress for a package of adjusted compensation—a dollar a day for each month of service plus an additional one-time payment of $100 for overseas service, along with help in buying a house or farm with a federal mortgage not to exceed $1,000. The American Legion pushed a plan that would offer every vet the chance to pick one of four options: a piece of land, substantial help in buying a home, free vocational training, or a dollar a day in adjusted compensation. Other veterans' groups either favored a dollar a day or, in the case of the Private Soldiers' and Sailors' Legion, a lump cash payment to each vet.[45]

By early May 1920 no fewer than seventy-five bonus bills were pending in Congress, and states, meanwhile, were creating their own bonuses. Voters in New York State were asked to vote on a $45 million bond to support a state bonus in 1920. In the weeks before the November 2 election, veterans demonstrated for the state bonus. On October 16, at least 50,000 veterans by police estimates—75,000, according to the parade's organizers—marched up Fifth Avenue in New York City, taking nearly four hours to pass the reviewing stand at Forty-second Street. They were cheered on by more than 100,000 spectators. Some five hundred vehicles carried about 2,000 wounded vets in a special section of the march, including, according to the *New York Times,* five Indian chieftains wounded in France. A large cannon, a replica of the famous French 75s, fired pro-bonus literature with the help of compressed air. There were sixty-two brass bands and "acres of drum and bugle corps." The signage tended to plead rather than demand: WE ASK VERY LITTLE FOR WHAT WE GAVE and BELIEVE US, OUR NUMEROUS UNITED STATES SOLDIERS CAN USE IT. Marchers were encouraged to show up at polling places on election day and let voters know how they felt about the bonus. It passed by a large majority. Although the parade was primarily a local event, it attracted the attention of the nation because of its size and the fact that it appeared in newsreels.[46]

The proposals in Congress ranged from flat lump-sum payments to government-financed loans. However, Shafer and his many followers insisted on a cash bonus granted to the veteran at the rate of a dollar a day for service at home and an additional twenty-five cents for each day overseas.[47]

Congress wanted to present some kind of money bill to the veterans in 1920, an election year. On March 11, in testimony before the House Ways and Means Committee, President Wilson's secretary of the Treasury, David F. Houston, said that "to float bonds in the amount of $2,000,000,000 or to meet such an additional expenditure out of taxes would present grave problems and might result in disaster." Despite this dire prediction, the committee forwarded an "adjusted compensation" bill to the full Congress in May 1920. The bill called for compensation for the veterans, not to exceed $500 for home service and $625 for overseas service, to be paid immediately.[48]

But two intertwined issues stood in the path of the bonus, the first economic, the second racial. The economic issue was familiar: Congress, still saddled with the cost of pensions from previous wars, did not want to authorize the additional burden of the bonus. By 1932, the amount paid to Civil War veterans and their survivors amounted to twice the cost of the war.

The other issue was something new. A letter to the *Cleveland Advocate*, an African-American newspaper, went right to the point: "For many months the bonus question has been see-sawing in our seat of government. It seems that the only opposition against it is the labor question—speaking more directly, Negro Labor."[49]

Many of the hundreds of thousands of Negro soldiers who came back to a white society in the previous two years were seen as a threat, competing for jobs and standing in employment lines that had long excluded them. Lynchings increased—from thirty-seven in 1917 to eighty-three in 1919—and in Washington, D.C., eight months before the May 1920 bonus hearings and a few blocks from the Capitol, roving mobs of white soldiers, sailors, and Marines attacked blacks in the wake of lurid rumors of blacks attacking white women. Armed blacks fought back in the shadow of the Capitol dome. By the end of the summer the rioting had spread to twenty-five cities, including Chicago, where a white mob stoned black youths who were swimming on the wrong side of a segregated beach. One was drowned. For those wondering why all of this was happening, the *New York Times* suggested that it was "Bolshevik agitation which had been extended, especially to those in the South."[50]

Although Houston's comment was little noticed at the time in the mainstream media, it was front-page news in the *Cleveland Advocate*. The African-

American newspaper was affiliated with the Republican Party and owned by Ormand A. Forte, who saw to it that his paper covered racial discrimination and lynchings as well as church news. Forte's connection to the bonus and black veterans was strong, and linking the bonus to the word *disaster* was ominously newsworthy. One of the *Advocate*'s contributing editors was Ralph W. Tyler, the only black correspondent given overseas accreditation during the war. He had been assigned directly to General Pershing's staff and was well versed in the contributions and sacrifices made by black soldiers.[51]

Earlier in 1920, Tyler had testified against General Pershing before a congressional committee looking into the deaths of soldiers of the Negro 92nd division who died on the first Armistice Day, November 11, 1918. He joined two officers of the 92nd who accused General Pershing of sending men to their deaths needlessly: "Every soldier who fell between 7 o'clock Sunday morning, November 10, and Monday morning, November 11, was needlessly slaughtered." The 92nd lost 498 men between the ninth and the eleventh, adding up to a total of 960 since October 8.[52]

Weeks later, the *Advocate* noted that the powerful U.S. Chamber of Commerce at its Atlantic City convention had entertained a resolution against the bonus for the reason that "the half million Negroes in the South, who probably would receive $500 or $600 each, would immediately quit work until the money was spent."

The *Advocate* responded editorially, "But the United States Chamber of Commerce, or at least those who sponsored that resolution, need not be solicitous about the Colored veteran quitting work until their bonus is spent. They need not fear any 'orgy of spending' simply because some half million loyal citizen soldiers may receive $500 or $600 each."

The paper took note of the fact that millions of acres of farmland were then owned and cultivated by a people little more than fifty years removed from slavery who were not prone to quitting work—and even if some of the bonus money was spent recklessly, white merchants would benefit. The *Advocate* was stunned that those who denied one Negro veteran his bonus would deprive four whites their payment, concluding that the resolution was "an insult to the race, and a most reprehensible injustice to the white world war veteran."[53]

Despite the racial issue, the 1920 version of the "Soldier Bonus Bill" did pass in the House, but it was shelved by the Senate, where key members of both parties opposed the idea, essentially because it would cost at least $2 billion. As Assistant Secretary of the Treasury R. C. Leffingwell put it in an article in the *Saturday Evening Post*, the money "is not in the Treasury and available for distribution." The only feasible way to pay for it, he said, was through new taxes.[54] And President Wilson let it be known that he opposed the payment as a matter of fiscal responsibility.[55]

America's elected leaders were not disputing the veterans' claim to back pay for wartime service. They just did not want to write the check.

The Tombstone Bonus

How Happy to be a soldier
Of the old Red, White and Blue
Paid like a banker in time of war,
And cared for afterward too,
With a job and a home in the city
Or a fertile farm in the dell,
For like Princes, we treat our Veterans—
We do, like Hell!

—Third stanza of "The Happy American,"
   Ballads of the B.E.F.

N EITHER PARTY SUPPORTED the bonus in the 1920 presidential election platforms; but noncandidate William Jen-
nings Bryan did suggest it be financed by a "war profits tax," and Republican
nominee Warren G. Harding suggested that he was ready to challenge the
platform.

As a senator, Harding had been one of the strongest supporters of Shafer's
proposal. During the campaign, Harding went to Norfolk on the yacht of
Ned McLean, owner of the *Washington Post* and husband of heiress Evalyn
Walsh McLean, for a boozy, Prohibition-defying $10-a-plate dinner where he

told Shafer that if elected he would sign the bonus bill even if the amount paid "doubled." (The dinner set the tone for the Harding presidency. Shafer later spoke of McLean's behavior at the banquet: "He had a habit of getting a seltzer bottle and squirting it on his friends, after a few drinks. The police picked him up and carried him out of the banquet to jail. Someone went and got him later.")[1]

After Harding was elected and in office, he still supported the idea of the bonus but suddenly turned against it, saying it would increase the national debt and thwart his plan to cut taxes. He had the support of business and the voices of major employers like George Eastman, the Kodak man, who claimed it would make "mercenaries out of our patriotic boys," and Pierre S. Dupont, whose chemical corporation was a major war contractor.[2]

Opponents pointed out that the cost of the bonus would be $2 billion to $4 billion at a time when the total federal budget was just over $4 billion. Cowboy humorist Will Rogers, who supported it simply because the boys deserved it, wrote, "Apple Sauce . . . this country is not broke, automobile manufacturers are three months behind in their orders, and whiskey was never as high in its life. . . . If we owed it to some Foreign Nation you would talk about honor and then pay it."[3]

The most powerful voices demanding passage of the bonus were the American Legion and the Veterans of Foreign Wars, which had popular support among members of both houses of Congress. But Harding and Secretary of the Treasury Andrew Mellon worked hard to get a bonus bill, which had been introduced earlier in the year, tabled. Harding intervened directly at a luncheon with his former Senate colleagues and personally delivered an anti-bonus message on July 12, 1921, saying that the first priority of Congress was tax reduction, not the soldier's bonus.[4] Congress tabled the bonus until the next session in 1922.[5]

Throughout the country the American Legion, the Veterans of Foreign Wars, and other veterans' groups held mass meetings in support of the bonus. Pressure was building against the bonus as well, with strong business opposition, especially from Wall Street. A New York American Legion chapter charged a leading brokerage house with compelling 247 of its employees to write anti-bonus letters to Congress. Thomas Edison weighed in on the issue during an interview on his seventy-fifth birthday: "I think we should postpone the bonus. The country is in no condition for it."[6]

The House vote—taken on March 23, 1922, with jammed galleries of supporters—disregarded party lines; the final count was 333 to 70, with 242 Republicans, 90 Democrats, and 1 Socialist in favor.[7] The Senate then passed it 47 to 22 and sent it to the president for his signature. After suggesting again that he was in favor of the bonus, Harding vetoed the bill on September 19, 1922, while heaping thanks on the veterans for their noble service: "The United States will never cease to be grateful."[8] He justified his veto by stating the country did not have the money. A tax cut, he said, was more important to veterans than a bonus because it would make America "a better country for which to fight, or to have fought, and affords a surer abiding place in which to live and attain."[9] Shafer, for one, was appalled by the veto and was told by congressional sources that the veto was written by "the fifth richest man in the world," Andrew Mellon. Pro-bonus legislators overrode Harding in the House but lacked the four votes needed to override in the Senate.[10]

The close veto-overriding vote worried the National Industrial Conference Board, whose thirty-one trade associations included the National Association of Manufacturers and the Institute of Makers of Explosives. The board produced a forty-eight-page booklet entitled *The Soldiers' Bonus*. It concluded that payment could not be justified on the grounds of economic equity and that its adoption might "tend to hamper the nation's efforts in behalf of incapacitated veterans at present and of the needy or aged veterans in the future." Now more than ever, it was clear that there was a growing opposition to the bonus from the same corporations that had received postwar compensation for their efforts in the "war to end all wars."[11]

By the summer of 1923 Harding had become totally dispirited by the corruption of his cronies, who were selling out the nation's naval oil reserve at Wyoming's Teapot Dome and Elk Hills, stealing from the Veterans Bureau, and diverting confiscated liquor into their own hands for resale. Friends said he was ill from the betrayals of his "gang." He embarked on a West Coast speech-making tour, hoping to determine what could be done about the scandals, the extent of which had not yet become public. On the night of August 2 he suffered a fatal stroke in San Francisco. The public would soon learn that his administration had been one of the most corrupt in history. Of particular interest to veterans was the fact that Charles R. Forbes, director of the Veterans Bureau, was found guilty of diverting $250 million into his own pockets and those of his friends.[12]

Vice President Calvin Coolidge was sworn in as president. A former governor of Massachusetts and U.S. senator, Coolidge had stood outside Harding's inner circle of cronies and was never tainted by their corruption. But he followed the same fiscal policies as Harding, and after some temporizing went on the record saying he opposed the bonus. The more prosperous states were providing for their own vets with bonuses. This seemed unfair to vets in the majority of states. By the end of the year nineteen states had authorized bond issues for $361,970,141 to pay state bonuses. The leader was Illinois ($55 million), followed by New York ($45 million), although the Empire State had run into legal problems and had yet to raise the money.[13]

In the early days of 1924, the bonus was again an issue, with parades and petitions to gain support for it. There was also strongly organized opposition, including nasty campaigning by business executives who threatened employees if they did not oppose the bonus. Coolidge denounced the practice as "utterly un-American." A Treasury whistle-blower claimed that his department had "juggled" numbers to make the estimated cost of the bonus appear bigger.[14]

A new bill was introduced on February 26 by Representative Hamilton Fish Jr. of New York, who had been one of the white officers of the "Harlem Hellfighters" regiment and winner of the Croix de Guerre and the Silver Star. He proposed that the cash bonus be paid not immediately but in 1945, with accrued interest. Veterans could borrow on their policies but not redeem them until 1945.[15] The twenty-year wait for cash was seen as a way to nullify Coolidge's promised veto. The American Legion supported the compromise.

Support for the bonus continued to grow. On March 1 between four and five thousand members of the American Legion and VFW paraded through the streets of Brooklyn in support of the bonus. The marchers delivered a petition with 130,000 signatures to Senator Royal S. Copeland.[16]

For the third time in four years the House passed a soldier's bonus bill—this time by a vote of 355 to 54 in the House, followed by a 67 to 17 vote in the Senate—but the delayed payment provision was not enough to keep Coolidge from vetoing the new bill for two stated reasons: he believed the budget had to be preserved, and it was not right to favor one group of people over all other Americans.[17] Coolidge then added, "Patriotism which is bought and paid for is not patriotism. . . . Service to our country in time of war means sacrifice. It is for that reason alone that we honor and revere it. To attempt to make a money payment out of the earnings of the people to those who are physically well and financially able is to abandon one of our most cherished American ideals."[18]

Coolidge's comment on patriotism backfired because it was superfluous to the veto, and doubly so because he had not been in uniform himself. He infuriated even those who were against the bonus. Congressman Fiorello La Guardia of New York, a veteran and a Republican, was hurt and offended by Coolidge's message, saying that it placed a "question mark" on the honorable discharges of four million soldiers. La Guardia, who had been elected in 1916 as America's first Italian-American congressman and who was known throughout his long political career as "the Little Flower," had taken leave from Congress to enlist in 1917 and served as a pilot and flight school administrator in the U.S. Army Flying Service in Italy. He returned to politics after the war with the rank of major, a brilliant war record, and living proof that "hyphenated Americans" could be both patriotic and heroic.[19]

Congress—encouraged by Coolidge's intemperate comments and La Guardia's anger—overrode the veto. The vote in the Senate was 59 to 26, two votes more than the requisite two-thirds needed.[20] Now, six years after the war had ended, the vets' demands that the nation fulfill promises to compensate them for their service—and to correct the disparity between civilian and military pay—had finally produced results: the World War Veterans Act was now law, granting "adjusted service compensation" to veterans of that war in 1945.[21]

The bonus issue could define or defile political careers—what politicians refer to as "a third rail." Republican Senate leader Henry Cabot Lodge of Massachusetts, the scholarly successor to Daniel Webster, had voted to override the veto. The party would not easily forgive him for this affront to a Republican president. Lodge claimed justification—a promise to the Massachusetts Republican Convention a year earlier.[22] The *Boston Globe* looked at Lodge and other Republicans who opposed Coolidge and saw "the amazing spectacle of a Chief Executive who has lost the backing of his own political majority in Congress." The *Boston Herald* saw New England failing a New England president and noted that three other Republican senators from New England—one from Maine and two from Connecticut—had worked against their leader.[23]

Under the terms of the new law, any veteran who had served in the armed forces between April 5, 1917, and July 1, 1919, was due compensation at the rate of $1 a day for home service and $1.25 a day for overseas service. From this was deducted sixty days' service because of $60 that had been paid to each veteran upon discharge. Those entitled to $50 or less were to be paid immediately, while the rest received certificates to be redeemed in 1945 with 4 percent interest. Since the note was issued in place of cash, an additional 25 percent was tacked on to the final payment in 1945. Three and a third million vets were issued certificates with a total face value of $3.5 billion—averaging a payout of about $1,000 per man.[24]

The so-called bonus was neither compensation nor a bonus. It was a twenty-one-year endowment life insurance policy payable at death or in 1945, whichever came first. But the term "bonus" had been ingrained in the national consciousness, and it was the label given to the legislation and the certificates. Veterans thought of it as just that—a bonus, an overdue monetary gift from a grateful nation. The misnomer was aided in part by Coolidge's in-famous words, "We owe no bonus to able-bodied veterans of the World War."

Confusing matters further was the way the certificates were imprinted: they showed the amount ultimately due in 1945 rather than its current value. A vet-eran, who would have been qualified to get $400 in 1925 if payment had been made then, carried a piece of banknote paper with green filigreed borders that said it was worth $1,000. For large numbers of poor vets, it was the only thing they owned that had value. Somewhere along the way, as it became more broadly understood that the only way one could cash out before 1945 was to die, it was dubbed the Tombstone Bonus.[25]

The bonus issue seemed to have been resolved as the Coolidge years played out, although the president's relationship with veterans remained cool, and he was not forgiven for his comments about them. In October 1924 it was dis-covered that he had exacted a fee of $250 for delivering a memorial speech to veterans in Bridgeport, Connecticut, when he was still vice president. It was alleged that "when money is in his own pocket" his attitude toward the veter-ans was a far cry from the one he conveyed at the time of the veto. "Every-body else donated his or her services for the meetings," said a formal notice from the Democratic National Committee about the Bridgeport incident. "Can the American people imagine Lincoln, Roosevelt or Wilson exacting a fee from soldiers and sailors for delivering a memorial address?"[26]

But the vets, for the first time since the war ended, seemed to have the upper hand. A week before the Bridgeport revelation was made, Frank T. Hines, director of the Veterans Bureau and later the head of its successor, the Veterans Administration, notified the undersecretary of the Treasury that ap-plications for bonus certificates were flooding his office and that 1,567,665 had already come in. Hines, who served in the Spanish-American War and was a brigadier general in the Great War, said that all veterans—about 4 mil-lion men—would probably apply for adjusted compensation.[27]

One veteran, a Texan named Wright Patman, was deeply bothered by the 1945 payment date—especially since the profiteers and large corporations had long since been paid in full with bonuses for their participation in the war. In July 1917, as a recent law school graduate, Patman had enlisted in the U.S. Army as a private and immediately began plumping for an overseas assignment but was rejected because of a minor heart ailment. He finished the war with a com-mission as a first lieutenant in the U.S. Guards, the only military group that would offer him chance for advancement. He left the Army with an awak-ened sense of moral outrage, especially about the money spent and corporate profits assured by the sales of weapons. He learned to fire an artillery piece with an eight-mile range, which he described to his sister in a letter: "What you would call a bullet is as big as a stove pipe and twice as long. It cost the government $1,250 to fire one of them." Patman then observed that the cost of firing the "bullet" was ten times the cost of a new schoolhouse.[28]

In 1928 Patman ran for Congress as a vet and an agrarian progressive who boasted that he had raised money for law school as a tenant farmer. His Texas district was so poor that fewer than 2,000 of his 255,452 constituents made enough to pay income taxes. *Time* magazine described his district as being "where hillbillies corner their rabbits in hollow logs and take Levi Garrett snuff . . . with their politics."[29]

During the campaign, a major issue for Patman was a "square deal" for American soldiers and sailors, an allusion to Theodore Roosevelt's 1903 statement that "a man good enough to shed his blood for his country is good enough to get a square deal afterward." As a former American Legion commander and a loyal member, he believed that the veterans of the Great War had been slighted and that the bonus was the first step toward correcting the injustice. Patman had lived on soldier's pay of a dollar a day when shipyard workers were making $20 a day.[30] "They [the average private] only got $21 a month and had to pay their own laundry bills. If they made an allotment to a wife or child they had nothing left," he said, adding that the soldier was expected to purchase Liberty Bonds with any money left over. To refuse was to be derided as a "slacker."[31]

Patman came to Congress as the undisputed leader of the pro-bonus forces. Two months after he took his oath of office and five months before the stock market crash, he first introduced a bill in the House calling for immediate cash payment of the bonus, to be financed by government borrowing at a cost of $3.4 billion. An identical Senate version came from Smith Wildman Brookhart, an Iowa Republican and a self-styled "cowhide radical."

As the American Legion and other political groups supported their own legislation before Congress, the Patman-Brookhart bill attracted little notice, and never made it out of committee. But Patman, who would soon make a name for himself as a scathing critic of the economic policies of Secretary of the Treasury Andrew Mellon, had gained the attention of the veterans. He was one of their own, willing to be their advocate.

When President Coolidge decided not to run again in 1928, the Republican Party's presidential nomination was won by Herbert Hoover, a California mining engineer and self-made millionaire who as wartime National Food

Administrator had been responsible for getting millions of tons of food to the Allies and to famine areas of Europe. In 1927 he headed the rescue of thousands of Americans driven from their homes by disastrous Mississippi River floods.

During the campaign, Hoover, heralded as the Great Engineer, proclaimed that Americans were "in sight of the day when poverty will be banished from this nation." Orphaned at nine, he was said by his supporters to know the meaning of poverty and hunger. Hoover carried forty of the forty-eight states, although this was his first campaign for public office. He had been aided by organized labor, which had campaigned against the two previous Republican presidents. Hoover, said union leader John L. Lewis, was "the foremost industrial statesman of modern times."[32]

In his March 1929 inaugural address Hoover proclaimed that the future of the country was "bright with hope." Seven months later, the economy collapsed, and Hoover was reviled by millions of Americans for what they believed to be his ineptitude and indifference to their plight. The 1929 crash, ushering in the most severe depression in American history, made a mockery of Republican claims to be "the party of prosperity."

Two problems dogged Hoover's administration: the descent into what became known as the Great Depression and the debilitating effects of Prohibi-

George L. Cassiday, a World War I veteran known as the "Man in the Green Hat," became a bootlegger, selling liquor in Capitol offices. Congressional customers included legislators who voted for Prohibition. (Underwood & Underwood/Library of Congress)

tion, which Hoover embraced with a renewed zeal. George Cassiday, who had been arrested in 1925 while wearing a green fedora and was henceforth known as the "the Man in the Green Hat," was targeted by the Hoover administration. Banned from the House of Representatives after his 1925 arrest, Cassiday had become the "unofficial-official" bootlegger to the U.S. Senate from 1925 to 1930. Then, under instructions from Hoover's vice president, Charles Curtis, and an ardent and resourceful federal prohibition agent named Roger Butts, Cassiday was arrested, convicted, and sent to jail.

Cassiday created a major scandal when he sold his memoirs to the *New York World* and *Washington Post*. He claimed, among other things, that he had the keys to more Capitol Hill desks and offices than any person in history. In the persona of the Man in the Green Hat, Cassiday became a national symbol of Prohibition's stunning hypocrisy and of the dilemma of the Great War veteran.[33]

When Cassiday was forced to drop his profession in 1930, Congress still had many bootleggers working its halls and offices. Bootleggers operated in front of the District police headquarters, in the Justice Department itself, and across the street from the White House. When *Washington Post* reporter Edward T. Folliard ducked out to buy a pint of gin from his favorite bootlegger, he found the supply had just run out. He jumped into the bootlegger's car and the two drove to the White House, where a large burlap bag was retrieved from the hedge. The bootlegger took a half-dozen bottles of gin out of the bag and told the reporter that was as safe a place as any to stash booze because nobody would expect anyone to hide liquor there. Folliard, unabashedly admitting his involvement in an illegal act, told the story in a short whimsical piece, picked up the Associated Press.[34]

A criminal class was being created in Washington, D.C. In 1929, a total of 19,273 District residents were arrested for alcohol-related crimes—roughly one out of every twenty-seven Washingtonians. Since all drinking was illegal, there was no legal drinking age and so no incentive to screen out minors. Women, who had not been welcome in the old saloons, were accepted in the new speakeasies, and the local smart set hung out at places like Le Paradise on Thomas Circle and Club Mayflower on Connecticut Avenue.

Prohibition turned the Capitol City into a place where ironies, contradictions, and hypocritical behavior were so common that it took a really rich item to attract attention. A drunken policeman was no longer news, but the fact that Evalyn Walsh McLean, the wealthy heiress to a Colorado mining fortune and owner of the famed Hope Diamond, bragged that she had her whiskey delivered to her Washington mansion by police escort was newsworthy, as were the lavish and zany parties she staged with her husband.[35]

In the America beyond Washington, unemployment was soaring to 8 million in 1930, and veterans were suddenly willing to agitate for prepayment of the bonus. To an increasing number of them, an adjusted service certificate was their only asset. At the depth of the Depression, Patman became the widely acknowledged leader of a large pro-bonus coalition in Congress and a nationally known spokesman for its immediate payment, which would then have meant an overall payment of billions of dollars. He had the support of the Veterans of Foreign Wars but lacked that of the American Legion, which at this point preferred to advance the causes of the disabled vet and the dependent wives and children of men killed in the war.

President Hoover addressed the issue of immediate payment in a speech to the American Legion National Convention in Boston in October 1930. The bonus, he said, could not be paid at that time because of the fiscal problems that the United States was facing. He pointed out that the government was spending $900 million on veterans, with $600 million going to veterans of the Great War. But he did break with tradition by suggesting that once the economic crisis was over, the White House would support new veterans' legislation, and the American Legion would be given a sympathetic ear.[36]

As the convention progressed, a power struggle took place, pitting Patman's followers against a pro-Hoover group led by the popular former Legion commander and Hoover's minister to Canada, Hanford McNider. When the Patmanites brought to the floor their minority report calling for debate on the issue of immediate payment, McNider and other officials got it tabled.[37]

Frustrated, Patman urged all of the Democratic candidates in the upcoming 1930 election to use the bonus as a campaign issue that, as he explained in a memo to the candidates, would force the Republicans to favor immediate payment. He predicted that Hoover would announce his support before the election.[38]

Not only did Hoover not change his mind, but at a press conference on December 9, 1930, he lashed out at groups that had introduced bills, including the bonus, that amounted to $4.5 billion "under the guise of giving relief of some kind or another," which if granted would require more taxes and thus slow economic recovery. He warned that prosperity could not be restored if there were raids on the U.S. Treasury by special-interest groups. Although he did not name the bonus in this outburst, that was how it was commonly interpreted.[39]

The bill that Patman reintroduced in early 1931 was termed a form of federal relief, granted on a discriminatory basis. Immediate payment got its strongest boost on January 21, 1931, when somewhere between five hundred and a thousand uniformed veterans paraded along Pennsylvania Avenue to the Capitol steps, where they were joined by Patman and a hundred or so more congressmen demonstrating for immediate payment.[40]

There was strong opposition to the Patman bill in the Senate, and Hoover let it be known that he would veto it. But the idea of Patman's bill had widespread support, generated by the Hearst newspapers and by Father Charles Coughlin, a priest who had a weekly radio show listened to by millions. Hoover faced a dilemma: the bonus was popular, but it would cost $4 billion, exceeding the income of the government, which meant that it would require a tax increase—the last thing the nation needed as the Great Depression worsened.

The House Committee on Ways and Means began hearings on "payment of adjusted compensation certificates" on January 29, 1931. The leadoff witness was Andrew Mellon, who asserted that veterans "would not seem to be a class which, as such, is in particular need." Life insurance executives and other businessmen joined in rejecting the idea.[41] But there was much support for payment: "This is not a dole, a handout; it is an adjustment in a very small degree of the soldier's pay while he served his country. We have adjusted all the claims of the war contractors," said John J. Cochran, a Missouri Democrat who was one of the many congressmen in favor of payment.[42]

An important moment in the hearings came when an official from General Electric, Owen D. Young, suggested that the loan basis of the bonus—the amount that could be borrowed with interest—be upped to 50 percent, giving the average vet about $500 if he chose to borrow while retaining the insurance provision of the bonus. It was a compromise that would put money—albeit borrowed money—in veterans' pockets.

The defining moment in the hearings, however, was reserved for a veteran. On Wednesday, February 4, 1931, Joseph T. Angelo, the man who saved the life of George S. Patton on the battlefield in 1918, testified.

At this time and place, he was an oddity—a living, breathing, appallingly thin, bona fide victim of the Depression, being given both the time and the respect to tell his story. He appeared with a comrade who was silent through the hearings. Angelo testified that the two of them left his home in Camden, New Jersey, on Sunday morning at nine o'clock and walked all the way to the Capitol. "I done it all by my feet—shoe leather. I was not picked up by any machine. I would not accept."

"Why?" he asked himself aloud.

Joe Angelo, who walked from New Jersey to Washington in February 1931 to testify about the bonus, wore his medals, including the Distinguished Service Cross, awarded for saving the life of wounded Major George S. Patton Jr. (Underwood & Underwood/Library of Congress)

"I come to show you people that we need our bonus. . . . I represent 1,800 from New Jersey. They are just like myself—men out of work. I have got a little home back there that I built with my own two hands after I came home from France. Now, I expect to lose that little place. Why? My taxes are not paid. I have not worked for two years and a half. Last week I went to our town committee and they gave me $4 for rations."[43]

Angelo pointed out that he was not asking for the full bonus, but enough to scrape through. Although he had borrowed some, he held a certificate with a face value of $1,444 and could not reconcile the amount on the certificate with the fact that he was broke, hungry, and unable to make the kind of money he had before he joined the Army. Angelo had been working in the Dupont Powder Works at $1.25 an hour—working as many hours as he wished—when he enlisted at a dollar a day.

"You took 10 percent of the amount you were making in civil life to take a position and go over and be shot?" asked Representative James A. Frear, a Wisconsin Republican.

"Yes, sir; absolutely; and I was proud of it."

He was then asked why he had enlisted.

Angelo said that a fellow worker had told him and some of his buddies that they were too yellow to join the Army. In response, Angelo and three others signed up the next morning. One was married with a child but claimed he was single to get in. Angelo had come close to being rejected because he weighed a mere 107 pounds. His married friend died in combat. Angelo came back with the Distinguished Service Cross.

He retold the story of his battlefield heroism—with a few over-the-top embellishments—and showed the committee both the pocket watch he had been given by Patton's wife and the stickpin that he had been given by Patton's mother.[44] He insisted that he had resisted the temptation of making money from bootlegging, which many other vets had resorted to, because that would be breaking the laws of the United States, which, as he put it, would not be "a fair deal."

"So, folks," he addressed the committee, ending his testimony with a plea for help with the bonus, "don't forget me for a job. That is all I care for."[45] Angelo made good newspaper copy and headlines, such as the one atop an Associated Press story: "Veteran, Wearing Medals, Jobless, Stirs Committee."[46]

Angelo repeated his testimony the next day for a Senate committee, and this time Patton's wife and children were in the hearing room because Beatrice Patton had wanted her children to see the man who had saved their father's life. At first she was upset because she knew that Angelo was "enlarging on the truth," and she dismissed him as "a catspaw—a pathetic type. Too bad." But later, when the family met with Angelo in a senator's office, he made a better impression on her. She wrote in her journal that night that he was a much nicer man than she had expected.[47]

On February 26, 1931, President Hoover vetoed the immediate-payment bill, arguing that the vets were being provided for in their local communities, that the "number of veterans in need of such relief is a minor percentage of the whole," that the concept of economic stimulus would not work because the vets would spend their cash on "wasteful expenditure," and finally that it would set a dangerous precedent, opening "the Federal Treasury to a thousand purposes," each of which "breaks the barriers of self-reliance and self-support in our people."[48]

The following day, a partial victory—approval to borrow on the certificates—was achieved by Royal C. Johnson, a South Dakota Republican who, like La Guardia, had taken leave from Congress to go to war. Johnson had enlisted as an infantry private. He came out of the war as a first lieutenant who had been awarded the Distinguished Service Cross and France's Croix de Guerre with gold star. As chairman of the House Committee on World War Veterans' Legislation, Johnson enlisted the aid of three other Republicans: Representatives Hamilton Fish Jr. and Isaac Bacharach of New Jersey, and Senator Arthur Vandenberg of Michigan. They crafted the Bacharach Amendment, which was hurried in and out of committee and onto the floor before the Seventy-first Congress could adjourn. On February 27, 1931, Public Law 743 sailed through both Houses—363 to 39 in the House and 72 to 12 in the Senate—and was signed by Hoover. To its supporters it looked like the ideal solution, giving the veterans cash, retaining the bonus, and stimulating the economy. The loan law allowed veterans to borrow up to 50 percent of the maturity value of their bonus certificates at 3 percent compound interest.

But Wright Patman and his followers were not happy—the interest charged on the loan would eat up any final payment. Immediate payment remained a major issue for Patman, and he redoubled his efforts to turn the whole bonus to cash, though the prospects were dim. Shafer, the man who started it all, had testified before the House Ways and Means Committee a few weeks before Hoover's February 26 veto. "I am in favor of paying the certificates now and I believe a majority of our citizens are," he had said. "However, the ex-servicemen have about as much chance of collecting in full at this time as a celluloid cat would have passing through Hades without being scorched."[49]

A Petition in Boots

Hark, hark hear the dogs bark;
Coxey is coming to town
In his ranks are scamps
And growler fed tramps
On all of whom working was frowned.

—*The Pittsburgh Press*, April 1894,
preparing for the arrival of Coxey's Army

FOR MANY AMERICANS in 1931, the only recollection that seemed to have any parallel was more than a generation removed. During the Depression of the 1890s unemployment was widespread, and many Americans came to the realization that even the hardest, most devoted workers were helpless when the economy turned sour—a lesson relearned by every generation living through a major economic downturn. Many Americans were starting to believe the core idea of the 1892 Populist platform: America had become a nation of two classes—millionaires and tramps. By early 1894, following the financial panic of 1893, the newspapers were filled with news of strikes, lockouts, general labor unrest, and millions of unemployed—comprising 20 to 25 percent of the nonfarm workforce. Many of the jobless had also become the homeless, wanderers looking for work.

But if there was one specific memory of that time that had not dimmed in the public mind, it was of a man who seemed to come out of nowhere: Jacob S. Coxey, an unsuccessful Ohio politician and successful owner of limestone quarries and breeder of thoroughbred racehorses who himself had been forced to fire forty employees because of the 1893 panic. Coxey declared himself the leader of the unemployed and demanded that the government embark on a vast public works program to provide jobs for the jobless by putting them to work building roads. He wanted this to be financed by debt in the form of federally subsidized bonds and the immediate printing of $500 million in cash for road construction. He had strong support, especially among farmers, who were clamoring for better roads.[1]

Joining Coxey in this endeavor was Carl "Old Greasy" Browne, a flamboyant stump orator who had earned his nickname honestly with a head of filthy, matted hair and a belief that one should never change one's clothes— in his case, rodeo clothes fashioned after those of Buffalo Bill Cody. Browne also believed in reincarnation and that a small portion of Jesus Christ was reborn in all humans—but he thought that a large amount of Christ returned in himself and in Coxey, whom he saw as the "Cerebrum of Christ." An avowed agnostic, Coxey was taken by Browne's theosophy and changed the name of his "Good Roads Association" to the "Commonweal of Christ." Browne, who had organized parades of the unemployed in his native San Francisco, inspired Coxey to announce a march on Washington. Coxey and Browne then called on the unemployed from all over the country to join them in the Army of the Commonweal of Christ, which would have enormous power. If enough men marched on Washington, they reasoned, a large portion of the body and soul of Christ would be there, and Congress could not resist its influence.[2]

Coxey announced that he and Browne would lead the main contingent from Massillon, Ohio, to Washington to present its demands to Congress on May Day. The press immediately dubbed the operation Coxey's Army, while Coxey called it a "petition in boots." Coxey and his family rode in a buggy drawn by Acolyte, a $40,000 thoroughbred pacer, with Browne riding a $7,000 stallion. The marchers were generally well received along the way, often fed by sympathetic farmers.[3]

As Coxey's Army left Massillon, as many as forty additional armies were assembling from all parts of the nation, each planning to join Coxey in Washington. In Los Angeles, one of Browne's old acquaintances, Lewis Fry, organized the "United States Industrial Army" and demanded that the railroads transport him and his men east. An army in San Francisco mustered two thousand men, including writer Jack London. Upward of ten thousand unemployed workers planned to join Coxey in Washington.

By the time Coxey and his group from Massillon finally made it to Washington on April 29, only about six hundred hard-core believers were in line. Many of the others ran into trouble along the way. A group out of Portland, Oregon, commandeered a Union Pacific train at Troutdale, Oregon. The U.S. Cavalry soon caught them and returned the 469 demonstrators to Portland, where they received a stern lecture from the U.S. district judge. Part of the New England army left by ship, only to run aground off Provincetown, Massachusetts.

Two days after his men arrived in Washington, Coxey marched them down Fourteenth Street and up Pennsylvania Avenue to the steps of the Capitol for a May Day rally, where he and Browne tried to speak. Prevented from delivering his speech on the steps of the Capitol, Coxey and his followers moved off Capitol Hill. More than four hundred, along with thirty horses, relocated to a swampy, gnat-infested lot southeast of the Capitol, without adequate food or shelter.

Coxey and Brown were later arrested for trespassing—the actual charges noting, among other things, that they "did then and there step upon certain growing plants, shrubs, and turf then and there being growing," a charge that in countless accounts has been reported as "walking on the grass."[4] On May 21 a judge sentenced the two men to twenty days in prison and a $5 fine.

But even in failure Coxey attracted new supporters. A small group from Harrodsburg, Kentucky, left in a balloon for Washington to support Coxey with a check for $1,000. "Coming by the Air Line" was how the *Washington Post* headlined the story. An English observer visiting America at the time noted that Coxey's "petition in boots" had attracted more free advertising "than any millionaire in America ever could have afforded."[5]

A number of marchers were stopped as they tried to take trains east. Because most of the railroads were in receivership in 1894 and under the protection of federal courts, whenever a train was hijacked, the U.S. Army was sent to stop, overtake, and detain it.[6] Soldiers were sent to train yards and sidings to prevent more seizures. It was estimated at the time that if Coxey's Commonwealers had been allowed the use of the trains, sixty or seventy thousand of them would have arrived in Washington.[7] More than a month after Coxey's May Day arrival at the Capitol, industrial armies were still on the move to support him. A group from Denver, kept off the rails, took the water route; 15 followers drowned in a Platte River boat accident, and some 350 survivors were stranded.[8]

By the time Coxey was finally released from prison, a major camp had appeared in suburban Maryland, and another, with about a thousand men, across the river in Rosslyn, Virginia. The Maryland group broke up after many members were jailed for stealing food from local farms. Virginia brought out the militia, which marched the men back into Washington. They settled on the grounds of the Naval Observatory until they were finally sent home by train at government expense.

Coxey's vast industrial armies did not make it to Washington because of the very thing that Coxey espoused—good roads. Not until World War I was the United States forced to realize how important roads were to the nation's needs. Some 30,000 trucks were used to ferry supplies to eastern ports for shipment to France, but they traveled over bad roads, often causing delays and disruptions. In 1919 the Army decided to demonstrate how deplorable those roads were by sending a convoy of trucks from coast to coast. It took sixty-three days of determined effort for the caravan to travel 3,251 miles: fifty-three miles a day. The convoy included twenty-eight-year-old Dwight David Eisenhower, a lieutenant colonel in the Tank Corps. Ike, as everyone called him, had spent the Great War in America and in 1919 was involved in a less than heroic struggle to keep trucks and tanks out of the mud.[9]

The point was made. A Good Roads Movement began as a moral, religious, and educational advancement for the nation. By 1925 the United States was spending a billion dollars a year on new roads, and the system was steadily improving. By 1931 the nation boasted 3,291,000 miles of public roads, of which 1,290,000 miles were paved.*[10]

This point was not lost on Coxey when, at the age of seventy-seven, he appeared on February 4, 1931, as the witness who immediately followed Joe Angelo at the Patman hearing. Coxey's testimony was about financing the bonus. But his presence was a reminder of his having established the new role of Washington as the place to go for the redress of grievances. Coxey was also a portent for a new invasion of the capital.

.   .   .

*Many years later, as president of the United States, Eisenhower wrote to Harvey Firestone Jr., the son of the founder of the company that bears his name. He had met Firestone along the army route in 1919, and in his letter Eisenhower noted that the caravan had "started him thinking" about the value of good roads and that it had planted in his mind the seed of an idea for an extensive system of highways. It bloomed thirty-seven years later, when Eisenhower as president led the legislative crusade for the Interstate Highway System we know today.

The group that most strongly supported immediate payment of the bonus was the Veterans of Foreign Wars, whose many allies included former Brigadier General Pelham Glassford. In September 1931 Glassford drove to Washington to help the VFW stage an Armistice Day Jubilee on November 11. A year earlier, Glassford, then forty-seven, had retired from the Army to move to Arizona, where he planned to serve in the state militia and help his father raise horses. Two weeks after his arrival, his father died suddenly; deeply depressed, Glassford gave up his plans to become a rancher. But he stayed in Arizona, where he went back to his avocation of painting murals, decorative screens, and watercolors.[11]

In Washington he was given a small office, immediately dubbed the Owl's Nest, under the rafters of the House Office Building. When word got out that he was in town, he was visited by a steady stream of old comrades as well as local artists who had known him in the mid-1920s, when he was stationed at the Army War College in Washington. Glassford, who had taught painting at West Point, had been very much a part of the local arts community. He had lived in a house in Georgetown festooned with art and artifacts and known affectionately as "the Borneo Embassy."[12]

One morning in late September Glassford visited the District Building, the local version of a city hall, to make traffic and parking arrangements for the Jubilee. While there he met with Herbert H. Crosby, a retired U.S. Army major general whom Glassford had known in France. Crosby was one of the three commissioners appointed by Congress to run the District of Columbia, which had no mayor or any other elected local official. He introduced Glassford to other city officials. In the midst of reorganizing the D.C. Metropolitan Police Department, demoralized and debilitated by scandals and corruption—among other things, it was still reeling from the nationally syndicated 1930 tell-all of the Man in the Green Hat—Crosby wanted to recruit a new leader who could regain long-lost public trust in the police department. Five minutes after Glassford left the building, Crosby and the D.C. Corporation Counsel decided to offer him the job of chief of police.[13]

The next day, Crosby visited the Owl's Nest and through the haze of Cuban cigar smoke announced, "I have a surprise for you. You are going to be our new chief of police." Glassford said he would have to go back to Arizona "to think this thing over and talk it out with my mother." After that talk, Glassford decided to take the job—but only with the promise that he would have a free hand in reforming the force. Although he was an outsider with no law-enforcement experience, his conditions were met, and he took the job. "I was practically 'drafted' as Superintendent of Washington police," he would later say.[14]

Glassford was appointed on October 21 under the condition that he would not take office until the VFW gala was over in mid-November. The "artist who became a cop" made good newspaper copy. A muscular, six-foot-three man with a constant smile and the nickname "Happy," he darted around town on his blue motorcycle, greeting everyone he encountered. When a reporter asked him what he knew of police work, he said, "Well, I've been arrested—once for driving through a red light and once for speeding on a motorcycle."[15]

But first came the Armistice Day Jubilee, which by any standard—let alone that of the Great Depression—was lavish, a production more 1920s Hollywood than 1930s Washington. Inside the cavernous Washington Auditorium was built a slice of Paris on Armistice Night, featuring a life-size replica of a section of Montmartre complete with narrow cobblestoned streets and balconied houses and a replica of the Moulin Rouge nightclub. Everyone of importance was there, including President and Mrs. Hoover, General Pershing, and General Douglas MacArthur, the youngest chief of staff in U.S. Army history and Glassford's friend since their days at West Point.[16]

After the gala, Glassford took command of policing Washington at a time when two alien forces struggled beneath the surface of the political discourse: American Communists on the left, and American Fascists on the right. Both looked beyond U.S. shores for drastic solutions—the dictatorships in Moscow, Rome, and Berlin. The U.S. Communist Party shouted for class warfare and revolution. The Right, entranced by the rise of fascism, spoke more softly but believed that power would come, as it had in Germany and Italy, when a strong state crushed the Left in the streets.

The U.S. Army had already fought Communists on their native ground. America had supplied the bulk of fifteen thousand troops in a coalition sent to Russia in 1918, when they intervened in the war between czarist forces and the Bolsheviks. Hundreds of American soldiers were killed fighting the Bolsheviks.[17] As Germany collapsed in 1918–19, U.S. Army observers in Berlin and other cities witnessed bloody street wars between Communists and the fascists who would put Adolf Hitler in power. The young American officers, rising in rank through the 1920s, retained as collective memory firsthand knowledge that insurrection was the ominous possibility in a nation under stress.

In the United States in the fall of 1931, there was open talk of domestic war, especially in the coalfields and industrial slums of major cities, which were scourged by unemployment and were also first to feel the impact of the great migration of African-Americans from the South, a migration that had started as a trickle in 1916. Both the right and left saw the vast cadre of unemployed Americans as potential political soldiers.

Glassford's first test as chief came on December 6, 1931, when members of a Communist-controlled "hunger march" began to arrive in the city. The march attracted just three thousand participants, who, as the conservative *Washington Star* angrily reported, sang "The Internationale, the hymn of Red Russia." Glassford kept close tabs on them, plying them with food and shelter, and giving them permission to march—or, more accurately, drive, as many were in trucks and cars. The one thing denied was permission for their leader, Herbert Benjamin, a Lithuanian immigrant and Communist organizer, to walk onto the floor of the U.S. Senate and present a petition. There were no arrests of demonstrators—the only one arrested was an unruly local who wanted to counterdemonstrate—and Benjamin and his lieutenants were given freedom to speak their minds.

At the same Washington Auditorium where he had run his VFW gala, Glassford appeared for a Hunger March rally as a nonauthoritarian figure in civilian clothes, puffing on his pipe. Benjamin told the rally that the next hunger march would bring "a force superior to the thugs of the ruling class." He also shouted to the assembled marchers, "Workers of this country must defend their fatherland, Soviet Russia, the country that has done away with unemployment."[18]*

Glassford treated hunger marchers as, to use his own word, "tourists" and served them a series of hot, huge, and hearty meals, many prepared by the chef of the Mayflower Hotel. Despite all the Red rhetoric, many marchers had been attracted to the event because they were legitimately hungry. The only marcher to be hospitalized had fainted from being malnourished.[19] The Army's Military Intelligence Division (MID) was at the scene in the person of Captain Charles H. Titus, an undercover agent who attended all the meetings and rallies. About half of the marchers, he reported, were non-Communists attracted to the group because they were simply "either hungry or interested in the trip." Titus looked over the group at the main rally and estimated them to be 35 percent Jewish, 35 percent Negro, 30 percent "miscellaneous white," and, "in all probability . . . about 25 percent women."[20]

---

*While this was going on, John Dos Passos, writing for the *New Republic*, noted that in another part of the auditorium a dance marathon was in its nineteenth hour and a man had fallen asleep on his partner's shoulder, prompting Dos Passos to mark the moment with the declaration "the jazz age is dead." *New Republic*, "Red Day on Capitol Hill," December 23, 1931, 153–54.

Although he was not connected with the hunger marchers, a sympathetic Jacob Coxey, the newly elected mayor of Massillon, Ohio, showed up with the marchers and was allowed to deliver his own personal economic plan, which included currency reform and payment of the bonus, to Theodore Joslin, Hoover's press secretary. Coxey stayed in the well-appointed Willard Hotel, a far cry from a prison cell.[21]

Edward T. Folliard of the *Washington Post* wrote that Glassford's policy of courtesy was "nothing short of magnificent," especially since the marchers were hoping to be "kicked, cuffed and clubbed" by the local police. Glassford, front and center during the whole episode, directed the entire operation from the saddle of his blue motorcycle. The only person who seemed to have suffered property damage during the incident was Thomas Damery, police chief of Somerville, Massachusetts, who was in town on police business but volunteered to be on the lookout for New England Reds. While he was patrolling the streets, someone smashed the window of his car and stole his camera, valued at $175.[22]

The hunger marchers left town on December 8, 1931, hurling jeers at the police escorting them, perhaps realizing that their goal of struggling against their oppressors had been foiled.[23]

Simultaneously, another group moved into town: eighteen war veterans from Seattle, who brought 45,000 signatures with them in favor of the bonus. They had started out with 25,000 from the state of Washington and picked up another 20,000 signatures on their trip east.[24] And before this eventful day was over, Patman reintroduced his resolution as the first of the new session: HR 1.

Less than a week later, Glassford received a letter from John Alferi of Philadelphia informing him that he was about to lead a group of a thousand veterans to the Capitol for a one-day march down Pennsylvania Avenue on Friday, December 18. Alferi's group was known as the Veterans' Bonus Brigade.[25] By the time Alferi left Philadelphia on December 14, he had only fifty marchers, and their issues had broadened to include repeal of Prohibition, which now more than ever was seen as a veterans' issue. "We are not Balsheviki [*sic*]," he declared before the departure.[26] Although the march had little impact at the time, the idea of a bonus march had been invented, and Alferi would lay claim to the title of "Mr. Bonus Army."

At the end of 1931, Wright Patman had both a cause and a foe to square off against—setting up, as one scholar saw it, a manifestation of the classic battle between "the debtor and creditor class."[27] Patman's personal nemesis was

Treasury Secretary Andrew Mellon, who for the last ten years had served three presidents in that capacity, working diligently to reduce the tax burden of the wealthy and keep the government out of the business of business. During the early years of the Depression, Mellon's oft-stated position was that no government action was called for to counter the economic calamity affecting the nation. Mellon made an ideal target for Patman and other Populists during the Depression. An art collector with the deepest of pockets, he had made his most spectacular purchases in 1930–31, when he acquired twenty-one paintings from the Hermitage Museum in Leningrad, including two Raphaels and five Rembrandts.

During the summer of 1931 Mellon had visited Europe on an economic mission, which resulted in the suspension of all remaining European war debts. Intended to soften the effects of the worldwide depression, the move angered pro-bonus forces and also helped mobilize them. Patman fumed, asking why, if there was enough money in the American economy to let Europe off the hook, there wasn't enough to pay the bonus.[28]

In support of the new attempt at legislation, another bonus demonstration was announced for February 6, 1932. This one was sponsored by the Army and Navy Union, a group founded in 1841 "to alleviate suffering and need among returning soldiers and sailors." Glassford, Vice President Charles Curtis, and Speaker of the House John Nance Garner had all given permission for the demonstration, which started out with organizers expecting to draw 8,000 veterans. Suddenly, though, there were signs that it might attract 100,000. After the legislative chairman of the Army and Navy Union, John H. Fahey, conferred with President Hoover and General Frank T. Hines, head of the Veterans Administration, the organizers decided to call off the event. Fahey told the *Washington Post* that the march would tax the city too greatly and that there could be friction with more "hunger marchers" who were talking about being in the city on the same date.[29]

At the beginning of 1932 the nation was in the nadir of the Great Depression; it would later be termed the "cruelest year" by both Frederick Louis Allen and William Manchester. Exactly 2,998 banks had failed in 1931, and they were still closing at an alarming rate. Foreclosures had become so routine and feared that in many communities bands of citizens set up armed roadblocks to prevent outsiders from coming in and buying up farms and homes. "Nobody is actually starving," President Hoover told reporters. But newspapers were publishing reports on starvation in San Francisco and New York City, where welfare officials reported that 110 people—mostly children—were dead of malnutrition.[30]

As more and more Americans settled in teeming communities of squalid tar-paper shacks known derisively as Hoovervilles, whatever levity could be found came in small doses and usually at the expense of the Hoover administration, which was vilified in song and verse.[31] One anonymous bit of doggerel, which began making the rounds in early 1932, seemed to sum it up for many Americans:

> *Mellon pulled the whistle,*
> *Hoover rang the bell.*
> *Wall Street gave the signal,*
> *And the country went to hell.*[32]

As for the veterans of the World War, many now in their forties, by 1932 a total of $896 million had been paid into the bonus fund; accrued interest added $95 million, bringing the fund's total to $991 million. The compensation certificates could be used as collateral for loans, at first up to 22.5 percent of their face value, then, under the terms of the 1931 legislation, up to 50 percent of face value, but at 4.5 percent interest. Those who took advantage of this new loan provision, in effect, cut their bonuses in half. No veteran who needed the money in loan form could conceive of being able to pay the loan back. Payments on the loan were deducted from the remainder of their bonus. By 1945 the cumulative interest would have entirely consumed the other half of their expected funds.

From the standpoint of most veterans, however, the U.S. Treasury had pocketed $2.39 billion of their money, which would not be released until 1945. Some, like *New York Herald-Tribune* columnist Walter Lippmann, tried to explain the fiscal facts of life to the vets. Lippmann pointed out that "to demand payment of the principal of a debt . . . before it is due is to demand money that is not owed at all now and to demand more money than is owed ultimately."[33]

As the year began, Hoover was steadfast in his belief that giving money to the veterans would encourage social-welfare advocates and deprive the government of funds needed for economic recovery. He had addressed the issue of legislation calling for immediate payment in speeches to the American Legion's national convention in Detroit in September 1931 and in Boston in October 1930. Hoover followed the policies of his predecessors, declaring that payment of the bonus could not be made at that time because of the fiscal problems facing the United States.[34]

The 1931 Legion convention was a split decision for Hoover. The delegates, by a vote of 902 to 507, supported him on holding off immediate cash payment of the bonus for economic reasons, but they were against him on Prohibition, opposing the law by a vote of 1,008 to 394. For the first time, the American Legion had put this to a vote, claiming it to be a veterans' issue. Many of the delegates believed that if they went along with the president on the bonus, he would go along with them on repeal.[35]

On January 6, 1932, a vast army of unemployed workers, mostly Pennsylvanians, arrived in Washington to demand jobs. They were led by Father James Cox of Pittsburgh, a Roman Catholic priest who had served as a chaplain in the war. Alarmed by the behavior of both the Communists and the Republicans, Cox had decided to organize his own march on Washington, inspired by Coxey. But unlike Coxey's Army, Cox's Army had cars and trucks and paved roads and grew as it moved on Washington, doubling, then more than tripling, from its initial core of 6,000, making it the largest march on Washington up to then.[36]

Early on the afternoon of their departure, Cox's Army arrived in Johnstown, Pennsylvania. They were met by Mayor Eddie McCloskey, a Democrat who had recently defeated the candidate handpicked by Bethlehem Steel. He greeted Cox and led him to a mass rally. McCloskey took the podium to denounce Bethlehem Steel's attempts to evade payment of property taxes. Then Cox rose to lambaste Hoover and his policies: "Our president is still trying to give money to the bankers, but none to the people. If I had my way, it would go to the people, who need it badly. There is plenty of money in this country, but try and get it. I do think that our mission to Washington will have its effect. The government sent Al Capone to jail for cheating it out of $100,000, yet John D. Rockefeller is giving $4,000,000 to his son to escape the inheritance tax."[37]

Cox wanted to meet with Hoover, but the White House opposed the idea. Lawrence Richey, the president's secretary, wrote an internal memo stating Hoover's position: "We will not see this man. If he has a petition we will be glad to receive [it], but he cannot see the president." Once Cox arrived in Washington on January 6, another Hoover aide contacted one of Glassford's detectives for assistance. He wanted to know if there really were any ex-servicemen with Cox or whether this march was merely another Communist propaganda ploy. The detectives reported that 20 percent of the marchers had fought in the Great War, and 10 percent had served in the Spanish-American War. The marchers, he reported, were in large part respectable citizens who did not want to overthrow the system but rather wanted the system to give them jobs.[38]

Given this positive report, Hoover invited Cox and a small delegation to the White House, where Cox lost no time in telling the president that the administration was acting "like an ostrich that sticks its head in the sand, believing that if he cannot see the hunter pursuing him or the trouble that is nearby, that the hunter or the trouble does not exist." Hoover expressed sympathy for the unemployed and then read a terse statement contending that the Depression had nearly run its course and that his administration had a program in place to complete America's economic recovery, and rejecting out of hand any massive federal spending on public works projects as a solution.[39]

There were no incidents during Cox's protest. Police and newspaper estimates of the crowds ranged from 12,000 to 25,000. Glassford again strengthened his reputation as a man who could control demonstrators.

With Cox's followers in the streets of Washington, Patman decided to legally attack Mellon, the greatest foe of prepayment, by introducing an impeachment resolution accusing him of "high crimes and misdemeanors." Patman also asserted that Mellon held his office illegally because of vast conflicts of interest between his private holdings and his role as a public servant. As early as the spring of 1931 Patman began his extraordinary campaign to impeach Mellon, claiming to represent those who believed that his acts were responsible for the Depression.[40]

Bringing formal charges against the Treasury secretary was a stunning move that quickly led to public hearings. Patman stated that the secretary was the owner of stock in 300 corporations with resources of $3 billion. Patman saw an immense conflict of interest in Mellon's engagement in "trade and commerce in every state, county and village in the United States, every country of the world, and upon the seven seas," while he was in charge of the tariffs and taxes imposed on those same corporations.[41]

The basis of the central charge of "high crimes and misdemeanors" was a 1789 statute that, among other things, prohibited any Treasury secretary from owning "in whole or in part . . . any sea vessel." Patman listed four Norwegian, fourteen Venezuelan, and thirty-six American ships used by Gulf Oil and the Aluminum Company of America as owned by Mellon in direct violation of the statute. He recounted that Mellon was in charge of tax refunds to Mellon companies, owned bank stock, was in the whiskey business, and had an interest in the Koppers Company, which was supervising the erection of gas plants in the Soviet Union—not yet diplomatically recognized by the United States—despite charges that goods imported from that country were made by convict labor. Impeachment hearings began less than a week later, at which point Patman added another charge: that the Mellon companies were given special treatment by the Internal Revenue Service, whose employees had been intimidated by Secretary Mellon. For all communications regarding these companies, said Patman, there was a special tag that read, "This is a Mellon Company."[42]

Hoover defused the situation by offering Mellon another position, U.S. ambassador to the Court of St. James in London. Ambassador Charlie Dawes had resigned on January 8. This was the perfect solution: it got Mellon out of Patman's hot seat.[43]

The delicate task of inducing Mellon to transfer from Washington to London was not made any easier by his belief that Hoover was capitulating to the demagogic congressman from Texarkana. But with his impeachment hearings under way on February 4, Mellon resigned and accepted the ambassadorial post.[44]

Deprived of his nemesis, Patman was furious. He insisted that the London job amounted to a "presidential pardon" that had "saved the Republican Party from a scandalous exposure that would have rocked the pillars of our Government." He added: "Mr. Mellon has violated more laws, caused more human suffering and illegally acquired more property to satisfy his personal greed than any other person on earth, without fear of punishment and with the sanction and approval of three chief executives of a civilized nation."

As soon as Mellon had been hastily confirmed as ambassador, the House Judiciary Committee withdrew from the impeachment proceedings, asserting that it was impossible to impeach a Treasury secretary who had resigned.

On January 22, 1932, the Reconstruction Finance Corporation was established by the Hoover administration. Hoover's most ambitious effort to deal with the Depression, the RFC started off by loaning money to banks and businesses, hoping that prosperity would "trickle down" through the economy. The $1.5 to $2 billion the RFC would eventually lend—the greatest peacetime outlay by the federal government to that point in history—would not be enough to reverse the economic collapse of the nation's banking and financial system. Patman insisted that this was nothing more than a gift to "the big boys" in New York, and he wanted to know why the same generosity could not be shown to the veterans.

Father Charles E. Coughlin, the "radio priest" who railed against "the vested interests of wealth" to a weekly network audience of between thirty and fifty million, said, "If the Government can pay $2 billion to the bankers and railroads [through the RFC], having had no obligation toward them, why cannot it pay the $2 billion to the soldiers, already recognized as an obligation?"[45] In his column of February 24, 1932, Will Rogers warned his readers that "you can't get a room in Washington. . . . Every hotel is jammed to the doors with bankers from all over America to get their 'hand out' from the Reconstruction Finance Corporation." The bankers, it seemed to Rogers, "have the honor of being the first group to go on the 'dole' in America."[46] Now more than ever, Patman believed, the time was right to push for immediate payment.

The White House and Secret Service, meanwhile, concerned about the bitterness that seemed to be growing on many fronts, anticipated civil disorder and attempted assassination. "Crank letters, threats, and eccentric visitors reached a new high," Edmund W. Starling, head of the White House detail, recalled. "Secret Service agents all over the country were busy checking on the people who felt an inclination to swell the White House mailbags."[47] New rules were created and the security detail beefed up to forty to fifty men per shift. No person was allowed to approach the president carrying a package. In January 1932 a confidential Secret Service memo, entitled "Riot Call Regulations," assigned battle stations for the agents and special police who would defend the White House from mob attack.[48]

Fear for the safety of public officials took a more sinister turn on March 1, 1932, when a nurse went in to check on the twenty-month-old son of Charles A. Lindbergh and his wife, Anne Morrow, only to find the child missing. A note near the nursery window demanded $50,000. Beneath the second-floor window were muddy footprints, a wooden ladder, and a carpenter's chisel. The case grabbed the attention of Americans like few before or since, and the fear of kidnapping—already a major concern throughout the country—was now ubiquitous.

Then, on the cold, gray morning of March 7, 1932, approximately four thousand men and women marched from Detroit to the Ford Motor Company's River Rouge plant in Dearborn to present a list of demands to company management. A fight broke out when the marchers were denied entry to the plant. Police opened fire on the unarmed mob. A photographer for the *Detroit News,* Ray Pillsbury, reported, "I would guess that hundreds of shots were fired into the mob. I saw their leaders drop, writhing with their wounds, and the mob dropped back, leaving their casualties on the road. . . . [People] were pitching forward every few seconds and lying still."[49] When the smoke cleared, four men lay dead or dying in what became known as the Ford Massacre. The four bodies lay in state for four days in Workers' Hall in Detroit under a huge red flag, a portrait of Lenin, and a banner reading "Ford Gave Bullets for Bread." The dead were accorded a funeral procession ten thousand people long and group interment, attended by thirty thousand, in a collective grave overlooking the River Rouge plant.[50]

The nation was in crisis. Fear of more violence and revolutionary unrest spread in the wake of the Ford Massacre. The anxiety was not new. It stemmed from a time soon after the Great War, when czarist Russia became Bolshevik Russia and communism came to America. The Red Scare, coupled with fear of anarchists and other radicals, had intensified in 1919 when a bomb exploded on the lawn of the Washington home of Attorney General J. Mitchell Palmer. He quickly formed an antiradical unit and put a young Department of Justice clerk, J. Edgar Hoover, in charge. Government agents arrested 6,000 aliens and deported 556.[51] The Reds wrote frightening manifestos and threatened revolution. But revolution never happened. As the 1920s roared in, the Red Scare faded.

The Depression brought new fears of menacing Reds. Communist Party officials in both America and the Soviet Union believed that unemployment and discontent had made the United States ripe for class warfare. Communists directed riots not only in Dearborn but also in New York City, Albany, Los Angeles, Akron, and Saint Louis, where rioters seized city hall and held it for several hours.[52] The new Red Scare also found its way into politics, for President Hoover, like every president since Wilson, decided against recognition of the Soviet Union, whose leaders called for the overthrow of the U.S. government and financed subversive activities by members of the U.S. Communist Party.[53]

The Red threat was taken very seriously by the U.S. Army, especially its Military Intelligence Division (MID), which had information that since February 1931 party leaders had been working on plans for a violent and mammoth bonus march to Washington.[54]

High-ranking Army officers were so convinced of a potential Red-led revolution that they ordered a study on how tanks could be used against potential revolutionaries. This was among the topics studied by officers attending the 1932 class at the Army's Tank School at Fort Benning, Georgia.[55] The officers were told that "radical manpower" in the United States numbered more than one million and included not only the estimated 380,000 members of radical organizations but also "unorganized" groups of aliens and criminals. The cities "most likely to become the scene of violent revolutionary activities" were Chicago, Cleveland, New York, Seattle, and San Francisco; other likely sites were Boston, New Haven, Buffalo, Philadelphia, Pittsburgh, Detroit, Dayton, and Baltimore. "Federal troops have been used in the suppression of domestic disturbances on more than a hundred separate occasions," the Tank School officers were told, "and there is every reason to believe that troops will be called on again, for the same purpose."[56]

The Army's plan of action benefited from lessons learned from Communist uprisings in Germany, beginning as the Great War was ending. Humiliated and hopeless in defeat, hundreds of thousands of German soldiers deserted and turned into revolutionaries of the Left and Right. Communists, fomenting riots and rebellion, seized power in dozens of cities. As a beleaguered Germany emerged from the war, former officers formed a Landesjaeger Corps—"national hunters"—who volunteered to fight the Communists, using machine guns, mortars, armored cars, and even aircraft against lightly armed, disorganized rebels, killing an estimated 15,000 of them.[57] U.S. military observers gathered detailed information on the Landesjaeger tactics, and the observers' reports made their way into Army files, including the Tank School document.[58] In a typical operation, Landesjaeger aircraft machine-gunned rioters on roofs and at the barricades, paving the way for armored cars and troops with machine guns and hand grenades. Sections of the city were cordoned off, and mortars lobbed shells into the areas.

The Landesjaeger's methods, according to the Tank School document, "merit rather close study because of the success achieved within a minimum of time, and with small damage to life and property." Tanks, the officers were told, should be used by U.S. Army troops only against "a major domestic disturbance which is well organized and led." Other weapons would include machine guns, hand grenades, mortars, artillery, and aircraft. "As a rule, firearms should not be used against a crowd if other weapons are available," such as tear gas.

"In the attack of a city controlled by radical elements," officers were advised,

> *an attempt should be made to obtain possession of as much of its territory as possible. . . . There will be many parts of the city where no resistance will be encountered and other parts where the rioters are strongly prepared to offer resistance. . . . [It] has been found advantageous to attack a mob on one flank, depending upon the direction it is desired to drive it, and in the rear, while being held in front. It may happen that those in front would like to retreat, but because of pressure from behind, are unable to do so. . . .*
>
> *A house occupied by rioters may be avoided if it is occupied only as a refuge. . . . If its occupancy menaces the . . . troops, or threatens their rear,*

it may become necessary to reduce it at once. Tanks are especially adapted for such attacks and can quickly reduce it to shambles.

The U.S. Army plans at that time were code-named in colors that labeled potential enemies, both domestic and foreign. War Plan Orange, for example, involved war against Japan.[59] White was assigned to the plan to defend Washington, D.C., against insurrection or serious riot.

4

Mobilizing a Bonus Army

Akron, Augusta, Austin, Baltimore, Boston, Bridgeport, Buffalo, Camden,
Canton, Chicago, Cleveland, Columbus, Council Bluffs, Denver, Des
Moines, Detroit, East Saint Louis, Erie, Fort Wayne, Hartford,
Indianapolis, Kansas City, Lancaster, Las Vegas, Los Angeles, New Orleans,
New York City, Newark, Omaha, Philadelphia, Pittsburg, Portland,
Raleigh, Reno, Richmond, Salt Lake City, Seattle, Springfield (Illinois and
Massachusetts), Stockton, Tampa, Wheeling, Wichita, Worcester,
Youngstown.

—Municipalities with large delegations to the BEF,
 based on police and news reports.

T HE THIRD CRUEL WINTER of the Great Depression faded
into the spring of 1932, bringing a new season of despair for
countless veterans. Like many, former sergeant Walter W. Waters was down
on his luck in Portland, Oregon. He had served his country well. Born in 1898
in Burns, a town that had sprouted in the heart of Oregon's open range, Waters moved with his family to Weiser, Idaho, on the Snake River.[1] When he
left school in May 1916, at the age of eighteen, he went to Boise and enlisted
in the Idaho National Guard. Shortly afterward his regiment of about 1,800
men was called to federal service as reinforcements for a punitive expedition

56

that President Wilson had sent to the Mexican border in pursuit of Francisco "Pancho" Villa.[2] A revolutionary turned outlaw, Villa was on a rampage against Americans. He and his band had killed sixteen Americans on a train in Mexico and raided the Texas town of Columbus and killed another nineteen. The U.S. Army, under Major General John J. Pershing, searched for Villa for eleven months. On February 5, 1917, President Wilson ordered the troops withdrawn.[3]

By then Waters's enlistment had ended, but on the eve of war he joined the Oregon National Guard, which, with units from other northwestern states, became part of the 41st Infantry Division. Waters was in the medical detachment of the 146th Field Artillery when the division sailed to France on Christmas Eve in 1917.[4]

Like most combat veterans of the Great War, Waters did not talk much about his days in France. He became a sergeant in April 1918, a good sign that he was a more than able soldier in fierce, and later storied, battles—Saint-Mihiel, Château-Thierry, Meuse-Argonne. A journal kept by Sergeant Harold Kamp, of the 146th Field Artillery, tells of artillerymen crouching "like animals of the forest" during their first gas attack, of the "stench of decaying human flesh and animals," of German machine gunners "chained to their guns, dieing [*sic*] with fear portrayed on their faces," and of Doughboys who "lived in dugouts for days, too frightened to come out of their hiding for food or drink."[5]

The 41st Division became part of the army of occupation. So Waters was not one of those Doughboys welcomed home in victory parades after the November 1918 Armistice. He did not return to the United States until June 1919. He was honorably discharged; on the line of his discharge paper labeled "Character," an officer wrote "Excellent."[6]

Waters, back in civilian life, tried to get going in some profitable business or position, as a garage mechanic, an automobile salesman, a farmhand, a baker's helper. Then, in 1925, as a twenty-seven-year-old drifter, he tried to change his luck by changing his name. Cutting all family and personal ties, he hitchhiked to Washington State and, as "Bill Kincaid," got a job picking fruit in Washington's bountiful cherry, peach, and apple orchards. He finally settled in Wenatchee, a fruit canning and shipping center at the confluence of the Columbia and Wenatchee rivers. He became a superintendent in a cannery and, still under his assumed name, married a cannery worker, Wilma Anderson.[7]

The cannery became a casualty of the Depression. After it shut down, Waters headed to Portland, where he got a job at another cannery. He and Wilma rented a two-room apartment on the wrong side of the tracks; by early 1932 he

Walter W. Waters, a veteran from Portland, Oregon, became commander in chief of the Bonus Army, but often faced opposition. "We will stay here until 1945 if necessary to get our bonus," he said. (Authors' collection)

was jobless again. But he had an idea: veterans should march to Washington and petition Congress for legislation that would give them the bonus immediately. He wrote out a speech and memorized it. On March 15, 1932, before several hundred veterans who had assembled in a hall in Portland, he made his speech as eloquently as he could. Essentially he told them: We should all hop a freight and head for Washington, D.C., to get the money that is rightfully ours. Waters attracted no followers, and he later conceded, "My speech fell flat."[8] George Alman, a cantankerous ex-lumberjack, remembered organizing several meetings at this time. At one, he spoke first and then asked if any other veteran wanted to come to the platform. "W. W. Waters came up," Alman remembers, "telling a story about himself and his wife having had only fried potatoes for Christmas dinner."[9]

Waters had become obsessed with the idea that the only way to get the bonus was to go to Washington and lobby for it. "During this time," he says, "I was anxiously watching reports in the newspapers of the progress of Bonus legislation. . . . I noticed . . . that the highly organized lobbies in Washington for special industries were producing results; loans were being granted to their special interests and those lobbies seemed to justify their existence. Personal lobbying paid, regardless of the justice or injustice of the demand."[10]

The idea of a march was not new in Portland. In November 1931 about forty Portland veterans hopped on the freights to Washington, met with Oregon members of Congress, and returned in passenger trains, thanks to a sympathetic fellow veteran, Oregon senator Frederick Steiwer, who had been a U.S. Army lieutenant in France.[11]

While Waters was in Portland talking about a march to Washington, the Veterans of Foreign Wars were planning their own march *in* Washington. The VFW demonstration was more a procession than a march. On April 8 more than twelve hundred veterans, with flags flying and bands playing, paraded to the broad steps of the U.S. Capitol. They presented Representative Wright Patman and other pro-bonus legislators with bundles of petitions calling for an immediate bonus payment. The VFW, which had organized the march, said there were 2,240,030 names in the bundles and packing cases of petitions that the veterans had carried to the Capitol steps.[12]

Included in the ranks of the veterans were large contingents from American Legion posts, marching in defiance of the anti-bonus stand of the national commander of the legion, Henry L. Stevens Jr., a North Carolina lawyer who had been elected by acclamation at the legion convention in 1931.[13] The Legion's legislative committee had obliged President Hoover by voting to keep all bonus resolutions off the floor of the convention.[14]

The impressive demonstration on the Capitol steps, along with the surge of bonus-now demands throughout the nation in the spring of 1932, produced widespread publicity. Radio personality Father Coughlin declared in congressional testimony in April that he had received some 2.5 million unsolicited letters on the bonus, which he said represented not just the vets but public opinion.[15]

The petitions and resolutions, however, were not producing results in Congress. Pro-bonus legislators were fighting to keep their bills from dying in committee. War veterans in Congress, including Fiorello La Guardia and Hamilton Fish Jr., argued vigorously against the bonus in bitter debates with pro-bonus representatives.[16] Watching newspaper reports and listening to radio news, Waters decided that Congress was ignoring the demands of veterans because members of Congress were seeing only signatures and pieces of paper—not hungry, jobless veterans.

On April 23, a one-paragraph story on page 4 of a Portland newspaper told of a planned veterans' rally a week later.[17] Again Waters spoke, and again he was rebuffed. But he kept talking, feeling he was getting better with each speech, even though no one leaped up and joined his cause.

Then, on May 1, newspapers across the nation carried an Associated Press report that the House Ways and Means Committee had voted against Patman's latest bonus bill. The committee had also called for the return and tabling of all bonus bills to the House with unfavorable reports—a death sentence for the bonus in 1932.[18] The committee had responded to reality: Hoover would veto any bonus legislation.[19]

Waters seized on this news. In his next speech he told a group of jobless veterans that "there was little difference between hunger in Washington and hunger in Portland." The men knew what he meant. By some estimates there were 4,500 jobless veterans in Portland.[20] Local relief funds were running out for them and everyone else. A Portland family of five—husband, wife, two children, and one grandmother, for instance—had to get by on a welfare food allotment of $4 a week.[21] Waters kept talking about going to Washington, and the crowds kept growing. The last meeting before finally setting out for Washington was on May 10.[22] The meeting was held outdoors in a park near city hall.[23] George Kleinholz, a veteran who was glad to have a job as a salesman, was walking by and stopped to listen. When he got home he told his wife, "I'm going to Washington."[24]

Around the same time, a footloose thirty-two-year-old who called himself Steve Murray arrived in Portland. He had been wandering around the Northwest for more than two months—catching freights, hitchhiking, and, in a firm, neat hand, always writing down his adventures in an extraordinary diary that would follow the entire campaign of the Bonus Army.[25] He had just received a pair of hand-me-down shoes from an American Legion post, and he decided to visit his uncle in Portland. By traveling in a boxcar and then hiking fifteen miles in his newly acquired shoes, he made it to Portland in early April and got a job painting and doing carpentry work in a hotel.

In his spare time, Murray often joined unemployed veterans who hung around the courthouse. Most of the talk was about Wright Patman's seemingly doomed bonus bill. Then one day he met Waters, who told him about the plan to march on Washington. Murray quit his job—"the work was about finished anyway," he wrote—and told Waters he would join up.

Other veterans who joined included George Alman, who had run several bonus meetings; Edgar W. White, who described himself as public relations manager; and Chester A. Hazen, an ex-sergeant whose asthma made him 10 percent disabled, by a Veterans Administration ruling. Hazen took over the march and gave himself the military title of commander in chief.[26]

The Oregon veterans joined hundreds of thousands of men, women, children, and babies who were already on the move in May 1932—walking, hitchhiking, hopping freights, heading somewhere, heading nowhere, looking for a meal, a job, a place to flop. During that year, by one count, America had a floating population of 25,000 families and 2 million boys and young men on the road. As for single women and girls, statisticians seem to have averted their eyes. There were only whispered tales of girls selling their bodies or disappearing into the hobo jungles carved out of the narrow wildernesses along railroad rights-of-way.

Kansas City counted 1,500 men and boys passing through the city every day.[27] Railroads were plagued by so many illegal passengers that many railroad cops were no longer arresting them for trespass. The railroad cops would just collar the trespassers and send them shuffling into the nearest town. And some towns reacted by having their policemen escort the trespassers back to the railroad tracks and order them to hop the next freight.[28] Every year at least a hundred people died under the wheels of freight trains, and hundreds of others were injured, many losing a leg.[29]

By 1932 newspapers and newsreels hardly noticed the poor, the evicted, the young tramps, as they were called. The dispossessed were no longer news. The same seemed to be true in Portland when the veterans marched off, "to the beat of a borrowed drum," as Waters described their departure. There was scant coverage in local newspapers. The men wore shiny old suits, bib overalls, or pieces of Army uniforms topped off by khaki overseas hats. They carried knapsacks or duffel bags or bedrolls, with tin cups dangling. They had $30 among them.

The men climbed into friends' trucks, which took them to the Union Pacific freight yards, where they waited for the night train. "We laughed and joked, like a crowd of children bound for a picnic," Waters remembered. "Then, from afar, we heard the whistle of the train. Here we were, ready to start, and here was the train. Its headlight fired the tracks far before it. The men tightened their knapsacks—here was the train. It passed us, at fifty miles an hour."[30]

Aware of the veterans' plans, railroad officials had ordered the train to highball through Portland too fast for anyone to hitch a ride. The veterans settled down in the freight yard, awaiting the next day's train.

Around 4:00 A.M., a bugler sounded reveille. Murray and the others woke up to find members of the local American Legion post passing out coffee and doughnuts. "Some of the men were so lazy," Murray wrote, "they would not get up even when mess call was blown, so the bugler decided to blow [the call for] pay day. Then they come thinking Old Man Hoover had paid us the *Bonus.* How discouraged they looked when they saw they were only getting coffee and doughnut for pay."

Waters and four others took up "the problem that faced the Bonus Army through its whole existence"—how to feed the men and, later, many wives and children. Nearby restaurants and bakeries donated food, the veterans scrounged coffeepots, and the men were soon sitting in boxcars and eating what the newly selected mess sergeants managed to produce. Some deserted the army that day, but new recruits appeared in their place. The count stood at about 280 when railroad officials appeared. Waters recollected this dialogue:

"We'll run the train right through the yards again without stopping," the officials said.

"We'll line up across the tracks," some of the men said. "Then try it."

"That won't do you any good. There are no empty cars on the train, and you can't ride on the roofs. There's a tunnel near here that will scrape you off."

"Put on some empties, then, or let the tunnel do its scrapin'."

"We can't—and it's suicide if you ride on top," an official said, ending the conversation.

The impasse continued until the train arrived. Seeing the crowd milling about, the engineer blew the whistle and slowed to a stop. Men jumped onto the boxcars' ladders and began to climb up. The officials told the engineer to wait. Then one of them said to the vets, "If you men will climb into some empty stock cars on that track over there, we'll hook them on the train for you. That's the best we can do."

The men scrambled down and ran toward cattle cars reeking of dung. ("We searched for a shovel and cleaned it all out," Murray noted.) The cars were coupled on, and the train headed east. Veterans who had ridden to battle in French "40 and 8" boxcars—meant to carry either forty men or eight horses—insisted that an American cattle car smelled better.

They were going east, but not according to plan. Chester Hazen and his buddies, who were supposed to drive ahead and solicit donations to buy food, failed at their mission. For three days and nights the men had to rely on handouts from fellow veterans and others as the train stopped or paused for short periods at little towns along the way through Oregon. Some locals rallied to help the vets: townspeople served them lunch in The Dalles, there were donations of food and a quick parade at La Grande, and then only a sandwich apiece and a little coffee at Huntington. "Please take note," Murray wrote in his diary, "how far apart our meals were and the amount we had to eat at each meal. The men would be just as hungry after eating as before." On a typical day, the veterans had only two meals.*

---

*When Waters's group was a few days out of Portland a pall was cast over them as the body of the Lindbergh baby was found on May 12, partly buried and badly decomposed, about four and a half miles southeast of his home.

At Pocatello, Idaho, in the western foothills of the Rockies, the men piled out of the boxcars and gathered in a windswept vacant lot, looking in vain for Hazen, who was supposed to meet them there. Local policemen and others found food for them. They huddled together through the night. By now they were calling themselves the Bonus Expeditionary Force, BEF for short. And they found themselves calling outsiders "civilians." They said they were in an army, the Bonus Army. But it was more of a disorganized, demoralized crowd than an army.

Commander in Chief Hazen appeared the next day, smiling assuredly but without food or money. George Alman and Hazen's other company commanders began to sharply question him about what had happened to the money he had collected: "We knew that not all the money so collected was going into food but some was going into his racketeering pockets."[31] According to Alman, Hazen tried to talk his way out of the confrontation, and when he threatened to pull a gun, local lawmen stepped in, disarmed him, and sent him back to Portland.[32]

Like so many incidents in the BEF trek, this one has more than one recollected version. Murray's diary entry for that day says that after a dinner of "good old Army bean stew," the bugler blew "assembly," a meeting was held, and "Hazen was found guilty of carrying a weapon on himself and tried to hold up our secretary, Mr. Taylor, the night before. What his idea was in trying to hold Taylor up I don't know, as it was only about $25 in our treasury. But at least he tried it and was disqualified and was kicked out of our outfit and turned loose. I heard later that he went back to Portland and started another bunch to go to Washington D.C. and he collected . . . $200.00 for expense money on their way. . . . He left the bunch stranded at La Grande, Ore., and he was gone."

The incident shattered the unity of the BEF. Some men huddled in small groups, muttering about the way Hazen had chiseled them and griping about having to take orders from anyone. Others slipped off to find likely places for panhandling. "Instead of becoming an army, under discipline, we were almost a completely disorganized mob," Waters recalled. His old sergeant's instincts took hold. He climbed to the top of a boxcar and started haranguing, using language that he declined to include in his restrained memoir. Whatever the words were, the men listened to them, and an election of officers was held on the spot.

Waters was elected regimental commander—not army commander—because he apparently thought of the marchers as a regiment on the move, perhaps with other regiments someday following.* The secretary mentioned by

---

*A Great War regiment had about 3,800 men.

Murray was A. F. Taylor, a stocky, well-liked man with a gift of gab who was elected the new commander in chief.[33] Like Hazen, Taylor was to go ahead of the marchers as an advance man. Waters, as second in command, created companies of forty men each, led by a captain with one lieutenant and one sergeant, all elected. Each company also was supposed to have a bugler and a first-aid squad. Alman became a captain, as did Murray. Recruits trickled in, but there were deserters, too. The Bonus Army's strength held at about 300.[34] Murray later tells of passing out potatoes to 350 men, by his count.

Orders from Waters—no drinking, no panhandling, no antigovernment talk—went directly to the captains. Waters also demanded that each man again show his discharge papers.[35] To enforce his rules, he appointed six military policemen, led by Mickey Dolan, a former West Coast prizefighter. Waters also appointed Jim Foley, a wartime supply sergeant, as regimental supply officer. Foley was to take charge "of all foodstuffs, tobacco, money, and supplies donated to us en route and to issue them proportionately to all the men."

Decreeing that the Bonus Army "was ready to move forward again," Waters obtained permission from Pocatello officials for a parade. The men marched through downtown Pocatello (to the beat of another borrowed drum) while four men walked along the sidewalk, hats in hand, collecting $20 for the BEF.

Although federal law forbade people to ride a railroad for free, whether in a passenger car or a boxcar, railroads varied in their enforcement of that law. The Southern Pacific Railroad alone was arresting or tossing off trains as many as 683,000 would-be freeloaders a year.[36] But a large number of railroad men were veterans themselves, and some found ways to wink at the railway laws, such as the fourteen empty boxcars the Northern Pacific Railway pulled into a siding in Pocatello. The men clambered aboard, more orderly now.

During a stop at Green River, Wyoming, the men staged a short parade before a crowd of about two thousand. "The American Legion gave us about $40.00 in smokes," Murray wrote in his diary that night, "and we took in about $25.00 in the parade. . . . We climbed into the train and went to bed as we sure were tired after all the drilling and parading." Next stop was Rawlings, where "we were short on food, as all we got was a cup of coffee and 1 sandwich each." There was another parade at Laramie, Wyoming. "We were all very hungry. So when mess call was blown all we got was a cup of coffee, 1 slice of bread and ½ a roll each. So we were still hungry." Looking out on the country flashing by, Murray saw "dead cattle and horses that had died from starvation and cold."

The train pulled into Cheyenne, Wyoming, in early evening and stopped at a sidetrack on an army post. "Here they fed us supper and, oh boy, it was good, as we sure were hungry," Murray wrote. They were even given seconds, "with ice cream after each helping. There were about 2,000 people here to watch this bunch of bums eat supper and, oh boy, how they stood around and watched us." Waters and Alman both mention a crowd—five to six thousand, by Alman's estimate. The BEF formed up for a parade, many of the men puffing in the thin mountain air.[37] Then they marched back to the freight yards and climbed back into the same boxcars, which took them to Council Bluffs, Iowa.

Here, a week after leaving Portland, they began to realize that people were welcoming them as warriors of the Depression, just as people in France had welcomed them as Yanks. Often a veterans' group in one town would notify a similar group in the next, requesting that they have hot meals available when the vets arrived. Unlike the countless streams of vagabond men on America's rails and highways, these were men with a purpose, men who were challenging the nation's creed of despair. The mayor of Council Bluffs presented them the key to the city. The town authorized a parade. American Legionnaires brought food. The police talked to officials of the Wabash Railway, and their boxcars took the veterans and their supplies out of Iowa and through Missouri to Saint Louis, then across the Mississippi River to East Saint Louis, Illinois.[38]

The veterans thought that the informal arrangements for boxcar transport would continue on the Wabash Railway line. But the Bonus Army was entering another province of the Depression as its men passed from the America of ranches and farms to the America of seething cities and shut-down factories. Communist-controlled hunger marches and demonstrations had shaken Detroit and touched off the bloody Ford Massacre in Dearborn, Michigan, two months earlier.[39] Chicago was bankrupt, with 624,000 out of work. After witnessing an angry protest from 20,000 people clamoring for food, Chicago mayor Anton Cermak had warned the state legislature, "Call out the troops before you close the relief stations"—the bureaucratic term for breadlines and soup kitchens. The alarmed legislators did send money, but money was running out by the spring of 1932. In Saint Louis, with a workforce of 330,000, only 125,000 had jobs, and one out of every eight residents faced imminent eviction. Across the river in East Saint Louis, where unemployment had reached 60 percent, a frightened mayor had issued an order prohibiting any meetings of the jobless.[40] East Saint Louis, a tough town going through tough times, did not want another 300 jobless men, even if they were veterans. At least, that was what the politicians and the railroad executives thought.

The BEF assembled at a depot about two miles out of Council Bluffs, where they were told to wait for empty boxcars. But what seemed to be an accomplished deal in Council Bluffs somehow evaporated under the glare of higher-ranking railroad officials with connections in higher places in Illinois. Suddenly, one of the local railroad officials mentioned interstate commerce laws that forbade railroads to give free rides. The trainmaster, who was to make up the train, said he had no empties but the veterans were welcome to ride on top of the cars—a potentially lethal way to travel. The men, wanting to move on, accepted the offer, but Waters refused because of the danger and because there would be no way to transport supplies or those veterans who were not physically able to climb to the tops of the cars.

Waters lined up the men along the track. The train started forward, then stopped because two cars in the middle of the train had become uncoupled. Trainmen went to recouple them while members of what Waters called the Transportation Committee slipped between cars and used their skills as laid-off railroad men. They again uncoupled cars or pulled pins from air-brake hoses. The train started . . . and stopped. Again trainmen hooked up the cars. The train started up and stopped again. The exasperated engineer said that was enough. He would not attempt to move the train unless the veterans were on board.

The angry trainmaster went to his office, accompanied by Waters, and made a long-distance phone call. "I have called the police, but they won't come down," Waters heard him say to someone. ". . . Yes. I did notify the sheriff, but he says that it isn't his job to prevent persons from riding on freight trains." The trainmaster slammed down the phone, led Waters back to the train, and pointed to four empties, telling him to load the men into them. Later that night, a few other empty cars were added and the train, fully coupled, headed for Saint Louis, Missouri.[41] There, the veterans expected to cross the river to East Saint Louis, Illinois, and get into boxcars provided by the Baltimore & Ohio Railroad, which would take them across Illinois and Indiana to Cincinnati, Ohio.

Commander in Chief A. F. Taylor, as the advance man, had gone on to Saint Louis by car. Meanwhile, word of the BEF was spreading, and even as Waters and his men were still sprawled on the floor of the Wabash boxcars, twenty-five vets from Tennessee were circling the streets around the White House in a truck bearing the sign "We Want Our Bonus."[42]

The train rolled through suburbs and northern Saint Louis, slowing down at a complex of tracks that branched into vast switchyards. The men awoke soon after dawn to see that the train had stopped alongside a vacant lot, surrounded

Among the Bonus Army's early arrivals in Washington were veterans from Chattanooga, Tennessee, who drove past the White House on May 18. The main contingent, formed in Portland, Oregon, was still en route. (Underwood & Underwood/Library of Congress)

by police brandishing nightsticks and shotguns. Waters, stunned by the sight, ordered his bugler to sound assembly. The men climbed out of the cars, lined up for roll call, and marched into the lot. The policemen did not move. Waters did not know that the Saint Louis police had been alerted by news stories saying that the veterans had "commandeered" freight cars and "forced the crew to take the cars along." A short while later, the chief of police arrived, looked over the quiet scene, conferred with Waters, and sent all but a half dozen officers back to their precincts. The chief gave five dollars to the veterans' mess fund. Having seen for himself that the veterans were orderly, the police chief had reacted the way other friendly officials had ever since the veterans had left Portland.[43]

Mess sergeants set up crude field kitchens in the vacant lot and cooked a lunch of beans, salt pork, potatoes, bread, and coffee. As the men ate, Waters decided to give them a rest while he and Taylor planned the next move. The men would spend Friday, May 20, in Saint Louis, sleep in the boxcars, then march off the next morning to the B&O freight yards, which were about twelve miles away, across the Mississippi in East Saint Louis. Taylor was to drive on and meet the marchers in Ohio.[44]

But B&O officials arrived at the vacant lot and presented Waters with a court order prohibiting the Bonus Army from using that railroad's boxcars.

The B&O and the Pennsylvania Railroad had asked Illinois governor Louis L. Emmerson to use the Illinois State Highway Police to keep the veterans from breaking the no-free-riders railroad laws. The chief of the highway police, sympathizing with the veterans, said that since they were not creating a disturbance on the highways of Illinois, he had no jurisdiction over what they might do on railroad property.[45]

Waters kept the men in the Wabash Railway boxcars in Saint Louis while he figured out what to do next. Rumors swept the ranks that anonymous politicians in Washington were somehow pressuring the railroads to stop the Bonus Army.[46] The Bonus March was in the headlines: Saint Louis newspapers, the Associated Press, and United Press were writing about the Bonus Army, not as another bunch of down-and-outers on the road but as men carrying with them the potential for conflict and violence. There might be a deadly riot, just as there had been in Dearborn. Newsreel cameramen headed for Saint Louis.

Waters and his marchers were no longer anonymous men on the move. Their next steps, across the Mississippi to East Saint Louis, would take them into history.

On Saturday, May 21, the buglers sounded the call for packing out. Waters had found a veteran with a truck who said he would take the food, field kitchens, and supplies separately to East Saint Louis if Waters would pay for the gasoline. Waters agreed, and the men began to march off.

One of the two bridges across the Mississippi was a toll bridge. Waters chose that one. "Looking neither left nor right, the men trudged along to the entrance to the bridge," Waters recalled. "Here they speeded their pace. The toll collector came out from his booth and, as if seeing a vision, watched the silent column pass. If he had had any thought of collecting a fee, he said nothing of it to us."

On the east side of the bridge, an Illinois State Highway Police officer on a motorcycle met them and escorted them through traffic and past the gawkers along Main Street, over Brooklyn Road to St. Clair Avenue and the B&O yards. On the way, Lester J. Ives, captain of F Company, staggered out of the line of march, feverish and weak. Ives, better known as Baldy, could walk no farther. A Good Samaritan in an automobile offered to take him to St. Mary's Hospital. Mickey Dolan, the tough boxer running the military police, helped Baldy into the car and jumped in himself.

"I don't want to go. I'm going to Washington," Baldy said.

"Don't worry, Baldy. We'll wait for you," Mickey said. The car headed to the hospital.[47]

When the marchers reached the B&O yards, they found about two dozen railroad policemen barring their way, alongside P. J. Young, superintendent of the B&O police. He told Waters that no marcher would be allowed on railroad property and no one was to ride a B&O train who could not pay the fare.

The men assembled in an adjacent field and began preparing their next meal while Waters negotiated with the railroad officials gathered around Young. Waters asked for eight boxcars. The request was denied. Then two coaches, for $75? The railroad men laughed, saying that the coaches would cost $5,000. There was no point in negotiating, Waters decided.

"We're going to Washington," he told the railroad men. "Nothing can stop us but bullets. We haven't bullets of our own, and we're not afraid of anyone else's bullets. We're going to Washington."

"To Washington they may go," Young said. "But they're not going on the B&O. If they try to take our train like they did that Wabash freight at Council Bluffs, we'll just sidetrack it and won't run it at all."

At one point in the debate, Waters pointed to one of the American flags in the camp and said, "We're traveling to Washington under the same flag we fought under . . . and we'll do nothing to disgrace that flag."[48]

Waters gave a short speech to his men about the need for courage and good behavior. Then, Murray wrote, "we put up our blankets on sticks to give us a little shade, as it was very hot that day, 98 in the shade." The men milled around, waiting for orders. Waters arranged for a parade through East Saint Louis. Most people there, suffering from catastrophic unemployment, had no love for the B&O or any other big corporation, and they liked the sight of these stubborn veterans. The mayor welcomed them and, according to Waters, said, "You can do as you please and stay as long as you like, as long as your conduct does not conflict with any of our laws."

Back at the yards, Young doubled his police guard. Strings of rail cars began shuffling up and down the many tracks. The savvy railroaders on the BEF Transportation Committee understood what was happening: yard workers, under orders to confuse the marchers, were playing an elaborate shell game with boxcars. Knowing that Waters had forbidden anyone to try to hop on a moving train, the workers kept as many empties as possible in motion. And, in the confusing shuttling of the boxcars, an eastbound train might suddenly move off unnoticed.

Around ten o'clock that night, word went around that an eastbound freight train had arrived. Waters led the men in two files across the yards. At his signal, they climbed into the cars. In moments scores of men were perching on top of boxcars, on coal gondolas, and on the sides of tank cars. They even hauled up their field kitchens. Young hurried to the cars and shouted up to Waters, "I thought you promised to keep your men out of the yards."

"I promised that I would until an eastbound train was ready to leave," Waters shouted back. "Then we are going with it."

"No train will move as long as you are on it," Young declared.

Someone shouted back, "No train will move *unless* we're on it."

No train moved. The men stayed on the cars through the night. Murray recorded in his diary: "A bunch of us slept on top of a car filled with cinders while the rest was scattered around in box cars and some were on police duty to guard the train so no seals [on the car doors] were broken by any one." At dawn, the men began climbing down, some of them falling asleep on the cross ties and cinders. They had a new name for the B&O: the Hoover Line.[49]

Young appeared, and negotiations started again. He told Waters that the men were interfering with yard work and had put themselves in danger of being run over. Waters agreed to retreat to the previously occupied field— provided members of the Transportation Committee could remain. Young agreed.

As the men reassembled in the field, more and more railroad policemen lined up at the edge of the B&O property. City police also were arriving—to handle the growing crowd of townspeople who had come to watch what Waters called "a struggle in passive resistance." The marchers dubbed their grounds Camp Bonus. Men from local posts of the American Legion and Veterans of Foreign Wars came bearing food and other supplies. About a dozen local veterans walked into the field, showed their discharge papers, and became members of the BEF.

Newspaper photographers and reporters now gave regular coverage of what looked like a great news story: a showdown between the veterans and the railroad. Stories about the marchers ran even when they were competing with headlines about the achievement of Amelia Earhart, who landed in Northern Ireland on May 21, becoming the first woman to fly solo across the Atlantic, a feat performed by Charles Lindbergh exactly five years before.

On Sunday, May 22, Charles Galloway, vice president and general manager of the B&O, arrived in a private railroad car. He was determined to get his trains running again. His arrival brought a new move in the confusing shuttling of boxcars in the yard. Small switching engines were pulling cars out of the yard. At first, no one paid attention. Switching engines could not pull mainline trains. Then a freight locomotive and a caboose sped out of the yard, heading east. Members of the Transportation Committee immediately realized what was happening. A full train was being made up *outside* the yard. They shouted: "Caseyville! Caseyville!" Men stumbled along the tracks in useless pursuit of the locomotive and caboose. Scores of other veterans ran toward the crowd and excitedly reported the railroad's trick. Sympathetic spectators offered to drive the veterans to Caseyville, eight miles to the east.

The highway ran parallel to the tracks. Some drivers shouted to the men running down the tracks and stopped their cars so they could hitch a ride. More and more veterans jumped into cars, squeezing inside or leaping onto running boards for the wild ride to Caseyville.

There they found the completed train, ready to pull out. The veterans ran from highway to railway, smashed down a fence, and sprinted to the train. Murray wrote, "We were forced to go up over a bank and across a bunch of tracks to get to the train, when the boys went over this bank and across them tracks just like going over the top in France. One yard cop tried to stop us, but he was knocked down and run over and never got a chance to get up until every one had gone by. There were a lot of people there to see us go over and they sure gave us a cheer."

While some men uncoupled cars or tampered with the air brakes, others climbed onto the cars and raised an American flag on the locomotive. Soon about one hundred marchers were on and around the train. It could not move. By nightfall, all the marchers were in Caseyville, where they would spend the night. But Waters had disappeared.[50]

By his own account, Waters strategically withdrew after giving Young an ultimatum: Let my men on the train, or I quit. In his recollected words, he told Young, "You can take your choice of letting a responsible group ride freight on your road . . . or having three hundred individuals to deal with." The railroad ignored the ultimatum, and Waters quit. He claimed in his memoir that the men knew he was only temporarily withdrawing as part of his strategy.[51]

However, Alman said Waters "slipped away . . . no one knew where." In Waters's absence, Alman took command of what would become a three-day stalemate while Waters quietly moved on to set up a camp in Indiana: the veterans would not let a train move without them, and the railroad would not move a train if it had veterans aboard.

By Alman's account, the men—"with steadily increasing militancy"—decided to elect a twenty-five-man Workers' Council that negotiated with local sheriff Jerome Munie, who seemed to be acting as a mediator between the veterans and the railroad. Newspapers said that the veterans soaped the rails, causing locomotive drive wheels to spin. This nondestructive sabotage, a sample of Waters's passive resistance, tied up at least thirty B&O trains for nearly twelve hours. The Workers' Council did allow a thirty-car refrigerator train, loaded with perishables, to leave.[52]

The veterans' increasing militancy was apparent enough for Lieutenant Governor Fred E. Sterling (Governor Emmerson was out of state)[53] to call out the Illinois National Guard. Six companies of guardsmen arrived in East Saint Louis, apparently unaware that the battleground now was Caseyville. A guard officer said that Sheriff Munie had asked for help. But Munie denied this. The guard's adjutant general later said that the request for aid had come from B&O officials "who said their property had been threatened."[54] Officers later found the veterans in Caseyville and talked with them, but a violent confrontation, so greatly expected by the newspapers and the newsreel cameramen, never happened.

In Caseyville, Sheriff Munie was not worried about the behavior of the veterans. "When it looked like trouble at Caseyville yesterday," he said, "it wasn't the veterans I was concerned about, but the sympathizers. There was a crowd of several thousand along the B&O tracks, all yelling and hollering for the veterans and telling them to stay on the train. . . . And later, when the vets passed the hat, you should have seen the dollar bills fall into it."[55]

The men hung on to the cars in rain and sun. Sometimes they sang a new version of their wartime song, "Mademoiselle from Armentieres":

We're going to ride the B&O
The Good Lord Jesus told us so.
Hinkey dinkey parlez-vous

In the temporary absence of Waters and apparently without the aid of Alman's Workers' Council, Sheriff Munie decided to end the stalemate. He contacted two local union officials and urged them to find cars and trucks to get the veterans onto highways, not railways. Businesses contributed more vehicles. The East Saint Louis Chamber of Commerce paid the expenses.

On the afternoon of May 24 the veterans packed themselves into eight trucks and eighteen cars, by Murray's count. The motorcade, paced by a slow dump truck full of veterans, passed through Caseyville's cheering crowds behind an Illinois State Police escort, sirens wailing. Rolling eastward once more, they sang a new verse based on the belief that Washington had somehow intervened against them and that Hoover was behind the hard line of the B&O.

We didn't ride the B&O.
The good Lord Hoover told us so.
Hinkey dinkey parlez-vous[56]

George Kleinholz, one of Waters's most trusted aides, later wrote, "It seems that the Chief Executive of the Nation had been reading about the March on Washington and decided to stop it. . . . Hoover had the whip hand over the officials of the B&O. They had applied to the Reconstruction Finance Corporation for a loan, and unless they did Hoover's bidding, they would receive very little consideration from the R.F.C."[57] The B&O had, in fact, received a $7 million loan from the RFC in March and was given another for $25.5 million on May 16—a few days before the incident with the BEF.[58]

By the time the BEF left Caseyville on May 24, official Washington understood that the Bonus Army was much larger than the 300-plus Portland group. For days now, radio and newspaper accounts of the BEF had been prompting thousands of other veterans from all regions of the country to form groups and head for Washington. The day that the BEF left East Saint Louis, police chief Pelham Glassford began to prepare for an unprecedented human onslaught. He appealed to first Secretary of War Patrick J. Hurley for funds and shelter, cots, and blankets for the bonus marchers. Hurley turned him down and told him that "the Federal government could not recognize the invasion." Hurley, Glassford told newspaper reporters, "was very reluctant to let any of his stuff go."[59] Unfazed, Glassford was then turned down individually by the Marine Corps, the Department of the Navy, the Washington Navy Yard, the Anacostia Naval Air Station, and area Army posts, which, unknown to Glassford, were already training to confront the Bonus Army.[60]

Details of the East Saint Louis standoff and its resolution had quickly reached the offices of the Army General Staff in the massive, ornate edifice known as the State, War, and Navy Building, across West Executive Avenue from the White House.[61] Here General Douglas MacArthur, Army Chief of Staff, presided over a shrunken peacetime Army that was continually being whittled down by Congress. Like all other officers assigned to Washington, MacArthur wore civilian clothes, presumably because his commander in chief, a Quaker, did not want the capital to have a military air.[62] In a nearby office was his principal aide, Major Dwight D. Eisenhower. To summon Eisenhower, all MacArthur had to do was raise his voice.[63]

In another, larger adjacent office was Major General George Van Horn Moseley, Deputy Army Chief of Staff, a close friend of MacArthur and a favorite of Hurley. When Moseley entered MacArthur's office on May 24, the departure of the Bonus Army from East Saint Louis had become a matter of urgency. Little formality prefaced Moseley's report. He said he was convinced that the Bonus Army was growing and would be a large presence in Washington. He told MacArthur that the Army should be ready to meet any emergency that might arise. MacArthur, however, did not believe there was an imminent crisis.[64]

In a letter to a friend written that same day, Moseley enumerated his fears: "We pay great attention to the breeding of our hogs, our dogs, our horses, and our cattle, but we are just beginning to realize the . . . effects of absorbing objectionable blood in our breed of human beings. The pages of history give us the tragic stories of many one-time leading nations which . . . imported manpower of an inferior kind and then . . . intermarried with this inferior stock." He added that "intensive investigations of the past months" showed that "we are harboring a very large group of drifters, dope fiends, unfortunates and degenerates of all kinds." They have become, he said, a "distinct menace."[65]

Colonel Alfred T. Smith, the Army's chief intelligence officer, also met with MacArthur that day to discuss what he saw as potential trouble. MacArthur began to come around to Moseley's way of thinking.

The next morning, MacArthur walked into Moseley's office. "George," he said, "I have thought over our conversation of yesterday, and you are right, and I want you to go ahead with all necessary arrangements to meet any possible emergency." Although there was no evident threat from Waters's three hundred–odd veterans heading for Washington, Moseley immediately turned to Plan White, developed in the 1920s to defend Washington from civilian attack.

Moseley had "a few tanks" secretly transferred from Fort Meade, Maryland, about fifteen miles north of Washington, to Fort Myer, Virginia, across the Potomac River from Washington. The fort supplied the men and horses for military funerals at the adjacent Arlington National Cemetery. On the Washington social circuit, Fort Myer was better known as the source of handsome officers who turned up as the extra men at dinner parties or, in dress blues, at White House receptions. By the early spring of 1932 wandering veterans had started appearing at the enlisted men's barracks at Fort Myer, looking for food and shelter. Sympathetic soldiers, some of them Great War veterans themselves, figured out a way to help the men and keep them from becoming beggars. Each month many soldiers chipped in a dollar apiece toward wages for veterans willing to work in mess halls or stables.

The fort was the home of the 3rd Cavalry, famous for exhibitions at society horse shows, where their specialty was acrobatics on horseback—"monkey drills," the troops called them. Washington society and military polo players met on Fort Myer's perfectly groomed polo field. One of the best-known soldier-players was Major George S. Patton Jr., executive officer of the 3rd Cavalry.[66]

Moseley also had trucks sent to Fort Washington, a few miles down the Potomac, with orders to stand by to transport troops to Washington. In cooperation with the Secret Service, he made arrangements "to put a small force upon a moment's notice in the White House grounds" and to "fully protect the Treasury," next door to the White House. He ordered Brigadier General Perry L. Miles, commander of Army forces around the capital, to secretly make detailed plans "to meet any emergency whatsoever."

Miles had been in command of the Washington Military District little more than a month when he got his orders from Moseley.[67] Miles's principal troops, stationed at Fort Meade and Fort Holabird, near Baltimore, were to be brought in to protect not only the White House and the Treasury but also the Capitol and the Bureau of Printing and Engraving.[68]

The military was prepared for civil unrest. Secretly, the Army's Military Intelligence Division (MID) had been keeping a watch on suspected radicals. The Army divided the United States into nine corps areas. For some time, the commanding officer of each corps had been sending a monthly secret "Special Report" to MacArthur's adjutant general, who ran the MID. The reports, called "Estimate of the Subversive Situation," were based on newspaper articles, tips from patriotic civilians, and intelligence from undercover operatives. A typical report, from the New England corps area, noted strikes in Boston and Darien, Connecticut, and mentioned ministers who preached pacifism in Boston, citing particularly a Quaker minister who "is an agitator and is being watched by civilian authorities." The report named several subversives and listed as "Centers of Unrest" Boston; Darien and Hartford, Connecticut; Manchester, New Hampshire; and Portland, Maine.[69]

The gathering of intelligence at that time was done by three agencies organized independently of one another: the MID, the Office of Naval Intelligence (ONI), and the Department of Justice's Bureau of Investigation. The ONI, which mostly kept watch over maritime matters, had a reputation for bold, and often illegal, operations. In 1930, for example, an ONI operative and an ex-detective had broken into the New York City offices of the Democratic Party. The assignment had come from Lewis L. Strauss, a naval intelligence reserve officer who said that "the President is anxious to know" what damaging information the Democrats had on him. No such information was found. The same ONI officer around this time broke into the headquarters of the Communist Party of America in New York, got unspecified information, made it appear that the break-in had been the work of a rival radical group, and stole checkbooks and bankbooks "to create even more trouble."[70]

Such desperate efforts to gather intelligence about Communist activities were intensified by reports of the coming of a Bonus Army riddled with Reds.

While the Army spent the day of May 25 on the first phase of the White Plan, Police Chief Glassford launched a one-day, one-man campaign to get Congress to take up bonus legislation immediately to stave off the delegations of veterans now heading to Washington from all points to join those already in town or its outskirts. In fact, Glassford, who had just returned from New York City, had encountered a group of veterans and their families on a road in New Jersey, walking to Washington to demand the bonus.

Glassford first went to the White House, thinking that if he could get Hoover to endorse his plan, it would help him when he went to Congress. He met with Walter B. Newton, a former Minnesota congressman who served as Hoover's secretary for political matters. All Glassford got from Newton was a promise to "think the matter over."[71] Glassford next called on Senator James Watson of Indiana, the Republican floor leader, pleading for quick action on the bonus bill. He also visited Representative Henry T. Rainey, the Democratic floor leader in the House, who had been in Congress since 1903,[72] and Wright Patman, who was looking for support to get his bonus bill out of committee.[73] These were audacious moves: a local police chief, without consulting his superiors, the District commissioners, was attempting to tell the U.S. Congress and the White House how to proceed with legislation.

The White House reacted swiftly. Glassford got a call from a Hoover aide, who said, "You are embarrassing the administration. . . . You should not have told the press what you were here for."[74]

Later in the day, Glassford called a meeting of veterans' groups, charity organizations, social agencies, and the Community Chest to discuss his dilemma: no food or shelter for an ever-growing army of veterans. The American Legion declined to help; the Veterans of Foreign Wars later donated $500.[75]

Herbert H. Crosby, the D.C. commissioner in charge of police and the man who had hired Glassford, attended the meeting.[76] Crosby was keenly aware that Glassford had embarrassed the commissioners by going to the White House without approval or even advance notice. Crosby broached the subject of the bonus marchers when he turned to Glassford and said, "If you feed and house them, others will come by the thousands."

Glassford shot back, "It would be far better to have 10,000 orderly veterans under control than 5,000 hungry, desperate men breaking into stores and committing other depredations."

"What is the police force for?" Crosby, a retired major general, snapped.

"Are you making a suggestion or issuing an order?"

"In the Army, it has been my experience that suggestion is obeyed the same as an order."

"We're not in the Army now," said Glassford. "This emergency places a tremendous responsibility for preserving law and order, perhaps protecting life and property, squarely on my shoulders. I cannot follow suggestions. If you desire to take the responsibility yourself for such a policy, all you have to do is to issue written orders and they will be carried out. In the absence of such orders, I shall take what I consider the correct course."

Crosby backed off, but he had lost confidence in Glassford's judgment.

Glassford had invited a member of Congress, Paul J. Kvale of the Minnesota Farmer-Labor Party, to the meeting with Crosby. Glassford trusted Kvale, who had been a sergeant in a machine-gun corps in the war, and he looked to him for guidance about the ways of Congress. Bringing the obscure Minnesotan to the meeting showed Glassford's lack of knowledge about the power structure of Congress. Still, Kvale did try to help. On the floor of the House he called on the leaders of what he called the "bonus brigades" to return home. A supporter of the bonus, Kvale said he spoke for the "hastily formed citizens committee" that Glassford had convened. These, said Kvale, were Washingtonians concerned "over the prospect of wholesale suffering and misery" that would arrive with the veterans.[77]

At the end of this long, frustrating day, Glassford realized he was on his own.[78] He now had a logistical headache of monumental proportions. Although he had found two abandoned buildings in which to house the first small groups of vets, he was suddenly hard-pressed for food, money, and shelter. And the day was not yet over.

That night he decided to attend an open-air meeting of about a hundred newly arrived veterans who had gathered to plan their next moves. The meeting was at Judiciary Square, which symbolically stood about midway between the Capitol and the White House.[79] By the time the meeting ended, Glassford had made two speeches, had been cheered, and had even been chosen secretary-treasurer of the group, which had a small mess fund. The veterans, taking the name from news reports of Waters's Oregon marchers, called their outfit the Bonus Expeditionary Force. They voted to institute military discipline, outlaw liquor, respect laws, and suppress panhandling. "I saw before me," said Glassford, "a group of poorly dressed men, many of them with medals, wound stripes and decorations for bravery."[80]

Earlier that evening, on his network radio broadcast, Lowell Thomas told his listeners, "The march of the Bonus Army on Washington, D.C., becomes more promising of excitement every day."

As the bonus marchers traveled across Illinois, people turned out to cheer them on. In Salem, a crossroads town in south-central Illinois, townspeople rounded up a band, struck up "Over There," and invited the veterans to parade through the business section. Flora, another crossroads town, came up with *two* bands and a parade.[81] Two young men, eager to meet war veterans, took Murray and a buddy to a café, bought them "a swell lunch," and gave them each a pack of cigarettes.

The motorcade was to leave Illinois by crossing the Wabash River at Vincennes, Indiana. Waters went ahead by car to a prearranged campsite in Washington, Indiana, about twenty-five miles east. When the Illinois motorcade stopped at the state line, an Indiana policeman beckoned the vehicles into his state. He escorted them to the Washington site. They arrived there at about four o'clock in the morning and tumbled to the ground, exhausted. The men fell asleep on the grass while the trucks and cars headed back to East Saint Louis.[82] For their noonday meal the city provided large portions of slumgullion—"slum" to the vets—a meat stew made with all available vegetables.[83] In early afternoon, tired and disheveled, the veterans shuffled in a ragged parade through Washington. Other veterans, walking along the sidewalks and asking for donations, collected a little over $32.

Next morning, the vets filled up trucks belonging to the Indiana National Guard that had been provided by the governor. The trucks rolled slowly along the hilly highways of southern Indiana and made an overnight stop at a city park in Seymour, a town about fifty-five miles south of Indianapolis. The governor of Ohio, aware that the motorcade would soon cross into his state near Lawrenceburg, Indiana, ordered up his own convoy of National Guard and State Highway Department trucks. On the first truck was a banner: "Veterans Bonus March. On to Washington."

Veterans from Cincinnati joined the march as the trip across Ohio began. Crowds cheered them in every town they passed through. The big, canvas-topped trucks stopped traffic on narrow streets.[84] The convoy halted for the night in a park at Zanesville, about seventy miles east of Columbus. There Waters was immediately handed a telegram that had arrived from Representative Wright Patman, asking him to go to Washington ahead of his men so that he could talk to officials there. Next, he received a message from a Secret Service agent asking Waters to meet him in a Zanesville hotel.

As Waters recalled the meeting, the agent asked him "a lot of questions" about his men and the motive for their march on Washington. Then he asked, "Is there anyone in your outfit you can't trust?"

"There are a few who don't agree with my principles of organization and discipline," Waters replied, "but I think they are all okay."

"Well, we've had you and your crowd under surveillance for some time and we'll keep you there," the agent said. "Personally, you have a clean sheet with us."

Waters showed him the telegram from Patman. The agent said, "Please don't leave your men, even for an hour. Our job is to protect Mr. Hoover, and remember, it takes only one man to do the damage. It would be dangerous for you to leave the men out of your control for a moment, here or in Washington. You've got to stay with them to see that strict discipline is kept."

Waters wired Patman to say he had to stay with his men.

The Portland contingent of the Bonus Army now numbered about 340, its ranks filled with members picked up along the way. In Ohio, the BEF split up for the first time, when about a hundred left the convoy near Cincinnati to hop freights or hitchhike. The rest stayed in State Highway Department trucks

State-owned trucks bearing Bonus Army members crawled through Montgomery, Ohio, on May 29. At the state line, West Virginia trucks picked up the veterans and deposited them in Maryland, the last stop before Washington. (Authors' collection)

in what was now the familiar system for getting the marchers through each state as quickly as possible.

They entered West Virginia near Wheeling.[85] Somewhere, passing through "some very beautiful country," Murray saw an old woman on the porch of a house. She "was crying and she kept yelling at us to bring back her boy. I expect she lost her boy in France."

They were taken into Pennsylvania by National Guard trucks on the National Road, America's first federal highway, which cut diagonally across southwestern Pennsylvania. A hilly, winding, undulating, gear-grinding road through spectacular spring greenery, since the early nineteenth century it had connected Wheeling to the headwaters of the Potomac River at Cumberland, Maryland.[86] Over one stretch, near the Pennsylvania-Maryland line, the veterans passed over what had been a military road hacked through the wilderness during the French and Indian War, a road that young George Washington had taken into battle in 1755.[87] At the state line, the veterans were passed to Maryland National Guard trucks, which took them to Cumberland, where they slept on the floor of an old skating rink. They had traveled some three thousand miles in eighteen days.[88]

Next day, the trucks would take them, not to the Maryland–District of Columbia line but right into the heart of Washington. The arrangement had been made by Governor Albert Ritchie of Maryland. Pelham Glassford had a natural empathy for the veterans, but he had done whatever he could to keep the marchers from coming to the capital. He had written to governors urging them to discourage the marchers—not only the Waters group but also those forming in other parts of the country. Most governors opted to move the veterans across their states rather than try to stop them. Glassford sent letters to VFW and American Legion posts, also to no avail. On his own, he announced, "If necessary, I will enforce my edict of forty-eight hours as the limit of their stay here. If Congress wants to foot their bills, they can stay as long as they like."[89]

Waters, despite the request of the Secret Service, decided to go ahead to Washington on an early-morning train on Sunday, May 29, leaving his men behind. He felt he had to meet Glassford before the BEF arrived.[90]

An Army of Occupation

*In the sad aftermath that always follows a great war there is
nothing sadder than the surprise of the returned soldiers when
they discover that they are regarded generally as public nuisances,
and not too honest.*

—H. L. Mencken, quoted in *B.E.F. News,* July 23, 1932

N WASHINGTON, Waters met first with Representative Wright
Patman, who, Waters later said, was "very nervous lest he be
credited in any way with having inspired the march."[1] Next, Waters met
Glassford and found him "friendly, courteous, and above all humanly consid-
erate." The ex-sergeant felt it hard to believe that he was talking to a former
brigadier general.[2]

Glassford took Waters to a vacant downtown department store at 8th and I
streets Southeast, not far from the Navy Yard, and told him that his men
could be sheltered there. The store's owner, D. J. Kaufman, had offered the
place as a refuge to the marchers, in the first of many such acts of kindness
performed by Washingtonians.[3]

"How many veterans will come here, do you think?" Glassford asked.

"There will be twenty thousand here within the next two weeks," Waters answered, coming up with what would be a prophetic number. Waters had been "flooded" with telegrams from groups of veterans pledging to join him in Washington.[4] And now he realized that he had launched a national movement.

Glassford let a cop who was a veteran, Patrolman J. E. Bennett, give the veterans the rules: "You're welcome here, but the minute you start mixing with Reds and Socialists, out you go. If you get mixed up with that gang, you're through here. The Marine barracks are across the street, the Navy Yard is a couple of blocks away, and there's lots of Army posts around. We don't want to call them, and we won't call them as long as you fellows act like gentlemen."

The vets agreed, and one of them said, "If we find any Red agitators, we'll take care of them ourselves."[5]

Waters's march had upstaged a bonus march that the U.S. Communist Party had been planning, similar to the 1931 Hunger March. U.S. intelligence sources[6] had a detailed special report from an agent identified as Operative HS, who had put the start of planning at January 15.[7] The organizers were leaders of the Workers' Ex-Servicemen's League (WESL for short, pronounced "Weasel" by foes).[8] Operative HS, without identifying them, said "five 100% Communists" had infiltrated the BEF.

The WESL was well known to Washington officials; its members had been singled out as picketers at the White House in October 1931. The U.S. Secret Service had tightened security around President Hoover at that time,[9] and the Veterans Administration had sent its own undercover man among the WESL picketers. He learned that three of them were teenage hobos, and the belief persisted that there were many nonveterans among the WESL members.[10]

Ever since the Hunger March, W. H. Moran, chief of the U.S. Secret Service, had feared an assassination attempt on President Hoover and had increased the White House guard force.[11] But despite his boss's continuing alarm, Colonel Edmund W. Starling, supervisor of presidential security for the Secret Service, now had a different opinion about the bonus marchers. It was Starling who had put undercover agents into the ranks of Waters's marchers. "Generally speaking there were few Communists," he later reported, "and they had little effect on the men's thinking. The veterans were Americans, down on their luck, but by no means ready to overthrow their government."[12]

Starling was in the minority in believing that the vets were not susceptible to the inflammatory language of the few radicals in the ranks of the Bonus Army. Most officials feared the radical rhetoric of Communist firebrands, especially William Z. Foster, who would become the Communist Party's presidential candidate in 1932. In a book published that year, he said that the only way out of the Depression was "the overthrow of the capitalist system" and the creation of an "American Soviet Government."[13] American intelligence officials were unaware that, in fact, Earl Browder, general secretary of the U.S. Communist Party, was in trouble with the Comintern, the Soviet organization that controlled national Communist parties, because he was not doing enough to foment revolution in America.[14]

Nonetheless, a WESL leader, John T. Pace, was en route to Washington when Waters's group was nearing the capital. A slim, hard-eyed ex-Marine who spoke with an Ozark drawl,[15] Pace, thirty-five years old, had joined the party about a year before and had just been made a WESL organizer when Communist officials in New York, on hearing of the BEF, ordered him to get as many followers as possible into the Bonus Army.

At 8:00 A.M. on Sunday, May 29, in Cumberland, Maryland, Waters's men climbed into an assortment of sixteen trucks provided by the Maryland National Guard. An American flag flew from the first truck. "We . . . rode all day until 4 P.M.," Steve Murray wrote in his diary. "We arrived at our destination after our long trek across the continent . . . and now when we arrived here at Washington, D.C., a bigger job was before us."

Reporters found many of the men sitting on a bench in front of their new home. "Steamy" Armstrong, who served in the British Army before joining the AEF in France in May 1918, had been a miner. When he joined the Bonus Army in Oregon, he had not had a job for two years. "We won't cause you any trouble," Steamy said, as if speaking to the people of Washington, "but we're going to get what belongs to us." M. M. Clark had been in the U.S. Navy. "I've got to have it," he said. "There's a wife and baby to think about." Relatives helped him keep his house during the two years that he had had only odd jobs. "But a man doesn't want that sort of a life. . . . All I want is what's coming to me"—his bonus would amount to $791—"and a chance to work." R. O. Awiswell was sitting next to Clark. Back home in Oregon, Awiswell had a five-acre farm almost paid for. A real estate company was letting him hold onto the land because it shared with him the belief that he would get his $656 bonus.[16]

Lacking the Army field kitchens he had expected, Glassford enlisted cooks at the Volunteers of America. To find food, he went to the commissary at Fort Myer, where, as a retired officer, he had the right to shop, and spent $120 of his own money.[17] Other shoppers would have included enlisted men and officers who had been restricted to base and were training to combat the veterans Glassford was going to feed. Glassford put one of his captains in charge of doling out the food, on a budget of seven cents per man per day. When the

marchers arrived they found a meal of hot stew, bread, milk, and coffee awaiting them. The next day at 7:00 A.M. they were fed breakfast, usually a small
bowl of oatmeal, a slice of bread, and a cup of coffee. At 4:00 P.M. they got
their second and last meal of the day, typically a small portion of meat, a potato, a slice of bread, and a cup of coffee.[18]

Since the first small groups of veterans began arriving in Washington in the
latter half of May, President Hoover had remained in the White House during
the week and journeyed on weekends to his hideaway, Camp Rapidan, in the
Shenandoah Mountains of Virginia. It was a presidential election year, and
during the week he was meeting with various groups for what are now called
photo opportunities. One day, for instance, he met with the representatives of
the National Association of Piano Tuners, then a group of young people from
Indiana on a "Prosperity Tour," and later he stopped by at a reception for girls
from private schools in the Washington area.[19]

He was expected to make a public appearance on Memorial Day, May 30, a
major holiday of parades and solemn oratory. On the previous Memorial Day,
President Hoover had gone to Valley Forge, Pennsylvania, on a special train and
made a speech.[20] But on the holiday in 1932, Hoover remained in the White
House, where, the public was told, he worked with political advisers on planks
for the platform at the upcoming Republican National Convention.[21]

The Secret Service had called in agents from throughout the United States
and reorganized the security arrangements at the White House.[22] A secret
plan, "Riot Call Regulations," had been drawn up in January 1932 in anticipation of Depression-inspired assassination attempts or civil disorder. The de-
ployment of security men seemed to have been drawn from that plan, which
set up thirteen guard positions in the White House and its grounds.[23] And
there was some concern about Hoover's health. Dr. Joel Thompson Boone,
who had looked after Harding and Coolidge, felt that President Hoover was
not in the best of health. Boone had a little notebook in which he jotted
down observations that he later typed up. On May 29, he wrote, "I have never
seen P. look so tired, haggard & mottled. I am concerned not alarmed [his un-
derlining]. I left him some allonal for bed time."[24] Allonal, a barbiturate, was
a mild sedative.

While Hoover worked on the Republican platform, Glassford fumed over
the treatment he had been getting from Hurley. He fired off a telegram to the
secretary of war and made sure copies went to the reporters who were nearly
always at Glassford's side: FAILURE OF THE WAR DEPARTMENT TO FURNISH
ONE THOUSAND BED SACKS AS PER MY WRITTEN REQUEST OF MAY TWENTY
EIGHTH RESULTED IN APPROXIMATELY FOUR HUNDRED VETERANS BEING

REQUIRED TO SLEEP ON HARD FLOORS LAST NIGHT. REQUEST ISSUE OF BED
SACKS TO POLICE DEPARTMENT IN THIS EMERGENCY BE EXPEDITED.

Hurley responded through an Army officer, who called Glassford and told
him that two thousand bed sacks were ready for pickup at Fort Myer. Then,
in a bureaucratic move that added to Glassford's frustration, the War Department issued a memo stating that the District commissioners had to cover the
loan of the bed sacks with a bond. The commissioners said they did not have
the authority to give such a bond, so Glassford accepted the responsibility.
Undoubtedly, President Hoover could have stopped the loaning of the supply
but chose to allow it to happen.[25]

Glassford did not mention his forty-eight-hour ultimatum again. He decided that the ever-growing army of occupation needed a general, and on
May 31 he issued to the press a handwritten notice: "W.W. Waters accepted
appointment as Comdr. in Chief Veterans Bonus expeditionary Force to organize all units arriving same as Oregon group—This accepted upon a strict
diciplinary [*sic*] agreement—including the elimination of radicals." Waters
never mentioned this "appointment" in his account. As he reported his rise to

Washington police chief, Pelham D. Glassford, on his blue motorcycle, routinely inspected the BEF
camp in Anacostia. Glassford, a general during the war, designed the camp with Army-style company streets. (Underwood & Underwood/Library of Congress)

power, he said that on May 30 he was "approached by representatives" from groups that had already arrived and they "asked me to be the commander of a united force." He said that he would take the command "only if these other units were willing to abide by the same strict measures of discipline as had the men from Oregon and agree to the use of passive resistance only." Next day, Waters said, he "accepted the position of 'Commander'" and named George Alman as his principal aide.[26]

To feed and house the BEF, Glassford again turned to Congress, publicly appealing for aid. Democratic senator Edward P. Costigan promptly introduced a bill that would add $75,000 to the $600,000 that Congress was giving the District of Columbia for relief work. At a hearing on June 1, Commissioner Luther H. Reichelderfer, a retired physician who had been a lieutenant colonel in France,[27] said the District desperately needed the $600,000. But he turned down the $75,000 for the veterans, saying that "thousands, and perhaps tens of thousands" of men would come to Washington if they were "assured of food and lodging," as the Costigan bill would guarantee.

The spokesman for the veterans at the hearing was Harold B. Foulkrod, who described himself as "chairman of the legislative committee of the BEF," although at that point he had no known connection with Waters. Foulkrod had been arrested in Philadelphia on April 7, 1932, on charges of unlawful assembly, inciting to riot, and making slanderous comments against the government.[28] The committee apparently did not then know about that recent arrest—or about Foulkrod's erratic life.

As Reichelderfer was speaking about the veterans' plan to petition Congress, Foulkrod interrupted him, saying, "These men are . . . here to compel the Congress of the United States of America to give consideration to the bonus bill, and get it on the floor, so that we can vote against these men in November."

"I notice you use the word 'compel.' I hope that will go into the record," Reichelderfer said.

Undaunted, Foulkrod talked on: "They have absolutely no other purpose in coming here but to see that House Bill No. 1 is acted upon; and they know, as we all know, there is a lot of shadow boxing going on, and these gentlemen [in Congress] do not care to place themselves on record. . . . we are the men who fought in France, and we are the men who gave everything we had—our bodies."

Foulkrod passionately continued, "I had a few hundred dollars, but the sheriff took my house in Philadelphia, and the household loan and finance company came along and took my furniture, and charged me 48 per cent interest. . . . I have nothing, and these men have not anything that they can call their own; all we have is poverty."

Glassford's testimony came next. The residents of the District of Columbia, he said, "would be very willing to give donations and accept the responsibility for hospitality up to a certain extent. This I am working on now, but I know full well that there is a point beyond which the residents of the District would not care to go, and that time may come within the next few days."[29]

On a wall in his office at police headquarters, Glassford put up a map of the United States and began to pin on it pieces of paper, each one indicating a group of veterans on their way to Washington. By the beginning of June there were twenty-two pieces of paper on the map.[30] Glassford, who had based his planning on newspaper stories and intelligence reports, expected that the total number of veterans in the capital would reach at least four thousand. Now, after talking to Waters, he looked at the map and wondered whether he was seeing twenty thousand.

The men represented on Glassford's map were hopping freights, driving jalopies, hitchhiking, or piling into National Guard trucks in a dozen cities, from San Francisco to Bennington, Vermont.[31] More than 800 veterans from Chicago and its suburbs had reached Whiting, Indiana, where they planned to board boxcars for the rest of the journey to Washington.[32] Forty veterans on their way from Evansville, Indiana, were camped in an old roadhouse in Louisville, Kentucky.[33] Two hundred had left Salt Lake City, Utah.[34] Some 300 had left Cincinnati in trucks.[35] About 200 veterans from New Orleans had reached Opelika, Alabama, in National Guard trucks with gasoline paid for by the city of Montgomery.[36] About 200 residents had taken leave from the National Soldiers Home in Johnson City, Tennessee. There were 50 in West Palm Beach, Florida, and political candidates in Wade County had sent another 50 on their way in cars. Five hundred Texans, who started each day with a prayer, passed through San Antonio, along with "Hoover's Goat" and its companion, "Herbie," so named because he was always kicking.[37] Three hundred vets left Little Rock, Arkansas, aboard a passenger train donated by the Missouri Pacific. From Oklahoma in Rock Island boxcars came 300, many of them jobless oil-field workers. Trucks carrying 400 veterans from Camden, New Jersey, were nearing Washington; 150 had set out from Albany; about 250 had left Minneapolis and were in La Crosse, Wisconsin. A hand-painted sign on a Wisconsin truck read, "We Done a Good Job in France, Now You Do a Good Job in America." And Portland was sending 200 men who had missed the first muster of Waters's BEF.

Rock Island Railway officials, without publicly admitting it, had agreed to let veterans in Texas board freight cars. In Great Falls, Montana, a railroad machinist led a group to the Great Northern yards and started them on their way. About 150 had come through Alabama in county and National Guard trucks. There were about 200 coming from Warrenville, South Carolina.[38] Stories began to circulate that railroad employees were actually adding cars to their trains to accommodate the veterans. "The conductor'd want to find out how many guys were in the yard, so he would know how many empty boxcars to put on the train," recalled a marcher named Jim Sheridan. "Of course, the railroad companies didn't know this, but out of their sympathy, these conductors would put two or three empty boxcars on the train, so these bonus marchers could crawl into them and ride comfortable into Washington. Even the railroad detectives were very generous." Sheridan's recollection also includes the death of a baby from starvation in a boxcar.[39]

Hundreds of veterans, split into feuding Communist and anti-Communist groups, were leaving New York City. As yet uncounted veterans were beginning to mass in Fort Worth and El Paso, Texas. In Great Falls, Montana, a railroad mechanic took charge of a group and said he would find a way to put them all on board trains of the Great Northern. Reports came in of 2,000 veterans in Nashville, Tennessee; 200 in Warrenville, South Carolina; and 300 in Oklahoma City.[40]

In the North Carolina Piedmont, people of Charlotte, Greensboro, and Winston-Salem marveled at the sight of veterans, black and white, coming down from the mountains and trudging up from the south, all of them with one goal, one place to go. Fourteen Carolinians marched with a slogan—"No Whiskey or Guns, but Our Bonus or Bust"—and carried a letter attesting to their good character. An Atlanta group, most of them white-collar men out of work and all of them veterans, had their own field kitchen and supply truck. One hundred and thirty-six men were led by Arthur B. Creagh, who carried with him the medal he had received from Congress for his expedition to the South Pole with Admiral Richard Byrd, who, incidentally, opposed the bonus. About 200 white veterans and 119 black veterans from Louisiana, Georgia, South Carolina, and North Carolina got as far as Raleigh, North Carolina, where they camped near the railroad tracks, stranded by lack of food. Nick Saparilas, owner of the Hollywood Café in Raleigh, brought them coffee, and townspeople put them on their way with donations of food and money.[41]

Increasingly news reports listed Negro veterans moving in large numbers toward Washington, some segregated, some mixed into predominantly white groups, and a few traveling alone. One of the latter was Sewilla LaMar, a black woman who headed for Washington by foot and freight from Los Angeles. She was brutally beaten and left helpless in a boxcar outside of Fostoria, Iowa, by "the men I had sought to help." She was robbed of her wedding ring, shoes, wristwatch, and $65 in cash by ex-convicts wearing tattered Army uniforms. "I did not mind the loss of these valuables so much but the bruises and humiliation I suffered on this mission of mercy will perhaps remain with me for the rest of my life," she reported shortly after the incident. One of the men was captured, convicted, and sentenced to jail in Fort Wayne, Indiana.

She stated her reason for making the dangerous trip: "I, like millions of mothers, have suffered the ravages of war. Somewhere over there lie the bodies of my husband and my brother, who gave their all in the World War. I have since remarried and my present husband, Robert Grant LaMar Jr., an enlisted man and overseas veteran, was spared the supreme sacrifice and returned to America, only after the Armistice was signed which declared that all fighting cease."[42]

Unmarked on Glassford's map were countless loners heading to Washington on their own. One of them was Henry O. Meisel, who left Clintonville, Wisconsin, astride a 1928–29 Indian Big Chief motorcycle. Out of work with "no prospect of getting a job," Meisel used his collection of foreign coins to finance his trip. Because his generator did not work, he could travel only in daylight.[43] Along the way, "nearly everybody I came in contact with was wholly in sympathy with the veterans and wanted to help me," he wrote. In West Virginia Meisel spotted a man who said he was a bonus marcher, too. The ex-Marine got on behind Meisel, and the motorcycle chugged on to Washington.

Looking at the map, remembering his days as a general, Glassford saw free-formed, free-moving masses in something like a maneuver of the Great War, when men of many units, coming from every direction, were on the march or in troop trains, all heading for one objective, all aware that others like them were on the move, and no one knowing what was going to happen when, finally, they had all assembled, awaiting the call to battle.

"Other lobbies had moved to Washington, supported by money" was how Waters put it. "We had no money, but perhaps a group, whose only support was in its numbers, might go to Congress and make some impression."[44]

The veterans under Foulkrod had a full-fledged lobbying operation under way by the end of May. Their first objective was to get the bonus bill to the full House for a vote by means of a petition that had begun circulating before their arrival. Fifty members of Congress were approached by delegations of veterans, who got seven signatures on the first day of lobbying. They now had 98 of the required 145 signatures.[45] The vets pledged to return the next day for more.[46] "They have the same right there as any other 'lobbyist,'" Will Rogers would write later in the summer. "They at least were not paid, they were doing it for themselves, which placed 'em right away about 90 percent higher in public estimation than the thousands of 'lobbyists' who are there all the time."[47]

Congress was now hearing from many special-interest groups, thus the bonus marchers' demand for the immediate payment of an estimated $2 billion in cash was far from the only request before it. Walter Davenport wrote in *Collier's* magazine at the time that "a change of spirit is noticeable on Capitol Hill. . . . Unhappily, the party leaders have now reached a point where they haven't the money to pay for what they are afraid to refuse."[48]

When Illinois veterans visited the office of Senator James Hamilton Lewis, himself a veteran of the Spanish-American War, he told them to "go to hell."

The vets kept coming, their demeanor and orderliness earning them much positive press coverage throughout the country. Every day Washingtonians looked out of their home or office windows and saw groups of men heading for their billets; those in trucks got police escorts.[49] The *Fort Wayne (Ind.) Journal-Gazette* even called the march a "pilgrimage."[50] The BEF continually presented itself as nonviolent and accommodating. Commander in Chief Waters demanded military discipline. His immutable rules: "No panhandling, no liquor, no radical talk."

That last rule reflected Waters's fears that the BEF would be infiltrated by Communists. His Oregon group was just getting settled when the first "Red" reports surfaced in Washington. Because Waters was not available, Alman responded to claims that the march had been inspired by Communists. "We are not infiltrated with any Communist group and we don't propose to join them," Alman said. Glassford backed Alman, but Red Menace propaganda was flowing and would taint the march. The adjutant general of the Veterans of Foreign Wars (VFW) said that Communists were "trying to create the impression that thousands of veterans are falling in behind the red flag. Nothing could be further from the truth."[51] The VFW, which backed the bonus but not the march, thus added to the Red Scare by giving the Communists more credit than their efforts deserved. Except for a Detroit contingent led by John Pace and a splintered unit from Cleveland, virtually all other groups coming to Washington were either spontaneously created in their communities or inspired by newspaper reports of Waters's march.

Under the banner of the WESL, there were, in fact, Communists on the move. On June 1, in a driving rain, Pace led 450 men, recruited with the help of women from the Young Communist League, to Detroit's city hall. There the men crowded onto streetcars, shouting that they were riding as guests of the mayor, although he had not authorized free rides.[52] The streetcars took them to the city limits. Then they walked a mile to the railroad yards. Pace argued with railroad officials that the veterans had protected the railoads during the war and now needed their help. They were allowed to board coal gondolas on a freight train that took them to Toledo, Ohio. There, like the marchers who had traveled with Waters, the next morning they negotiated with city and railroad officials, who were only too glad to get them on their way on ten freight cars hitched to an eastbound train headed for Cleveland.[53]

In Cleveland, longtime Communist leader C. B. Cowan had set up a tent where he signed up anyone who called himself a veteran. By the time the Detroit group arrived at the Cleveland railroad yards, hundreds of Ohio marchers were already there. Among the Cowan-led marchers were some who announced that they were anti-Communist and bona fide veterans.

Now came another railyard confrontation. But this time, with the marcher force steadily increasing and the Communist and anti-Communist groups eyeing each other suspiciously, the tough tactics of Pace and Cowan were setting up a complex conflict that was moving dangerously close to violence. Cowan ordered his men to prepare to "storm" an Erie Railroad freight heading for Pittsburgh.[54] Pace egged on his men by telling them the government "had all kinds of money" to spend on the railroad during the war but veterans who fought in that war were not allowed to ride on them. So, he said, the men's only alternative was "to ride them without permission."[55]

After railroad police prevented the men from boarding any train, they took over the roundhouse and several switch engines. Railroad workers, sympathetic to the cause, did not resist. About twenty triumphant marchers climbed on a locomotive and, overseas caps on their heads and clenched fists raised in a radical salute, posed for a defiant portrait. That news photo, far more than the earlier coverage of East Saint Louis, linked bonus marchers to Communists in the minds of intelligence officials in Washington.

In the tense railyards, the tired, hungry men began quarreling. Fistfights broke out. Veterans from Michigan and Toledo called the Cleveland men Communists. "That's not true," Pace shouted. "I am not a communist. I don't believe in it, and we're all loyal to the government."[56] Cleveland police arrived. Frank J. Merrick, Cleveland safety director, knew he and his men stood on the threshold of violence. "If they decide to take matters into their own hands and commandeer the freight car," he said, "we can't shoot them down like dogs." By now the estimates of veterans in Cleveland had reached two thousand.[57]

Defiant veterans celebrated their takeover of a roundhouse in Cleveland, where railroad officials and police tried to keep them from riding boxcars eastward. The confrontation helped to alert newspapers to the Bonus Army story. (Brown Brothers)

Next morning, June 5, Merrick herded the men into a nearby field. Suddenly someone shouted, "Are we going to get our train to Pittsburgh?" Men rushed toward a string of empty cabooses. Police on horseback charged the men. The horses crowded the men, pressing so close that vets could smell the horses' sweaty flanks. The men were routed. They ran back across the rails, over an embankment, and returned to the field.[58] Then another group, urged on by an unidentified man, charged the roundhouse. This time police on foot confronted them. Some men ran on and were clubbed. That group also retreated, and the violence ended as quickly as it had begun.[59]

On June 6, the mayor of Cleveland walked into the area where the marchers were gathered and offered $100 and transportation across the Ohio line to Pittsburgh to any group that stepped forward. About a hundred men gathered around Doak E. Carter, a thirty-six-year-old veteran of both the wartime Army and the peacetime Navy. He was living in a Cleveland hotel[60] and was identified by some old-timers as a former railroad detective. Carter led the men away and said he would get them to Washington.

The rest of the men left the yards and walked south about eight miles to New Bedford, Ohio. They then moved by vehicle and foot to Pittsburgh. There on June 9 police arrested Cowan on a general charge of suspicion, based on his known criminal record. Pace managed to slip out of town and continue on to Washington.[61]

WESL claimed the march as its own inspiration, disregarding Waters and all other leaders. The initial claim of Communist inspiration was made by Joseph Singer, an official of WESL, and it was repeated by Emanuel Levin, who called himself chairman of the National Bonus Army Committee of the WESL. The same day that Pace left Detroit, Levin, an energetic Communist from New York, arrived in Washington, D.C., casually claiming that the Communists had

J. Edgar Hoover, as he appeared at the time of the Bonus Army, was director of the Justice Department's Bureau of Investigation—forerunner of the Federal Bureau of Investigation—which he would head for forty-eight years. (Underwood & Underwood/ Library of Congress)

in fact created the bonus march and were planning to stage a mass rally and parade on June 8. Immediately police chief Glassford let it be known that he wanted to "get in touch" with Levin for questioning.[62] June 8 was also the day of a planned BEF parade, which Levin claimed would become "a red letter day." Agents from J. Edgar Hoover's Bureau of Investigation now began their search for Communists in the Bonus Army.[63]

Glassford knew that conflict between Communists and non-Communists could touch off street warfare and the kind of uprising the Communists were hoping for. Worried, he secretly sent a memo to the District commissioners recommending that they be prepared to "declare an emergency," possibly order the use of military force, and even invoke the White Plan to quell widespread rioting. Maintaining a confident demeanor, he expressed private fears in the memo:

> *Although no disorders have occurred, the plan of the Police Department is to assemble all disaffected groups at Anacostia Park and should emergency arise to hold the Eleventh Street Bridge against a riotous invasion across the Anacostia River. Plans and preparations are being made to this end, including plans for the use of tear gas; at the same time a force of police will be held in readiness on the east side of Anacostia River in order to localize any riot that may occur, and to prevent access to the bridges further north.*
>
> *As soon as funds available have been exhausted and no more food can be furnished by this department we believe that an emergency situation will exist. Such a situation may develop as early as noon tomorrow.*
>
> *Recommendation: That preparations be made by the Commissioners to declare an emergency, and to provide for the use of the National Guard, or to place in effect "the White Plan."*

Glassford said he was working to split the vets into two groups: "one comprised of bonafide veterans who have elected a commander and call their organization The Bonus Expeditionary Force—the other a group . . . believed under communist control."[64]

Glassford publicly announced his plans for Anacostia on June 2, merely mentioning the site and not his strategy involving the convenient drawbridge.[65] He said he had received permission from the Office of Public Buildings and Public Parks to use a large expanse of Anacostia for the camp he was planning.[66] The camp was to be a tent city to shelter the 4,000 vets reportedly en route, 1,200 of whom were expected that night to augment the 2,000 already in town.[67] The billet at Eighth and I streets was jammed, as was a second billet at Seventh and L streets SW.[68] Although veterans would continue to find places to stay in downtown Washington, Anacostia would become the principal camp and the center of Bonus March activities.

The site picked by Glassford, across the Anacostia River but a few blocks from the Capitol, was on riverside land that had once been a village of the Nacotchtank Indians—anglicized to Anacostan and the place to Anacostia—then, as now, one of the neighborhoods of Washington little known to outsiders. The opening of the Washington Navy Yard in 1799 across the river from the flats spurred residential growth, which was again given a boost in 1867 when the Freedman's Bureau settled freed slaves and their families on the James D. Barry Farm, a neighborhood of single-family houses. Eventually 500 families built houses here. Just to the north of the black area was Uniontown, a planned community that barred any "Negro, mulatto or person of African blood." Understandably, the streets of Anacostia in 1932 were mixed—a black grocer on one corner and a white grocer on the next—but not integrated.[69]

"I was around eleven years old, I guess, when the marchers came here," says Charles T. Greene, then an eighth-grader who lived just a few blocks from the camp in 1932. "The interesting part of it was that the bonus people occupied the Anacostia Flats, a park where one side of it was for whites, the other side of it was for Negroes. And the only thing on the site of the camp

Veterans' sheds, tents, and shanties sprawled across the Anacostia Flats. On the horizon to the left the three masts of the U.S.S. *Constitution* are visible. The ship was in the Navy yard during a bicentennial celebrating George Washington's birth. (National Archives)

(the Negro side) was a baseball diamond and four tennis courts." Greene, who is African-American, was familiar with the Negro side of the park. He said that if one was riding a trolley across the drawbridge crossing the river, and "looked to the right, you could look right into the site they picked for the bonus camp."[70]

Among the first veterans to arrive in Anacostia—in pouring rain, escorted by police on motorcycles—were men from Camden, New Jersey. They formed lines, went to a registration tent manned by a police officer, and gave name, serial number, and discharge information. They built the first bunk-house from lumber and tar paper that Glassford had obtained, using three Army field kitchens that Glassford had found. On these stoves the veterans cooked their first hot meal since leaving home. They washed themselves in the river, washed their travel-stained clothes, and hung them on riverside trees. They spent their first night sleeping on wet ground covered with huge puddles. Next day, they went to dumps to salvage materials, brought them back to Anacostia, and began the continual expansion of what they called Camp Camden.[71]

On June 6, bonus marchers from New Jersey start to build what they called Camp Camden, across the Anacostia River from downtown Washington. The site later was named Camp Marks in honor of a friendly police officer. (Authors' collection)

Among the visitors to the camps was Senator James Hamilton Lewis, who had recently told the veterans to go to hell. He drove out to Camp Camden and found the the Illinois delegation, which had about nine hundred men. Lewis stood up on the top of his car, identified himself, and, speaking over a chorus of booing, said that he had thought his visitors had been Communists. And now, after seeing the camp, he knew he was wrong. He asked the men to make a list of what they needed most. The booing stopped. Veterans looked at one another quizzically.

The Illinois committee drafted a letter and sent it to Lewis. "A great number of men are without shoes," they wrote; "there are practically no blankets; the food is not near enough; soldiers are sleeping on the ground on ticks filled with hay; we have no tents, just a barracks which leaks; . . . the rest are scattered around on the ground. . . . The boys would also like facilities for writing home and procuring tobacco for chewing and smoking."

Lewis, a Democrat, forwarded the letter to Assistant Secretary of War Frederick H. Payne with a request that the War Department do what it could to help the veterans at Anacostia. He was told that the War Department was not authorized by Congress to loan tents.[72]

Glassford was adept at getting food donated: four 150-pound turtles were delivered for soup, and the Dixie Barbecue Company showed up with enough pork to feed dinner to the estimated 1,500 vets and family members in town on the night of June 1.[73] On that same day came the first perceptible editorial anger about the hordes of uninvited guests and what they would do to the city: "Responsibility for this futile march on Washington rests squarely on the shoulders of demagogues who have led veterans to believe that if they howled loud enough Congress would pass the bonus measure," said the *Washington Post*, insisting that the marchers had been duped and that "their only way to avoid further hardships . . . is to retreat homeward."[74] Some Washingtonians felt differently, including the wife of Ned McLean, owner of the *Washington Post*.

The free-spirited Evalyn Walsh McLean possessed a legendary desire to help others and, according to friends, once went out into a blinding snowstorm, albeit in a chauffeured car, because she thought people out there might need help. Predictably, she felt compelled to help the bonus marchers, just as she had turned over her seventy-five-acre estate, a former monastery called Old Friendship, to the Red Cross to use as a convalescent home for sick and wounded soldiers during the war. Earlier in 1932 she had naively given Gaston B. Means, the notorious swindler and con man (who had once actually worked as an investigator for the Justice Department) $105,000 to rescue the

Evalyn Walsh McLean
befriended the bonus marchers.
(Harris and Ewing Collection/
Library of Congress)

Lindbergh baby from its kidnappers. When the baby was found dead, Means was charged, and his trial was going on during the time that the bulk of the BEF was setting up camp in the Anacostia Flats.

McLean was awakened to the plight of the bonus marchers when she first saw a truck rumble past her Massachusetts Avenue mansion on Embassy Row in early June: "I saw the unshaven, tired faces of the men who were riding in it standing up." As more truckloads passed her house, she looked to the sidewalks and saw ragged hikers walking where diplomats normally strode, wearing scraps of old uniforms and using sticks to walk with that seemed "less canes than cudgels. It was not lost on me that those men, passing any one of my big houses,* would see in such rich shelters a kind of challenge—2020 [Massachusetts Avenue] was a mockery of their want."

That night, after 1:00 A.M., she drove down to where the veterans were, near Capitol Hill and at the Anacostia campground now being established, and came upon Chief Glassford, who knew her socially. Glassford was about to leave to buy coffee for the men. She drove with him to the all-night counter at Child's restaurant and addressed an awestruck counterman.

"Do you serve sandwiches?" she asked. "I want a thousand and a thousand packages of cigarettes."

---

*McLean had a mansion in Newport as well as other properties.

"But, lady—"

"I want them right away. I haven't got a nickel with me, but you can trust me. I am Mrs. McLean."

Glassford got the thousand coffees (which, McLean noted, he paid for out of his own pocket), and well into the early morning the two of them fed all the hungry marchers in sight. McLean recalled later, "Nothing I had seen before in my whole life touched me as deeply as what I had seen in the faces of the Bonus Army."[75]

The next day she went to see Judge John Barton Payne, head of the Red Cross, and tried to convince him that a national crisis was unfolding, and it was the responsibility of the Red Cross to get involved. All he could offer was a little flour, "and I was glad to accept it." Her next stop was the Salvation Army, which, she found, was already doing all that it could. She asked the commander if he could suggest how she could help the families, and he said that he would find out. He came the next day to say that they needed a big headquarters tent to serve as a welcoming point for new marchers as they arrived. She ordered the tent from Baltimore and had it delivered to Anacostia along with books, radios, and cots.

McLean also befriended Waters, whom she invited to her home several times. One day she checked out the house that Glassford had reserved for women and children who chose not to live in the outdoor camps. She found the residents sleeping on the floor. She bought beds and later delivered cast-off clothing from her own children. One day one of the women picked up a dress from McLean's daughter and said, "I guess my child can starve in a fifty dollar dress as well as in her rags."[76]

On June 4 Glassford appeared to present an ultimatum that came not from him but from the District commissioners. George Alman was in charge because, as at the first encounter with authorities back in East Saint Louis, Waters had once again resigned and disappeared, saying he was ill. Speculation was that he was—for reasons unclear—holed up in a relative's house in the Washington area.[78] Alman relished the leadership that Waters had handed him. The tough-talking ex-lumberjack stood toe-to-toe in confrontation with Glassford.

"The situation is becoming acute—both as respects food and money," Glassford told Alman. "The Health Department is clamoring for us to close up these places." He said that on June 9, District of Columbia trucks would arrive at the encampments and take the veterans as far as fifty miles in the direction of their homes. At the fifty-mile mark they would be dumped back into the lives they led before they came to Washington. They would be warned that anyone who did not get into a truck would not get any shelter or food from the District of Columbia. The commissioners of the District of Columbia had, they thought, solved the problem that Glassford had created.[78] Glassford promised to notify nearby governors about the plan in the hope that they would "pick you up where we leave you."

"You realize that by the eighth of June there will be a hell of a lot of men here, don't you, Mr. Glassford?" Alman asked, alluding to the eve before the departure of the trucks and a day after a planned twilight rally and parade.

"Sure I do," Glassford replied. "But I want your cooperation and the cooperation of your men toward getting all of you out of town. If you won't go, I'm not making any threats. I shall simply close up these quarters and discontinue furnishing food. The people of the District no longer feel they should feed your men."

"Well, I don't feel they should, either," Alman said.

"And you understand, I hope, that there is no feeling of antagonism on my part, that what I am telling you comes in a friendly vein."

"I understand your attitude and the attitude of the government so far, and I shall give you the answer of the men as soon as I can."

When the conversation ended, Alman talked to newspaper reporters. "We came here to stay until the bonus bill is passed," he said. "And neither General Glassford, nor anybody else, is going to run us out of town."[79]

Waters himself reappeared as leader later that day to say, "Whenever the bonus is voted, we will be very glad to accept the police offer of free truckage out of the city."[80] A veteran who heard about the ultimatum added his reaction: "Out of here by Thursday? Huh! Kaiser Wilhelm didn't do it in eighteen months." A vet from Newark said, "If they don't feed me, I'll go on the streets and beg. Then they'll lock me up and have to feed me."[81] Many veterans did venture into Washington neighborhoods, begging door-to-door, breaking the Waters rule prohibiting panhandling.[82]

The veterans may have been cheered by the news of an ever-expanding BEF army, but every newcomer meant a cut in rations for the men already in Washington. Police, sifting through dozens of reports, counted up 3,207 veterans heading to Washington.[83] These included 200 American Legionnaires from Brooklyn who were determined to keep their distance from a Communist-led New York City group.[84] In Harrisburg, Pennsylvania, police escorted 400 Illinois marchers who were transferring from the freight cars of one railroad line to the cars of the line they would take to Washington. In Decatur, Georgia, 137 vets from New Orleans—100 of them African-Americans—were

Boston veterans headed for Washington to join the Bonus Army. They left on June 2, as publicity about the Bonus March spread, inspiring similar groups. By June 12, some ten thousand veterans had arrived in the nation's capital. (Traveler Collection/Boston Public Library)

strung along a highway, hitchhiking north.[85] In Fort Wayne, Indiana, police and the Knights of Columbus fed 71 veterans from the Seattle area; a police vehicle hauled their food and footsore members to a rail yard, where they awaited the next available string of boxcars. Six members were expelled after a brief hearing determined that they were Communists.[86]

In Los Angeles, 1,300 veterans enlisted in a California bonus brigade being organized by Royal W. Robertson, a flamboyant leader who wore a cagelike back and neck brace.[87]

Glassford knew the veterans were not going to retreat before zero hour on Thursday. Running out of ways to feed them, he decided he had to raise money any way that he could. His first move was to organize a large boxing benefit to raise money for food. He recruited a Marine Corps major to set up a card of at least fifteen bouts. The boxing would be on June 8, the day following an event Washington awaited with apprehension: the twilight parade that would put thousands of veterans in a march to the Capitol.

While there was a constant attempt to keep a tally of vets arriving and already in town, accuracy was almost impossible because they were quartered in so many odd places, perhaps the most unexpected being in a burlesque house.

The colorful Jimmy Lake, raconteur and promoter of prizefights, owned the Gayety Burlesque on Ninth Street in Washington's tenderloin. Lake was a showman who seemed to know just about everybody he felt was worth knowing. He was a good friend of Irving Berlin, had worked with W. C. Fields, and had booked the best into the Gayety: Will Rogers, Abbott and Costello, Bert Lahr, and Mickey Rooney, to name a few. He also featured the greatest striptease artists of his time: Ann Corio, Georgia Sothern, and Gypsy Rose Lee.[88]

Lake got one look at the men when they first started piling into town and noted that unfortunate souls in New York's Bowery flophouses "were in the lap of luxury compared to the human element in the Bonus March." As the Anacostia camp was being established, he took pity on a camp forming in Potomac Park, known then in Washington as the Speedway and today as Haines Point, a spit of land jutting into the Potomac with a road around its outer edge. "It's a delightful drive for lovers in the moonlight, but in those days there were areas of plain, unadulterated mud," Lake later recalled. "There had been several days of rain. And it was in the mud that the men were sleeping."

He assembled the men and got them to march from the park in two platoons, one for night and one for day. From then on, the two platoons alternated sleeping in the balcony at the Gayety. "The theater seated 1,550, so I just closed up the balcony to the public," said Lake. "Although quartering the men in the theater was a violation of sanitary laws, it was no time to think like that. Suffering humanity was more important than law."

The men slept and snored in shifts and provided background noises so loud that the strippers and vaudevillians started rumors that the place was haunted. Lake kept what he was doing secret because he feared that the vets would be out in the mud again if the authorities found out.

Shortly, he was summoned by the police to headquarters to speak with the chief. Fearing he was in trouble and in for a hefty fine or worse, he told the men to stay away from the theater until they heard from him.

Ushered into Glassford's inner sanctum, he was greeted with a powerful voice.

"Jimmy Lake?"

"Yes, sir," he replied meekly.

"For God's sake, what can we do to get some smokes for the mob you are quartering in your theater?"

"Let's give a benefit performance!"

Without any fanfare or advertisement, Lake staged a "quickie" performance at the Gayety, netting enough money to buy cigarettes in abundance from several tobacco companies at heavily discounted prices. Lake then wanted to do more, so he went to see Clark Griffith, an imaginative baseball player, manager, and then owner of the Washington Senators and the proprietor of Griffith Stadium.*

"Clark, how would you like to have the opportunity to sell 50,000 bottles of pop, 50,000 bags of peanuts, as many packages of Cracker Jacks, and probably 10,000 cups of coffee? And cigars and cigarettes, too?"

"Out with it, Jimmy, what do you want?"

Lake wanted to stage a mammoth benefit boxing match—the one Glassford had envisioned a few days earlier—and the night of June 8 was set for the big event, the day after the twilight parade.[89]

More than 100,000 Washingtonians lined the streets to see what the *Post* called the "strangest military parade the Capital has ever witnessed." The BEF was marching in full force: 8,000 men, and if there were any secret Reds among them, they were there under rules that said the parade was open to any man who showed an honorable discharge from the armed forces. About 100 admitted Communists were in the ranks of the marchers, each one known and watched by BEF stalwarts.[90]

George Alman, calling himself commander, led the parade. Also up front was Harold Foulkrod, the eloquent lobbyist with the murky past, now a contender for leadership in the BEF. The lobbying had worked. There now were 145 names on the petition. The bonus bill would reach the floor of the House to be voted on.

Waters had hoped that the parade would pass the White House, but Glassford ordered a route he could control: from Seventeenth and Constitution Avenue to Pennsylvania Avenue and down the great ceremonial boulevard to the Peace Monument at the foot of Capitol Hill.[91] Police lined the street, watching for the rumored Communist disruption that never happened.

Marching behind the leaders were heroes of the Great War, led by a man who had been awarded the Medal of Honor. Others wore the Distinguished Service Cross, the Silver Star, the French Croix de Guerre. Among the heroes was an African-American from Washington, William A. Butler, who wore a Distinguished Service Cross and the Croix de Guerre and served as a symbol of the unpublicized integration of the BEF.

The parade stepped off at twilight to the music of a local American Legion band, its members in black-plumed hats and golden capes, marching in defi-

*Griffith would be elected to the Baseball Hall of Fame in 1946.

ance of the Legion's opposition to the bonus and to the Bonus March. Disabled veterans rode in open trucks and drew the heartiest cheers from the crowd.

The men marched by state, beginning with Oregon, just as the Bonus March had begun, and every unit followed an American flag. Many flags were tattered, worn out like so many of the men who walked behind them. Sprinkled through the parade were men carrying signs: "Here We Stay Til the Bonus They Pay," "Georgia Vets Rebels-Yanks United We Stand," "Millions for War Not One Cent for the Hungry Vet," "Who Won the War? We Haven't Won Anything," "Cheered in '17. Jeered in '32."

The parade was a triumph for the vets, who showed that they were not a menace to the city. But most of the veterans now knew, as Waters and Glassford certainly did, that the city, in the person of the District commissioners, did not want them there any longer. They were about to be politely invited out, and the commissioners would provide the trucks.

The benefit boxing night arranged by Glassford and Jimmy Lake—"the greatest array of boxing talent ever brought to Washington," said the *Post*—drew a record crowd of fifteen thousand fans. They saw some fifty fights, ranging from matches between well-known professionals to bouts between amateurs. "Sitting side by side," wrote *Post* sportswriter Jack Espey, "were overalled laborers and daintily clad ladies, men in tattered sweaters and young fashion plates." A ring had been erected over the infield of Griffith Stadium's baseball diamond, and a parade of boxers climbed in and out.

A bout between Stanford Carrier, representing the American Legion, and Lou Jameson, representing Walter Reed Army Hospital, brought the fans to their feet. Carrier won the decision. Jimmy Lake announced the fights, each a bout of three two-minute rounds, and when he felt that he had the cheering fans in a giving mood, he asked for contributions for the BEF.

They collected about $3,000.[92]

Hooverville, D.C.

All you here—here and there
Pay the bonus, pay the bonus everywhere
For the Yanks are starving,
The Yanks are starving,
The Yanks are starving everywhere.

—Camp Marks song, to the tune of "Over There"

AT EIGHT O'CLOCK on Thursday morning, June 9, the District trucks rolled onto the Anacostia Flats encampment, which was within the Eleventh Precinct, under the command of Police Captain Sidney J. Marks. As a group of vets crowded around the trucks, Marks spoke in a booming voice: "If you are tired or distressed, if you want to get back to your homes, we have trucks—"

Laughter drowned out his speech. Marks smiled and went on, "Well, I suspected that. And so far as I am concerned, I don't want to see you leave. I hope you stay and get your bonus."

The applauding vets were not surprised. Marks had been a kind and accommodating cop from the beginning. His humanity had already produced a name change: from Camp Camden to Camp Marks.[1] Captain Marks's performance reflected what he saw as his chief's attitude toward the marchers—an attitude that was infuriating Glassford's boss, Commissioner Crosby. Although Crosby did not publicly reprimand him, he reportedly told Glassford that the chief faced "peremptory dismissal" by President Hoover for his efforts to feed and shelter the BEF. Crosby denied the published report, but there seemed no doubt that the two men were heading toward a collision, with the vets as innocent bystanders. Complicating the situation was the fact that Glassford's friendly public relationship with the vets cloaked private fears of disorder, as he had revealed in his secret memo to the commissioners.[2]

Encouragement at this key moment came from Father James R. Cox, the priest who had led an unemployment march earlier in the year. He had flown in from Pittsburgh, along with his chauffeur, attorney, and secretary. In the uniform he had worn as a chaplain in the war, he strode to the speakers' platform in the camp and shouted, "Stick it out! You will never get what you're entitled to unless you stick. Men are coming from every corner of the country and if you stick it out, before this is over there will be from 500,000 to 1 million of you.

"If they won't give you this little bonus—offered you because your wartime pay was less than common labor—turn them out of office. Go home and organize against them. Send men here who still look after the people, not the 500 millionaires who control the national wealth."

Another priest came through with more than words. Father Charles E. Coughlin, the Detroit radio priest, sent the BEF cash. In a June 9 telegram he said, "Cunning Communists are dicing for the leadership of these World War Veterans, and tonight, both to cheer the hearts of the bonus army and to show that Communism is not the way out, I am donating $5,000."[3]

The men also heard from Norman Thomas, Socialist Party candidate for president, who distributed leaflets to the veterans. In vain, Thomas urged them to abandon their fight for the bonus and begin instead a crusade for a permanent government relief effort. "We address you not only as veterans of the World War but also as veterans of that larger and unending war against poverty—a war which . . . finds millions of workers facing starvation in the midst of plenty." Thomas called for an extensive public works program and universal unemployment insurance to take care of all workers when they are "thrown upon the scrap heap by their employers."

The eviction did not occur on June 9. As more and more vets continued to pour into Washington, Waters reiterated, "We're here for the duration."[4]

While the money from Coughlin staved off immediate starvation, the BEF had to find a way to get a dependable supply of food. Contributions came in from local merchants and well-wishers. Some groups arrived with their own rations. The people back in Camden, for instance, sent a truck full of food and pledged to support their men.[5] At least four organizations promised large donations.[6] They would have to be large. There were thousands of mouths to feed, and no longer could the veterans count on Glassford, the one local official who had helped them but now, under pressure, had to leave them on their own.

Soon after the first veterans began to appear in Washington, Glassford, apparently without authority from anyone, had arranged for local Marines to set up a Bonus Clinic, staffed by physicians and medics, at the Indiana Avenue headquarters of the 6th Marine Reserve Brigade. Major Don S. Knowlton, brigade surgeon, had taken charge. Working with him were four medical officers and six naval hospital corpsmen assigned to the Marines. He sent a daily sick-call report to Glassford. On June 3, Knowlton reported, he had treated 104 men, and the dental officer extracted ten teeth, one each from ten patients; there were "no complaints or growls, morale good." Some of the Marines' patients had already been treated by first-aid teams at their camps. Knowlton complained about "a very incompetent crew" in the camps who were "causing a large number of iodine poisoning cases." The ailments included colds, rheumatism, blistered feet, trench feet, pleurisy, bronchitis, acute tonsillitis, poison ivy, toothache, constipation, sprains, stomach disorders, and body vermin—American cousins of the "cooties" of French trenches. By June 11 Knowlton was treating more than three hundred men a day, and he knew he could not handle such a patient load for long. On that day General MacArthur authorized the setting up of an Army field hospital at Fort Hunt, an abandoned military site across the Potomac River and about eleven miles south of Washington.[7]

The establishment of the field hospital came in the wake of a report by the District of Columbia's chief medical officer, who feared that primitive sanitary conditions—swarms of flies, half-buried garbage, mosquito-breeding puddles, mess kits passing from hand to hand—could bring on an epidemic.[8] Waters believed that a typhoid epidemic never happened because all the veterans had been inoculated when they went to war. There were no amenities. Folded newspapers served as plates for those without mess kits. Spoons and forks were rare. But, as Waters philosophized, "No landlords came daily threatening eviction. No bill collectors called. . . . the absence of gas and electricity had at least the compensating comfort that neither could be cut off for non-payment of bills."[9]

Long mess lines wound through the Bonus Army's Anacostia camp. Food was donated by Washingtonians—including Police Chief Glassford—and by hometown supporters. Veterans usually ate only two meals a day. (Theodor Horydzak Photograph/Library of Congress)

Rising from the vast Anacostia Flats was a hill where local residents dumped their junk. That was where the veterans of Camp Marks got most of their building supplies: cardboard and wooden boxes, egg crates, rusty bedsprings, fence stakes, bits of lumber, wrecked cars. From a car a vet could get a seat to make into a bed or a bumper that would become a shelter's curved roof. A salvaged blackboard, with a child's scribbles still on it, made another kind of roof. There were also roofs made of rusty bedsprings thatched with tufts of the long-stemmed grass that sprouted here and there on the flats. One lucky junk-picker found a chicken coop that he carried off for his new home.[10] A man from Ohio lived in an oil drum, another in a barrel filled with grass, another in a burial vault set on trestles, another in a piano box, with a sign, "Academy of Music."[11] Some vets had burrowed into the hill, making dugouts like the ones that had sheltered them in France.[12] A family of five made their car a home.[13] There were tents that Glassford had managed to wrangle from the Army and National Guard, and there were shelters made from tents and odd bits of canvas or oilcloth. Somebody planted a tiny tree and hung a sign, "We'll have shade by 1945."[14]

Veterans used the Anacostia River as a bathtub. Some local citizens, while not "hostile to the veterans," worried about sanitation problems and the health of men who "bathe in the polluted water below the mouth of a sewer." (Underwood & Underwood/Library of Congress)

Men bathed and washed their clothes in the Anacostia River. Laundry hung from tent ropes, from clotheslines strung everywhere; clothespins were an absent luxury. They cooked their typical meal of mulligan stew (recipe: place whatever edibles available into boiling water) in large iron pots or former garbage cans or on old army wood-burning field-kitchen stoves, also produced by Glassford's scrounging. Drinking and cooking water came from two lines of fire hoses hooked up to fire hydrants a few hundred feet away. Garbage was buried in trenches.[15] There were latrines, routine facilities for a bivouac. Anacostia gas stations got used to having lines of veterans waiting to use the restrooms.[16]

Many men slept in the open, chilled by rain and the fog drifting in from the rivers. A New Yorker told a reporter how he had spent the night: "It got dark and I couldn't move around without stepping on somebody and getting cussed out. I just had to lay down and shiver. Finally I thought I couldn't stand it any more. But I was lucky. There was one fellow with a blanket. Three of us crawled under it with him, and the four of us just hugged together all night—so it wasn't so bad." He wore a silver button that showed he had been wounded in combat.[17]

Day after day men tramped into the hot, muddy flats. They usually arrived by freight train; most railroad detectives were not badgering vets anymore. Fifty-five Minnesotans, for instance, arrived in a car marked "Livestock" and carried with them a Pennsylvania Railroad bill of lading on which a friendly railroad man had written: "Livestock, 55 veterans."[18] Another car arrived in Washington with a sign on the side: "Cattle who escaped the slaughter—17 veterans."[19]

As Glassford had originally envisioned it, the camp was laid out in company streets. He had acquired lumber for what he called barracks, which were more like sheds without walls. But as the army rapidly grew and the food supplies just as rapidly dwindled, he stopped buying lumber and used the money to buy groceries.[20] The vision of an army-style camp had to give way to the reality of a junkyard city, one of many "Hoovervilles" like it throughout the nation. At the Hooverville on the Flats, no one had an accurate count of the wives and children, but a visiting writer told of seeing many veterans arriving with their families. "The wailing of ill-nourished youngsters became common," he wrote. "Milk was scarce."[21]

Waters's Oregon group and early arrivals had been billeted in abandoned buildings. Then, as more and more veterans arrived, Glassford sent them, with police escort, to Anacostia. When Waters first took over the BEF, he remained in a downtown building, setting up his headquarters there and dispatching "billeting officers" to meet the new arrivals, usually at the Washington freight yard, and send them on their way, in straggling columns behind an American flag, to the Anacostia Flats. Cheers inevitably greeted them, and they found their way down the flag-bedecked company streets to their state's area.

They were all thin, and most were gaunt. Nearly all the men wore hats—gray fedoras with the front of the brim snapped down, or caps, or an occasional straw or overseas hat from the war. They wore long-sleeved shirts, either a white dress shirt (kept white as a matter of pride, and usually with a dark tie in a four-in-hand knot) or a blue or gray work shirt. Many wore vests and, for special occasions, suit coats. The men from farms or small towns wore bib overalls. The only sign of informality was rolled-up sleeves. Parts of old uniforms—trousers, shirts, even puttees—appeared here and there. Trousers looked as if they had had as tough a life as their wearers. Shoes were scuffed with run-down heels and thin soles, reinforced with inner strips of newspaper that blocked the dime-size hole that was an emblem of life on the road. Hardly anyone had a watch; these had long since been sold or pawned.[22]

Waters chose to wear a uniform that gave him the air of an officer: polished cavalry boots and khaki jodhpurs, topped by a white shirt, black bow tie, and a military-style tunic with a whistle on a lanyard in his left breast pocket, over which he had pinned two military ribbons. He affected a walking stick and did not wear a hat. Like Glassford, Waters had envisioned an orderly, army-style encampment and a registration system that would sift out nonveterans and Communists. To enter the camp, a man had to prove that he was a veteran. Waters strictly enforced the veterans-only rule and recruited a squad of MPs to maintain order and heave out real or suspected Communists.

Life at Camp Marks was enhanced by the Salvation Army, which maintained "The Hut," a gigantic green sailcloth tent near the entrance to the camp. It was staffed by female workers, known affectionately as "Sallies," who provided small comforts: a lending library, a place to write and send letters, and tables at which to play checkers. Periodically there would be a distribution of playing cards, tobacco, magazines, and clothes.[23]

For their part, Washingtonians saw the camps as an attraction: a place to visit on the weekends. Austin Kiplinger, son of journalist and publisher W. M. Kiplinger, recalled being taken downtown as a child by his father to walk

Veterans lined up for books at a camp library run by the Salvation Army. Also distributed here were writing paper and envelopes. Veterans could then mail their letters at an official post office set up at the camp. (Underwood & Underwood Collection/Library of Congress)

among the bonus marchers on Pennsylvania Avenue; they would move across the river to see others in their makeshift shelters—"tin huts in the mud of the Anacostia Flats."[24]

Writers passed through Camp Marks and wrote articles that began to put a positive, human face on the BEF for the public. On June 10 John Dos Passos, then at work on *The Big Money*, came and compared them to the army of 1917–18. Dos Passos had worked in an American hospital in France and driven an ambulance in France and Italy. The horrors he saw there would inform his writing for the rest of his life. After the American offensive at Château-Thierry, he recalled in his memoir, the wounded were being evacuated directly to Paris, and an urgent call was sent out for Americans on leave or on duty in the city to volunteer for hospital service: "The night I particularly remember it was my job to carry off buckets full of amputated arms and hands and legs from the operating room."[25]

Now in 1932 he looked at the men anew: "There is the same goulash of faces and dialects, foreigners' pidgin English, lingoes from industrial towns and farming towns, East, Northeast, Middle West, Southwest, South." But he saw them as older—"sunken eyes, hollow cheeks off breadlines"—and they reminded him of how quickly the lean years consume the fat ones.

Dos Passos, like so many others covering the camps, reserved the highest praise for Glassford ("the perfect host") and his men ("The cops and the ex-service men play baseball games in the afternoon; they are buddies together"). He was most taken by the centerpiece of the Anacostia camp: "a big platform with a wooden object sticking up from one end that looks like an old fashioned gallows. Speaking goes on from this platform all morning and afternoon."[26]

Thomas R. Henry, writing for the *Evening Star,* was constantly surprised by the speed with which this "rag-and-tin-can city" was growing, seeming to have doubled overnight between the Friday and Saturday nights of June 10 and 11: "New streets with their nicely aligned junk-pile shelters appeared as if by magic as more and more veterans seemed to get the knack of making themselves comfortable." Henry saw this as "a remarkable achievement of self-discipline," a place where there was "no crime, no dissension, no rebellion."[27]

He seemed most fascinated with the children of the Bonus Army, whom he characterized as "having the time of their young lives in this muddy junk pile jungle where there are no school bells, where the best of everything is reserved for them and where they are welcome in any hovel."[28]

"We used to watch them build their shanties," says Charles T. Greene, an eighth-grader living a few blocks from Camp Marks in 1932.

They had their own MPs and officers in charge, and flag-raising ceremonies, complete with a fellow playing bugle. We envied the youngsters because they weren't in school. Then some of the parents set up classrooms.

You had another set of the bonus marchers who didn't want to be identified with those people who camped out there on the Flats. They tried to impersonate just normal citizens. My mother had a very large house—we had a very large family—and she rented a room to a bonus marcher. I didn't realize that he was a bonus marcher because I knew he had a job pressing in the cleaners. I didn't know he was a bonus marcher until I started in the Cadet Corps in high school and he's going to teach me the Manual of Arms. So, that's when I found he was a bonus marcher.[29]

Besides the neighborhood kids who visited the camp, there were many kids who lived there. Nick and Joe Oliver, seven-year-old twins, had finished school in Belle Vernon, Pennsylvania, when their father said he was going to take them to Washington. Their father had gone to war as Antonio Oliverio, an Italian immigrant in a Doughboy's uniform. He fought in a tank battalion, was promoted to corporal, and was gassed. After the war he changed his name to Anthony Oliver, found a job as a bricklayer, got married, started a family, and became a charter member of American Legion Post 669. In the spring of 1932 the post endorsed the bonus and asked Tony and another veteran, Sam Ditz, to represent the post in the Bonus Army.

Tony decided to take the twins with him, leaving his wife and the six other kids at home. For two years Nick and Joe had been prizefighters, managed by their father, who set up matches in makeshift rings before small, enthusiastic audiences for whatever change landed in the hat that Tony passed around after the three-round match. Their father called them "my bread-and-butter boys," kids who had fun while earning a little money for the family. "We really boxed, but we never got hurt," Nick says.

Tony would look for work in Washington—bricklaying or whatever he could get—and leave the twins in the camp. They could box there just as well as in Belle Vernon. He told his wife to go to the drugstore every Friday night at nine o'clock and stand by the telephone, awaiting his call so they could talk about the kids.

"We started off just after school ended in May," Joe remembers. "My father had a Model A Ford, the kind you had to crank to start. We left at daybreak."

They headed south on an American road that dated to the eighteenth century, the National Highway across the mountains. "Sam Ditz brought a peck

Nick and Joe Oliver, seven-year-old twins, boxed in the Anacostia camp, where they lived while their veteran father went into Washington looking for work. By passing the hat after a match, they sometimes earned as much as a dollar. (Underwood & Underwood Collection/Library of Congress)

of potatoes with him in a burlap bag," Joe continues. "Every time we stopped, Sam would roast some potatoes. And we had some bread and salami."

His brother remembers that they stopped every once in a while to pick berries and snatch apples. "I guess it took us about twelve and a half hours for the 250 miles to Washington," Nick recalls. "My father was always afraid of running out of gas. He took a ten-dollar bill and hid it under the dash and said that's going to get us home."

"I remember when we saw the Capitol. My eyes popped out," Joe says.

The twins' father drove them directly to Anacostia. They found the company street where the Pennsylvania vets stayed and lived in the car for a couple of nights. Then they made a shelter—"a kind of lean-to"—out of pieces of cardboard. One day, Nick says, "my dad squared off a place and said we're going to do us an entertainment. He passed the hat around. One time, I remember, we got one dollar and thirty-seven cents in dimes, nickels, and pennies."[30]

They wandered the camp all day long while their father found work as often as he could, at about $2 a day. Their landmarks were the river and a pole with a sign that read "Pennsylvania." Sometimes they would get lost for a while because the camp was changing every day. But there was always the Pennsylvania pole.

They both vividly remember the absolute darkness of the night, with no flashlights or lantern to pierce it. "There were campfires here and there," Nick says. "But all around it was pitch-black. All you could do was hit the sack."

Alexander S. Colevas, eleven at the time, was another Camp Marks kid: "We used to go over to the flats and put on wrestling matches with the other kids and families from SE [southeast Washington]. These vets would toss us pennies and nickels. . . . You must remember that this was Depression time, and anywhere we could make a penny, we went."[31]

Henry Meisel, the motorcycling vagabond from Wisconsin, described the camp as "a lake of mud" after a hard rain, and cracked and rutted in dry weather. But he liked the place. The Salvation Army's big tent, which had a "goodly supply of books and magazines" and chairs and tables where he could write letters home, "tended to bring back the memories of those days served in France some fourteen years ago."

Anyone, he wrote, "could get a real thrill by going to the top of the bluff and looking over the entire camp below. American flags could be seen flying from every possible point of vantage so that hundreds of flags were unfurled to the breeze. Certainly these people were all good Americans, and there was no radicalism whatever."

Everyone was on the lookout for infiltrators. One night, Meisel wrote, "somebody began shouting: 'Every one out. The reds are coming.' The bugler was then ordered to blow 'assembly' and the veterans all rushed from their quarters armed with clubs, iron bars, bricks, etc. Men went to where the women and children were, and all approaches were guarded." It was a false alarm and everyone went back to their bunks. "The veterans at Camp Marks were certainly far from being in sympathy with any of the radical elements in Washington."[32]

About 1,100 wives and children populated the main camp, making it, with more than 15,000 people, the largest Hooverville in the country. Hundreds—and eventually thousands—of other veterans were scattered around Washington in more than two dozen billets, most of them in deserted and half-demolished buildings.[33] But Camp Marks was the heartland, where the vets set up a library and barbershop and staged vaudeville shows at which they sang such ditties as "My Bonus Lies over the Ocean." Almost daily, Glassford visited the camp, riding his blue motorcycle.

James G. Banks remembers that neighborhood people "took meals down to the camp. The veterans were welcomed." Far from feeling threatened, most

A miniature bungalow rose from the Anacostia shantytown, where many families lived. The Pennsylvania woman who inhabited it with her five children said of her makeshift shelter, "This is the only home we have." (Underwood & Underwood/Library of Congress)

residents saw bonus marchers as something of a curiosity. "On Saturdays and Sundays, a lot of tourists came down here," says Banks. The veterans and the people of Anacostia got along well, he remembers. "The guys used to come out and date girls in the neighborhood. In fact one of them married the sister of one of our friends. Sometimes they would play ball. There was a little semi-pro ball field up on Sumner Road where they came to see ball games."[34]

Frank A. Taylor had just gone to work in the summer of 1932 as a junior curator in the Smithsonian's Arts and Industries Building. "People in Washington were quite sympathetic [to the veterans]," Taylor remembers. "They [the veterans] were very orderly and came in to use the rest room. We did ask that they not do any bathing or shaving before the museum opened."[35]

Charles T. Greene, James Banks's pal, loved hanging out in the camps. "They would talk down there," he recalled, "and have entertainment for the people there, plus some of that entertainment was to draw people down there who could donate money or bring things to them. I remember the time they had this fellow—a bonus marcher—who they buried alive down there. We would go down there to see how long he was going to be able to stay underground. Couple of times they had people sitting on poles to attract people."

Washington newspapers relished life in the camps, and their reporters produced almost daily dispatches on camp life, writing about flagpole sitters, Indian chiefs, and one bona fide relative of Abraham Lincoln. Yet they largely missed the biggest story of camp life in this more-southern-than-northern city, where schools, buses, restaurants, and movies remained segregated. John Dos Passos mentioned the fact that whites and Negroes were mixed in the large audiences that clustered around the large stage at the center of the Anacostia camp,[36] and the *Evening Star*'s Thomas Henry was the first to mention this in print when he observed that there were "white men and colored men crowded together under the same shelters, but few others pursued the story."[37]

In the years between the Great War and the early 1930s, hundreds of thousands of African-Americans moved from the rural South to the industrial North; estimates range from 300,000 to a million. The North's black population, drawn to such cities as Chicago, Detroit, New York, and Cleveland, increased by about 20 percent between 1910 and 1930. In the early days of the great migration, race riots racked several cities.[38] Proposals for a federal anti-lynching law, killed by the Senate in 1922, came up again during the Hoover administration in reaction to fifteen lynchings between December 1929 and July 1930.[39] Hoover appointed African-Americans to federal commissions and urged an end to discrimination in federal agencies. But, in the face of opposition from southern legislators, he chose not to support legislation to stop lynchings.[40]

In June 1932 W. E. B. Du Bois's *Crisis*, the magazine of the National Association for the Advancement of Colored People (NAACP), carried an article entitled "The Secret City," alluding to the fact that Washington was 27 percent black, but little was said or written about these 132,000 souls. The color line was tightly drawn, especially at the White House door, where since the inauguration of Woodrow Wilson only two blacks had been invited to regular social functions, Minister Dantes Bellegarde and Congressman Oscar De Priest.[41] Negro groups were allowed to visit, but pictures were absolutely forbidden. One day in June President Hoover met with and had his picture taken with a group of motion picture engineers and members of the Yo-Yo Club of Raleigh, North Carolina. The next group through the door was the internationally acclaimed Fisk Jubilee Singers, who were given a cordial greeting but no photograph.[42]

In Anacostia and in the other camps, the color line seemed to have been erased. Jim Banks, the grandson of a slave and a resident of Anacostia, looked back on the camp as "the first massive integrated effort that I could remember. . . . They [blacks and whites] were eating and cooking together. They were segregated in the Army, but they weren't segregated here."[43] Charles Greene recalled the same thing: "You could see blacks and whites, and they were living as a unit."[44]

Sewilla LaMar said, "It was Jim Crow ships that took our boys over there, and under the Hoover administration, it was Jim Crow ships that took the Gold Star mothers to the graves of their sons who were left in Flanders' Fields. Jim Crow, it seemed, stood out above all else. It was only the denial of the bonus plea which affected both black and white veterans alike." And she added, describing the camps, "There was no Jim Crow there."*

Roy Wilkins, a rookie reporter for the *Crisis*, suggested that the NAACP monthly move away from its lofty "ebony tower" approach to issues and report them firsthand rather than write essays about them. Putting words into action, he headed from New York by train to Washington's Union Station and then to the teeming Camp Marks in Anacostia for a few days and nights in June. "There I found black toes and white toes sticking out side by side from a ramshackle town of pup tents, packing crates, and tar-paper shacks. Black men and white men, veterans of the segregated army that had fought in World War I, lined up equally, perspired in sick bays side by side. For years the U.S. Army had argued that General Jim Crow was its proper commander, but the Bonus Marchers gave lie to the notion that black and white soldiers— ex-soldiers in their case—couldn't live together."[45]

At Camp Marks, he noted, "there was one absentee, James Crow." If the bonus marchers could unite across racial lines, Wilkins asked, why couldn't the entire fabric of American life be desegregated? He hunted for several days and nights to find an example of segregation and finally found one at Anacostia, where a small group of "colored bonuseers" from New Orleans and other towns in Louisiana had erected a section of shacks for themselves, insisting on their own mess kitchen.

He was also taken by many other things: the organization of the camps, the discipline (enforced by black and white MPs), the ingenuity employed to turn junk into shelter, and mostly the music. "Over in one corner a white vet was playing a ukelele and singing what could have been the theme song of the

---

*Since so many American dead were buried in France, the U.S. government established a program to periodically allow mothers to visit the graves of their sons.

Roy Wilkins, a writer for the *Crisis,* the magazine published by the NAACP, shown in 1932. He visited the bonus marchers and found no Jim Crow in the Anacostia camp—despite, he wrote, many U.S. Army officials claiming that "whites and blacks could not function together." (NAACP Collection/Library of Congress)

camp: 'In a Shanty in Old Shanty Town.' On a Sunday afternoon the camp piano was played alternately by a brown lad with a New York accent and a red-necked white boy from Florida, while a few rods away Elder Micheaux's visiting choir was *giving* voice, in stop-time, to a hymn, 'God's Tomorrow Will Be Brighter Than Today'; and whites availed themselves of the free choice of patting their feet either outdoors to the piano or in the gospel tent to the choir."[46]

Wilkins's article was accompanied by an editorial box stating that the integration of the Bonus Army was evaded "gracefully" by the white press, which would go no further than to indicate that "a Negro was present" at a given event. One of the only white reporters to pick up on the "polyglot army in which Negroes and whites mingle without restriction" was Gardner Jackson of *Survey* magazine, who saw something else there: "The men . . . indeed, practiced the first large scale attempt to mimic Mahatma Gandhi's passive resistance." He added in parentheses, "I might be thrown out as a red if I told them that in person." These men and their families were characterized with many labels, including, now, "nonviolent."[47]

Native Washingtonians who visited Anacostia on the weekends were, to use the words of Constance McLaughlin Green in her history of race relations in Washington, "astonished" to discover white veterans from Alabama and Mississippi as well as northern and western states sharing billets, rations, and chores with Negro veterans. Like Wilkins, Green could find no evidence of Jim Crowism among the vets.[48] Another phenomenon recalled by both Banks and Green was that individuals and families of the Bonus Army broke through the color line in the Anacostia neighborhood. Greene recalls that near his house in a black neighborhood, a white family moved in. Girls in that family became friends with his sister.

The racially integrated camps were a challenge to the status quo, and their very existence flew in the face of the conventions of 1932, a year that would end with W. E. B. DuBois creating a list of Hoover's offenses against blacks. One of them had to do with the Gold Star mothers. In DuBois's indictment, Hoover ordered "colored Gold Star Mothers on separate ships with inferior accommodations" to France.[49]

Wilkins in his article in the *Crisis* hurled a major challenge at the military, which, he said, had been diligently spreading the doctrine that whites and blacks were unable to work together in uniform: "Why can't the United States army with its equipment and its discipline enlist Negroes and whites together in all branches of the service?" he asked. "It can, but it will not. The army is concerned with refined democracy, with tabus, with the maintenance of poses. The B. E. F. is concerned with raw democracy and with reality. But hereafter the army will have to hide behind its self-erected tradition, for the B. E. F. has demonstrated, right under the August army nose, that the thing can be done."

At the very end of his visit Wilkins stood on a little rise of land overlooking Camp Marks and observed, "Men and women can live, eat, play and work together be they black or white, just as the B. E. F. demonstrated. Countless thousands of people know it, but they go on pretending, building their paper fences and their cardboard arguments. Back home in Waycross, Miami, Pulaski, Waxahachie, Pine Bluff, Cairo, Petersburg, Des Moines, Cincinnati, Philadelphia, Kansas City and St. Louis, they go on pretending, glaring, jabbing, insulting, fighting."[50]

When Roy Wilkins made his visit to Anacostia, he did not see or meet all of the Negroes in the Bonus Army because a number of them had already been driven out as Communists; some were, some were not. Plainclothes police and federal undercover agents considered two things sure indicators that a person was a Communist: a Jewish name or a black face. And there were plenty of each there, stirred into the vast human melting pot seasoned with equal parts of despair and goodwill. By early June, the Communist label on the bonus marchers was gaining credibility—despite Waters's clearly anti-Communist remarks and his insistent demand that no Communists be admitted into the BEF. Rumors about Communist revolutionaries swirled through the city.

Meanwhile, anti-riot training was under way at nearby Fort Myer, where the continued arrival of bonus seekers created mounting apprehension. "There was a feeling of unease in official circles, and a restless, troubled feeling throughout the city," Lucian K. Truscott Jr., a young lieutenant at Fort Myer, sensed. "No one knew what to expect."[51]

Officers and enlisted men at Fort Myer restricted to base, conducted secret training on how to quell riots or armed rebellion. Troops took turns playing rioters and riot controllers. Some stood behind a corral fence, flailing pick handles, beating sticks, yelling, and flapping slickers or blankets. Troopers on horses charged the fence, conditioning the horses to stay calm in a maelstrom of noise and violence.

At edgy Fort Myer, communism became a trespasser. Although the garrison troops and officers were confined to base, the gates remained open, and through them came civilians who saw the riot training. Soon Communist-published handbills were being found in barracks and stables. Similar handbills were distributed in the Marine barracks in Washington. One read:

> *SOLDIERS AND MARINES: The higher Army and Navy authorities, acting for the Wall Street–Hoover government are taking steps to use you against the Ex-servicemen who are now in Washington. Your officers expect you, if the government considers it necessary to club or shoot down the Veterans to protect them from carrying on their struggle and getting the bonus. . . .*
>
> *Soldiers! Marines! You are workers! No real red-blooded American soldier will allow himself to be used to shoot down fellow workers—his war-time buddies—his father or brothers who are unemployed.*[52]

The handbills infuriated Truscott and most of the other officers and men, leading them—along with the Army's Military Intelligence Division—to believe that the Bonus Army was full of Communists, or even Communist-controlled.

Communism was very much on the mind of General Douglas MacArthur on June 8, when he was in Pittsburgh making the commencement speech to the largest class ever graduated by the University of Pittsburgh. "Pacifism and its bedfellow, communism, are all around us," he said. "In the theatre, newspapers and magazines, pulpits and lecture halls, schools and colleges, it hangs like a mist before the face of America, organizing the forces of unrest and undermining the morale of the working man. Day by day this canker eats deeper into the body politic. . . . We should be at all times prepared to defend ourselves. . . . It is undefended riches which provoke war. The wealth of the United States presents a tempting spectacle which may ultimately lead to another world war."

MacArthur's speech to 1,326 graduates and their kin and friends was politely received in the bowl of Pitt Stadium. But in the university activities building, police hauled away three antiwar protesters, members of a group that had objected to having MacArthur as the commencement speaker.[53] And even as MacArthur was warning about omnipresent communism, 400 bonus marchers—most of them led by admitted Communists—were clogging the streets of Pittsburgh; some had arrived by freight train, others in a string of trucks. John T. Pace of the Workers' Ex-Servicemen's League led one group; C. B. Cowan, the firebrand Communist who had masterminded the railroad confrontation in Cleveland, led another. Pace eluded Pittsburgh police and slipped out of town, arriving in Washington on June 9. But Cowan was arrested on "suspicion." Police cars sped around the city, herding the two groups toward McKees Rocks, a small town northwest of downtown Pittsburgh. There they were all put in the basements of the municipal building and a furniture store. Down-and-out residents, who would have been surprised at MacArthur's allusion to the wealth of America, managed to find enough coffee and food to feed the unexpected strangers.

Many of the marchers spending the night in Pittsburgh vehemently denied that they were Communists. Among them were those in a California contingent that had mingled with the Pace group in McKees Rocks. Mrs. William Perrotta, who was called the "Joan of Arc of the West" by her companions, led the 350 Californians with her husband. They left their two sons, four and seven years old, at home. The Californians headed off on a Pittsburgh & Lake Erie Railroad freight train and planned to change to a Baltimore & Ohio or Western Maryland freight at Connellsville, Pennsylvania. As they headed east, about 150 Pittsburgh-area veterans got ready to leave in a motorcade of six trucks supplied by area businesses, with gasoline donated by other local supporters.[54] Neither the Californians nor the Pennsylvanians were Communists. But they, like so many veterans already in Washington, were being tarred with the red brush. Allegations of Communist sympathies were, to use MacArthur's words, hanging like a mist over the entire BEF.[55]

· · ·

Few of Washington's civilian movers and shakers felt the kind of compassion shown by Evalyn Walsh McLean. More typical was the response of Gilbert H. Grosvenor, president of the National Geographic Society, who saw the veterans as a threat. On June 9 he wrote to his father, saying he was concerned that President Hoover might not be able to go to Constitution Hall, a short distance from the White House, to present the National Geographic Society Gold Medal to aviatrix Amelia Earhart. Grosvenor accepted the baseless, but widespread, canard that most of the men were not veterans, writing, "A large number of so-called veterans never saw service, or if they did, did not cross the seas. The promoters of the gathering here were Communists. The entire program was carefully prepared at Communists' headquarters in New York." The "invasion of Washington by the veterans may precipitate unbelievable catastrophes."[56] (John O. La Gorce, associate editor of the *National Geographic Magazine*, agreed with his boss. In a letter to Hoover he complained about veterans who would accost shoppers as they came out of grocery stores and "in an insistent voice ask if they really needed all that food at home when there were hundreds of people starving.")[57]

Grosvenor's letter shows that even in early June the veterans, who were struggling for survival, were viewed by some residents as Communist-led and a threat to the city. Taking his cue from federal agencies, Police Chief Glassford quietly turned his Special Investigations and Missing Persons Squad into an undercover unit. Its officers attended Communist meetings in Washington, infiltrated suspected Communist groups, and began to assemble what became a "confidential administrative file" of 15,000 index cards and 5,000 dossiers on persons and organizations. The files even contained the license numbers of cars parked near places where Communist meetings were held.[58]

Two days after MacArthur's appearance in Pittsburgh, the U.S. Army began a secret project to ferret out Reds among the marchers elsewhere. The order, undoubtedly seen by MacArthur, came from Secretary of War Hurley, who sent radiograms in secret code to the nine officers commanding troops spread across the United States in the nine corps areas: "With reference to any movements of veteran bonus marchers to Washington originating in or passing through your corps area, it is desired that a brief radio report in secret code be made to the War Department indicating the presence, if any, of communistic elements and names of leaders of any known communist leanings."[59]

Reports trickled in for weeks: "Marchers leaving Rochester, New York; known communists among them"; "Guns and ammunition stolen from an ROTC building in Albany"; "Five admitted communists agitating recruits preceding 2,500 Los Angeles now vicinity El Paso."[60] Most corps commanders did not report seeing many Reds. The commander of the 3rd Corps Area in Baltimore, however, reported that although he knew of no Communists in the Baltimore group, he believed there was a "general feeling of unrest . . . to the general effect that some serious trouble is likely to arise at an early date."[61] Eighth Corps Area headquarters at Fort Sam Houston, Texas, reported that in the California delegations there were Jewish Communists financed by Metro-Goldwyn-Mayer.[62] And from the 9th Corps Area in San Francisco came a note about Waters's Oregonians: "There was no evidence of Communist penetration of this group, except for one of its members, George Alman." Even before Hurley sent his order, an intelligence officer telephoned an "unconfirmed report from a reliable source," which said that "a detachment of Reds were concentrating in the vicinity of Herkimer [New York], that they had thirty-one machine guns and two pieces of artillery, caliber not stated."[63] J. Edgar Hoover, director of the Justice Department's Bureau of Investigation, sent the Army's Military Intelligence Division a report saying that some of the marchers were alleged to have "dynamite in a plan to blow up the White House."[64]

Undercover operatives from the District police and MID infiltrated meetings of suspected Communists. After John Pace was released in Pittsburgh and reached Washington, the agents tailed him, once getting close enough to overhear him talking to other men about the "big show." In a report he was quoted as saying that authorities would be "afraid to put us out" of the abandoned government-owned building they occupied, "as it would be starting something, and, that, Comrade, is what we want. Let the big guy start first, and we will finish the doings."[65]

Such reports produced an air of crisis, especially in the Army. The police, MID, and Secret Service officials worked closely together. The MID, for example, routinely provided information from army records so that dossiers could be produced on BEF leaders, and copies of District police reports went to the White House.[66] MacArthur began getting daily intelligence reports.[67] Moseley got a tip from a reserve officer in Detroit saying that Communists from that city "planned to take forcible possession of one of the government buildings, raise a Red flag from the flag staff, and declare a government of the Soviet Union of the United States."[68]

Waters boasted of the BEF's attacks on Communists, the first of which took place on June 10, when the police were called out to protect some two hundred Communists who were evicted from the Anacostia camp. Pace's group turned up the next morning and along with the evictees occupied a vacant building, one of many that had been bought by the federal government for demolition in connection with the Federal Building Program at Thirteenth and B streets SW.[69]

From this point forward, the Communists were not only shunned but also abused by the BEF. Several men found inside Camp Marks were tried by a "kangaroo court" and sentenced to fifteen lashes across the back.[70] Communists told of beatings and kidnappings, and hinted that two men whose bodies were found in the Potomac had been beaten and thrown into the river.[71] Two young women with Communist literature—"boudoir Bolsheviki," Waters called them—were accosted by his MPs in Camp Marks and turned over to local police but not charged for any crimes.[72]

Ostracized by the BEF and under constant surveillance by the Army, Pace and his followers were handled differently by Glassford. "Pace had participated in the Dearborn riots and had the reputation of being a dangerous and fearless leader," Glassford wrote in his diary. "Waters refused to supply food for Pace's group from the central commissary which had been established, so I went over to Pace's billet, not only to straighten out the sustenance difficulty, but also to get acquainted with Pace. I felt that the better I knew Pace the better I could anticipate his moves. . . . Much to my surprise I found him to be an affable good natured individual, with a very engaging smile."

Glassford found that most of Pace's men were "colored." He promised to get them food, and thought they were far more interested in food than in communism. When Glassford, who had gotten Pace's police record from Detroit and found he had once been arrested for attempting to chloroform an alderman, asked him about this, Pace smiled and said, "You're damn right. That alderman deserved to be chloroformed."[73]

Rumors about Communists did not hurt the lobbying of the BEF, which produced an incredible achievement. Challenging the American Legion, one of the most powerful lobbying machines in Washington, the veterans managed to restore life to a bill that appeared to be dead. Back on May 6, the House Ways and Means Committee had voted against Wright Patman's cash-now bill. Ordinarily, this would have killed a bill, and Patman knew he faced a formidable parliamentary struggle. To get such a bill out of committee and onto the floor for a vote, the bill had to be formally tabled for seven meeting days. Then a petition had to be made for the invoking of a special rule. That was granted by the Rules Committee for Patman's bill.

After all this was done, Patman had begun buttonholing colleagues to get the 145 names needed to bring the bill to the floor, when the vets arrived. Their amateur lobbying technique consisted mainly of confronting hundreds of representatives, face-to-face. The well-fed, well-tailored members of Congress saw before them hungry, tattered, but unbowed men with empty pockets. The sight of those men was far more powerful than the messages from American Legion lobbyists. From those encounters, the bonus marchers produced many of those 145 signatures.[74] But the bill still could die, murdered by the calendar. Because bills could be brought out by petition only on the second and fourth Monday of the month, the next time the bill could be put before the House was Monday, June 13. And the House was scheduled to adjourn on June 10 so that Republican members could attend the Republican National Convention, which was to nominate President Hoover for his second term. In order for Patman's bill to reach the floor, the scheduled adjournment would have to be postponed. Patman put it succinctly: "a vote to adjourn is a vote against the bonus."[75]

Speaker of the House John Garner saw to it that the House was not adjourned. He believed that a vote on the bonus had to be taken.[76] On Tuesday, June 14, Wright Patman's cash-now bonus bill, authorizing an appropriation of $2.4 billion, was finally headed toward a vote on the House floor. Democratic Representative Fred Vinson of Kentucky began the debate. Arguing that the bill would put billions of dollars into circulation, he said that it "goes at the basic conditions underlying our weakened economic structure." Two other representatives, loyal to President Hoover, rose to oppose the bill. One of them called the Bonus March "a foolish trip and one which should not have been undertaken."

Representative James Frear of Wisconsin, who had served in the Army from 1879 to 1884,[77] chided his colleagues: "Those who here enjoy $30 a day or more should not denounce these wet, ragged, bedraggled men soaked for days in the rain, who only ask for a dollar a day. They ask for bread for themselves and their families. They ask it from the wealthiest country in the world, for which they fought. Among those who came back, a million or more are in dire need. They ask for bread, and Congress should not offer them a stone." Democratic Representative Charles Crisp of Georgia, who had been in Congress since 1913, emphasized the need for maintaining fiscal integrity and did not believe the bonus was just because "the masses of the American people" would "have to pay the bill."

Next on his feet was Edward Eslick of Tennessee, a Democratic congressman since 1925. He was going to make an important speech, and his wife was in the gallery for the occasion. So were many members of the BEF, disobeying an order from Waters, who did not want it to appear that veterans were trying to pressure Congress. "Uncle Sam," Eslick said, "the richest government in the world, gave sixty dollars and an IOU 'that I will pay you twenty-seven years after the armistice.' But, Mr. Chairman, I want to divert you from the sordid. We hear nothing but dollars here. I want to go from the sordid side—"[78]

Eslick gasped and slumped to the floor. Representatives rushed to him and carried him to the lobby, where the House physician tried to revive him. His wife rushed to the lobby and found her husband dead of a heart attack.[79]

Next day, five thousand bareheaded BEF men lined the streets as Eslick's body was taken from a funeral home to Union Station for the train home to Tennessee. Others, led by holders of the Distinguished Service Cross, marched in Eslick's cortege.

On June 15, the House of Representatives passed the bonus bill by a vote of 211 to 176, with 40 not voting. For the bonus were 153 Democrats, a Farmer-Laborite, and 57 Republicans; opponents included 51 Democrats.[80] The BEF had won a battle, but another awaited in the Senate.

On June 17, more than 6,000 veterans[81] thronged Capitol Hill to maintain a vigil on the Senate, which was scheduled to vote that day on Patman's bill.[82] One of the senators was Senator Thomas P. Gore, a populist from Oklahoma—the state's first senator and the first blind senator. He was driven to Capitol Hill by his black driver. Next to Gore sat his grandson, seven-year-old Gore Vidal. All summer the boy had been hearing about the "Boners," as some Washingtonians called the Bonus Army. Grown-ups talked about the rumors sweeping Washington: the Boners had attacked the White House, torched the Capitol, were looting stores. Vidal, as he later wrote, "thought that the Boners were just that—white skeletons like those jointed cardboard ones displayed at Halloween. Bony figures filled my nightmares until it was explained to me that these Boners were not from slaughterhouses but from poorhouses."

As the car approached the Capitol, "I stared out the open window, looking for Boners. Instead I saw only shabby-looking men holding up signs and shouting at occasional cars. At the Senate side of the Capitol there was a line of policemen. Before we could pass through the line, Senator Gore was recognized. There were shouts; then a stone came through the window of the car and landed with a crash on the floor between us. My grandfather's memorable words were 'Shut the window,' which I did."[83]

The shouts and songs of the veterans—"The Yanks are starving, the Yanks are starving"[84]—could be heard in the Senate chamber as the debate went on. Liberal senators, conceding that the veterans' cause was just, nevertheless said they would vote against it because the bonus bill would kill off one for un-

More than six thousand bonus marchers took over Capitol Hill on June 17, awaiting the Senate vote on the bonus bill, which the House had passed. To the tune of "The Yanks Are Coming," veterans sang, "The Yanks are starving, the Yanks are starving." (Underwood & Underwood/Library of Congress)

employment relief. Democratic Senator Elmer Thomas of Oklahoma, who would vote for the bonus bill, told the Senate that whatever the vote, the Bonus Army "would commence immediately to make their plans for evacuation" of Washington.[85]

Veterans sprawled across the Capitol Plaza and the lawn. Others filled the Senate gallery, listening to every word. Senator Hiram Johnson, a California Republican, did not feel threatened, he wrote his son, but he felt the veterans' presence ominous: "If the farmers of this Nation who are suffering united, as these men have united, and with the same abandon, started a march upon the Capitol, and joined ranks with those of the city whose souls have been seared with misery during the past few years, it would not be difficult for a real revolution to start in this country."[86]

Some thirteen thousand men in Camp Marks were preparing to join their comrades on Capitol Hill. Assistant Superintendent L. I. H. Edwards—a rival for the job Glassford was given in 1931—panicked when he realized the Camp Marks vets were ready to march. On what a local paper called "the tensest day in the capital since the War," Edwards ordered the Eleventh Street drawbridge raised. John D. Weaver described the scene in the novel he based on his summer with the Bonus Army: "The policemen, standing shoulder to shoulder, formed a blue picket fence in front of the raised drawbridge, thrust up into the darkening sky like a giant hand. Police cars were parked along both sides of the street, and Lorry [a character in the book] could see their tommy-guns."[87]

Scores of police blocked the other two bridges. Edwards's move stopped the flow of veterans to Capitol Hill but also increased the smoldering anger in Camp Marks.[88]

On Capitol Hill, neither Waters nor Glassford was immediately aware of what had happened. Waters had ordered all men in Camp Marks to come to the Capitol. "I noticed very few additions to our numbers as it grew dark," he recalled. "Suddenly one of my aides rushed through the crowd, to where I was sitting on the Capitol steps with the men." The aide told him that the drawbridge had been raised. Waters, stunned, wondered what would happen if the thousands of men around him heard about their penned-in comrades.[89]*

Glassford had given standing orders that the drawbridge could be raised

---

*Despite the growing anger of the veterans on the bridge, there was a moment of levity: a pair of vets doused themselves in chicken blood and convinced an ambulance driver to take them across the bridge.

and the other bridges sealed only if any demonstrations broke out in Anacostia or on the Hill, where he had hidden police reserves in the belowground labyrinth of the Capitol. The Marine Barracks had been put on alert.

Irate commuters, unable to cross the Potomac on any bridge, complained bitterly to police. Edwards ordered the drawbridge lowered and the other bridges opened. Veterans began streaming in from Anacostia. Glassford called for the reserves to appear.[90] A senator asked Waters what would happen if the bill should be defeated. "Nothing will happen," Waters said, "unless something stupid is done to stir up the men."[91]

Debate continued into the evening. Waters had arranged for a mobile kitchen to bring the veterans a hot meal of stew and coffee. Except for some angry words directed at news photographers, the men remained calm. The U.S. Army Band, which played a concert on Capitol Hill on Friday nights in the summer, appeared, to everybody's surprise.[92] Finally, around 9:30, Senate aides summoned Waters inside. He reemerged moments later to break the news to the crowd: the bill had been defeated—a "temporary setback," he said, promising again that the BEF would "stick it out" until 1945.[93] The men roared at that, and for a moment it looked as if the veterans would attack the Capitol. Then Elsie Robinson, a nationally syndicated Hearst columnist and friend of the BEF, whispered something in Waters's ear. He shouted to the crowd: "Sing 'America.'" They started to sing, and the Army Band struck up the song. When the last notes drifted over the plaza, the veterans began to head back to their scattered billets and back to Camp Marks.

While this was going on outside, on the Senate floor there was a move to reconsider the bonus and a second to table the bill. By a vote of 44 to 26 the bill was tabled, which effectively meant that the issue of the bonus would lie dormant until the Seventy-third Congress convened in 1933.

It was finally over, Washingtonians thought the next day. Now the veterans could all go home. But before the Bonus Army could make its next move, Waters and Glassford had unfinished business. The veterans' anger over the raising of the drawbridge seemed to be increasing by the hour, and the feeling was that the BEF had been double-crossed by Glassford. Waters asked for and got an apology. "It was a mistake to have done so and the entire Police Department recognizes it as such," was how Glassford put it in a letter.[94]

The Death March

Four abreast they marched—
five thousand strong. . . .
All were down at the heel.
All were slim and gaunt and their eyes had a light in them.
There were empty sleeves and limping men with canes. . . .
They did not march in the light of day. They marched in darkness. . . .

—Floyd Gibbons, *Literary Digest,* June 18, 1932.

FOLLOWING THE VETS' SINGING of "America" and peaceful return to their camps, the *Evening Star* editorialized, "These men wrote a new chapter on patriotism of which their countrymen could be proud." To which the *New York Times* added, "Even in the stress of the Senate debate and vote they kept the order which has been one of the most amazing qualities of this march on Washington." Both papers also said that it was time for the veterans to admit they had made a mistake and accept defeat.[1]

Nothing was further from the minds of the vast majority of the veterans occupying the city. The BEF began settling in for what looked like a long-term presence in the city, and the small band of Communists met daily to target the White House in the belief that demonstration and disruption would force

President Hoover to demand a special session of Congress. For this reason, both the Army and the police had Pace's men under constant surveillance.[2]

In the days following the vote, some BEF men and their families left— 1,000 by police estimates; only 200, according to Waters, who called for new recruits: "Have 150,000 here by fall," he said to recruiters he sent to key cities. The first recruiter was a woman from Wisconsin who went to Richmond for reinforcements and supplies. To find recruits in the Northeast, Joe Angelo was sent out with the head of the Utah delegation. Another duo was sent south. A truck left for Long Island, New York, with BACK TO WASHINGTON WITH RECRUITS chalked on its side.[3]

To remove any doubt that the BEF intended to become a permanent force, Waters and his executive committee printed membership cards. Wright Patman was issued card No. 1, and Glassford, No. 2. The cards contained a pledge of allegiance to the United States and its Constitution, as well as to the BEF.[4] At about this same time Waters and Glassford began talking with John Henry Bartlett, former governor of New Hampshire and former postmaster general, about setting up a plan for a "semi-permanent" colony for homeless vets on thirty acres of District land owned by Bartlett.[5]

The remainder of the month of June favored the BEF with new recruits, food, and countless column inches of upbeat newsprint. From New York, for instance, ninety-four cabdrivers arrived in taxis borrowed in Baltimore. "Their sang-froid and their arrival a la mode de Gallieni at the Marne[6] sent rumors through town that a battalion of New York gangsters had come armed with bombs for some desperate purposes," reported the *New York Times,* adding, "but they turned out to be entirely harmless except for their vocabularies."[7] Eight former German soldiers brought a ton and a half of food from Jersey City. Now naturalized Americans, all had fought against the Americans, all had been wounded at least twice, and all had won decorations. The food was offered as "slight reparations for the shiploads of food sent to starving Germany by the United States after the war" and caused Henry O. Meisel to comment, "I never did hear of any such being done by any of the British or French veterans who were our allies during the war."[8]

A well-known local art collector and veteran auctioned off a famous bronze statuette to enhance the mess fund, and an Oregon woman, the self-styled Mother of the Bonus Army, married a forty-year-old vet in New York, where they had gone for a visit. As their permanent address they gave BEF headquarters in Washington. The first baby, "Baby Pipp," was born to a BEF couple (Mr. and Mrs. Edmond Pippenbring of Jacksonville, Florida) who lived in Camp Marks, which now had its own comedian (Sandy "Scottie"

Gibson, who convinced a local company to give the camp a new piano), and its own poet and official photographer (Eddie Gosnell). A couple (the Swartworths of Pittsburgh) hitchhiked with their children to Washington, having convinced the kids (Billy, five, Buddy, three, and Cissy, one) that they were on vacation and that Camp Marks was "a big park."

The BEF also had its own newspaper, the *B.E.F. News,* which debuted on June 25. It was created and edited by Joseph L. Heffernan, former mayor of Youngstown, Ohio, who was addressed by the title of Judge. He had come with the Ohio delegation looking for material for a series of magazine articles. Early issues were mundane, akin to a small-town weekly with poetry, camp gossip, and the odd bit of unintended irony—reporting, for instance, on vets leaving camp to do their National Guard duty back home. The paper's first press run was 25,000, and 597 vets sold it out in eight hours.[9] By the middle of July the *B.E.F News* claimed street sales of 50,000 and out-of-town sales of 25,000. Judge Heffernan said he was planning to line up 30,000 vets to sell it in New York and that he soon hoped to have a circulation of 1 million.

Heffernan chronicled life in the camps, interpreting the Bonus Army for others—telling, for example, a reporter for the *Star* that most people did not understand its diverse composition.[10] "With the Texas outfit for example, are five rodeo riders," he said. The *News* became the glue that linked the camps to the local public. But if these stories received ink, they were not getting celluloid. At a time when newsreels were part of the usual program in the nation's movie theaters, newsreel cameras rarely showed everyday Bonus Army camp life, though cameramen were told to cover any outbreaks of violence. Under orders from New York headquarters, Fox and Hearst cameramen shunned the vets, while Paramount carried one short item and Pathé two.[11]

The major still-photo companies did circulate images of daily life in the camps, depicting everything from a replica of the White House erected in Anacostia to images of men tending communal caldrons of stew. One image showed a family that built and lived in a scaled-down house replete with chimney and front porch; others showed Anacostia as a place with streets, albeit muddy ones, a library, a post office, and its own boxing ring. Images of the Oliver twins slugging away in that ring were sent around the country. Local photographers—including Harris and Ewing, a company known for its soft-focus portraits of Supreme Court justices and debutantes—produced high-quality photographic postcards, which were mailed from the camp post office and kept by locals as souvenirs of this unusual summer. Other, crudely printed postcards found whimsy in such subjects as a cluster of hovels created from old car bodies and fenders, a black barber shaving a white patron in an

This image of a "southern-style" barbershop was on one of the many postcards depicting camp life in Anacostia. Veterans could make money selling postcards on the streets of Washington. (Authors' collection)

open-air barbershop, and a group of jolly men lined up in front of their pack-ing-crate-and-tar-paper tenements. These were not images of despair and de-pravity, but rather portraits showing the down-at-the-heels dignity and sense of humor that made the BEF camps seem appealing, even romantic, and sug-gested that the ban on newsreel cameras kept them from becoming even more attractive to the American public.[12]

During this time, Moscow, in the form of the Comintern, was urging Com-munists in the United States and other countries to rise in global revolution. From Moscow, the BEF looked like the best possible source of insurrection in America. Earl Browder, head of the U.S. Communist Party (and a spy for the Soviets), was being pressured to mobilize the unemployed. In a desperate move, he went to Camp Marks, even though he had been a draft dodger, spending most of the Great War in jail for refusing to register for the draft and for opposing the war. He did not make much of an impression at Camp Marks. But in a dispatch to the Communist *Daily Worker* he said that, come the revolution, the marchers would be the "shock troops" of America's unem-ployed masses.[13]

Washington police undercover operatives, along with informers for both the police and Army intelligence, kept meetings of left-wing vets under surveillance. Secret reports carried a heavy dose of stereotyping, one describing a participant as having a "Jewish nose and appearance" and a "negro" with "dark colored skin."[14]

At the same time, leadership of the BEF was in flux. After the Senate vote against the bonus bill, Waters found himself in the midst of a power struggle exacerbated by his own petulance and desire for more and more power. Reports from the BEF "secret service" informed him that his camp commanders and a self-appointed executive committee were holding secret meetings in hotel rooms around town.[15] Finally, on June 25, he decided to force a showdown by again resigning. For several days the BEF was leaderless and confused. The Communist *Daily Worker* jumped into the void, suggesting that this was a revolt staged by the rank and file because Waters had cut off the food supply to the WESL; the *Worker* confidently predicted that Pace would be swept in as the new leader.[16]

Early on the morning of June 29, following Waters's third resignation in three weeks, his secretary, Owen W. Lucas, reported to police that a shot had been fired at a car Waters usually rode in during his rounds of the camps. "I am positive that the shot was intended for Waters," Lucas said. The car was passing down East Capitol Street, near Capitol Hill, when the shot was fired, Lucas said.[17]

Hours later, at a tumultuous meeting at Camp Marks attended by 10,000, Waters climbed to the roof of a shed and spoke, saying that he would return but only if given "complete dictatorial powers." As he jumped down, the cry went up, "Let's vote now! Waters again!" By the acclaim of those present, Waters was reinstated as leader of the BEF. But this time he demanded—and was given—broad, total control over the veterans. Within minutes of his ascendancy he pledged that he would immediately abandon all committees and ban his rivals from any office. He ordered morning military drills for everyone and declared that he would build a force of five hundred "shock troops" to maintain discipline in a new BEF, which he termed "a mobile military machine" that would be ready to serve the country in any "national emergency," refusing to say what emergency he had in mind. "I'm going to be hard-boiled with the B.E.F.," he said. "If any man refuses to carry out my orders, he will be dragged out of Washington by the military police. To hell with civil law and General Glassford. I'm going to have my orders carried out!"[18] At this point Waters was openly flirting with fascism, imagining himself a leader of millions rather than thousands. In the days that followed a name would be given to this movement: the Khaki Shirts, an American adaptation of Italy's fascist Black Shirts and Germany's Nazi Brown Shirts.

The following day, Glassford responded. He declared that Waters would not be allowed to exercise unlawful powers and that nobody was going to be dragged out of D.C. by Waters's shock troops. Glassford followed up by refilling the BEF's larder with 3,000 pounds of meat, 500 pounds of sugar, 4,000 loaves of bread, and much more. He paid the $773.40 bill out of his own pocket.[19]

That night Glassford told a conference on emergency unemployment relief that even if Congress voted to offer money for the veterans to return home, he did not expect many of them to take the offer. A large number had no homes or came from places where the unemployment problem was so severe that they were not wanted. "Thousands of these veterans will stay here until something is done to break them up," he said. He ended by stating that more veterans would come and that tolerance had to be shown to them. "They are no longer young," he reminded his audience. "They gave their best to their country and are doing their best to act creditably while here."

As June turned into July, several hundred bonus marchers returned to their homes, but several hundred new men replaced them, perhaps enticed by Waters's declaration that he and others intended "to stay here until 1945 if necessary to get our bonus." The police estimate of veterans in Washington on the

President Herbert Hoover and aviatrix Amelia Earhart are flanked by Gilbert H. Grosvenor, president of the National Geographic Society, and his wife at the presentation of Earhart's gold medal on June 28. Hoover had feared the veterans would prevent him from attending this event. (Library of Congress)

first of July was 21,100, with more on the way. The cooler-than-normal summer days were characterized by an almost continual alternation between drizzle and downpour, creating, as a veterans' magazine put it, the "same slimy soup of mud to wade through, eat and sleep in" that had plagued the men in France. The mud and body lice, along with the general worsening of sanitary conditions and the dwindling supply of food, began to wear heavily on the men, women, and children of Anacostia.[20]

On the first of July, Glassford dug into his pocket for the second time in a few days to provide food—this time spending $600. Late that night, word came that twenty tons of meat was on its way from New York, a gift from the city's meatpackers. Hunger had become an issue that overrode all others. "Through sheer force of personality, I talked with men high in national affairs at Washington and was told that the government was absolutely unable to pay the bonus now, no matter what happened," said Sewilla LaMar, by now a BEF leader. "And I believed them. I went back to the men and told them. My words were scoffed at, and I was greeted with derision. I found out for the first time that hunger knew no reasoning."[21]

Waters led a group of five thousand to the Capitol on Saturday, July 2, to

Bonus Army commander Walter W. Waters, in his officer-style uniform, led five thousand veterans who gathered at the Capitol on July 2 to protest the decision to adjourn Congress without taking action on the bonus bill. (General Douglas MacArthur Foundation)

protest the planned adjournment, scheduled to take place in two weeks—before the date that the bonus bill was to come onto the floor for debate. Once Congress shut down, it would not reconvene until December, after the elections. The men arrived only to find Congress had gone home for the long holiday weekend. Waters, who had led his men on an apparent wild-goose chase, promised to return on Tuesday, July 5, when the House reconvened. Waters's rally moved ahead anyhow, droning on for four hours. Foulkrod reported on his futile trip to Chicago, the site of both presidential conventions where he had tried and failed to get the two parties to insert a pro-bonus plank in their respective platforms. Waters, flanked by four MPs and dressed in riding breeches, boots, and a khaki shirt, celebrated the good news that Franklin D. Roosevelt had received the nomination of the Democratic Party hours earlier, and said that he had already secured an audience with Roosevelt on the issue of the bonus payment. It would take place sometime in the next week, "and when I see him," he told the cheering crowd, "I will get a statement which I will bring back to you and repeat word for word."[22] It was no secret that Roosevelt was on record opposing the bonus, and Waters had no reason to suspect otherwise. In April Roosevelt had released a statement: "I do not see how, as a practical business sense, a government running behind two billion dollars annually can consider the anticipation of the bonus payment until it has a balanced budget, not only on paper but with a surplus of cash in the Treasury."[23]

On the eve of his nomination, sitting with Samuel I. Rosenman and several other members of his "brain trust" in the governor's mansion in Albany, Franklin D. Roosevelt was preparing the final, rhetorical flourish for his acceptance speech—what traditional orators and politicians refer to as the peroration—even though the nomination was not yet sewed up. But the direct-line telephone kept ringing as people called in from the Democratic Convention in Chicago, and the summary lines were not getting written.

"I remember one of those interruptions very well," Rosenman later recalled: it was Senator Huey Long of Louisiana, a man Roosevelt had never met.

"Hello, Franklin—this is the Kingfish."

"Hello, Kingfish, how are you?"

"I'm fine and hope you are. I have a suggestion for you which will clinch the nomination."

Roosevelt was "all attention," according to Rosenman, as Long continued.

"I think you should issue a statement immediately, saying that you are in favor of a soldiers' bonus to be paid as soon as you become President."

"I am afraid I cannot do that because I am not in favor of the bonus."

"Well, whether you believe it or not, you'd better come out for it with a strong statement, otherwise you haven't got a chance for the nomination."

The governor explained that he could not say he was in favor of something he was opposed to.

"Well, you are a gone goose," said the Kingfish as he hung up.[24]

As night turned to morning, and as one ballot followed another, Roosevelt's staff began to think that the Kingfish might have been right. Rosenman, a former legislator and confidant of the governor, took a pot of coffee and several hot dogs to a private dining room, where he sat down to write the missing peroration—even though the nomination was still hours from being locked up. Rosenman came out of the room with a draft of the peroration that included the line: "I pledge you, I pledge myself, to a *new deal* for the American people." Neither Rosenman nor Roosevelt took special note of the two words intended to symbolize "bold, persistent experimentation" on behalf of "the forgotten man"—also Rosenman phrases—but within a few days, this had become one of the most powerful labels of the twentieth century.[25]

On July 2, the same day that Waters led his men to Capitol Hill and promised a private meeting with Roosevelt, Major George S. Patton Jr. reported for duty as executive officer of the 3rd Cavalry Regiment at Fort Myer, where secret anti-riot training had been going on for weeks. Patton shared Moseley and MacArthur's belief in the Red Menace and had his own ideas on how to deal with defiant citizens: "If you must fire do a good job—a few casualties become martyrs, a large number an object lesson. . . . When a mob starts to move keep it on the run. . . . Use the bayonet to encourage its retreat. If they are running, a few good wounds in the buttocks will encourage them. If they resist they must be killed."[26]

On the night of July 2, five hundred new vets, mostly from Michigan, showed up at Camp Bartlett on Alabama Avenue SE as plans for a great Fourth of July parade fell apart. Local veterans' marching bands and sympathetic drum and bugle corps had been dropping out of the march for days, and now none remained. The futile trip to the Hill earlier in the day had sapped the hungry veterans of their energy. Glassford paid another $600 for food.

Glassford braced for the parade, which was to march from the Capitol to the White House. He canceled all police leaves until the parade was over. His men, he said, would carry the usual billy clubs and side arms. On the eve of the scheduled parade, President Hoover said that he would spend the Fourth at his Rapidan camp. This meant that both ends of Pennsylvania Avenue would be vacant. Rain canceled the long-feared parade, and it was rescheduled for July 5, merging it into Waters's planned demonstration at Capitol Hill when the members of Congress returned.

Next morning's papers reported that a grave site had been donated for a four-year-old boy who had died of measles and pneumonia induced by malnutrition. He had lived with his parents and an aunt in a house near Camp Marks that sheltered fourteen other children.[27] The boy's death and the mention of malnutrition underscored the fact that the BEF could not feed itself. Making matters worse, con men found a new racket. They roamed the city and the countryside begging for food in the name of the Bonus Army and then keeping it or selling it. Two of the con men were arrested. Both were vets, but neither had anything to do with the Bonus Army.[28]

Waters headed to New York on the Fourth of July to take possession of 1,500 pounds of meat that had been donated by the Adam Hat Stores. While Waters was in New York, the planned parade had turned into a march on the Capitol and another rally—this one led by Foulkrod on the Senate side of Capitol Hill.

The rally, staged to protest the announced adjournment of Congress on July 16, turned into an angry, bitter tirade against Hoover, Mellon, Congress, the Red Cross, the way veterans were treated, and the absent Waters, who was attacked for his burgeoning dictatorship and the use of his MP shock troops.

Foulkrod, in charge in Waters's absence, lashed out at everything that seemed to stand between him and the bonus. The Red Cross was cited for its failure to help with the food crisis. With Herbert Hoover as its honorary chairman, money coming in from the hated Reconstruction Finance Corporation, and a brand-new building on E Street, the Red Cross was a highly visible target for the ire of the vets, who remembered all too well paying for doughnuts and coffee at Red Cross canteens outside combat areas.* Local American Legion Post 8 had just gone on record condemning the Red Cross for its lack of concern, demanding that Red Cross workers step up and help the veterans. Foulkrod called the head of the organization, John Barton Payne, "a political parasite, and a dirty contemptible cur."[29] (Payne had gone from short-term secretary of the interior under President Wilson to Red Cross chairman in 1921.)

Hoover was derided by the demonstrators and loudly booed for not feeding them. This was an extraordinary moment, a far cry from the booing that

---

*Few realized that this modest fee for food was imposed on the Red Cross by the Army, which had listened to the complaints of local merchants who claimed they were losing business.

had evolved into the less-than-angry chant "We want beer! We want beer!" that had greeted the president at the World Series the previous October.[30] The veterans believed that Hoover was keeping food and beer from them—and paying thousands of agents to enforce Prohibition with money that could be used to pay the bonus.[31]

As Foulkrod railed on, a Military Intelligence Division officer, Major Paul Killiam, listened and later noted in his report that the "marchers could easily be swayed to action one way or another, and that if some magnetic speaker had demanded an invasion of the Capitol and violence, he would probably have gotten support with serious trouble resulting." Killiam also revealed that the Metropolitan Police on duty had been disarmed by Glassford, creating "resentment and disgust" among police on the scene. Killiam reported that the police said Glassford had "got away with it" this time and might again, but that it was not fair to the police, Congress, or the public. The MID officer reported that Glassford had assured him that these men were not criminals, and that he was afraid that a minor disturbance could cause a policeman to lose his head, forget orders, "and shoot somebody or hit somebody in the head."[32]

In New York, Waters had planned to make appeals for cash in theaters and over a major radio network. "When I went to the studio I found that pressure from higher up had canceled my appointment," he said, adding that the same thing happened at the theaters. Waters, the promised meat, and a thousand pounds of coffee all arrived in Washington by plane on July 5, with more food to arrive later by truck. The food crisis had been given only a short-lived hiatus, for the meat would be gone by the next night and the camps would be back on short rations. "Mutiny Feared in Bonus Army," read a *Washington Daily News* headline.

Wilma Waters arrived from Portland while her husband was returning from New York. As soon as they were reunited, he took her to the home of Evalyn Walsh McLean, who described her as "a little ninety-three-pounder, dressed as a man, her legs and feet in shiney boots. Her yellow hair was freshly marcelled." The heiress had become a friend of Waters and allowed him to use her million-dollar mansion as "a sort of headquarters." She took Wilma Waters upstairs to a bedroom that McLean's father had designed for King Leopold of Belgium, sent for her maid to draw Wilma a bath, and told her to take a nap.

"You get undressed and while you sleep I'll have all your things cleaned and pressed," McLean said.

"Oh, no, not me. I'm not giving these clothes up. I might never see them again," Wilma replied. Her grueling trip had begun with a hop in a plane, which had been forced down by engine trouble in the Dells of Wisconsin. For the rest of the way she had hitchhiked and ridden buses.[33]

Wilma threw herself on the bed fully clothed; McLean tiptoed out of the room and had a talk with Waters.

"I'm desperate," he confessed. "Unless these men are fed, I can't say what won't happen in this town."

McLean telephoned Vice President Charles Curtis, who had attended dinner parties and poker games at her mansion. She told him that she was calling for Waters, who was standing by her side: "These men are in a desperate situation," she said, "and unless something is done for them, unless they are fed, there is bound to be a lot of trouble. They have no money nor any food."

Curtis told her he was calling a secret meeting of senators to urge immediate passage of a bill that would send the bonus marchers back to their homes. This was hardly news, as the bill had already passed the House and was scheduled for an early vote in the Senate.

At this moment she wished that her drinking buddy, Warren G. Harding, was still president: "Harding would have gone among those men and talked in such a manner as to make them cheer him and cheer their flag," she later wrote. "If Hoover had done that, I think, not even troublemakers in the swarm could have caused any harm."[34]

Wilma and Walter headed for the apartment that was paid for by McLean. "I could have lived in Anacostia, but things were bad there—there were always upheavals," Wilma Waters would later say.[35]

Of all that occurred on July 5, 1932, nothing was odder or more incendiary than a long radiogram, stamped SECRET, from an operative named Conrad H. Lanza to the Army's adjutant general, who was responsible for intelligence. The message, which foretold a revolution involving veterans and active-duty personnel of the U.S. Armed Forces, was read by MacArthur and other high-ranking officials.

Lanza's message asserted that a member of the BEF, Charles M. Bundell,[36] was leading a group back to Washington from upstate New York and claimed that the BEF had machine guns and the support of some U.S. Marines—who were said to be ready to turn bridges over to the Bonus Army—and soldiers in Fort Ontario, New York. A revolution was about to begin, Lanza said.

Specifically cited was a contractor—a former commander in the U.S. Navy—who said he had been told by members of the BEF that it was their intention to occupy the Capitol permanently and that when attempts were made to oust them, blood would be shed. At this point Waters, with the assistance of gunmen from New York and Washington, would create armed conflict in the streets of Washington, signaling a Communist uprising in all the large cities, "thus initiating revolution."

The Army now had information, passed through channels without comment, that a revolution was imminent and that "at least a part" of the Marine Corps garrison in Washington would side with the revolutionaries. It was one of the most remarkable documents ever to wind its way through the Army chain of command. If nothing else, it would go a long way to suggest why the Army would not rely on the Marine Corps in the days ahead.[37]

On July 7 Congress appropriated $100,000 toward getting the veterans out of town. Frank T. Hines, administrator of veterans' affairs, was authorized to provide funds for gas and oil, together with a 75-cents-a-day "travel subsistence," or railroad fare at one cent per mile. The appropriation further stipulated that whatever was paid "shall constitute a loan without interest which, if not repaid to the United States, shall be deducted from any amount payable to such veteran on his adjusted-service certificate." The deadline for accepting travel funds was July 15.

The congressional vote followed, by a few hours, an outbreak in Anacostia that seemed to emphasize the need to move veterans out of town. A group of Communists had gone from their Pennsylvania Avenue billet to Anacostia to deliver speeches against the dictatorial rule of Waters (who, at WESL meetings, was now known as Mussolini Waters or simply Mussolini) and to advance the idea that more of the veterans should camp near the Capitol, as the Pace group did, instead of in the mud of Anacostia. When John Pace launched into an anti-Waters tirade, some of Waters's shock troops closed in on him, threatening to injure him. Pace was shielded by Glassford, who said, "There is not to be a fight among the veterans. Pace has a right to speak. He is not in your camp. If you don't want to listen, go back and play baseball."[38]

The police then issued Pace and WESL a permit to demonstrate on Pennsylvania Avenue the following day. On July 8, some 2,000 members of the BEF lined the avenue, armed with bricks and cobblestones, to break up the WESL demonstration. Pace, outnumbered twenty to one, canceled the demonstration.[39]

With $100,000 now available for return trips, there seemed to be no valid reason for the veterans to remain. From all sides voices demanded they leave. "It is very evident that the bonus army can not remain in Washington much longer without becoming involved in serious trouble," warned the *Washington Post* on the morning after the money was appropriated. Later that day the *Evening Star* editorialized that "to urge them to stay here is to keep them in deeper and deeper distress and perhaps to bring them to face utter disaster." These and other editorials were quoted in a memo, written and signed by Glassford, who had copies distributed to the BEF camps. The veterans' presence, the memo said, was "seriously effecting local relief" by diverting contributions that would have been going to the poor people of Washington. "Congress is about to adjourn," Glassford continued. "It is futile to expect favorable bonus legislation at this session. No political advantage can be gained by remaining longer in this city."

Many of the men who took the tickets—600 of them on the first day—walked to Union Station, sold them to travelers at cut-rate prices, and then returned to camp.[40] Reports quickly circulated that some of the men leaving Washington were actually recruiters, sent home to bring back fresh troops. There also were incidents of veterans claiming to be from far-off places to get railroad fares, as no documentary proof was required. Cunning drivers claimed they had a carful of returnees heading for the West Coast, collected all their stipends, and headed back to Anacostia.

As the plan to send the vets home began to reveal its shortcomings, odd schemes were hatched to lure the veterans out of their camps and back to their home states. At the suggestion of Randolph Walker, associate editor of Pathé News, Glassford had an electric power line run out to the baseball diamond at Camp Marks and set up a movie projector and screen. On the night of July 10 he showed five thousand vets an eight-minute newsreel of placer gold mining in western states, "to get the men's minds on some other line of activity."[41]

While the film was being shown, Joe Angelo had himself buried alive four feet below the ground at the corner of Thirteenth and D streets SW. He pledged to stay there until the bonus bill was signed. But the night superintendent of police ordered him disinterred.[42] The custom of live burial was a common stunt at Camp Marks. A coffin was built large enough to give the "corpse" enough room to sit up. It was fitted with a stovepipe so that the person inside could breathe, and spectators who were willing to contribute twenty-five cents could see inside.[43]

By July 11, Hines was able to tell the president that 1,100 had taken advantage of the get-out-of-town offer.[44] But as those vets departed, others were arriving. Besides the 350 Californians led by the "Joan of Arc of the West," another, larger group was on its way from California. Ever since June 10, when the large new band of bonus marchers left Los Angeles with a motorcade parade and a city hall sendoff by the mayor,[45] coded Army intelligence reports, tracing the Californians' movement, had been transmitted to Washington.

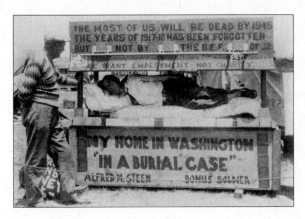

A veteran at Camp Marks demonstrated for the "Tombstone Bonus" by living in a coffin. Someone else charged viewers to look at a veteran lying in a buried coffin and breathing through a funnel. (Underwood & Underwood/ Library of Congress)

The California group, which originally numbered 2,600, had quickly and literally begun to run out of gas, leaving 1,500 of their number stuck in Tucson with empty gas tanks.[46]

The California army had dwindled to 450 by the time it arrived in Washington on July 12 under the leadership of Royal W. Robertson, a rail-thin man whose neck was encased in a steel brace attached to his head with a leather strap under his chin.[47] He was immediately favored by the news media for his cool leadership qualities, projected with the skill of a Hollywood actor— which he was, when he could get work.*

Robertson and his men set up camp on Capitol Hill, immediately presented petitions to Vice President Curtis and Speaker of the House John Nance Garner, and then announced that they would occupy the Capitol grounds until the adjournment of Congress. If the bonus was not paid by then, they would go home and work to defeat anti-bonus politicians in the November election. This new group became an immediate attraction for Washingtonians who had never seen Capitol Hill under siege before. By the end of the day, police estimated that 10,000 automobiles and trucks packed with sightseers had passed the Capitol to see the encampment.[48] That night, the Californians lay down on the grass around the Capitol to sleep. Glassford's men looked the other way.

Robertson was less than cordial to Waters, who asked him if he would like to join the BEF and move to its camps. "Well, I'm going to wait a few days

---

*Robertson's Hollywood career consisted of mostly minor roles, which included a disabled French soldier in *The Four Horsemen*, starring Rudolph Valentino.

until I see what it is all about," Robertson replied. "We came to Washington to petition Congress, not to picnic."[49]

The following night the U.S. Capitol Police turned on the sprinklers. Glassford, acting independently from the Capitol police, told Robertson that his men would have to keep moving if they wanted to remain on the Hill. Robertson, immediately realizing the publicity advantage to this order, decided to have his men march back and forth around the Capitol, single file, in a slow, solemn shuffle. This was almost immediately dubbed "the death march," and Robertson played the idea for all it was worth. "When you get just so sleepy you can sleep standing up," Robertson said. "Many of the fellows did it in France and they can do it again."[50]

One man, his head swathed in bandages, was being held up by two companions as he walked. Spectators handed him coins and cigarettes. "It's for my buddies," he responded in a barely audible voice. When a reporter asked the man what outfit he was in overseas, the bandaged vet gave a spurious reply. The reporter noted that, except for such "transparent faking," the bulk of Robertson's men were legitimate.[51]

Attracted by the simple and effective drama of the march, several hundred members of the BEF joined it. Even though Waters and Robertson would not meet a second time, there was a chilly, unwritten truce between them. Waters, who saw Robertson as "a spectacular addition to the bonus seekers," was strangely absent during the first days of the death march.[52] Waters, especially as a totalitarian leader, was being upstaged by Robertson. Thomas R. Henry of the *Evening Star* wrote that Robertson was "one of those natural-born leaders with a confidence inspiring positiveness who arise suddenly out of obscurity in times of crisis and whom men will follow to the death." He added, taking a clear jab at Waters, "He is a man's man—but none of your tin-soldier sort."[53]

All through Wednesday, July 13, the men shuffled in the sticky, 89-degree heat. Many had not slept for thirty-six hours. Men occasionally slumped onto the grass in front of the Library of Congress, exhausted, begging Robertson to let them sleep for a few minutes.

"Get up," he shouted to one of the men within earshot of a reporter. Prodding him with the toe of his boot, he added, "What do you think we are, sightseers?"

When he finally realized that his men were at the breaking point, Robertson, with support from Glassford, quietly divided the marchers into two groups so that while one group snaked around the Capitol, the other slept in a vacant lot outside congressional jurisdiction.[54]

As the day progressed, police wreckers crisscrossed Capitol Hill, hauling away the battered cars that had crossed the Rockies to deliver Robertson's army. More and more veterans and locals were drawn to the scene by the fortitude of Robertson and his men. By evening, the crowds watching the death march—at times it was a more animated affair that the papers called a "snake dance"—had become so large and unruly that the Capitol had to be closed. It was a tense evening, made tenser when a woman accused a policeman of pushing her. Camera flashbulbs went off everywhere, and a veteran, said to be shell-shocked, fell to the ground when one went off near him. Later pronounced fit by a doctor on the scene, he rejoined the march.[55]

On July 14, the anniversary of the day the mobs stormed the Bastille in the French Revolution, Vice President Curtis, vexed by the sight of even more veterans continually filing past the window of his Capitol Hill office, without precedent and without informing anyone of his decision, called out Marines from the Navy Yard to protect the Capitol. When they arrived, many by streetcar, with full equipment and fixed bayonets, the death-march vets cheered them, and according to George Kleinholz, "many struck up old acquaintances." The marchers, imagining that the Marines were sent there to entertain them with fancy drills, dipped their soiled American flags in tribute to them.

Glassford was in a meeting with MacArthur and Crosby at the War Department when Admiral Henry V. Butler, commandant of the Navy Yard, walked in to report that sixty Marines were on the way to the Capitol.[56] Glassford got Butler to recall the Marines, who were already at the Capitol.[57] Speaking of Curtis, Glassford said he was "fed up with hysterical meddlers." It was the first time since the Civil War, when the city was under attack at Fort Stephens, that the Capitol was protected militarily, and calling out the Marines was a most unpopular move. The *Daily News,* in an editorial entitled "The Curtis Blunder," said that the vice president's actions could have produced "bloody and tragic" results.[58]

Glassford, though chief of police of the District of Columbia, had to recognize and deal with the District's separate power centers: Congress and the White House. Theoretically, the Capitol and the area around it—Capitol Hill—were under the jurisdiction of the U.S. Capitol Police, a patronage police force controlled by a three-man police board consisting of the sergeant at arms of the Senate, the sergeant at arms of the House, and the architect of the Capitol. All three were appointed by Congress and subject to its whims. The sergeants at arms were usually ceremonial figures but could exert power, especially through the police board. The architect of the Capitol had absolute power over architectural and landscape issues having to do with the Capitol, its utilities, and its grounds. Thus, he could make decisions about what happened on Capitol turf. (Glassford had specifically defied the architect by revoking his order banning photographs or newsreels of the marchers.) At the White House, the Secret Service controlled the security of the president and the White House. Besides dealing with the Secret Service (and its uniformed police), Glassford also had to acknowledge the authority of one of President Hoover's chief aides, Lawrence Richey, a former Secret Service agent who now guarded Hoover's political moves.[59]

Officials in the White House and on Capitol Hill were jittery about July 15, Congress's deadline for the veterans to leave Washington. Congress and the Hoover administration had done all they could. They expected that when that day dawned, the end of the Bonus Army problem would be in sight. The police board chose the deadline day to issue a statement charging that when Glassford gave permission for the "death march" on Capitol Hill, he had acted "wholly without authority" and that the veterans had been violating an 1882 act of Congress forbidding anyone "to parade, stand, or move in procession or assemblage."[60] Glassford said that the situation had been "fraught with danger," making it "necessary for some one man to assume authority." Glassford added that Vice President Curtis "told me in person that he did not desire violence."[61]

By deadline day, Glassford had effectively taken charge of the city, including Capitol Hill—and the two dozen BEF camps scattered around the District. His biggest worry was Camp Marks. In a letter to Glassford, the Anacostia Citizens Association expressed worry about sanitation problems caused by the camp, but they added that they did not "wish to be understood as hostile to the veterans."[62]

On Capitol Hill, the dominant sound was the shuffling of feet and the clinking of tin cups and canteens that hung from the belts of the death marchers. At midnight on July 15, the offer for go-home funds was due to expire. Only 1,736 had taken Congress up on the offer, and only $26,820.27 of the $100,000 allotment had been spent. Of those who had taken the money only 1,545 had actually departed—by all accounts fewer than the number of new veterans, including Robertson's 450, who had come into the city since the offer was made. After seeing that the deadline had passed without the large numbers of expected departures, at the last minute President Hoover extended the deadline to July 25.[63]

At dawn on July 16 the death march was temporarily suspended to make room for the thousands of veterans assembling in front of the Capitol—5,000 by ten in the morning, up to 10,000 by the noon police count, 17,000 as the day progressed, according to Waters.[64] Originally a parade had been planned for the day of adjournment. But Glassford had convinced Waters that his policemen were, in Waters's words, "tired after a week of almost unbroken day and night duty," so there was no parade.[65]

Waters reached the Capitol at 10:00 A.M. to find his men cordoned off behind lines of police that stretched across the black asphalt of the broad Congressional Plaza, where the demonstration was scheduled to take place. Glassford appeared on his blue motorcycle, to cheers from the veterans.[66]

Waters, standing in a corner of the plaza, made his move: "When I was ten feet from the front line I turned and without a word, but signaling with my arm, I started towards the Capitol. I heard a roar behind me and saw that the men were quickening their pace after me."[67] Waters was leading his men in a dogtrot charge on the Capitol.

Halfway across the plaza Waters stopped. Glassford, stunned by what he took to be a hostile move, ordered Waters arrested, along with Waters's current deputy, Doak Carter, who had led a Cleveland contingent to Washington. The arrests intensified the anger of the veterans.

"We want Waters!" the veterans shouted. Glassford momentarily released him, but he became so belligerent that Glassford arrested him for a second time. The police chief seemed to have lost control of the crowd.[68]

"It looked for a moment like stark riot ahead," said newspaper reporter Bess Furman, who was watching the moiling scene below from a window in the Capitol, "but a quick-witted trained nurse who had been aiding bonus families and therefore was known to the leaders grabbed a megaphone and shouted: 'Let's all sing "America"!'"[69] Sing it they did, as well as many other songs— "Hail, Hail the Gang's All Here," "Over There," "The Old Gray Mare," and many others, ending with "My Bonus Lies over the Ocean." The woman, blond and wearing a blue-and-white nurse uniform, identified herself as Lauretta D'Arsanis, once known as the Flower of Saint Theresa. "I had a little flower shop in New York but they closed me out," she told a reporter. "So I came down here to help out because I have dedicated my life to Saint Theresa."[70]

Waters emerged during the singing, further quieting the mob, and, flanked by police, shouted to the crowd: "I have permission for you men to occupy the center steps of the Capitol. I have promised the police to keep the sidewalks in front of the building clear, so come up to the steps." The men pressed forward, and Waters then announced that he been granted a long interview with Speaker of the House John Nance Garner and that he planned to call on President Hoover.

At noon, a delegation of BEF members went to the White House in an attempt to see the president but were turned down by presidential secretary Theodore Joslin, who said the president was "too occupied" at that time.[71] The president, meanwhile, was preparing to go to Capitol Hill and preside over the closing of Congress.

At 12:40 Garner was presented with a petition demanding that Congress not adjourn until "some material aid" was given to the BEF. Waters then gave his men a choice: follow him back to the camps or, pointing to Robertson's resumed death march, "join that outfit over there," which many of them did.[72]

Shortly before ten o'clock that night, with Capitol Hill now under control, trouble broke out at the other end of Pennsylvania Avenue. About fifty men, mostly Communists, were heading toward the White House. As their approach was reported, police prepared for trouble. They closed the gates of the White House grounds and cleared Pennsylvania Avenue and adjacent streets of all pedestrian and vehicular traffic. More than four hundred policemen—the largest massing of police in one place since Washington's 1919 race riots—were summoned to surround the Executive Mansion. A police inspector quoted President Hoover as saying that if the police could not clear the streets within a few minutes, he would call out Regular Army troops.

The police acted swiftly. As demonstrators entered Lafayette Square, across Pennsylvania Avenue from the White House, the police drove them back and forced them to disperse in small groups. Police arrested three holdouts. One man vigorously resisted, and Glassford plunged in to aid the five policemen fighting him. He was one-armed Nathan Kalb, also known as Shorty.[73]

In the White House, the president's physician, Navy Captain Joel Thompson Boone, stayed at Hoover's side, "not knowing what services might be required of me" because he believed that demonstrators would overpower the police and attack the White House.[74] At 10:30 P.M. the White House announced that President Hoover would not be taking the traditional trip to the Capitol to mark the adjournment of Congress. At 11:26 the Seventy-second Congress adjourned. Most of the congressmen left through back doors and the underground tunnels under the Capitol to avoid any confrontation with lingering groups of veterans. On hearing that adjournment had been called, Robertson turned to his men and said, "If that is the case, our work is done."[75]

The next morning, a Sunday, President Hoover was whisked out of the city for a few days of vacation. Waters held drills and a military parade in which regiments of the BEF passed in review.[76] Washington was beginning to get used to the idea that Congress had gone home, leaving the bulk of the BEF and Pace's Communists behind. That evening, Pace announced a new program: he would picket the homes of congressmen living in Washington as well as city officials to compel Hoover to call Congress back into session.

Two days later, on Tuesday, July 19, amid fresh reports that new groups were forming and heading to Washington, Major General Smedley Darlington Butler, a Quaker, a U.S. Marine, a veteran, and the son of a former congressman, arrived in his limousine to speak at Camp Marks. He had been invited by Waters, who rode with him into camp, to stem the tide of desertions. Some 460 veterans had asked for return funds the previous day, bringing the total to 3,056.[77]

Butler, the holder of two Medals of Honor for heroism in the "Banana Wars" of the 1920s—U.S. intervention in conflicts in small Caribbean nations—had a distinguished Marine career, going back to the Boxer Rebellion. Teddy Roosevelt called him "the ideal American soldier." Butler had expected to become commandant of the Marine Corps, but President Hoover passed him over and selected an older, far less colorful general. Rough in the ways of Washington, Butler had infuriated the Italian government with a derogatory remark about fascist dictator Benito Mussolini. In the midst of formal U.S. apologies, Butler was threatened with court-martial. He got off with a reprimand, but, angry and bitter, he retired from the Marines in 1931.[78] Because Butler had long fought the military hierarchy on behalf of the enlisted man and because of his ongoing campaign to keep the country aware of tragic war casualties hidden away in Veterans Administration hospitals, Waters could not have made a better choice to rally the BEF.

As Butler stepped out of his limousine, men who had been under his command greeted him. Then Butler leaped to the rickety stage and addressed five thousand veterans: "Men, I ran for the Senate in Pennsylvania on a bonus ticket. I got hell beaten out of me. But I haven't changed my mind a damned bit." The vets roared their approval. "I'm here because I've been a soldier for thirty-five years and I can't resist the temptation to be among soldiers."

He next addressed the theme of the evening: "Hang together and stick it out till the gate bars of hell freeze over; if you don't, you are no damn good. . . . Remember, by God, you . . . didn't win the war for a select class of a few financiers and high binders." A lifelong Republican, he told the veterans to go to the polls in November and change things. He ended with an admonition: "Don't break any laws and allow people to say bad things about you."

He was followed by a twelve-year-old girl dressed as Uncle Sam, who sang patriotic songs. The great pep rally came to a close with the singing of "Sweet Adeline," a Butler favorite. He was mobbed by those who wanted to speak with him, and he sat on the ground until 2:30 A.M. listening to their stories.

He slept for three hours and, after a spartan breakfast of coffee, potatoes, and hard bread with the men, took the stage again to warn them: "If you slip over into lawlessness of any kind you will lose the sympathy of 120 million people in this nation."[79]

His warning came as Glassford, MacArthur, and men close to the president were all reading secret intelligence reports that told of Communist hopes to bring violence to the streets of Washington. At the same time, Waters was openly embracing fascism. The *B.E.F. News* published his plans in a front-page article headlined "Khaki Shirts—W. W. Waters Imagines One Million—Waters Outlines Road Ahead for New Organization." The article said, "Inevitably such an organization brings up comparisons with the Facisti of Italy and the NAZI of Germany. . . . For five years Hitler was lampooned and derided, but today he controls Germany. Mussolini, before the war was a tramp printer driven from Italy because of his political views. But today he is a world figure. . . . The Khaki Shirts, however, would be essentially American."[80]

With Congress adjourned until December, and Waters and Pace both vowing to stay until the bonus was paid, Washington was increasingly worried about violence or an epidemic breaking out in the veterans' camps.[81] Most anxiety focused on sprawling Camp Marks in Anacostia. Even as the *Washington Post* was reporting that Camp Marks appeared to be growing,[82] however, official concern suddenly shifted to a Bonus Army shantytown closer to the heart of federal Washington. Ever since the first veterans had begun arriving in Washington, many had been occupying dilapidated, government-owned buildings on Pennsylvania Avenue.

President Hoover told the commissioners that he wanted those downtown veterans evicted. The commissioners set the ouster for July 22.

Tanks in the Streets

*When I marched off to war in 1917, I remember a Civil War veteran,
over seventy years old, telling me, "Son, you are all heroes now.
But some day they'll treat you like dogs."*

—Benjamin B. Shepherd of the BEF

ALONG A STRETCH of Pennsylvania Avenue, about half a mile east of the White House and three blocks west of Capitol Hill, stood half-demolished buildings, their outer walls ripped away and their rooms open to view. Other buildings already had been torn down, leaving behind cellars and vacant lots full of bricks and rubble. When the first wave of bonus marchers arrived in Washington, Glassford had billeted many of them in the deserted buildings. The old structures, some dating to the Civil War, were owned by the U.S. government and were being razed to clear the way for a complex of massive government buildings that would become known as the Federal Triangle.[1]

As more and more veterans poured into Washington, they were sent off to Camp Marks, but many chose to move into the downtown camp. When the buildings filled up, the vets who shunned Camp Marks built shacks and lean-tos and pitched ragged tents beyond the buildings designated by Glassford,

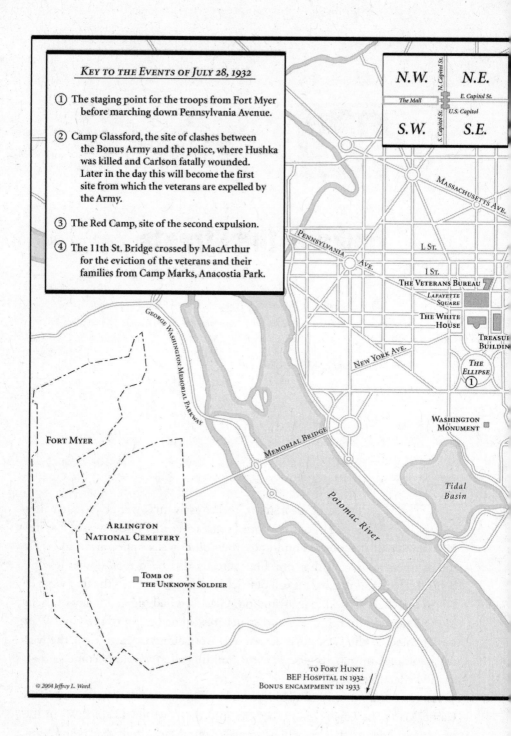

Key to the Events of July 28, 1932

① The staging point for the troops from Fort Myer before marching down Pennsylvania Avenue.

② Camp Glassford, the site of clashes between the Bonus Army and the police, where Hushka was killed and Carlson fatally wounded. Later in the day this will become the first site from which the veterans are expelled by the Army.

③ The Red Camp, site of the second expulsion.

④ The 11th St. Bridge crossed by MacArthur for the eviction of the veterans and their families from Camp Marks, Anacostia Park.

N.W.   N.E.

The Mall   E. Capitol St.

N. Capitol St.

U.S. Capitol

S.W.   S.E.

S. Capitol St.

MASSACHUSETTS AVE.

PENNSYLVANIA AVE.

L ST.

I ST.

THE VETERANS BUREAU

LAFAYETTE SQUARE

THE WHITE HOUSE

TREASURY BUILDING

NEW YORK AVE.

THE ELLIPSE ①

WASHINGTON MONUMENT

GEORGE WASHINGTON MEMORIAL PARKWAY

FORT MYER

Potomac River

MEMORIAL BRIDGE

Tidal Basin

ARLINGTON NATIONAL CEMETERY

TOMB OF THE UNKNOWN SOLDIER

© 2004 Jeffrey L. Ward

TO FORT HUNT:
BEF HOSPITAL IN 1932
BONUS ENCAMPMENT IN 1933

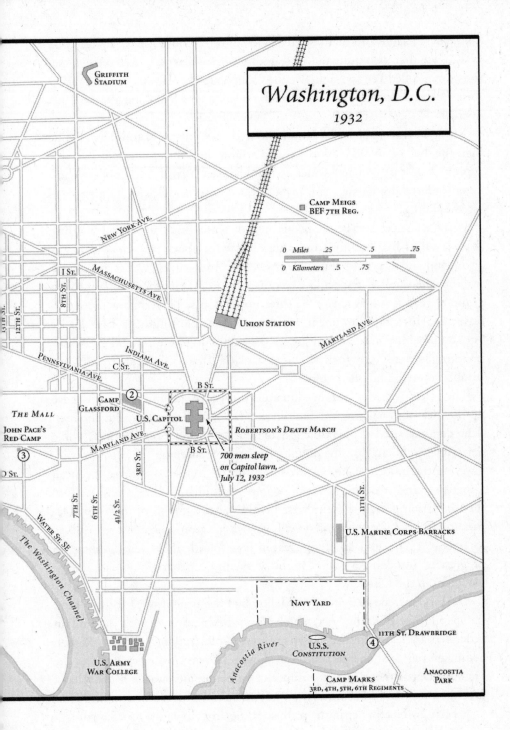

GRIFFITH STADIUM

Washington, D.C.
1932

CAMP MEIGS
BEF 7TH REG.

NEW YORK AVE.

MASSACHUSETTS AVE.

I ST.

8TH ST.

13TH ST.

12TH ST.

0   Miles   .25   .5   .75

0   Kilometers   .5   .75

UNION STATION

INDIANA AVE.

MARYLAND AVE.

PENNSYLVANIA AVE.

C ST.

B ST.

CAMP
GLASSFORD   ②

THE MALL

U.S. CAPITOL

ROBERTSON'S DEATH MARCH

JOHN PACE'S
RED CAMP

MARYLAND AVE.

B ST.

③

D ST.

700 men sleep
on Capitol lawn,
July 12, 1932

3RD ST.

7TH ST.

6TH ST.

4½ ST.

11TH ST.

U.S. MARINE CORPS BARRACKS

WATER ST. SE

The Washington Channel

NAVY YARD

11TH ST. DRAWBRIDGE

Anacostia River

U.S.S.
CONSTITUTION

④

U.S. ARMY
WAR COLLEGE

CAMP MARKS
3RD, 4TH, 5TH, 6TH REGIMENTS

ANACOSTIA
PARK

taking over a large area that centered at Third Street and Pennsylvania Avenue NW. More than two thousand veterans, mostly southerners, lived on this site, sometimes called Pennsylvania Avenue Camp and also known as Camp Glassford.[2] A few blocks away, at Thirteenth and B streets SW, John Pace and his Workers' Ex-Servicemen's League men were billeted.

Rising in this small-scale Hooverville were the remains of four large buildings: the shell of an old National Guard armory, and three others, including a gaping, four-story concrete structure that had been a Ford automobile agency. Lee's Undertaking Garage, still in business, shared a wall with another half-razed building.

At Third Street and Pennsylvania Avenue was a brick-and-wood building that served as BEF headquarters and a home for about 150 veterans. It was also "condemned as a fire trap," Henry Meisel observed. He was there one day in June when police, responding to orders from the Fire Department, told a group of veterans to evacuate the three upper floors. The veterans refused to leave, and in a tense moment a police captain confronting a BEF leader "stood up behind his desk and shouted, 'I want you to understand the Washington police are ready for any emergency and if you fellows are looking for trouble you will find plenty of it.'"[3]

The veterans at the BEF headquarters did not yield, and authorities gave up the idea of evacuating the building on fire-hazard grounds. But the incident demonstrated a phenomenon of that long, hot, wet summer: while newspaper publicity and the public's sympathy focused on the vets who wallowed in the mud or baked in the sun of Camp Marks, the focus of official impatience and frustration was on Camp Glassford. To the administration, the veterans and their shanties were highly visible symbols of the Great Depression and did not belong in downtown Washington. There had to be a way to remove them, and an ironic reason was found: they were holding up progress by impeding a major public-works project that would ease unemployment in the District.

Treasury Secretary Andrew W. Mellon had been the driving force behind the 1926 Public Buildings Act, which led to the creation of the $300 million Federal Triangle, one of the nation's biggest public building projects. Mellon had taken personal charge, and even though he was no longer running the Treasury Department in the summer of 1932, the area was still considered Treasury turf.[4] And so it was that on July 20 an assistant secretary of the Treasury, Ferry K. Heath, began the process of shutting down Camp Glassford.

Heath had given Glassford permission to use the buildings as long as occupancy was "not extended beyond the actual need."[5] Now, on July 20, in the eyes of officialdom, the veterans had had their day in Washington, and since Congress was adjourned, they no longer had a need to be there. Heath, who ran the Federal Triangle program, sent letters to Glassford and Commissioner Herbert H. Crosby asking that the veterans leave the old Ford building and the area along Pennsylvania Avenue between Third and Fourth streets by July 25. Heath also wrote to Rhine & Company, the firm that had the demolition contract, saying that the area was being cleared and the razing of the buildings could soon resume.[6]

The day that Heath ordered the eviction was also the day that John Pace chose to storm the White House. Because Pace knew the police would stop any mob of veterans heading toward the White House, he told about two hundred men to approach singly or in twos and threes. Scattered groups began walking north along Fourteenth Street, and, by entering the District's northwest quadrant, crossed the border into executive Washington. They then turned westward toward Fifteenth Street and reached the majestic, multicolumned Treasury Building, where Pennsylvania Avenue turned the corner to the White House. Here Police Inspector Albert J. Headley and forty police officers blocked their way. Headley raised his hand and said, "You may not go through."

"We are not marching," Pace said. "This is not a parade. We are walking on the public streets as individuals."

Ignoring Pace, Headley pointed to where he stood and told his men, "Get everybody back of this line."

Pace's men pressed forward. Headley grabbed Pace and shouted to a patrolman to blow his whistle—the signal for reinforcements to arrive on the double. Pace retreated and, leading a band that dwindled to about fifty, probed for another route toward the White House. He found policemen and police cars everywhere. Traffic had been cut off around the White House. The gates were chained and locked. Policemen and men of the Secret Service were stationed at thirty-foot intervals around the White House. As the *New York Daily News* would announce in a screaming headline, "Hoover Locks Self in White House."

At Twelfth and D streets NW Pace tried again. His vets and police collided. Policemen seized Pace and two others, then chased the rest of the men back to their billet, where there were more police.[7]

On July 21, soon after Glassford told Waters about the eviction notice, the District commissioners summoned Glassford to their office and told him to clear out a larger area bounded by C and D streets SW and Twelfth and Thirteenth streets SW. Some 1,800 BEF veterans and about 500 women and children lived in that area, along with Pace's 200 Communist followers.[8] Lieutenant

Colonel U. S. Grant III, director of public buildings and public parks and a Hoover confidant, extended the expulsion orders to encompass all federal land occupied by the BEF, including Camp Marks and adjoining Camp Sims in Anacostia, and Camp Meigs in far-off northeast Washington. Veterans and their families in Camp Bartlett were exempt because they were on private property, a plot of wooded land about three miles from downtown Washington.

The commissioners told Glassford that the veterans had to be out of the Pennsylvania Avenue buildings by July 22; that the tents and rolling kitchens belonging to the District of Columbia National Guard had to be returned by noon August 1; and that Camps Marks, Sims, and Meigs had to be evacuated by August 4.[9] (Coincidental with the stick came a carrot: President Hoover signed into law a bill that allowed some veterans to borrow up to half of the maturity of their bonuses at an interest rate of 3½ percent.)

Responding to news of the eviction, Waters said, "They can issue orders, but I don't know how they are going to enforce them. Wait until they start moving out the women and children. . . . That will make swell pictures." Food stocks were so low that Waters ordered the feeding of women and children first. "If anything remains," he said, "the men will eat."[10]

Robertson decided it was time for him to take his Californians out of Washington. Police lined up trucks to haul them to the Maryland line, but no one would climb in. So Robertson, with a cheery wave of his hand, got into his car and headed back to California.[11]

By police count on July 21, there were 11,698 men in twenty-four separate camps in Washington. No one knew the number of women and children scattered through the camps. Glassford had a plane fly over the camps and drop leaflets about the looming eviction. After he sought a legal opinion from the District corporation counsel, the commissioners temporarily postponed the eviction while they found a legal way to do it.[12]

Waters went to Camp Glassford and told his men to "stand your ground." If "the police get rough," he said, "I, as your commander in chief need only to raise my hand above my head and my following of 12,000 men will either fight or frolic, according to my wishes."[13]

Pace, well aware of the rising tension, decided to make another White House foray at noon on Monday, July 25. That morning Hoover, under heavy guard, had returned from a weekend at his Rapidan camp. Pace's idea was to pick up sympathizers among lunchtime workers—most of them government employees—and stymie police. As he and about 150 followers set out, plainclothes police slipped into the group and tried to talk the would-be picketers into dispersing.[14]

Again they met a phalanx of police at the Treasury Building. This time, however, police and veterans clashed in a running street battle. Walter Eicker climbed a tree and urged on the men, shouting, "Comrades! Comrades!" Two detectives started shinnying up the tree as Eicker climbed higher. "We want our bonus! To hell with Wall Street!" Eicker yelled from his perch. "This is only the beginning of the uprising of the rank and file!" While many in the crowd booed, one of the detectives grabbed Eicker. They pulled him out of the tree and into the hands of policemen who shoved him into a patrol wagon. Pace and Eicker were arrested.*

The melee went on, police swinging nightsticks and veterans fighting back with their fists. A veteran slugged a newspaper photographer and ran off toward a fashionable shopping district. A passerby shouted, "He grabbed a copper's gun!" Dozens of police ran after him. Vets and policemen knocked down pedestrians; officers ripped a shirt off a veteran's back before subduing him and several others. Another group ran off and got as far as the east gate of the White House grounds. As the few officers there stood off the mob, a squad of motorcycle police, led by Glassford, roared up and dispersed the last of the vets.

Until July 22, Glassford had complete control of the day-to-day fate of the Bonus Army. Although he had endorsed the idea of the Hoover administration's go-home payments scheme, the administration no longer trusted him. This had been true as far back as June 10, when Joel Thompson Boone, presidential physician and confidant, scribbled into his little notebook, "Pres. says Glassford has been insubordinate & that the Commissioners have had a hell of a time with him. That he will find himself out when this is over; that he seems to be another [Smedley] Butler."[15]

Like Hoover, MacArthur had been getting impatient about the way the police had been handling the BEF, which, to Army intelligence officers, was at least riddled with Reds and probably controlled by Communists. The veterans' refusal to leave Washington, along with the Pace-led moves against the White House, convinced MacArthur that the Communists were on the brink of violence.[16] By then, the Army had secretly moved two combat vehicles from a base in Aberdeen, Maryland, to nearby Fort Myer: a truck-mounted 75-millimeter gun with about 100 rounds of shrapnel ammunition and an armored car with .30 and .50 caliber machine guns and "full loads" of ammunition. The Army drivers had been ordered to avoid "the center of towns and cities, especially

---

*Pace and Eicker were charged with inciting to riot. For Eicker, there were two extra charges: making a speech in a public park without a permit and destroying public property—specifically, breaking twigs in the tree he had climbed to make his speech.

Washington," and if questioned to say that these were merely experimental vehicles to be shown to "interested personnel in Washington."[17] The vehicles were American versions of the kind used by German Landesjaeger officers against urban revolutionaries.

Besides ordering riot training at Fort Myer and secretly transferring the combat vehicles, along with tanks from Fort Meade, MacArthur and Moseley met with Major General Blanton Winship, as adjutant general the Army's top legal authority. Winship, both a lawyer and a battle-tested officer, had won the Distinguished Service Cross and Silver Star in France.[18] By Winship's interpretation, if the president called in the Army, "a mere scattering of the members of this force at the places of their present encampments, or driving them beyond the borders of the District of Columbia, would not effect a permanent dispersion of the force, so as to bring the insurrection or threat of insurrection . . . to an end." As Winship interpreted the reality of such a presidential order, MacArthur would have to load the veterans into Army trucks and haul the prisoners, under armed guard, to state after state, potentially extending the crisis in Washington far beyond its borders.

There was also the problem of Plan White, which required a presidential proclamation to be put into action. In MacArthur's strategy talks, President Hoover was represented by Secretary of War Hurley. A combat veteran, Hurley had served as an adjutant general for a time after the war, and had very close ties to both MacArthur and Moseley. He had argued for MacArthur's appointment as Army chief of staff after Hoover questioned it, and he had appointed Moseley assistant chief of staff, calling him "the most brilliant mind in the entire Army."[19]

Aware of the proclamation trigger needed for Plan White, Moseley had twice in June ghostwritten a presidential statement that presumably would do the trick. He showed the first statement, which he called a "memorandum," to Hurley, who, Moseley recalled, said it "contained not only a good idea, but that it was good politics as well and would have a good effect." Moseley did not disclose what happened to his second statement. There is no record of Hurley's showing the Moseley statements to President Hoover, but Moseley says he was told (presumably by Hurley) that Hoover believed the Bonus March was "simply a temporary disease of the individuals concerned and it would have to work itself out in the normal way." Moseley's second statement made no mention of federal troops but has the president order the District commissioners to do what was necessary to stop "the concentration" of homeless veterans. The White House still had no interest in this milder Moseley statement.[20]

There is no indication that Hoover's White House advisers realized, as

Moseley, MacArthur, and Hurley did, that the White Plan called for a presidential proclamation to launch military intervention and martial law. Although Moseley's proposals cited the constitutional right of petition and showed the proper respect for the presidency, the Bonus Army had put him in a mutinous mood. The marchers were "Communists and Bums," he had said in a letter. And he had called for a military coup d'état if politicians could not solve America's problems.[21] Like MacArthur, Moseley believed that Communists were a clear and present danger that politicians were ignoring, imperiling the nation.

By July 26 both Waters and Glassford knew that they had little time to stave off disaster. Both men wanted an eviction free of bloodshed, and so both recognized the need to preserve their working relationship. Waters realized that unlawful behavior would ruin the reputation of the BEF.[22] But the political drama was being overshadowed by the fact that people were starving.

A Washington dairy had been donating forty quarts of milk a day to Camp Marks. One of the vets went to the dairy to fetch the milk, which was doled out to children.[23] There was not enough to go around. Mrs. George Hogan, a mother in Camp Marks, had a three-year-old and a ten-month-old. They needed three quarts of milk a day, she said, and now she was lucky to get one.[24]

The eviction orders mentioned men, not women and children. Both Glassford and Waters knew that these nonveterans were the wards of whatever fate descended upon the BEF. Waters had a new ally, Herbert S. Ward, a local attorney who had volunteered to work for the BEF. Ward had met with Secretary of the Treasury Ogden Mills, stressed the need to care for 500 women and children, and got the deadline extended to midnight, July 26, on humanitarian grounds.[25] Waters followed through by trying to get help from unlikely sources. He called on Judge John Barton Payne, head of the American Red Cross, who reiterated what he had told Evalyn Walsh McLean: the Red Cross would not get involved with the BEF. But Payne did call MacArthur, who in turn sent Waters on to Hurley. Waters, accompanied by Ward and Doak Carter, the BEF chief of staff, met with Hurley in his office in the State, War, and Navy Building near the White House. As Waters recalled, during the five-hour meeting General MacArthur "never once stopped his ceaseless tread around the room."[26]

Waters wanted tents to temporarily house the evacuated men, women, and children on the private land at Camp Bartlett while the vets built barracks there. Camp Bartlett had become a Valhalla vision for Waters, who hoped to ensconce his veterans and their families there and become a permanent Washington presence. Waters, however, had not yet made any arrangements. Since

May, Glassford had been thinking of Camp Bartlett as a fine site for the BEF after eviction. By July, Camp Bartlett housed about 1,200 vets, including some thirty families in regulation army squad tents. The camp had electric lights, two kitchens (one general and one used by the units from Detroit), and even a baby grand piano.[27] Glassford had been talking to the owner, John Henry Bartlett, but nothing had yet been worked out.

When Waters asked Hurley for tents, the secretary of war turned to MacArthur and asked, "Is there any tentage available?"

"No," said MacArthur.

Hurley turned back to Waters and said, "Waters, the War Department has no tentage available, and if it did have we certainly would not place it at your disposal. . . . We are interested only in getting you out of the District. At the first sign of disorder or bloodshed in the BEF, you will all get out. And we have plenty of troops to put you out."

The conversation between Hurley and Waters dragged on while MacArthur continued silently pacing. Finally, as Waters and his associates were about to leave, Waters directly addressed MacArthur. "If the troops should be called out against us, will the BEF be given the opportunity to form in columns, salvage their belongings, and retreat in orderly fashion?"

Waters later recalled that MacArthur replied, "Yes, my friend, of course."[28]

On the afternoon of July 27, Waters summoned 182 men he had designated as BEF officers and told them that he believed that a peaceful evacuation of the Pennsylvania Avenue area might be imminent. He asked them to try to keep the men of Camp Marks and other billets away from the evacuation area. As he was completing that meeting, Glassford called him and asked him to come to the office of the District commissioners. Waters, who had never met the commissioners, was taken to a waiting room and told by Glassford, "The commissioners have sent for you to discuss orderly plans of evacuation."

Waters did not meet the commissioners face-to-face. In shuttle-diplomacy fashion, Glassford went into one room to talk to them, then came back to Waters's room to tell him what the commissioners were proposing. After a series of messages, Glassford came back to say he had a plan. According to Waters, Glassford said, "I promise to evacuate two hundred men by six o'clock tomorrow morning. Thereafter I will evacuate groups of forty or larger each day until I have the area completely cleared within the next two weeks."

Waters accepted the plan. But Glassford came back to say that the commissioners, while agreeing to the two-hundred-man evacuation the next day, would only give Glassford until Monday, August 1, to completely clear the area. Waters reluctantly agreed to that plan as the best he could do; it gave him a little time, but it did not involve federal troops.[29] That same afternoon, Doak Carter informed Bartlett that Waters wanted to move the entire BEF to Camp Bartlett. Bartlett was told that an unidentified donor had promised funds for the purchase of lumber for a barracks. Bartlett said he would cooperate only if Glassford approved the plan. Bartlett reached Glassford on the morning of Thursday, July 28, and learned that the chief not only approved but said he hoped that by Monday he would have all the men and their kin—about 7,000 people, he estimated—out of federal property and into Camp Bartlett.[30]

Shortly after getting the call from Bartlett, Glassford stood in front of a blackboard in the Traffic Bureau squad room at police headquarters and, before about one hundred police officers, drew his plan for the day's operation: The entire area between Third and Four-and-a-half streets NW would be roped off and cleared of spectators, men placed at five-foot intervals, and two policemen assigned to escort each of the Treasury agents. Inspector Lewis Edwards, an assistant superintendent, would command the hundred men at the scene. Inspector Ernest Brown, also an assistant superintendent, would lead a detail of forty men, placed at key intersections in the large area bounded by Maryland Avenue, Indiana Avenue, Second Street, and Seventh Street NW near the foot of Capitol Hill, to divert veterans and rubberneckers from the evacuation scene. When the blackboard session ended, Edward, Brown, and Glassford and their men rushed off for Pennsylvania Avenue.

Waters, in full boots-and-jodhpurs uniform and accompanied by similarly costumed aides, had already arrived at Pennsylvania Avenue. He ordered a bugle to blow "Assembly" and stood upon an improvised speaker's platform. Amid heckling—"Give us our bonus!" "Let 'em come and take us away!" and "We'll fight the whole damn works!"—Waters urged the men to accept the evacuation. "Glassford and his policemen are pretty good fellows, but when you start defying the federal government, which don't take any consideration of the human element, you're going to get licked. We can't lick the United States Government, but when the United States troops are called to escort me out, I'm going out."

He rambled on, saying he had the money—donated by an unidentified Washington woman who "has plenty"—to build shelters at Camp Bartlett for at least two hundred people immediately. "Will you move or won't you?" he asked, ending his speech. A chorus of "No!" answered him. The men drifted off to join the growing crowd. Veterans were coming in from all directions.[31] That morning, phone calls had gone out to the camps, ostensibly from Waters's headquarters, to send men to the evacuation area on Pennsylvania Avenue—but neither Waters nor any of his aides had issued such orders.[32]

At 9:50 A.M., Glassford contacted Waters through Aldace Walker, a Washingtonian who had recently become Glassford's "special secretary and aide."[33] Walker handed Waters a copy of the Treasury Department order: *all* the veterans in the area were being evacuated at 10:00 A.M. Waters, jolted by the news, realized that Glassford had betrayed him during the negotiations with the commissioners. (Glassford later insisted that he had to keep Waters in the dark because the commissioners had ordered the police chief to keep the real plan secret.) Waters read the order aloud and shouted to the men: "There you are! You're double-crossed! I'm double-crossed!" The men, angry and confused, headed back into the buildings.

The Rhine company had moved large cranes with wrecking balls to the area, but the cranes remained parked because the firm's insurance company said it would not cover any work until the veterans and their families had been evacuated.[34] At ten o'clock, six Treasury agents appeared, and Glassford put his plan into action. One of the agents announced that the Treasury Department was taking over the building—the old Armory—and handing it over to Rhine & Company. The Armory was the headquarters of the 1,600 predominantly southern men of the 6th Regiment of the BEF, whose leaders said that every one had been honorably discharged and that 85 percent had served in France.

Glassford, Assistant District Attorney John Fihelly, the agents, and their police escorts entered the building. On the first floor were about a dozen men and a California woman, who smiled as a Treasury agent took her arm and walked her out. Jerry Wilford, the commander of the 6th Regiment, left just as peacefully, as did the other first-floor residents.

The procession then filed up a wooden stairway that had been braced against the second floor on a wall-less side of the building. The eviction team found a basketful of bricks, about twenty empty beds, and an African-American man lying on the floor. He refused to stand. When two agents started to drag him toward the stairway, he started swinging at them. Fihelly ordered him arrested for resisting a legal eviction order. Policemen dragged him down the stairs, carried him across a stretch of rubble, and pushed him into the back door of a patrol wagon.[35] The vets kept streaming out of the building, some walking, some pushed along by policemen who had arrested them. A Pennsylvania veteran had his artificial leg propped against a wall and demanded that he be carried out. The police refused, and he had to go out on his own.[36]

The first phase of the evacuation went on smoothly for nearly two hours, before Glassford decided that he would suspend the evacuation while he broke for lunch. He planned to complete the evacuation by the end of the day.[37] The

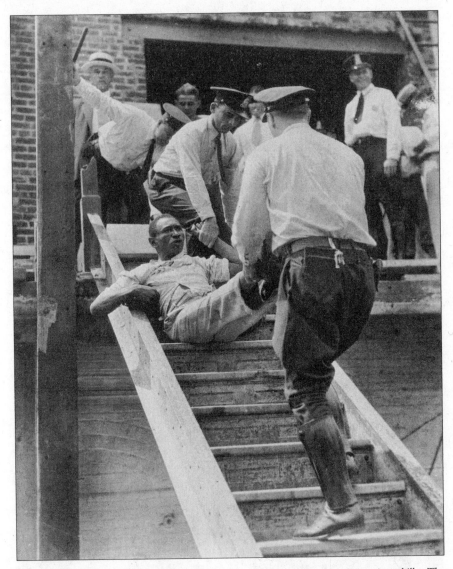

Police hauled a resisting veteran out of a government-owned building used as a Bonus Army billet. The eviction began peacefully at 10 A.M. on July 28. Near noon, attorney general William D. Mitchell ordered veterans expelled from all camps on U.S. property. (General Douglas MacArthur Foundation)

crowd of bonus marchers and curious onlookers was growing steadily. Inspector Brown sped off on a motorcycle down Pennsylvania Avenue, past the Capitol, and saw trucks full of Camp Marks men. Brown whirled around, headed back to the evacuation site, and ordered traffic cops to fan out and detour all traffic heading toward the area.

As an old soldier, Glassford well knew the military adage "No plan sur-
vives initial contact with the enemy." But he had never seen the vets as the
enemy, and he did not expect trouble. Suddenly trouble came, in the form of
a group led by a man who carried an American flag. The men emerged from
the crowd, surged through the police rope, and began to cross a patch of
rubble-strewn land behind the building. Glassford ordered them to stop. Patrolman J. O. Patton, who for weeks had been assigned to watch over the
area's BEF billets, identified one of the men as a Communist. He was Bernard
McCoy, a Navy vet from Chicago.

Someone—Patton said it was McCoy—rushed forward and tore Glassford's badge off his shirt.[38] Vets began hurling bricks and rocks at the police,
who fought back with nightsticks. When an officer grabbed the flag, a veteran
hit him with a lead pipe. Police and veterans took cover behind shanties.[39]
Bricks or rocks hit Glassford on the shoulder and on a leg protected by his
leather puttees.[40] A brick hit a police officer—a decorated combat veteran—as
he went to the aid of his chief. The officer slumped to the ground and was hit
again in the head. His skull fractured, he was carried off for medical aid, along
with four other officers.[41] "I was standing about forty feet away," wrote reporter Paul V. Anderson, "and it looked like an ugly mess, but the cops kept
their heads and no shots were fired. Glassford dashed into the heart of the
melee, smiled when a brickbat hit him in the chest, and stopped the fighting
in a few seconds."[42]

Violence suddenly flared during the attempt to evict veterans from abandoned government-owned
buildings on the morning of July 28. The clash began when men carrying an American flag tried to
break through police lines. (General Douglas MacArthur Foundation)

Glassford climbed up on a pile of bricks and shouted, "Come on, boys. Let's call an armistice for lunch." Some men laughed and some cheered.[43]

In those wild five minutes, police arrested McCoy and three others who were believed to have been in the group that had rushed in with the flag. Others arrested included John O. Olson, who had been awarded a Distinguished Service Cross for valor in France, and Broadus Faulkner, a Kentucky man who had also served in France. Faulkner had a criminal record—he had spent four years in prison for housebreaking. Olson, claiming that he had not been in the group that had fomented the brick-throwing, later said he had rushed out of the crowd that had arrived at the scene from Camp Marks and tried to grab the flag. As McCoy told it, as police grabbed the flag bearer and fought the others, "I went to the aid of my buddies. A half dozen cops jumped on me. One of them hit me over the head with his club and knocked me out. They say I grabbed General Glassford's badge. I don't know. I was out. . . . General Glassford is a fine fellow. Why should I grab his badge?"[44]

Waters claimed that the flag-carrying group were "Reds,"[45] but Glassford, who later interviewed the three men arrested, did not find them to be so.[46] Still, the idea persisted that Communists had started the five-minute melee.

The drawbridge to Anacostia, which the police had raised in June to keep veterans confined, was not lifted this time. Veterans packed it, and all morning and into the afternoon it remained a path for veterans streaming to the scene of action. As veterans poured into the Pennsylvania Avenue area, Inspector Edwards called on all precincts to send every man they could spare. More than five hundred more policemen rushed to the area on foot, in patrol cars, and in patrol wagons.[47]

Without Glassford's knowledge, Commissioner Crosby had a spy on Glassford's evacuation team. After the brick-and-nightstick battle, the spy, Lieutenant Ira E. Keck, slipped off to the District Building—Washington's equivalent of a city hall—at Pennsylvania Avenue and Fourteenth Street NW. Keck told Crosby and Commissioner Reichelderfer that "a riot had occurred," that the police "had been attacked with bricks, clubs, iron bars, concrete and similar articles," that "several thousand marchers were on their way from other camps," and that Keck, along with Inspectors Brown and Edwards, believed that "the situation was beyond the control of the Police and bloodshed could be averted only by the presence of Federal troops."[48] Reichelderfer sent Keck back to the scene with instructions to tell Glassford that the commissioners wanted to talk to him before calling for military aid.

As Keck approached Glassford, he saw him and his secretary, Aldace Walker, talking to Waters. As Waters recalled the conversation, Glassford said, "It's looking serious."

"What shall we do about it?" Waters asked.

"If I'm not asked to increase the area of evacuation," Glassford replied, "I'm satisfied that there will be no more trouble."

Waters said he agreed, adding, "But if things go ahead like this morning, then I can't control these men, and no one else can, either."

Meanwhile, shortly before noon, Attorney General William D. Mitchell, independent of the commissioners, told reporters that he had decided to order the evacuation of veterans from *all* government property, not just the buildings that Glassford had been evacuating.[49] Mitchell, as a Cabinet officer, had to be acting with White House approval, but there was no indication that his action was coordinated with those of the commissioners.

About 1:00 P.M., Keck returned to the District Building with Glassford, who brought along Walker, probably as a witness. What happened at the meeting depends upon who described it. The commissioners said that Glassford repeated Waters's admission about losing control of his men, that Glassford had agreed that federal troops were needed, and that he was present when Crosby called MacArthur and requested that troops "be held in readiness."[50] Glassford, however, told reporters waiting outside the District Building that he had not asked for federal assistance "at this time," though he did not want "to go against the seething mob" again. He said he had told the commissioners that his men could maintain order.[51]

Glassford and Walker returned to the evacuation scene, which by now was jammed with about four thousand arriving veterans and hundreds of spectators.[52] The roped-off area was clear of everyone except police, looking vulnerable in their summer uniforms of white shirt, black tie, and black trousers. Crosby and Reichelderfer soon arrived, briefly looked around, and left. Shortly after 1:45 P.M., Glassford heard an uproar in front of the Ford building, about fifty yards away. Glassford and several policemen rushed to the building and ran up a makeshift outside stairway to the second floor to get a better view of a scuffle on the ground below.

Someone in the crowd yelled, "Let's get him!"

As officers George W. Shinault and Miles Znamenacek followed their chief to the second floor, men shoved them down. A brick hit Znamenacek. Someone grabbed Shinault's nightstick and hit him with it. A garbage can, hurled from above, crashed near Znamenacek. Glassford, looking down on the fallen policemen, saw Shinault draw his gun and fire two shots. Two men fell. Other policemen rushed up, guns drawn.

Angry veterans and police officers faced off at the rope that police stretched around the original eviction scene. As crowds of veterans poured into the area from other camps, every available policeman was ordered to the area. (General Douglas MacArthur Foundation)

"Stop that shooting!" Glassford shouted. Dazed, Shinault raised his gun and aimed at Glassford, who ducked behind a pillar.

On the ground lay William Hushka, a thirty-five-year-old veteran from Chicago, who died almost instantly.[53] Eric Carlson, a thirty-eight-year-old veteran from Oakland, California, was mortally wounded. Ambulances carried them away, along with three injured police officers.[54]

"A breathless silence of horror, as in the presence of death, seemed to depress the thousands of bystanders," recalled John Bartlett, who had arrived shortly before and saw the shattering of his dream of providing a peaceful bivouac for the BEF.[55] A few minutes later, Raymond P. Brandt, a reporter in the Washington bureau of the *St. Louis Post-Dispatch,* went up to Glassford and jolted the chief with the news that federal troops were massing on the Ellipse, the circular greensward south of the White House.[56] Then Assistant Attorney General Nugent Dodds formally told Glassford that the troops had been called out.

"When will the troops arrive?" Glassford asked. "What will be their mission?"

Dodds said he had delivered the message that had been given to him, then walked away.

MacArthur had been meeting since morning with Moseley and Major General Blanton Winship, the judge adjutant general. Winship decided that the president could—and should—declare martial law; once that happened, Winship said, the situation was entirely in the hands of the military.[57] The military was going to be MacArthur. His low-ranking aide, Major Dwight D. Eisenhower, recalled later that he diplomatically tried to tell MacArthur that quelling a riot was beneath the dignity of the Army chief of staff. "But," Eisenhower remembered, "he said that this was a very serious test of the strength of the Federal Government; that he was going, and that I was going as his aide."[58]

MacArthur sent an aide to his quarters—a twenty-one-room Victorian-style home on General's Row at Fort Myer—and told him to return immediately with the general's dress uniform and boots. He then told Eisenhower to go home and get his own uniform. Eisenhower rushed to the Eisenhowers' apartment near DuPont Circle. Cursing and throwing civvies and boxes around the

"Where Veteran Was Killed" is a grim postscript to a peaceful portrait of the veterans' billet where police fatally shot not one but two veterans on July 28. One was killed instantly; the other suffered mortal wounds. (Authors' collection)

room, he found his rarely worn uniform and sprinkled talc on his legs to ease the donning of his stiff leather boots.[59]

At 1:35 P.M., General MacArthur telephoned Brigadier General Perry L. Miles and told him to alert the troops at Fort Myer and at Fort Washington, about eighteen miles down the Potomac on the Maryland side, opposite Mount Vernon. Five minutes later, MacArthur again called Miles and ordered him "to assemble on the Ellipse at once."[60] At 1:50 P.M., Major George S. Patton Jr., at Fort Myer, called the commanding officer of the 2nd Squadron to say that the squadron had been ordered to Washington and that the troopers were "directed to saddle and be prepared to move as soon as possible."[61]

Captain Lucian K. Truscott Jr. led 213 cavalry troopers who "pounded down through Arlington National Cemetery, over the recently completed Memorial Bridge, and halted on the Ellipse at about 2:30."[62] They were the first to arrive. Fort Myer infantrymen were being brought in trucks, and coming up the Potomac from Fort Washington was a steamer carrying about 250 infantrymen and their officers. While awaiting the infantry, Major Patton rode off alone down Pennsylvania Avenue to Third Street NW to reconnoiter the terrain. He returned to the Ellipse with the crowd's cheers and jeers in his wake.[63]

Glassford rode his motorcycle to the Ellipse, where he found MacArthur in full uniform. When Glassford asked him what he planned to do, MacArthur said, "We are going to break the back of the BEF. Within a short time we will move down Pennsylvania Avenue, sweep through the billets there, and then clean out the other two big camps. The operation will be continuous. It will all be done tonight."[64]

Glassford asked MacArthur for a ten-minute head start and roared back to the Pennsylvania Avenue billets, where he had his men spread word among the veterans. He also sent warnings to the other camps and urged the evacuation of women and children before the troops arrived. Expecting that the troops were only minutes from going into action, Glassford cleared Pennsylvania Avenue, which had been filling with spectators. He kept them on one side of the broad ceremonial avenue, opposite the veterans and their billets. "Absolute order prevailed," Glassford recalled. "Veterans in their billets on the other side of the avenue awaited with eager curiosity the arrival of the soldiers."[65]

It would be a long wait. The steamer bearing the Fort Washington troops sailed up the river to the Washington Channel and—not far from a small BEF camp at an abandoned warehouse—docked near the Army War College. The soldiers boarded trucks that took them to the Ellipse. Another fifty men and five officers came from a Fort Myer unit that usually guarded the Tomb

Douglas MacArthur (center, with handkerchief) and Dwight David Eisenhower (right, smoking) on July 28. The two leaders became increasingly distant over time. Writing about July 28 in his memoirs, MacArthur said, "I . . . brought with me two officers who later wrote their names on world history," referring to Eisenhower and Patton. (General Douglas MacArthur Foundation)

of the Unknown Soldier and provided pallbearers for funerals. Flatbed trucks appeared carrying five tanks that had been secretly transferred to Fort Myer in June. After stocking up on tear-gas grenades and tear-gas candles, the force was ready to move out.

At 4:10, with General MacArthur at his side, General Miles stood in the Ellipse and addressed the cavalry, tank, and infantry officers assembled before him: "Gentlemen, the so-called Bonus Marchers are occupying certain Government properties in Washington and are successfully resisting efforts by the police to evacuate them. This command has been called upon by properly constituted authority to clear those properties. . . . You will use such force as is necessary to accomplish your mission. Tear gas will be used. Women and children who may be found in the affected area will be accorded every consideration and kindness."

The force stepped off at 4:30. More than two hundred cavalrymen, carbines at the sling and sabers drawn, spread across Pennsylvania Avenue, rank upon rank, trotting from the Treasury Building at Fifteenth Street NW toward the Capitol. The trucks carrying the tanks rolled slowly behind the cavalry. Then came about four hundred infantrymen.[66] Bringing up the rear were two staff cars, one bearing Miles and MacArthur, the other Eisenhower and Captain Thomas Jefferson Davis, MacArthur's longtime aide.[67]

Bartlett, still near the Pennsylvania billets called Camp Glassford, looked in the direction of the White House and saw "a force of Cavalry with sabers glistening, making the ominous click of iron feet on the pavement, which sounded so much like war."[68] Spectators on the north side of the avenue wondered if this was a show of force, a parade of military strength. On the south side, in the shacks and rubble of the billets, some veterans thought the same. "Let's give them a big hand," one of them said, and many of them started clapping. Morris Reynaud, a black vet who had come to Washington from New Orleans with two hundred white and black vets, didn't clap. "They're going to come back and give us some trouble," he said.[69]

The size of the crowd—some ten thousand, by army estimates—surprised Miles, who was in command, but with MacArthur at his elbow.[70] Captain H. W. Blakeley looked around and saw "a fantastic mixture of rioters, spectators, shoppers, streetcars, baby carriages, police, infantry, and officers from the War and Navy Departments in civilian clothes."[71]

The infantrymen came to a halt, turned smartly, and fixed bayonets. Miles labeled his two adversaries "the crowd" and "the mob" and ordered some of the cavalry troopers to herd the crowd out of the way to the north while other troopers and infantrymen worked on the mob, driving the veterans southward.

From the roof of the Ford building, where the evictions had begun in the morning, Richard L. Strout, a reporter for the *Christian Science Monitor,* looked down to see the soldiers assembling on the avenue and fixing bayonets, while in the rubble of the billets some veterans were lining up for mess call. Just below Strout, a veteran yelled down to the soldiers, "The last time I saw them bayonets I was going through Marne." An officer stood in the center of Pennsylvania Avenue and shouted up: "You got three minutes to clear out! Three minutes! I warn you!"

The soldiers donned gas masks. Strout saw a stone fly. "Then the riot started."[72]

Without warning, the soldiers started hurling gas grenades at the vets. Troops drove Strout and other onlookers off the roof and through gas-clouded floors to the street. An infantry squad rushed into another wrecked building still housing veterans, ran to the roof, and hurled tear-gas grenades down the stairwells, clearing the place.[73] But the wind was from the south, and clouds of tear gas wafted over the crowd.

The cavalry "made war" on the spectators gathered to watch the eviction, J. F. Essary of the *Baltimore Sun* reported. "Men and women were ridden down indiscriminately," he wrote. "Nothing like this cavalry charge has ever been witnessed in Washington. The mad dash of these armed horsemen against twenty to thirty thousand people who were guilty of nothing more atrocious than standing on private property observing the scene was bitterly commented

Soldiers, ordered by President Hoover to evict the Bonus Army, herded veterans and onlookers alike out of downtown Washington. "God, that I should see such things in the United States," said a reporter. (General Douglas MacArthur Foundation)

on by spectators." Senator Hiram Bingham of Connecticut, wearing a Palm Beach suit and Panama hat, had a tear-gas bomb thrown at his feet.[74]

When eight-year-old Naaman Seigle and his father left their home at Four-and-a-half and M streets NW that afternoon, they saw soldiers marching, and Naaman thought it was a parade. They went to the F. P. May hardware store at Sixth and C streets to buy a Philco radio. When they stepped out of the store, they suddenly began crying and coughing. Naaman was frightened and bewildered. Solomon Seigle, a pharmacist and part-time newspaper reporter, knew they had been gassed and, Naaman remembers, "He was mad as hell."[75]

Most of the veterans broke and ran. But some remained, taunting the soldiers and throwing bricks and stones. Cavalrymen tried to drive them north with slaps of their sabers. The tank trucks let down their ramps, and five small tanks rumbled onto the avenue. The infantrymen, wearing gas masks and with bayonets fixed, advanced toward the billets, hurling gas grenades. Vets threw some of the soup-can-size containers back, burning their hands.

The cavalry, on the flanks of the infantrymen, moved ahead in line. "Most of the marchers gave way and fell back," wrote Joseph C. Harsch of the *Christian Science Monitor*. "In front of me, one stood his ground. A saber flashed in a swinging arc and grazed the cheek of the marcher. Blood flowed. The marcher backed away holding a hand to his bleeding ear."[76]

A. Everette McIntyre, a member of the Federal Trade Commission, saw the infantrymen in gas masks advance on the veterans, jabbing with bayonets to move them on. "Soon, almost everybody disappeared from view, because tear gas bombs exploded," he remembers. "The entire block was covered with tear gas. Flames were coming up, where the soldiers had set fire to the buildings to drive these people out."[77]

"I watched the soldiers moving from hut to hut, starting the blaze," Strout reported. Shanty after shanty went up in flames, along with the meager belongings of the vets and their families. "Be careful, men. Don't burn any flags," an officer said. But the camps were full of flags, and they burned as well as scraps of wood and cardboard that had sheltered the vets. As cavalrymen headed into the camps, most vets and their families fled across the Mall. Some men stood in defiance. "Hit me, you yellow bastard!" shouted a vet carrying an American flag.

"If we had guns—" said another. A buddy agreed, saying, "Jeez, if we had guns."

The father of six children roped orange crates onto the fenders of his battered car. His wife ran up with her arms full of clothes.[78]

Soldiers in gas masks drove veterans away from their billet near Pennsylvania Avenue. Bonus marchers had been allowed to live in abandoned buildings on a site that would become the Federal Triangle. (General Douglas MacArthur Foundation)

Paul V. Anderson heard an officer bark a command and then saw cavalry-men charge the crowd with drawn sabers. "Men, women and children fled shrieking across the broken ground," Anderson wrote, "falling into excava-tions as they strove to avoid the rearing hoofs and saber points." A woman at a shack pleaded for permission to go inside and snatch a suitcase with all the clothes she had for herself and her child. "Get out of here, lady, before you get hurt," the soldier said. He then set the shack on fire.[79]

As Major Patton saw it from his saddle: "Bricks flew, sabers rose and fell with a comforting smack, and the mob ran. We moved on after them, occa-sionally meeting serious resistance. Once six men in a truck threw a regular barrage of bricks, and several men and horses were hit. Two of us charged at a gallop, and had some nice work at close range with the occupants of the truck, most of whom could not sit down for some days."[80]

A veteran wearing the Distinguished Service Cross and the Croix de Guerre stood his ground when a soldier advanced toward him and pointed his bayonet at the vet's chest. The veteran made a quick motion with his hip and sent the soldier sprawling. He stood and was about to lunge when an officer stopped him and, nodding toward the medals, said, "Have some respect for those." Then he said to the vet, "Buddy, I'd go along if I were you. It will be better."[81]

Anderson followed infantrymen who were casually tossing tear-gas grenades. "Some fell in front yards jammed with Negro women and children," he reported. "One appeared to land on the front porch of a residence. Two small girls fell to the sidewalk, choking and screaming."[82] An infantry officer felt he was getting more opposition from spectators than from vets, particularly in a neighborhood "occupied by colored people" who "joined with the bonus marchers in insulting language toward the troops."[83]

After clearing the vets from Camp Glassford, infantrymen and cavalrymen headed for Fourteenth and C streets SW. "Now you'll see some fun," someone yelled. "They're heading for the Reds' camp."[84] Tanks clanked toward the shacks as men scrambled over rubble in retreat. A reporter spotted people carrying babies, oil lamps, sacks of bread, and a black cat. Flames rose from the deserted shanties. MacArthur appeared and ordered counterfires to keep the fires from spreading.[85] Few veterans were seen, and the word was passed that the Communists had fled.

When all the veterans had been chased away from downtown Washington and the soldiers could take a break, a couple of them were approached by an older man.

"Were you in France?" he asked.

"No," one of the soldiers said.

"No, you were running around in short pants. Well, I was. And if we had guns we'd show you something. We're just as good shots as you are. Better maybe."

The young soldier mumbled something.

"This ain't going to stop here," the veteran said. "The whole country is gonna hear about this."[86]

As a soft summer evening closed over Washington, flames silhouetted the Capitol and the Washington Monument. The day had ended—but not the Army's battle against the BEF. At 9:00 P.M., after he and his troops had eaten, MacArthur told the ranking infantry and cavalry officers that "this command will proceed to Anacostia Flats and evacuate Bonus Marchers from that property."[87] Ten minutes later, the troops were on the march.

Morris Reynaud, who had not joined his applauding buddies on Pennsylvania Avenue earlier in the day, was one of the thousands of men, women, and children driven southward toward the Anacostia River. Now, in the dark of night,

Smoke veiled the Capitol dome as flames engulfed veterans' shanties, set afire by soldiers. Later that night, General MacArthur, defying presidential orders, would send soldiers into Camp Marks, which would also go up in flames. (General Douglas MacArthur Foundation)

he was standing near the bridge when he saw soldiers approaching. He rushed back to Camp Marks and shouted, "They're coming! They're coming!"[88]

As the cavalry passed on its way to the bridge, Walter Griffin, a black veteran from Chattanooga, stood in front of the Navy Yard at attention, holding an American flag, with three or four companions in formation behind him. When the last of the cavalry reached the bridge, Griffin and his pals fell in behind, along with a band of cheering, jeering bystanders. They followed for a few paces. Then the rear guard of the unit wheeled and hurled a gas bomb at them, forcing them to retreat back onto the sidewalks.[89]

The infantry next passed with fixed bayonets. The crowd began to boo. "As we were going across the Anacostia Bridge, they had their bayonets on their guns and they were really prodding them," wrote Raymond P. Brandt of the *St. Louis Post-Dispatch*. "And . . . a Negro was there and he got stabbed in the back, badly stabbed. He said, 'Well, I may not be an American, but I'm a Virginian.'"[90]

A civilian jumped out and began pulling soldiers out of line, causing the march to break up momentarily. The crowd scattered in the confusion. Through all of this, and for as long as troops passed by, Griffin held his flag high, still at attention.

When Griffin's story was retold a few days later by I. S. David, a reporter for the *Washington Tribune*, the city's only African-American newspaper in 1932, it ended with these lines: "Company after company marched by. . . . Not an officer looking up. Many of the soldiers looked scared and most of these mere boys hung their heads as if in shame." Added in italics by David or his editor was a postscript to the story: "*For the first time in American history, American troops on duty passed the colors held in loyal hands without being called to attention and without giving a salute.*"

In Camp Marks, Police Lieutenant Ira E. Keck saw a crowd gathered around Eddie Atwell, the camp commander. Keck heard Atwell say, "I have never advocated violence. Violence is knocking at the back door. We wish to protect ourselves. We have already lost one man [Carlson was still alive] and several police are in the hospital. We do not blame the municipal police department for what is happening. But we blame the Army and the President. . . . If they come to this camp tonight, I will meet them at the gate. . . . I will give you a promise to kill the first man to put his foot across the line."[91]

Keck left, continuing his eyes-and-ears mission for the commissioners. But police officers from the local precinct, who had worked with Atwell and respected him, tried to reason with him. He knew and they knew that there were about seven thousand people in Camp Marks, and six hundred were women and children.[92]

MacArthur and his men paused to regroup at the northern side of the bridge. General Moseley, who had spent the day in his office, appeared with an urgent message from Secretary of War Hurley to MacArthur. "As we walked away, alone, from the others, I delivered that message to him and discussed it with him," Moseley recalled. The message was from Hoover, stating that he did not wish the troops to cross the bridge that night to force the evacuation of Anacostia. MacArthur, according to Moseley, "was very much annoyed in having his plans interfered with in any way until they were executed completely. After assuring myself that he understood the message, I left him."

Moseley went back to his office and soon got a call from a White House official, who had been keeping abreast of the situation. He asked if the message had been delivered and understood. Moseley called in Colonel Clement H. Wright, the secretary of the Army General Staff, and ordered him to go to MacArthur "and explain the situation as I had it from the White House." Wright reached

MacArthur and conveyed Moseley's message. Wright reported back to Moseley that it was too late—"the troops had not crossed the Anacostia Bridge, but were advancing on the bridge," and MacArthur soldiered on.[93] Both Eisenhower and Miles also later recalled that Hurley's verbal message had been delivered to MacArthur.[94]

Shortly after 10:00 P.M., Atwell, carrying a white flag, approached an Army staff car. He pleaded for an hour's truce so he could evacuate the camp. MacArthur granted the request.[95]

At Camp Marks, Nick and Joe Oliver, the seven-year-old boxing twins, were asleep in the lean-to near the family car. Their father woke them up, shouting, "Come on! Come on! The soldiers are going to kill us. Let's get out of here. The soldiers are going to kill us."[96] In the darkness, Tony Oliver found his friend Sam Ditz, loaded him and the boys into the car, and headed out of the camp. Steve Murray, who had witnessed the routing of the bonus marchers downtown, believed Camp Marks would still be safe. Some of Murray's North Carolina friends had formed "The Friendly B.E.F. String Band" and driven with him to Washington to entertain the vets. Murray rounded up the band members, piled them into the car, and drove to Anacostia. "When we were just swinging into the camp grounds, a cop stopped us and said the only entertainment the camp would get tonight would be bullets. So we were forced to go back, but I went down to the camp and helped get the women and children out before the soldiers would get there."[97]

A unit from the District of Columbia National Guard arrived with a large searchlight, which played its beam around the dark camp, picking up scenes of panic—men trying to start jalopies, mothers calling for children, men and women carrying children toward the far hills of the camp.

Tanks took up positions on the bridge to block traffic in and out of the camp. Then, as the infantrymen entered the camp, stones flew out of the darkness, along with one word from one man: "Yellow-w-w-w-!" Reporter Joseph C. Harsch, who was standing near MacArthur, saw him summon a sergeant and give an order. "I watched," Harsch wrote, "as the sergeant collected a squad and started down the row of makeshift huts. They wadded newspapers into a corner and set them alight. The row of huts was soon blazing."[98] Thomas Henry of the *Evening Star* also followed the infantrymen, who at one point threw gas grenades into a crowd of booing citizens. Henry saw a truck from the District Fire Department shine its headlights to illuminate the first row of tents and hovels. "They are deserted now," he wrote. "The soldiers apply the torch to them. They are like tinder."[99]

Reporter Bess Furman, who had seen the Camp Glassford evacuation, drove with her newsman husband to Anacostia but found the bridge raised. They turned around and drove to Haines Point, once the site of another small camp and a good vantage point for looking across the Washington Channel toward Anacostia. They saw "a blaze so big that it lighted the whole sky . . . a nightmare come to life."

On the Potomac River, under a crescent moon, a moonlight excursion boat, outlined in bright lights, was returning from a cruise to Fort Washington. "It had been a perfect evening," recalled Elbridge Purdy. As the boat neared its landing dock on Water Street SE, the band was playing the last dance. Then, near the mouth of the Anacostia River, passengers saw a red haze, then a mass of flames. The whole riverbank seemed to be burning. Passengers rushed to the starboard side, and the crew began pushing them back because the boat was listing under the shift of the rubberneckers.

An Army captain who was Purdy's sister's date on the cruise realized what was happening and knew he had to join the troops at Anacostia. As soon as the boat docked, all three hopped into a car and drove the short distance to Anacostia. They were stopped at the now-lowered bridge, showed identification, and got permission to drive to the camp.

"There were continuous flames," Purdy recalled. They saw soldiers carrying torches made of rolled-up paper. "Veterans were packing and rushing about. Tear gas, which was being used to drive them out, made it difficult to see. . . . It was like riding through the steam of a teakettle. . . . There were pregnant women and some babies. . . . They were grabbing and packing their meager belongings." When some vets saw the captain's uniform, they "began throwing rocks and pieces of brick at our car." But they made it to where MacArthur stood—"I will always remember the staunch outline, the erect figure"—and dropped off the captain. Then soldiers directed them out of the "tear gas, dust, and filth."[100]

The long day ended in a press conference that lasted until past midnight. MacArthur, back at his headquarters, stood before a crowd of reporters. Oddly, there were no newsreel cameras, which had been on the scene earlier in the day. Reporters speculated that the newsreel cameras had been barred from Camp Marks's blazing final night just as they had been barred, by gentleman's agreement, during Camp Marks's summer days.

MacArthur called the veterans "insurrectionists" and declared that "if there was one man in ten in that group today who is a veteran, it would surprise me." Reviewing his day's work, he said, "The mob down Pennsylvania Avenue looked bad. They were animated by the spirit of revolution. The gentleness and consideration with which they had been treated had been mistaken by them as weakness and they had come to the conclusion that they were about to take over the government in an arbitrary way or by indirect methods.[101]

"It is my opinion that had the President not acted today, had he permitted this thing to go on for twenty-four hours more, he would have been faced with a grave situation which would have caused a real battle. Had he let it go another week I believe that the institutions of our Government would have been very severely threatened. It can be said that he had not only reached the end of his extraordinary patience but had gone to very great lengths to avoid trouble.

"Had the President not used force he would have been derelict indeed in his judgment regarding the safety of the country because this country is the focal point of the world today. Had he not acted with the force and vigor which he did, it would have been a bad day for the country tomorrow.

"I have never seen greater relief on the part of the distressed populace than I saw today. . . . At least a dozen people told me, especially in the Negro section, that a regular system of tribute was being levied on them by this insurrectionist group."[102]

By the time the conference ended, the evacuation of Camp Marks was almost complete. Veterans who had cars had headed off to somewhere. Many veterans and families had got only as far as the hills that rose behind the camp, and there they huddled until morning, children coughing from tear gas. Hundreds had fled into the streets of the neighborhood and had been taken into homes. At midnight one resident found eight small children and infants lying in the doorway of a five-and-ten-cent store, their mothers putting wet cloths over their eyes.

One fleeing family, the Meyers from Ephrata, Pennsylvania, had been taken in by another family several blocks from the camp. Some soldiers charged into the neighborhood, flinging the last of the two thousand tear-gas grenades used that day. One landed beside an open window. A cloud of gas wafted into the bedroom where twelve-week-old Bernard Meyer lay coughing and gasping. His parents took him to a hospital, where he died. The father said that the boy had been sick when he was gassed. The hospital said that the gas possibly aggravated the illness. Government investigators, including the chief medical officer of the Army Chemical Service, concluded that the baby died of enteritis, an inflammation of the intestines, possibly caused by bacterial diarrhea. But, a hospital spokesman said, the tear gas "didn't do it any good." The Army and the Justice Department investigated and found that tear gas had not killed Bernard Meyer, but to many in the BEF, he was the last casualty in what they called the Battle of Washington.[103]

The Long Morning After

There was an old Hoover
Who Lived in a Shoe.
He had so many veterans
He didn't know what to do.
So he gassed them and tanked them,
And burned up their beds
And then told all the people
The vets were all Reds.

—*B.E.F. News*, September 17, 1932

O N THE MORNING of July 29, with the *New York Times* spread open on his bed at Hyde Park, Democratic presidential nominee Franklin D. Roosevelt told an aide that there was no need now to campaign against Hoover. "Flames rose high over the desolate Anacostia flats at midnight tonight," read the first sentence in the *Times* account, "and a pitiful stream of refugee veterans of the World War walked out of their home of the past two months, going they knew not where."

After studying the paper for a few more minutes, Roosevelt asked, "Why didn't Hoover offer the men coffee and sandwiches, instead of turning . . .

Doug MacArthur loose? They're probably camping on the roads leading out of Washington. They must be in terrible shape."

Terrible was an apt adjective.

"When the veterans of the Bonus Army first tried to escape," wrote Malcolm Cowley in his role as a reporter for the *New Republic* magazine, "they found that the bridges into Virginia were barred by soldiers and the Maryland roads blocked against them by state troopers. They wandered from street to street or sat in ragged groups, the men exhausted, the women with wet handkerchiefs laid over their smarting eyes, the children waking from sleep to cough and whimper from the tear gas in their lungs. The flames behind them were climbing into the night sky. About four in the morning, as rain began to fall, they were allowed to cross the border into Maryland, on condition that they moved as rapidly as possible into another state."[1]

The dispersed were supposed to return to their homes, which most of them did not have. So when a rumor was heard that Mayor Eddie McCloskey of Johnstown, Pennsylvania, would welcome them, they took up the cry "On to Johnstown!" McCloskey, a veteran, had been a frequent weekend visitor to

The day after destroying Camp Marks, soldiers posed at a shattered piano. The veterans, a witness said, were "treated like a tramp dog some man picks up in the alley, feeds, gives a bed in his house, and then shoots the next morning when he finds it has got lice." (General Douglas MacArthur Foundation)

Camp Marks. He had even brought his daughters, who danced on the rickety stage. He had become friends with Waters and other BEF leaders, and when he made his offer, he expected no more than a few hundred. He was shocked to learn early on July 29 that something like eight thousand more were on their way to his city.[2]

Cowley, heading toward Johnstown, came upon a group of three hundred and agreed to take two of the refugees in his car. The vets picked the two by a quick informal vote. The first had been gassed in the Argonne and teargassed at Anacostia; he, Cowley said, "breathed with an effort, as if each breath would be his last." The second man had been separated from his wife and six children during the retreat from Camp Marks and hoped to find them in Johnstown. "He talked about his service in France, his three medals, which he refused to wear, his wounds, his five years in a government hospital. 'If they gave me a job,' he said, 'I wouldn't care about the bonus.'"[3]

Waters emerged on the morning after the expulsion to order all remaining veterans out of the city and proclaim himself a leader in a new movement, assuming, in the words of the *New York Times*, "the role of an American Hitler." As his BEF headed to Johnstown, Waters was setting up national headquarters in Washington for the Khaki Shirt movement to "clean out the high places of government" and return government to the masses. The men of the BEF, he told the *Times*, are torchbearers for the "inarticulate masses of the country." The short-lived Khaki Shirts would soon begin a slide into fascism, which Waters would disavow. But his creation of the organization displayed the degree to which he was attempting to become a national political figure, even if it meant comparing himself to Mussolini and Hitler.[4]

As for President Hoover, reporters were told that he had met with MacArthur and Hurley the night before, around 10:30 P.M., in the second-floor Lincoln Study, which Mrs. Hoover had restored as an office for her husband. By looking out the windows of the study, Hoover and his late-night visitors could see the red glow of the Camp Marks fires. The *Evening Star,* without giving a source, stated authoritatively that "the President and those with him went to the window and for some moments looked in the direction of the flames."[5] Then Hoover retired for the night, and MacArthur and Hurley went to the nearby State, War, and Navy Building for a press conference that MacArthur dominated.

Whatever thoughts Hoover may have had that night,[6] he knew that he had to explain the sabers and the tear gas and the flames to the nation. On July 29 he dictated a letter to Commissioner Reichelderfer. In the first draft of the letter, Hoover said, "I complied with your request for aid from the Army to the

Smoke could be seen rising from the ruins of the Bonus Army's Anacostia camp on the morning after troops—using tear gas, bayonets, and torches—drove out the veterans and their families. "And this," said a veteran's wife, "because they cry for food. . . . Because they beg for work." (General Douglas MacArthur Foundation)

police. It is a matter of congratulation that, after the arrival of this assistance, the mobs which were defying the municipal government were dissolved without the firing of a shot or the loss of a life." He also wrote that "most" of the members of the mobs were not veterans. In the second and final draft, "congratulation" was changed to "satisfaction" and "most" was changed to "a large part."[7] Those two changes marked the first stirrings of what would become the Hoover administration's official stance on the expulsion of the veterans and their families: there would be no gloating, MacArthur-style statements from the White House. And the BEF would become a mob full of men who were criminals, Communists—and not veterans.

The president also issued a public statement on July 29, saying, "A challenge to the authority of the United States Government has been met, swiftly and firmly," adding that the government could not be "coerced by mob rule." But he sharpened his nonvet claim in a letter to an influential American Legion post in Boston, one of the largest in New England. Responding to a telegram commending him for his action, he wrote, "I would be glad if the veterans throughout the country would know the character of the men claiming to be their representatives who have been in Washington since the adjournment of Congress. It is the impression of our Government services that less than half of them ever served under the American flag."[8]

By Hoover's accounting, most of those in Washington before adjournment were veterans, but those who lingered were dominated by non-vets. Hurley followed through on August 3 with a lengthy statement in which he estimated that only one-third of the men were veterans, adding that "many veterans themselves became more and more under the influence of the number of so-called red, radical agitators after many of the genuine veterans had left." The government sent troops on July 28, he said, after a "definite organized attack of several thousand men was then made upon the police." Hurley blamed the fires, including the conflagration in Anacostia, on "retreating radicals"—except for some torching by troops "in the interests of sanitation."[9]

The flaming shacks had made spectacular newspaper photographs, particularly a nationally published photo showing a soldier lighting a shanty with a torch. The Army did its best to explain that the torching was a misunderstanding: a lieutenant at the beginning of the action downtown, seeing that many of the shacks around him were already afire, believed that an order to burn them had been given. Then several policemen approached him, handed him matches, and said, "Those shacks should be burned also." The lieutenant accepted the suggestion—and the matches—and gave the order to set the fires. This order, the army said, was then passed down the line. (In fact, Army reports about actions downtown frequently tell of the destruction of shacks as part of the military operations.) The Army claimed that the vets, not the soldiers, had burned the camp in Anacostia, insisting that the occupants did the burning. Witnesses said that the troops in Anacostia had set fires for illumination. What seems to have happened next is that when the vets saw those fires, they believed that the soldiers were going to set the whole camp afire and decided to finish the job.[10]

While the remnants of the Bonus Army trudged to Johnstown, the U.S. Army began cleaning up in Washington in the early hours of Friday, July 29. One of the troops' missions was the eviction of women and children from an old government-owned redbrick house that had been used as a BEF shelter. On the street outside the house, charity workers found ninety children and many mothers and reported, "Babies, with uncovered heads, no shade, no care or food, were held in the laps of their shocked, suffering mothers."[11]

On July 30 John Henry Bartlett witnessed a roundup of park sitters and homeless people by the police. "Many who had not been identified with the

On the day after the expulsion of the Bonus Army, a U.S. Army sergeant—with a tear-gas grenade still dangling from his belt—checked passengers on a Washington bus in search of veterans who might have been lurking in the city. (General Douglas MacArthur Foundation)

bonus army were caught in the drive," he said. "Police patrols and commandeered taxis ran, in a steady stream, to Judiciary Square, which a police cordon had transformed into a human corral. There all who could not establish definite means of support were reloaded into cars and taken to the district line, where they were again transferred into trucks and whisked away and dumped. A police count showed 502 poor people, none criminals, had been evicted."[12] Bartlett also watched as the Army set fire to huts that had been missed the first night. Again soldiers used sabers, bayonets, and tear gas to move veterans, spectators, and jeering schoolchildren, who were chased by mounted cavalry. "An old man laboring along with two sacks of potatoes did not step lively enough to please a cavalryman. I saw he was cut, his hand bleeding by a sabre thrust," Bartlett said. A longtime African-American resident of Washington— and not a bonus marcher—was put in a truck and wound up in Indianapolis, along with another man who said he had been on his way home from a dance when soldiers and police forced him into a truck.[13]

The Army drove out the 1,500 veterans and their families who believed they were safe at Camp Bartlett. Vets at Camp Sims left before any soldiers arrived, as did about 250 veterans in small waterfront camps along the Washington Channel. In the afternoon, soldiers hurled tear-gas grenades to drive off a score

Army trucks carrying machine guns stood ready during the eviction. No shots were fired, but Police Chief Glassford saw "brutality," not by the Army but by "the Hoover Administration's attempt to make political capital out of hunger, misery and despair." (General Douglas MacArthur Foundation)

of veterans who had returned to Pennsylvania Avenue, probably to search for belongings that had survived the fires.

About two hundred veterans from Texas, California, and Missouri got across the Potomac to Virginia but were driven back by Virginia police. The veterans then headed up Wisconsin Avenue to Maryland, whose governor was providing trucks that would take them to the Pennsylvania line.[14] A policeman on a motorcycle led a procession of other vets, many carrying American flags, to the Maryland line for further expulsion. Thousands of vets were transported out of Maryland. State after state then provided trucks to ship the BEF remnants westward, using the same technique of border-to-border vet-passing that had moved the Bonus Army into Washington back in May and June. Countless veterans and their families had melted into the Depression underworld of the District, living on the street, among residents who took them in, or in missions and other charity residences.

Three BEF families were officially allowed to remain in Washington, at least for a little while. They had ill children in hospitals or private residences and under the care of the Red Cross, which considered them emergency cases and thus acceptable under guidelines that had kept the Red Cross out of the BEF camps.[15] On August 1, one of the children, two-month-old Gertrude Mann, died in a hospital; her death was attributed to intestinal disorders. Again, authorities ruled that tear gas had not played any role in her death.[16]

That same day, a meeting was held in the office of Assistant Attorney General Nugent Dodds. Attending were J. Edgar Hoover, director of the Bureau of Investigation, along with representatives of the Secret Service, the Army's Military Intelligence Division, the Veterans Administration, the Immigration Service, and the District police. The Veterans Administration agreed to provide veterans' names to Hoover, who would then search his fingerprint files to see if any of them had been arrested. Those statistics would provide the foundation for the administration's claim that the BEF was riddled with criminals, but since the VA fingerprints would also prove that the men were veterans, it would be difficult to use the VA's names to prove the nonveteran charge. Nevertheless, the VA and J. Edgar Hoover began the task.[17]

Another issue had to do with how and when the troops were called in. As laid out in a packet of official papers from the White House, the process had begun when Luther Reichelderfer, chairman of the Board of Commissioners, sent a letter to President Hoover sometime on July 28. The letter said that after the morning conflict during the evictions, Glassford believed that it would "be impossible for the Police Department to maintain law and order except by the free use of firearms," and so the commissioners requested "that they be given the assistance of Federal troops." Next, according to the official papers, Hurley ordered MacArthur to send troops "immediately to the scene of disorder." Hurley also ordered MacArthur to cooperate with the police and turn over "all prisoners to the civil authorities." His men were also to show "every consideration and kindness" to all women and children, adding, "Use all humanity consistent with the due execution of this order."

Many accounts published after July 28, 1932, say that the troops were not summoned until the shooting of the veterans by police. But the commissioners' letter to the president mentions only the morning fracas with police, not the shooting of the veterans in the afternoon. And the timing of the mobilizing phone calls, as stated in the official U.S. Army "Report of Operations against Bonus Marchers," shows that MacArthur's call for troops went out at 1:35, before the shooting.[18]

The District commissioners fired off telegrams to the governors of Virginia and Maryland, telling them that "all organized bodies or groups of persons attempting to enter the District shall be prevented from doing so" unless they can prove that they "have a lawful purpose." Leo Rover, U.S. attorney for the district, bypassing Glassford, called Inspector Ogden T. Davis of the police's Crime Prevention Bureau and told him to join immigration officials and Secret Service agents in a raid on an abandoned church, where alleged Communists were meeting. Police arrested about thirty men, including Communist Party vice presidential candidate James W. Ford.[19]

The dragnets infuriated Glassford, who questioned their legality. "I am chief of police," he said, "and I intend to enforce the laws here to the best of my ability. By enforcement, however, I do not mean persecution."[20] Even as he spoke, he was preparing to testify before a coroner's jury looking into the police killing of two veterans and a grand jury investigating how he and the Army had handled the ouster of the BEF.

Early on Tuesday, August 2, Eric Carlson died from gunshot wounds he sustained when William J. Hushka was killed. Hushka was buried in Arlington National Cemetery with full military honors a few hours later. The soldiers who fired the farewell volley over his grave included men from Fort Myer whose bayonets and tear gas had driven the Bonus Army from Washington. More than two thousand people, many from local veterans' groups, attended the ceremony, along with Hushka's family and Walter and Wilma Waters.[21]

Across the river later in the day, as Carlson's body was being wheeled into the dingy Washington morgue, a coroner's inquest into the killing of the two men was in progress. Patrolman George Shinault was charged with the killing of Hushka and patrolman Miles Znamenacek with the killing of Carlson. Twenty witnesses were heard. Znamenacek, in a statement read by his attorney, told of following Glassford up the steps of the abandoned building when "a crowd followed us up, shouting, 'Get the major [Glassford]." Then, Znamenacek's statement continued, "I spread my arms to hold the onrushing bonus marchers back, and noticed a bulge in one of the men's shirts. I felt to see what it was. The mob rushed me and knocked me down. I got up and something hit me on the head. It felt as though my head was sailing through the air. I broke loose and drew my gun. Down at the foot of the stairway, Officer Shinault was battling with a number of men. One of them had him by the throat and was trying to strangle him. Dodging bricks, I aimed at and shot that man. I found out later it was Carlson."

Glassford testified that he had seen Shinault being clubbed and then, from the ground, firing and killing Hushka from a range of four feet. A bystander named Armstrong testified that he had seen a man in civilian clothes with a gun in the building before the disturbance began. But a lawyer from the American

Civil Liberties Union established that Armstrong's testimony might have been tainted because he was "beginning to make contracts" with the Treasury Department. Several other bystanders testified that bricks were in fact being thrown at the police. After a five-minute deliberation, it was decided that the two patrolmen had used their weapons in self-defense, and they were returned to duty.[22] Shinault, who had received threatening letters, was assigned to a radio patrol car, in which he would be accompanied by another officer.[23]

A grand jury, empaneled by U.S. Attorney Rover, avoided looking into the killing of Hushka and Carlson. In his instructions to the jurors, District Supreme Court Judge J. Oscar R. Luhring referred to the BEF as a "mob" and said it reportedly "included few ex-servicemen, and was made up mainly of communists and other disorderly elements." When the jurors finally did indict three men for assault to kill and assault with a dangerous weapon, all three turned out to be combat veterans, as were Hushka and Carlson, and one had been awarded the Distinguished Service Cross for bravery in France.[24]

Over the next few days, newspapers advertised theater newsreels that promised graphic images of fleeing veterans and their families, blazing shacks, clouds of tear gas, soldiers wielding fixed bayonets, and cavalrymen waving sabers. The ad in the *Washington Post*, for example, called the Pathé News's *Washington Bonus Army Riots* the greatest news spectacle "you have ever seen."[25]

In movie theaters all across America the unthinkable happened: the United States Army was booed and MacArthur jeered. Evalyn McLean was in California when the expulsion took place. She recalled going to a movie and seeing the newsreel of the tanks, cavalry, and "the gasbomb throwers" running Americans out of "our" capital. "I was so raging mad I could have torn the building down," she wrote. "They could not be allowed to stay, of course, but even so I felt myself one of them." Apparently many other Americans thought they too were one of them. The images and the lurid words—"a day of bloodshed and riot"— contributed to a caricature of Hoover as a cold and heartless man, unable to cope with the needs of the hungry and dispossessed.

A woman from Portland, Maine, wrote Hurley to say that when the newsreel came on the screen she heard a gasp go up from the audience. To make sure she heard right, she waited and saw the newsreel again. And again came the gasp.[26]

If the expulsion needed a human face, it came in the person of not Hushka or Carlson—men at the wrong place at the wrong time—but of Joe Angelo, whose story in the *New York Times,* headlined "A Cavalry Major Evicts Veteran

Who Saved His Life in Battle," told of Angelo's eviction by the man whose life he had saved in the Great War.[27] The *Philadelphia Public Ledger* ran a Joe Angelo story, as did the *Washington Daily News,* among others.[28]

On the morning of July 29, in the smoldering ruins of Camp Marks, Major George Patton and several other officers were sitting on bales of hay, drinking coffee from an Army field kitchen, and talking about their long day-and-night battle against the BEF. Another officer, Captain Lucian Truscott, looked up to see "a tall sergeant of the Twelfth Infantry . . . with a small civilian in tow." The sergeant, Truscott later wrote, "asked for Major Patton, saying that the man claimed to be a friend of the major's. When Patton saw them, his face flushed with anger. 'Sergeant, I do not know this man. Take him away, and under no circumstances permit him to return!' The sergeant led the downcast man away."

The man was Joe Angelo. As he left the group, Patton told the officers, "That man was my orderly during the war. When I was wounded, he dragged me from a shell hole under fire. I got him a decoration for it. Since the war, my mother and I have more than supported him. We have given him money. We have set him up in business several times. Can you imagine the headlines if the papers got wind of our meeting here this morning? Of course, we'll take care of him anyway."[29]

The Joe Angelo story was an exception; the newspapers had tended to look at the veterans as a large, unruly group without names or faces. Probably because of the power of the images in newsreels and newspapers, however, the mood of at least some of the press turned from applauding the Hoover administration to questioning its decision. "What a pitiful spectacle is that of the great American Government . . . chasing unarmed [veterans], women and children with army tanks," observed the *Washington Daily News.*[30] A growing number of editorialists and citizens, while abstractly agreeing with the need to remove the veterans from Washington, were also disturbed by images of the expulsion. In an editorial the *Boston Globe* invoked "the distressing picture" that had been spread in front of a nation whose "nerves and resources have already been severely strained by the struggle for economic recovery." The paper called for a "painstaking investigation" into the expulsion.[31] There were also calls for investigation in Congress, but none ever came.

The thousand-odd refugees who first arrived at Johnstown set up camp on the grounds of the abandoned amusement park on the edge of town. They dubbed it Camp McCloskey, and it filled up at the rate of two hundred per

Driven from Washington, veterans and their families fled to an abandoned amusement park in Johnstown, Pennsylvania. When social workers asked where they would go next, many replied, "I do not know" or "We have no home." (Authors' collection)

hour. There was little food and no coffee. Local charities sustained them as the camp grew to an estimated peak population of nearly 9,000.[32]

Pennsylvania social workers went to the park and, as they surveyed the refugees, also inadvertently refuted the administration's view of the BEF as a gang of Reds and criminals. "Every one of the approximately 75 men I questioned specifically as to their service records, produced his service papers, showing honorable discharge," wrote J. Prentice Murphy, a member of the state welfare committee who visited the camp. At least fifteen men he interviewed had medals for valor.

"There were graduate physicians, nurses; a graduate pharmacist; passenger conductors; locomotive firemen; artisans, such as structural iron workers; carpenters; white collar people, such as clerks, down to the casual and irregularly employed worker. They spoke with restraint; some certainly were folks who read and liked books."[33]

Murphy found many families who had no place to go. One he cited consisted of a mother, father, and three children: "The mother is the daughter of a professor at an Indiana college. This family . . . had no particular destination." Another family—father, mother, five children, mother pregnant—had a girl who had suffered from convulsions the night before. The father was a baker. The family had been evicted from their house in New York State and was hoping to find refuge with the wife's relatives in Virginia. The BEF members and their families, Murphy decided, were ordinary Americans who "could tell of more sufferings and hardships during the past two years than could be told by any other group of like numbers because the BEF is pretty much a cross-section of the citizenry of the whole country." Mrs. Helen Glenn Tyson, Pennsylvania's assistant deputy secretary of welfare, likewise saw the refugees as representing "a cross-section of America just as truly as the army in 1917–1918. . . . There was no doubt that the majority of them were bona fide war veterans. . . . American flags were everywhere, repudiation of the 'reds' was violent; though the speakers often added that 'that night in Washington was enough to make anyone a Bolshie.'"[34]

The public health investigations also produced medical reports. One, reporting on a wound on a boy's leg, added a poignant detail: the boy had been stabbed with a bayonet wielded by a soldier who had stopped him from going back to his burning shack to save a pet rabbit.

From the beginning, McCloskey had been under intense local pressure to close down his namesake camp. Layoffs at Bethlehem Steel had made Johnstown a city full of unemployed men—and a city whose own relief system had broken down. The Salvation Army had been serving four thousand meals a day before the Bonus Army arrived. A newspaper editorial warned of the need to protect the community "from the criminal fringe of the invaders."[35] Yet the town had shown its heart as in 1889 it had shown its grit, after more than 2,200 people died in the Johnstown Flood, one of the worst disasters in American history.[36] The local hospital treated dozens of refugees and posted volunteer doctors to the camp.[37]

The BEF was virtually leaderless. Doak Carter, who had arrived on July 29 and set up the camp, was living in a hotel in Johnstown. Waters was on a futile search for a permanent site even as he urged his followers to go home. Mayor McCloskey organized a committee to solicit money and food, and opened an account in a local bank to handle donations and to account for expenditures on food and other necessities.[38]

Finally, with some hidden assistance from Washington, Daniel Willard, the president of the Baltimore & Ohio Railroad, offered the veterans free rides as far west as Chicago and Saint Louis in the coaches—not the boxcars—of the B&O. (They were moved at a cent-a-mile rate, which may have been paid by members of the Chamber of Commerce or by Washington sources, depending on who was explaining the exodus from Johnstown.) Those who had cars were given free fill-ups of gas and $1 each for food.

McCloskey, an ex-prizefighter with a cauliflower ear, explained the need to leave to his erstwhile guests, one of whom he socked in the jaw for heckling: "God sent you here and I'm sending you away. . . . That's more than Hoover did for you. . . . What do you say?" Hearing a murmur, he paused and then continued: "Then you bums can walk and I'll see you get a damned good start. I won't call in any troopers to massacre you. I'll put you the hell out myself. . . . I'll knock the teeth out of anybody who hangs around here."

In a calmer moment, McCloskey said, "We of Johnstown have now partly paid our debt to those who sent us help" at the time of the great flood. The last stragglers out of Camp McCloskey burned Hoover and Mellon in effigy before leaving.[39]

On the morning of Monday, August 15, Washingtonians awoke to read in their morning newspapers that Officer George Shinault, who had fatally shot William Hushka of the BEF, had been killed when he went to a house to investigate a domestic disturbance at 39 F Street SW. Shot twice as he entered the house, he died almost instantly. According to his partner, a fight was going on in the house between "a colored man and woman," and it was the man who shot Shinault and then escaped. The killer was alleged to be Willie Bullock, and within two days two black men with that name were in custody—neither the right one.[40]

The Hoover administration continued its campaign to get out its own version of the evacuation. On September 12 the White House released a report from Attorney General William D. Mitchell, who accused the Bonus Army of bringing to Washington "the largest aggregation of criminals that had ever assembled in the city at one time." The report, based on J. Edgar Hoover's analysis of BEF fingerprints, said that "a very much larger proportion of the Bonus Army than was realized at the time consisted of ex-convicts, persons with criminal records, radicals, and non-servicemen."[41]

The report bristled with statistics stemming from the Veterans Administration's list of 4,723 veterans who had been given transportation home. Although these were veterans and were presumably not in Washington on July 28, Mitchell still used them as his models, noting that when those names were checked against J. Edgar Hoover's fingerprint and criminal records, 829 (or 17.4 percent) were shown to have been "convicted criminals." Mitchell supported his "aggregation of criminals" charge by claiming that if there were that many criminals in this VA sample, then the same percentage probably held for the entire Bonus Army.

To arrive at his claim that a large number of BEF members were not veterans, Mitchell used a list that Glassford had compiled. In the beginning of the Bonus Army invasion, Glassford had police register the veterans as they arrived. The practice stopped after June 12 because the police were overwhelmed; by that time the names totaled 3,656. Of those men, 877 did not identify themselves as veterans. Frank Hines, the head of the VA, said in a letter about this list, "It is possible that some of the 877 were ex-servicemen and could not be identified because of meager information, but the bulk of them were evidently imposters."[42] Hines later contradicted himself when he said that he believed the overwhelming majority of the men were veterans.

Many vets who were on the road or hopping trains did not carry documentation. (One of those was Steve Murray, who lost his papers in a scuffle involving a railroad cop.[43]) Other vets, lacking papers, went to the VA's Washington office, got their credentials, and probably did not get their identities corrected. When Waters was running the BEF, he demanded identification before issuing passes to the camps. He later said that he had roster sheets listing the names of 28,540 veterans.[44]

Among the crimes listed in the Mitchell report were both military offenses, such as unauthorized absences, and civilian crimes, many of them minor but exaggerated, such as "offenses against the family and children," which turned out to be nonpayment of support. There were also arrests for drunkenness, for violating the notoriously unenforceable Prohibition laws, for gambling, and for an all-inclusive police charge called "suspicion and investigation." Most of the dispositions of the arrests were not known, but the attorney general treated all arrested men as having been convicted.

Refutation of Mitchell's charges came swiftly and massively—just in time for an important date on presidential candidate Hoover's campaign calendar: the American Legion convention in the city where the Bonus Army began, Portland, Oregon. Secretary of War Hurley volunteered to speak to the legionnaires and lay out the administration's line on the expulsion. In a dinner address to past national commanders, he specifically denied the deliberate firing of the veterans' camps. "I say to you upon my honor," he said, "that those billets were set on fire first by the people who occupied them."[45] But newspapers had already printed the damning photo of a soldier setting fires and had obtained an affidavit from him attesting to his actions.[46]

Nationally known correspondent and broadcaster Floyd Gibbons, whose eye patch bespoke his wounds in France, went to Portland because of the "war . . . on the convention floor." Gibbons ripped into Mitchell, asking, "If these men were such dangerous criminals, why were they not arrested?" Turning to

A parade opened the 1932 American Legion convention in Portland, Oregon. Here the Bonus Army began its march—and here Secretary of War Patrick J. Hurley would claim that the Bonus Army was riddled with criminals and Communists. (Oregon Historical Society)

Mitchell's list of crimes, Gibbons wrote, "As I figure it, the proportion of 829 'convicts' out of forty thousand men that passed through the camps, is something like under three per cent." President Harding's own cabinet (in which Hoover had been secretary of Commerce) had a criminal record of at least 10 percent, Gibbons wrote: "and it wasn't for parking in front of a fire plug either."

Joining Gibbons in the refutation of the report were Elsie Robinson, who wrote for the Hearst papers and was the reporter closest to the Bonus Army, and George R. Brown, a former war correspondent and the star reporter for the *Washington Herald*. "Smugly satisfied, one Government official after another has risen to justify that shameful day," Robinson wrote. "And this week the whole Administration united in an attack on the honor of American ex-soldiers which is unparalleled in heartlessness and arrogance and deliberate misinformation."

Brown, taking a more measured tone, pointed out that VA chief Hines had said earlier in the year that "ninety per cent of the bonus army were ex–service men." Brown also noted that every BEF member with a public identity—from Waters to Hushka and Carlson—was a veteran with an honorable record. "This writer," Brown continued, "has personally come into contact with certainly not less than two hundred of the men of the Bonus Army, both before and since the eviction. In nearly all cases, in the course of conversation about the war service of the men, he has been shown their discharge papers. In no instance was there any reluctance to show them."[47]

Mitchell's report gave Pelham Glassford a chance to rebut the issue of criminal records. Of 362 arrests of bonus marchers by D.C. police, Glassford said, only twelve were for "offenses of a criminal nature." While the BEF was in Washington, there was less crime overall in the city—and crime increased in August, after the Bonus Army had been driven out. By Glassford's estimate, based on police censuses of billets, the "Communist camp," meaning the one occupied by the WESL group, numbered about 150 men. The largest groups of "radicals" assembled at one time numbered 210, he said.[48]

He also questioned the use of troops. "I was never apprised by the Commissioners that troops had been called," he said in a formal statement. "Although it has been stated that the police were threatened with a mass attack, the actual encounter was halted almost instantly."

Having challenged the attorney general of the United States and indirectly the president, Glassford did not look forward to a long career as police chief. In what looked like a deliberately staged controversy to get rid of him, the commissioners refused to back him in his decision to demote the chief of detectives as part of a reorganization of the Detective Bureau. "I find myself . . . holding a position of great responsibility but deprived of the essential authority to discharge it without fear and without favor," he said in his letter of resignation on October 20, 1932. He had been chief of police eleven months.[49]

During the presidential election campaign, the expulsion of the Bonus Army haunted Hoover—and the Secret Service, whose chief of the White House detail, Edmund W. Starling, worried about the behavior of hostile crowds. When Hoover went to Detroit to speak on October 22, Starling later wrote, "the city was in an ugly mood. . . . For the first time in my long experience on the Detail I heard the President of the United States booed. All along the line there were bad spots, where we heard jeers and saw signs reading: DOWN WITH HOOVER; HOOVER—BALONEY AND APPLESAUCE. The President looked bewildered and stricken."

The presidential party got back on the train and headed for Hoover's next appearance, in St. Paul, where he said, "Thank God we still have a government in Washington that knows how to deal with a mob."

"A ripple went through the audience and I broke into a cold sweat," Starling continued. "After the speech a prominent Republican took me aside and said, 'Why don't they make him quit?'"[50]

On November 8, 1932, Americans, desperate for change, elected Governor Franklin Delano Roosevelt president by seven million votes. George Patton, discounting the effect of the Great Depression on voters, later said that the army's "act[ing] against a crowd rather than against a mob" had "insured the election of a Democrat."[51]

On election day, the *Washington Herald* published a startling photo with a headline that echoed Hoover's campaign remark: "How to Deal with a 'Mob.'" The photo showed Hushka lying on the ground outside the building where he was shot. It looks like a tableau—more than a dozen veterans gather around Hushka, who lies in the V formed by two planks that served as a stairway. Propped up on his arms, he leans his head on one of the planks. One man, who apparently stands where Shinault stood, points his right hand at Hushka, as if he were aiming Shinault's gun. Beneath Hushka is what looks like a blot of blood. There is no blood on his white shirt, though the coroner said he had been shot through the heart.

The same photo appeared in Waters's book with the caption "MURDER William Hushka, freshly killed by police bullet during 'ferocious riot.' 'Riot' was so ferocious that this picture could be taken a minute after shot was fired!" The photo was credited, "By permission of Eddie Gosnell, Official Photographer, B.E.F."

·　·　·

William Hushka, shot by a policeman during the July 28 clash,
lies dying. The strange photo, by
"official" Bonus Army photographer
Eddie Gosnell, was published
four months after the shooting,
with no explanation for the delay.
(*B.E.F., the Whole Story of the
Bonus Army*)

On November 11, J. Edgar Hoover advised Assistant Attorney General Dodds that "various marches" were about to descend on Washington.[52] The Military Intelligence Division put out a call to all corps commanders for reports on marchers. From Kansas City came a secret message saying that the National Guard armory there had been broken into, and seventy-five pistols and two thousand rounds of ammunition had been stolen. "There is good reason to believe," the report said, "that the bulk of these pistols are now in the hands of the 'Bonus elements' of the Bonus, Hunger, and Farm Marchers passing through and starting from the 7th Corps area."[53] Estimates of the number of marchers ran as high as 100,000. At Fort Myer, troops, using tear gas, again staged riot-control drills.[54]

On December 4, about 3,000 marchers from eastern cities, including 200 women but no children, arrived on the outskirts of Washington. Police directed their motorcade to an area along New York Avenue NE, a cul-de-sac that was cordoned off. Police kept them surrounded through the night. A western unit of about 1,700 and a smaller southern group arrived later. People slept in their cars and trucks or on the cold pavement[55] and next day staged a short parade that was hooted at and booed by the police, who kept the marchers under tight control. In their wake, WESL members calling themselves the Radical Bonus Marchers appeared on December 14, claiming to have nearly 500 members scattered around the city. A committee of five met with Vice President Curtis, and when one of them refused to shake his hand, he said, "Well, you can go to the devil!"

In the final Bonus Army event of the year, Representative Louis Thomas McFadden, a Republican from Pennsylvania who had called the eviction "the greatest crime in modern history," stood in the well of the House and began, "Mr. Speaker, I rise to a question of constitutional privilege. On my own responsibility as a member of the House of Representatives, I impeach Herbert Hoover, President of the United States, for high crimes and misdemeanors and offer the following resolution. . . ." As soon as the resolution was read, a Democratic representative moved to table it—to the cheers of the Democrats, who controlled the House. The tabling motion was accepted by a vote of 361 to 8. The eight nay voters included Wright Patman.[56]

At the beginning of 1933, many veterans still banded together against the Depression, clinging to the hope that the bonus could be paid. On a patch of urban wilderness along the Hudson River below Riverside Drive in New York City, about eighty men struggled through the winter in shanties hammered together from crates, sheets of tin, and whatever else could be found in junk piles. They raised a flag each morning, and a bugler blew reveille and taps. These men relied on the sale of pro-bonus literature and begging to stay alive. One of the refugees from Washington became a professional panhandler and later recalled, "I had quite a few steady clients. One of them was Heywood Broun. Every time I'd put the bite on him, he'd say, 'For Chrissake, don't you know any other guy in the city beside me?'"[57]

There were other vets, and some families, in shantytowns in Omaha, Pittsburgh, Detroit, and Cleveland. Most shantytowns had no name, but Chicago's was called Camp Hushka, and near San Antonio, Texas, there was Camp Diga (for Agricultural and Industrial Democracy, spelled backward). Diga was the idea of former first lieutenant and future congressman Maury Maverick, who set it up in an abandoned oil plant. The camp was run as a cooperative with a population of about 160, including wives and children. Families lived in boxcars donated by Missouri Pacific Lines, and meals were cooked on army field stoves salvaged from the trash at Fort Sam Houston.[58]

The year 1933 was only seven days old when Washingtonians learned that the Bonus Army was mustering again. Veterans were already reported assembling in Philadelphia for what appeared to be an advance guard of the march. About two hundred gaunt men did begin the 136-mile walk from Philadelphia, but only six were left when a Washington newspaper reporter found them in Elkridge, Maryland, thirty miles from the capital. Five were sitting on a curb, having a lunch of bread and water, while the sixth stood, clutching a pole on which was hung an American flag. If they ever did reach Washington, their arrival was not noted. Presumably they joined other down-and-outers who were sleeping in Washington flophouses and eating in missions, awaiting the deliverance that the New Deal was expected to bring.[59]

But the news of another Bonus Army was hardly heard over the steady drumbeat that marked time for the coming of Franklin D. Roosevelt. The nation waited impatiently for his inauguration on March 4, the date decreed by the U.S. Constitution.[60]

During the long interregnum, Hoover spent his borrowed time quietly wrangling with Roosevelt, offering his economic ideas to the next president, who politely ignored them while working on how he would produce his New Deal. Adding to the tension of this period was an assassination attempt on President-elect Roosevelt. He had been on a cruise aboard the yacht of his friend Vincent Astor. After the yacht docked in Miami on February 15, Roosevelt headed for Bayfront Park, where he was to make a speech. A short man standing on a wooden chair about twenty-five feet from Roosevelt aimed a .32 caliber pistol he had bought in a Miami pawnshop. As he fired five shots, a woman pushed him. He missed Roosevelt, but his bullets struck five people, including Chicago mayor Anton Cermak, who died two weeks later.[61]

Few Americans noticed and few cared that the bonus marchers might descend again on Washington.[62] Intelligence operatives in the Army and the Department of Justice, however, were gravely concerned; this time the leaders of the veterans were known "radicals," the catchall word that once included Bolsheviks, Communists, and anarchists and now sometimes was extended to American fascists.

The Khaki Shirts, the fascist group that Waters had espoused in Washington in 1932, now had followers in other cities, although Waters was no longer active in the organization.* Art J. Smith, head of a California group that came to Washington, had become the commander in chief of the Khaki Shirts, modeled on Hitler's Black Shirts, Mussolini's Brown Shirts,

---

*Since the exodus of the Bonus Army from Johnstown, little had been heard from Commander in Chief Waters, who had gone into seclusion in Florida. In January 1933, when plans for a new march were reported, he denounced the idea of a return of his army to Washington.

and the Silver Shirt Legion, founded by William Dudley Pelley of Massachusetts. The Khaki Shirts were driven by their leader's belief that fascism was the only way out of the Depression. However, the Khaki Shirts had a streak of the Left, giving as its mission the waging of "relentless war on economic crime, political graft, and judicial corruption," with a special interest in building "the strongest army, navy and air corps in the world" (with the air corps to be a separate service).[63] Smith had founded his version of the Khaki Shirts in Philadelphia, beginning with veterans from that city who had been in the BEF. To show his Khakis' true colors, he also called his organization the U.S. Fascists and at first centered his activities among Philadelphia's Italian immigrants, who idolized Mussolini.[64]

Meanwhile, the Left took hold of plans for the 1933 march through the Veterans National Liaison Committee, which claimed that it had no political affiliations but was a Communist-front organization. One of its members was James Ford, the U.S. Communist Party's candidate for vice president in the 1932 election. (He and presidential candidate William Z. Foster received 103,253 votes.) Other members belonged to the Workers' Ex-Servicemen's League.

The Veterans National Liaison Committee had enough financial backing, from undisclosed sources, to rent an office in a building on Capitol Hill. Members included George Dewey Brady of Newark, New Jersey, who had been the registration officer of the BEF, and delegates from the Khaki Shirts, giving the committee at least the appearance of a broad-based group and not a Communist front.

The committee called the march a "national veterans convention" that would demand the bonus, fight any attempts to cut disability benefits, and seek immediate relief for farmers and the unemployed. The convention was to be held in Washington from May 12 to May 15, which the committee declared "Veterans Justice Day." Notices were sent out to "rank and file" members of the American Legion and other veteran groups.[65]

An Army intelligence report named ninety-six alleged Communists from nineteen states and the District of Columbia who had been given instructions about the planned march. The WESL was no longer a renegade outcast of a Bonus Army. Looking very much in charge, it was raising money for the march by selling five-cent pamphlets, *Veterans, Close Ranks*, which, the report said, called for "payment of the bonus, at the expense of the rich."[66]

While the left-wing group planned the march, John Alferi, the man who carried the title of the first bonus marcher because of his 1931 trip, once more arrived in Washington, but not for another march. He came out against the 1933 march, while praising the 1932 actions of President Hoover and General MacArthur. (He had written Hoover on May 8, saying, "I want you to know that 4,000,000 Veterans would like to have you back as our President."[67]) Alferi, though, was still demanding immediate payment of the bonus.[68]

The Return of the Bonus Army

CAN THERE BE A MORE WORTHY CAUSE?
Let your conscience make the answer
Then we know there'l be no pause.
Help them in their time of trouble
Hear their earnest pleading cry
While others you are aiding
DO NOT PASS THE VETERANS BY.

—Last stanza of a poem sent to Franklin D. Roosevelt
on January 6, 1935, by Nelson E. Lund, USMC 1917–1919

O N MARCH 9, 1933, five days after his inauguration, President Roosevelt called several members of his cabinet and other officials to a White House meeting to discuss an idea he had to put 500,000 young men to work on conservation projects. He said he wanted his idea transformed into the draft of a bill, and he wanted the draft submitted to him that night. At 9:00 P.M. he had the draft. On March 31 the law creating what became known as the Civil Conservation Corps, the CCC, went into effect.

Members of what became known as Roosevelt's Tree Army had to be single men between the ages of eighteen and twenty-five, and willing to go off to work in the woods. They were to be paid $30 a month and had to allot at least $22 to their families; more than 75 percent of them would send home $25 or more. The U.S. Army would run the CCC camps under a civilian administrator. Roosevelt, responding to organized labor's complaints about the $1-a-day pay, gave the administrative job to a union official: Robert Fechner, a vice president of the International Association of Machinists. Fechner, a veteran of the Spanish-American War, had a blue-collar background, unlike most of Roosevelt's "brain trust" advisers. "Most of my clerks are better educated than I am," he said.[1]

The Tree Army was created for young men and felt like a slap in the face to the men of the Bonus Army; obviously too old to qualify, they became the first victims of Roosevelt's war against the Depression.

During his election campaign Roosevelt had promised a balanced budget, and as soon as he became president, he started a process that would eventually produce the balance by slicing $480 million from veterans' benefits. The director of the budget was a Democratic Arizona congressman, Lewis W. Douglas, who had advocated a slash in appropriations for benefits during the Hoover administration. Douglas, millionaire heir of the Phelps Dodge copper mining fortune, resigned from Congress to take the budget post.

Douglas, who had been gassed and decorated for bravery in France, believed, as a veteran, that service in uniform did not guarantee special privileges, especially since veterans garnered 24 percent of the budget while representing only 1 percent of the population. He went to work on Roosevelt's major proposal to Congress, the Economy Act, fashioning the $480 million cut.[2] The act was rushed through Congress and signed by Roosevelt so swiftly that veterans' organizations did not have time to mount a full-scale lobbying campaign against it. Even if they had, Roosevelt's momentum and popularity undoubtedly would have overcome the veterans' lobby. And the national commander of the American Legion, Louis Johnson, backed Roosevelt, saying, "The Legion wants nothing more than to be of service to America in this situation, as our members were in 1917–1918."[3] Johnson, a Washington insider with back channels to the White House, would become assistant secretary of war in 1937.[4]

Too late, lobbyists flooded congressional offices with heart-wrenching stories of veterans hurt by the Economy Act. Arthur Krock, chief Washington correspondent for the *New York Times*, wrote that "down many Main Streets go armless veterans who used to get $94 a month from the Government, and now get $36."[5] Men who had lost two arms, two legs, or two eyes would have their pensions reduced; those with service-related illnesses would lose up to 80 percent of their pensions; veterans with such diseases as tuberculosis and neurosis would lose their entire pensions if their conditions were not un-equivocally connected with their service in uniform.[6]

"I know many many veterans will soon be laid in there [*sic*] graves, death being brought on by the additional worry which is bound to come," an Ohio official of the Disabled American Veterans wrote to a member of Congress, who passed it to the White House.[7] Death did indeed come to troubled veterans. A Philadelphia man killed himself and left a message to President Roosevelt saying that because his benefits were gone, he had no way to provide for his family except through his death, which would give his wife the remaining $275 from his bonus. A patient in a Dayton, Ohio, veterans' hospital killed the chief of the medical staff after being told that because he no longer got a $60 benefit check, he had to leave the hospital.[8]

Reports of suicides poured into congressional offices, and members of Congress began to regret their hasty endorsement of the Economy Act. Roosevelt held firm and appealed to the veterans' patriotism in a special message. "I do not want any veteran to feel that he and his comrades are being singled out to make sacrifices," he said. "On the contrary, I want them to know that the regulations issued are but an integral part of our economy program embracing every department and agency of the government to which every employee is making his or her contribution."[9]

In late April the old BEF reappeared, minus Waters, and an organization calling itself the Veterans' Relief Association claimed that 30,000 veterans were ready to march—both for the bonus and the restoration of benefits.[10]

Four leaders from the 1932 march met in the White House to negotiate with Louis McHenry Howe, Roosevelt's longtime confidant and his principal political adviser. Howe, an ex-newspaperman, had known and counseled Roosevelt when he had been governor and when he had been stricken with polio. No one in the White House in 1933, with the exception of Eleanor Roosevelt, knew Roosevelt better. Mrs. Roosevelt and Howe had formed a bond during her first shaky days after Roosevelt's victory. In a letter to a friend, she had said she "could not live in the White House." Confidentially shown the letter by the friend, Howe had torn it up and thrown it away,[11] then took it upon himself to guide and counsel the woman, who would become the most influential and celebrated First Lady of modern times. The first test of their bond would come with the second bonus march.

Harold B. Foulkrod, formerly the "legislative agent" or chief lobbyist for the BEF, now became the spokesman for the self-anointed BEF leaders. In their public statements, they showed themselves as pro-Roosevelt by sidestepping the hot veterans' benefits topic. They listed their demands as: payment of the bonus immediately to two million unemployed veterans; preference in federal, city, and state jobs for veterans; the immediate removal of General MacArthur as Army chief of staff and Frank T. Hines as administrator of Veterans' Affairs—and the firing of all married women employed by the federal government to make way for veterans.

Foulkrod claimed that four thousand veterans were already in Washington, ready to go "to their tents." But he assured Howe that he and the other leaders would try to hold off their march because of the president's troubles, a tactful reference to the firestorm over Roosevelt's slashing of veterans' benefits. "Mr. Howe told us that he was not in a position to give us an answer today," Foulkrod reported. "He told us to come back in two weeks and therefore we will hold up our plans to move on Washington until after that time. He was very sympathetic with us, but added that nothing is ever accomplished by a club."[12]

Whereas in 1932 legislators favoring the bonus were introducing legislation as the marchers arrived, the 1933 Congress saw itself, in the words of historian Arthur Schlesinger Jr., "staving off violence—even (at least some thought) revolution." In what would become Roosevelt's epic First Hundred Days, from March 9 to June 16, he would send Congress a record number of bills, and, like the vet-targeting Economy Act, all of them would pass.[13] Even such stalwart bonus advocates as Representative Wright Patman and Senator Elmer Thomas joined their colleagues in a congressional statement urging "all buddies who are really sincere and want to see the bonus pass to think carefully before joining any movement which will hurt our cause." The statement urged veterans not to march again.

After learning of the White House meeting, J. Edgar Hoover, director of the Bureau of Investigation, passed on to his new boss, Attorney General Homer Cummings, a warning about Foulkrod, whose past had been only partially revealed the year before.[14] Hoover reported that Foulkrod had five aliases and a criminal record that included convictions for burglary, passing bad checks, and forgery.[15] Oddly, he did not add information about Communist influence on the march. For months Hoover had been aware of plans for a Washington march by Communists. "Organizers of the so-called 'Purple Shirts,'" the "Mystic Multitudes," and 333,000 delegates of the "oppressed people of the Nation" were also planning to descend on the city, Hoover said in one of his reports to Ernest W. Brown, Glassford's successor as Washington's chief of police. Another report told of 473,000 "trained men ready to take action" with their 116 airplanes and 123 machine guns. None of Hoover's reported invaders were ever sighted.[16]

The day after the Foulkrod group met with Howe, the Veterans National Liaison Committee wrote to President Roosevelt, "Large groups of veterans are now en route, and thousands more are preparing for the trip to Washington and will arrive on or about May 12th." Howe invited the committee to the White House even though MID reports had identified the committee as a Communist front. Emanuel Levin, while admitting he was a Communist, tried to show Howe they were not a gang of Reds. He introduced the men in this way: George Dewey Brady, a Democrat, a Catholic, and the father of two children, was named after the great American hero Admiral George Dewey. Edward J. Williams voted Democrat, was the father of two children, and was active in relief work for Disabled American Veterans. Harold Hickerson was the father of one child in a family whose menfolk had fought in the Revolution, on both sides of the Civil War, and in every war since. Hickerson was also the coauthor, with Maxwell Anderson, of a Broadway play.[17]

Several meetings were held over the next few days. At one point, Frank T. Hines, administrator of Veterans' Affairs, was called in. He began by saying he hoped that they would not "get tied up with that terrible fellow, Levin." Williams interrupted Hines to say, "General, we took that bull by the horns six months ago. Let me introduce you to Mr. Levin. He sits right here." Hines, a consummate politician, turned to Levin and remarked on how the press "distorts a person's reputation."[18]

So Howe found himself involved with two bonus marches—one obviously from the Left, and one that would soon evolve into a right-wing group. In 1932 Police Chief Glassford had dealt directly with Waters and other march leaders, including Communists. Now Glassford was gone, and there was no one to stand between the White House and the rival planners of the second bonus march. Howe—and ultimately Roosevelt—decided to bestow extraordinary privileges on Levin's Veterans National Liaison Committee, which started calling itself the Veterans Expeditionary Force, the VEF.[19]

Howe, certainly with Roosevelt's blessings, had allied the administration with Levin's group, despite the fact that Levin was a Communist and not a veteran of the Great War. The Navy Department made public records that showed Levin had served in the Marine Corps, albeit before the war. According to the records, he was born in Russia on November 10, 1884, and had been living in Cleveland when he enlisted in the Marines on May 9, 1906. He was discharged on May 8, 1910, and enlisted again on November 29, 1915, but he had secured a "purchase discharge"—meaning that he had been able to end his enlistment by paying an undisclosed sum—on March 24, 1916, saying that his mother had died of tuberculosis and he had to take care of his sisters.[20] Even though it was a matter of public record, the Navy's revelation was largely forgotten; most accounts referred to Levin as a veteran, implying he was a veteran of the Great War. Unlike Foulkrod's BEF, which was composed of veterans of the Great War, the VEF admitted any veteran or dependent with a grievance.[21]

Howe, willing to face criticism from anti-Communists, decided to accept the VEF's agenda for a national veterans' convention and began making plans to feed and shelter about 9,000 veterans at Fort Hunt, an old abandoned Army post that had been the site of an Army field hospital that cared for bonus marchers in 1932.[22] As for the cost, word leaked that Wright Patman— even though he had said he opposed a second march—had introduced a congressional resolution drawing expenses for the convention from a fund that Congress had authorized in 1932 to pay for a Washington reception for French veterans that had never been held. The expenses included free bus transportation between downtown Washington and Fort Hunt.[23]

On Thursday, May 9, 1933, Washingtonians, begrudging hosts for another bonus march, once again saw U.S. Army troops moving into the city. This time, however, the fifteen army trucks, escorted by police motorcycles, kept on moving, crossing the Potomac on the Arlington Memorial Bridge into Virginia and heading down the George Washington Memorial Parkway to Fort Hunt.

At first, neither the White House nor the Army would disclose why the trucks, carrying a company of infantry—about 230 men—had traveled from Fort Meade to Fort Hunt. Soon, though, Washingtonians learned that Louis Howe[24] had selected Fort Hunt as the place where the second march would be housed. The Fort Meade infantryman would put up a tent city for the 8,700 VEF veterans expected for their national convention, which was to begin on Saturday, May 11. The precise number came from a political move that had a Howe look to it: the White House–VEF agreement called for twenty men from each of the 435 congressional districts. Foulkrod, seeing that his men were not included in the agreement, demanded that his thousands of followers get their own food and shelter.[25] But in a statement printed on a White House mimeograph machine and distributed by Levin's committee, it was quite obvious that the food and shelter would go only to "properly accredited delegates"—and Levin's group was doing the accreditation.

Foulkrod said that 4,000 "right-wing" veterans were on the march from

Baltimore. George Alman assembled 1,000 men in New York City, and one of them said, "No matter how many police are in front of the White House, we will walk in." Five hundred VEF members were reported on their way from Chicago, and 150 more from Indianapolis.[26] The stage was being set for a confrontation between the Left and the Right, for the White House agreement covered only the VEF.

While the troops were putting up tents and setting up field kitchens at Fort Hunt, Washington police cleared the city of crooks, robbers, and agitators. Some fifty "undesirables" were rounded up and "held for investigation." Under the White House–VEF agreement, tents were set up on Pennsylvania Avenue near Sixth Street NW—a few blocks from the spot where Hushka and Carlson had been killed—for the registration of accredited veterans. They were to have their convention at the Washington Auditorium on Saturday, May 11, and leave the city on May 19. Only VEF members would be admitted to the convention.

Veterans Bureau buses or army trucks took the registered members to Fort Hunt, where they found a tent city laid out in company streets of forty tents each. The eight-man tents had electric lights, and at the end of each street were sinks and running water. Army cooks worked in field kitchens and served the meals on mess kits issued to each camp guest. Latrines had been dug by infantrymen from Fort Meade. There was a large tent, with loudspeakers, for meetings. Overlooking the Potomac River was a bathhouse with one hundred showers. Fort Meade troops patrolled the perimeter of the camp—and dozens of Virginia state troopers were strung around the sovereign soil of Virginia beyond the camp. The governor of Virginia said that nearby citizens were fearful, and he wanted to make sure that when the vets left, they would not threaten the Old Dominion.[27]

Instead of the club-carrying MPs of Commander in Chief Waters's days, men assigned to a "safety committee" walked around wearing blue armbands marked "SC." Instead of boot-wearing officers with assumed military ranks, there were "committeemen" and elected "street leaders." On a typical day the men had oranges, eggs, potatoes, bread, butter, and coffee for breakfast; a lunch of baked ham, potatoes, peas, rice pudding, bread, butter, and coffee; and a supper of sliced bologna, potato salad, apple butter, bread, and coffee.

The first group of about two hundred BEF veterans arrived in a rainstorm on May 10. Wet, ragged, and angry, they set up a soggy camp on Capitol Hill in a vacant lot that was used as a neighborhood dump. They built a large campfire, and through its flames and smoke could be seen the dome of the Capitol. Foulkrod and his aides said they would go to the White House and demand separate—and presumably equal—accommodations for their right-wingers.[28]

The men awoke to find themselves being ogled by staffers in the nearby House Office Building. Ordered to leave, the vets stumbled off in columns of four and were taken, under police escort, down Capitol Hill to a park near the Botanical Gardens. Like an apparition from the past, Pelham Glassford appeared before them and told them they had been "duped by Levin and his crowd" into coming to Washington. Glassford's words fell on rain-soaked ears, and the veterans paid him little heed. But during the day, about half of the BEF contingent drifted away, presumably to their homes or to the open road.[29] (Waters also was reported to be in Washington, but his presence had no effect whatsoever on what was happening.[30])

Later, when BEF veterans did go to the White House, Foulkrod was not among them; Howe, apparently acting on J. Edgar Hoover's information, had decided that he would meet only with men who held honorable discharges. The White House tried to get the 200 or so right-wingers to agree to go to Fort Hunt, where 1,110 of Levin's men were living.[31] Talks dragged on while the right-wing veterans, dogged by police, wandered Washington in search of a place to call their own. Believed to be among the right-wingers was Eddie Gosnell, the poet-photographer who had snapped the controversial death photo of William Hushka during the violence the year before. Gosnell, who had the only photographic negative of Hushka's killing, said he had other photographs and documents that would embarrass people connected with the march.[32]

Thanks to Howe's extensive experience with thorny Albany politics, a solution was found to the Left/Right impasse. Levin and Harold Hickerson resigned. Foulkrod was ousted in an election. Under a new leader, the BEF agreed to join the VEF in Fort Hunt. But about twenty-five right-wingers refused to go to the camp. They headed off to find sympathizers in Washington, led by a Brooklyn vet who had deserted the VEF, saying he would rather "die in the mud" than remain with the Reds of Fort Hunt.[33]

Henry Meisel, who had arrived at the first bonus march on a motorcycle, got to the 1933 event by riding in boxcars and talking his way onto airplanes. After landing at Washington-Hoover Airport,* he hitchhiked to Fort Hunt, arriving just in time for supper. He was fed, but because he was unregistered, he had to take a free bus back to Washington. He returned to the camp by bus

---

*Hoover Field, located near the present-day site of the Pentagon, was the capital's first major air terminal. In 1930 it merged with Washington Airport.

and ate a second supper. Meisel's tent was in what he called the neutral ground between the two factions. Meisel disliked the dull-bladed razor he had been issued, so he took the bus into Washington and picked up his safety razor and camera at the office of his congressman, Gerald J. Boileau, a Republican and a veteran, to whom Meisel had forwarded them. He lingered in Boileau's office, discussing the bonus and other matters, then returned to the fort, where the food was "very wholesome" and came with extra helpings.[34]

The convention, which originally had been the object of the VEF march, produced shouting matches as the two groups collided in debate. There was also a parade of exactly 626 veterans—"there were almost as many police and detectives following the parade as there were veterans in it," according to Meisel. The parade passed the White House, where a petition for the bonus was presented, and the Capitol, where no petition could be presented because Congress had adjourned for the day.[35]

The most dramatic event came at the camp, in a carefully orchestrated public relations move by the White House.

"Go out and see the men at the camp," President Roosevelt had told Howe.

Members of the 1933 bonus march were housed by the government in tents at Fort Hunt in Virginia near Mount Vernon. They were well fed, provided with unlimited amounts of coffee, and were honored with a visit from the new First Lady, Eleanor Roosevelt; but they got no further than their predecessors in gaining the bonus. (Authors' collection)

"See that they have good food and shelter and above all good, hot coffee to drink. There's nothing that makes people feel as welcome as a steaming cup of coffee."

Howe asked Mrs. Roosevelt to take him for a drive into the Virginia countryside. He directed her to a road that led to Fort Hunt.

"Louis! What is this place and what are we going to do here?" she asked.

"This is where the Bonus Army is quartered," he answered, "and you are going in there and talk to those men, get their gripes, if any, make a tour of the camp and tell them that Franklin sent you out to see about them. Don't forget that—be sure to tell them that Franklin sent you. Inspect their quarters and get the complete story."

"But, Louis, what are you going to do?"

"Me? I'm going to take a nap," he said, curling up in the seat of her red roadster.

Stepping onto the muddy road, Mrs. Roosevelt made her debut as an active-duty First Lady.[36]

Mrs. Roosevelt did what Howe told her, adding her own touches, as she would do throughout her career as First Lady. She made a little speech about her own work as a volunteer in the war, had coffee with the men, and led them in a wartime favorite, "There's a Long, Long Trail a'Winding." There was not much to the visit itself, but it produced a grace note that summed up President Roosevelt's masterful handling of the veterans. He did not back the bonus. He was still holding firm about the cut in veterans' benefits. Yet, at no cost to the budget, he had won them over. As a vet said as Mrs. Roosevelt was leaving, "Hoover sent the army. Roosevelt sent his wife."[37]

Roosevelt found a way to give something to the 1933 bonus marchers while still opposing the bonus. He issued an executive order that authorized the enrollment of about 25,000 veterans of the Great War *and* the Spanish-American War in the CCC, waiving age and marital restrictions. There were gripes—"Not for me. It's like selling yourself into slavery," one vet said. And many cheered when a VEF leader shouted, "To hell with reforestation!"[38] But more than 2,500 signed up immediately, crowding around tables set up for their enlistment into the Tree Army. About 700 veterans turned down the CCC job offer but accepted free transportation home, paid for out of the same French reception fund that had financed the Fort Hunt encampment.[39]

In the wake of the march came a sinister and mysterious event. Eddie Gosnell died early on Memorial Day, and members of the right-wing group charged that suspicious circumstances surrounded his death. Washington police said that Gosnell's death was a suicide by self-administered poison in a furnished room he had rented sometime before. But two veterans said that just before he was taken to a hospital, feverish and writhing in agony, they had given him a telephone message from an unidentified foe. "Tell him I'll see him in hell," Gosnell said. He told another friend that he feared for his life and had twice been attacked.

A member of the right-wing group began an investigation, claiming that Gosnell had been driven to his death by unnamed persecutors. Nothing came of the private investigation, and the mystery lingered on; Gosnell's photos and documents never surfaced. Investigators did, however, learn that Gosnell was not his name. He was buried with full military honors at Arlington National Cemetery under his real name, Edward Steinkraus, after two ex-wives approved.[40]*

In Philadelphia in June 1933, the Khaki Shirts fought a street battle with local Communists. One of Art Smith's fascists was killed; Smith staged a well-publicized funeral, claiming that he had a well-armed army of millions.

Rumors swirled around the city that Smith planned to take over the National Guard arsenal in a plot to seize Philadelphia on Columbus Day, 1933. Police struck first, raiding Khaki Shirts headquarters and seizing a number of weapons. Eventually Smith disappeared with $25,000 in Khaki Shirts funds, but his organization lived on to become part of the Christian Front, a notorious anti-Semitic, pro-Nazi organization.

Although it would not be declared publicly until later, General Smedley Darlington Butler, the bonus marchers' comrade in Camp Marks days, claimed that he had been asked to lead an army of veterans in a coup d'état at this same time. The plotters, Butler said, were powerful businessmen who wanted to get rid of Roosevelt before he had a chance to run for a second term.

It had all begun in the summer of 1933, Butler said, when he had been asked by Gerald MacGuire, a Wall Street bond trader, to speak out for the gold standard, which President Roosevelt had abandoned soon after taking office, believing that a flexible dollar, rather than one based on gold, was the key to recovery from the Depression. MacGuire, according to Butler, tied a

---

*A year later the final words were published on Gosnell's death with the publication of Jack Douglas's *Veterans on the March:* "Still another mystery was the killing a year later, of Eddie Gosnell . . . who had gotten a picture of Hushka just after the murder and other 'intimate' pictures many of which later disappeared. He died after drinking acid. It was said he took it by mistake while drinking. Intimate friends of Gosnell's said he never drank intoxicants of any kind" (235).

back-to-gold campaign to the bonus, saying that his group wanted the bonus paid in gold-backed money.[41]

MacGuire, Butler said, represented powerful Wall Street financiers, including Robert Sterling Clark, heir to the Singer sewing machine fortune, and Grayson Murphy, a director of the Guaranty Trust Company, a wealthy stockbroker and, as an officer in the Great War, one of the founders of the American Legion. They were, MacGuire said, among the financial backers of a "superorganization" that would be unveiled shortly.

Butler said he soon learned that MacGuire and the financiers he claimed to represent wanted more from him than merely some lobbying for a bonus paid in gold. Butler said he was asked to lead an army of 500,000 veterans to Washington as part of a coup to take over the government. Butler warned James E. Van Zandt, national commander of the Veterans of Foreign Wars, that he would be approached. And when Butler spoke out about the plot, Van Zandt revealed that he had also met with MacGuire. Van Zandt quoted MacGuire as saying his group wanted "to get rid of this fellow in the White House."[42]

The superorganization that MacGuire had foreseen in his talks with Butler did emerge, strengthening Butler's belief in the plot. It was the American Liberty League, whose members included Duponts, other wealthy supporters, and conservative Democrats who opposed Roosevelt.[43] MacGuire had also accurately predicted that Roosevelt would soon get rid of General Hugh Johnson, head of the National Recovery Administration. MacGuire's gift of political prophecy convinced Butler that he had inside knowledge, and, in Butler's mind, this gave credence to the plot. Butler insisted that he objected to the plot, reporting that he had finally told MacGuire: "If you get these 500,000 soldiers advocating anything smelling of fascism, I am going to get 500,000 more and lick the hell out of you, and we will have a real war right at home."[44]

As with the Khaki Shirts, America's flirtation with fascism simply faded away; by the time Butler told his story to a new congressional committee, formed to investigate Nazi activities in the United States, it had little impact.*[45]

---

*The committee was cochaired by Representative John McCormack of Massachusetts and Representative Samuel Dickstein of New York. Testifying before the committee, MacGuire denied the plot, saying that he had been merely lobbying for the gold standard. What would be called the McCormack-Dickstein Committee and eventually the House Un-American Activities Committee issued a relatively mild report in November 1934. McCormack said he would return to an investigation of the plot in the future, but questions about the plot's scope and the plotters' identities remained unanswered. The committee turned to other matters in the wake of MacGuire's death and a lack of interest on the part of the press and the Roosevelt White House.

When a much smaller contingent of bonus marchers arrived in the spring of 1934, they seemed to epitomize a lost cause. Many of these men would end up in veterans' rehabilitation camps in Florida and the Carolinas. (Authors' collection)

The same could not be said of those demanding cash payment of the bonus, which continued to bedevil the Roosevelt administration.

On March 16, 1934, Louis Howe wrote to the Office of the Adjutant General to say that he had information from CCC Camp 375 in Virginia that veterans there were planning a march to Washington to protest the end of their one-year enlistments. Fechner, director of the Office of Emergency Conservation Work (the official name for the administrator of the CCC), also told Army officials that members of the Communist-led Veterans National Rank and File Committee were "urging a militant action on the part of the veterans for a Bonus March." The commanding officer of a CCC camp in Tolland, Connecticut, sent the adjutant general the names of veterans "who have been identified with agitation" and who were involved in the 1933 march.[46]

A third bonus march was just over the horizon, and as in 1932, Congress was looking at a bonus bill. Wright Patman had introduced it as soon as Congress reconvened in January 1934. It was stalled in committee because, as everyone knew, if it reached the floor for a vote, anyone in favor would be defying Roosevelt—and if by some miracle it passed, he would veto it. In a "Dear Henry" letter to Speaker of the House Henry T. Rainey, Roosevelt had said he would veto any bonus bill, "and I don't care who you tell this to."[47]

In an election year for all of them, members of Congress were well aware that a vote against the veterans could mean no votes from veterans in November. Van Zandt telegraphed the president, urging him to "make public your objections . . . in fairness to approximately three and one half million veterans who believe they have been made victims of discrimination."[48] The House voted Patman's bill out of committee, then passed it in a wild debate and sent it to the Senate, knowing the senators would not challenge Roosevelt.[49]

Bonus marchers came back on the Washington stage in the spring of 1934, joining those transients who had remained in the city from previous marches. They had no more chance of getting a bonus from Roosevelt than from Hoover. When Roosevelt pushed through Congress the Economy Act, slashing veterans' benefits, he had simultaneously offset the budget savings by getting from Congress the Federal Emergency Relief Administration (FERA), launched with $500 million from the Reconstruction Finance Corporation, created by President Hoover primarily to help banks and corporations. FERA would give federal grants to states for relief to needy citizens, especially the unemployed. Harry Hopkins, a career welfare worker who had been the head of Governor Roosevelt's New York State relief organization, was given the job of running FERA,[50] and he decided to use FERA funds for the lackluster bonus march of 1934.

Hopkins directed what was essentially a replay of 1933: an encampment at Fort Hunt and a convention, where veterans could talk and pass resolutions. Back for another visit was John Alferi, the self-proclaimed "one-man bonus army" who urged the 1934 marchers to be orderly lest they be seen as "a bunch of bums and troublemakers."[51] Alferi, who in 1933 had praised ex-president Hoover, changed his mind and now believed that if President Roosevelt "keeps up his good work, he will be reelected for twenty years more."[52]

This time the WESL claimed a membership of only 127 of the 1,500 veterans accommodated at Fort Hunt. But the left wing dominated the convention. Levin and Hickerson were back, and they invited Communist Party candidate James W. Ford. "Keep away from the CCC camps. They are the forerunner of Fascism," Ford had advised the delegates. Fort Hunt was, in fact, a CCC camp. In 1933 many of the first veterans had begun their Tree Army stints there, and Fort Hunt had been officially handed over to the CCC.[53] This time, nearly 600 men signed up for the CCC, but only about half were accepted, probably because recruiters knew about Robert Fechner's attitude toward vets in the CCC.

In a letter to Louis Howe, Fechner had said, "It is my opinion that a feeling generally prevails among War Veterans throughout the country that if a sufficient number of them congregate in Washington they can get almost anything they demand so far as the CCC is concerned."[54] Fechner obviously disliked the idea of mixing worn-out veterans in their forties with the energetic youngsters who were making the CCC one of the administration's most popular creations. In the glowing official accounts of CCC accomplishments, the veterans were hardly mentioned.

Hopkins apparently shared Fechner's sentiments, for he seems to have decided that there would never again be a bonus march. He had set up FERA transient camps in nearly every state to handle the swarms of men, women, and children wandering America's highways and railways. Hopkins's Federal Transient Bureau in 1933 estimated that there were between 1 and 1.25 million transient and homeless persons in the United States. Other, unofficial estimates put the total as high as 5 million.[55]

Many of the transient camps were at the bases of the U.S. Army, which, suffering from Depression budget cuts, welcomed the chance to find a use for its vacant buildings. Fort Eustis, Virginia, near Norfolk, for example, housed more than 3,600 men in 1933. They worked a five-and-a-half-hour day, with half of Saturday and all day Sunday free. Among the jobs was setting traps for animals with marketable pelts and growing cabbage, which was made into sauerkraut for other camps. Besides getting food and shelter, they got work clothes and $1 a week.

White and black campers were segregated, which was typical in transient camps,[56] as it was in CCC camps. Segregation in CCC camps and the failure to promote black enrollees led to complaints from African-Americans, particularly officials of the NAACP. In one case the NAACP intervened to obtain an honorable discharge for a Harlem youth who was dishonorably discharged after refusing to fan flies away from a white Army officer at a CCC in New Jersey.[57] Roosevelt himself, in a handwritten note to Fechner, said, "In the CCC Camps, where the boys are colored, in the Park Service work, please try to put in colored foremen, not of course in technical work but in the ordinary manual work."[58]

Writing to Senator Robert J. Bulkley of Ohio in 1936, Fechner said, "Whether we like it or not, we cannot close our eyes to the fact that there are communities and States that do not want and will not accept a Negro Civilian Conservation Corps company." In one place, "When the citizens of the community learned that a Negro company was to be sent to the camp, they absolutely refused to permit the company to occupy the camp and we were forced to completely abandon the project. I therefore adopted the policy of having our representatives consult with the Governor of the State before attempting to assign a Negro Company to any locality."[59]

The transient camps solved a larger problem of homelessness, but did not specifically address the pesky issue of the veterans still showing up in Washington to submit their bonus demands. Many found themselves at a house at 2626 Pennsylvania Avenue, where they could get a free meal, a place to sleep, and, if needed, legal advice.

For the leaders of the New Deal, this small group—most of whom had been driven out in 1932—was a constant reminder that the very men who had served in the defeat of Herbert Hoover were now in a position to create great damage to an administration that would be seeking a second term one year later.

Hopkins came up with a plan, based on the model of the transient camps but totally separate from them. As veterans straggled into their Washington refuge, a mere eight blocks down Pennsylvania Avenue from the White House, they were given passage to special Veterans Rehabilitation Camps, where they could be put to work as FERA employees at a dollar a day. From the outset these camps would be entirely separated from the CCC camps now being filled by much younger men. President Roosevelt approved the plan, and on October 12, 1934, the first veterans were shipped south.

Some of the vets in Washington agreed to be shipped to camps in South Carolina. Others accepted shipment to Florida, where they would go into a period of "conditioning" at a FERA transient camp and then to Fort Jefferson, once the prison for Lincoln assassination conspirators, on the remote island of Dry Tortugas, south of the Florida Keys. The fort, said to be badly in need of repair, would give the vets work far from Washington. The first three hundred bonus marchers were sent to the Jacksonville camp awaiting shipment to Dry Tortugas, but the transfer of responsibility for Fort Jefferson from the Navy to the Interior Department was taking longer than expected.* Then, on October 18, 1934, their mission was changed. They would be sent to camps in Florida's Upper Keys, where they would work on a road construction project that would link the Upper Keys to Key West.[60]

On January 4, 1935, President Roosevelt alighted from his car and began entering the U.S. Capitol by way of a passage cleared in the crowd waiting to greet him. He was to deliver his opening message to the Seventy-fourth Congress. A large man with heavy black stubble, dressed in a ragged coat and a muffler made from a blanket, jumped out in front of Roosevelt, his right arm raised in a gesture that a reporter on the scene said "might have appeared violent but was meant to be arresting."

---

*By December 1934 the Dry Tortugas started being used as a penal colony for vets accused of "drunkenness, insubordination and theft."

In a deep, heavily accented voice, the man bellowed, "Hol' on there—waita that min, Mr. President! How about the bonus?"

In the instant between his statement and what would have been certain death from the guns of the Secret Service and police, he identified himself as John Alferi, the head of the 1931 bonus march. This was his fourth trip to Washington to demand his bonus. He was well known to the police as a "sore thumb," a persistent but harmless pest. Alferi, forty-five years old, was quickly wrestled to the ground and dragged away to a room in the Capitol. When he was searched, all that was found was a ragged honorable discharge, some news clipping from his previous trips, his bonus certificate, and a pass for the opening of Congress and the president's message. The pass had been given to him by Senator Huey Long's office, but the guards had refused to seat him, presumably because he had made such a pest of himself lobbying individual members of Congress, and it was feared that he would disrupt the president's speech.[61]

Deemed not to be a threat by the authorities, Alferi was discharged and told to go home; but he and the five men he brought with him—all veterans of the 1932 march—demonstrated that the bonus was still a very live issue and that, in the person of a veteran willing to risk his life to confront the president, it was now Roosevelt's issue.[62] A week before the Alferi confrontation, the president had replied to the head of an American Legion post in Henderson, Texas, who had asked him to support immediate payment. Roosevelt stated in a letter, released to the press for publication on New Year's Day, that he opposed the bonus for a host of reasons, including his belief that the bonus was the only life insurance that many of the veterans had and that, of the 3,500,000 veterans who had been issued certificates, 3,038,500 of them had borrowed against them from the U.S. Treasury.[63]

Suddenly, the bonus had little to do with Republicans—Hoover, Coolidge, Harding, or Mellon. Now it was an old albatross hanging from the neck of the New Deal. The now familiar Patman Bill demanding immediate payment of the bonus, resubmitted for the sixth time in January 1935, sailed through the House. The vote brought renewed hope to veterans—especially those in the rehab camps in the Carolinas and the Florida Keys, where there had been reports of recent trouble.

Labor Day Hurricane

The Unknown soldier? Not at Arlington,
But forgotten at Matecumbe Key;
Not crosses row on row in Flanders fields,
But bodies row on row at Matecumbe.

Just bums you say? the flower
Of the nation when they marched away
The Bonus Bill? Death signed it,
But it's hell to pay!

Literally, now the stench of the nation,
Raises to high heaven!
My God! can prosperity ever come
To a nation so forgetful,
So bereft of love for its native sons?

—Last three stanzas of an unsigned poem, "To My
    Buddies at Matecumbe Key," found in a scrapbook of
    hurricane material at the Helen Wadley Branch of the
    Monroe Public Library, Islamorada, Florida.

THE GREAT DEPRESSION had forced the county containing the Florida Keys into total bankruptcy, and the man handed the job of solving the problem was Julius Stone Jr., who had run New York State's welfare program under Governor Franklin D. Roosevelt.

Beginning in March 1934, when he arrived in Key West, Stone planned to take the crumbling town and restore it to an earlier state of prosperity by making it a major tourist destination. The city was unable to pay police, fire, and sanitation workers; 80 percent of the local residents were on welfare, and the per capita monthly income was $7. Things had become so bad that before Stone came up with the option of tourism, there was serious talk of abandoning the place—removing the residents of the city to a place where there were jobs (Tampa was mentioned) and then closing down the local government. As late as July 1934 Key West was in such a dire state of emergency that the mayor and county commissioners turned over all their legal powers to the governor. The reason was expressed in a headline in the *St. Petersburg Evening Independent* of July 5, 1934: "Key West People Face Starvation, Governor Is Told."[1]

The governor immediately passed the affairs of Key West and Monroe County to FERA in the person of Stone, who was given 2 million New Deal dollars and czarlike powers to transform Key West into what he predicted would become "The Bermuda of Florida."[2]

To make the plan work, automobile traffic had to move more smoothly; the car ferries that linked the Florida Keys would have to be replaced with highway bridges. The bonus veterans who had been sent from New Deal Washington for "rehabilitation" were first sent to Jacksonville and then assigned to work camps along the Upper Keys. The greatest concentration of vets was on Lower and Upper Matecumbe Keys. The first fifty bonus vets arrived at the work sites in early November 1934, and by the beginning of 1935 there were seven hundred men in three work camps. Camp 1, the northernmost, was on Windley Key, sometimes referred to as Upper Matecumbe Key, seventy-eight miles south of Miami; Camp 5, at the northern end of Lower Matecumbe Key, was about eight miles south of Camp 1 and four miles north of Camp 3 at the end of the Key. Headquarters for all camps was at what had been the Matecumbe Hotel on Windley Key. The men were housed in tents and quickly constructed barracks, mostly at the water's edge, that could be taken down and moved as the roadwork and bridge building progressed southward toward Key West.

New Deal planners thought they had finally found a way to end the problem presented by the wandering remnants of the original Bonus Army. But not everyone was happy with the solution. Ernest Hemingway was particularly angry at what was happening to Key West under the directorship of Stone. Hemingway, a Republican, did not like the government, especially the New Deal under Roosevelt, whom Hemingway termed "the Paralytic Demagogue."

In order to attract more tourists, Stone organized a massive force of four thousand local volunteers who were to spruce up the town, put in a sewer system, rid Key West of outhouses, renovate more than two hundred guest houses and one major hotel, and bring in theater groups and other cultural attractions. Trash disappeared as flower gardens were planted. The jobless were hired to catch stray dogs and cats, which were exterminated.[3]

Stone also published a list of forty-eight local sights of interest, including, as number eighteen on the list, Hemingway's home on Whitehead Street. This attracted gawkers who would peer in his window and—thinking it was an official attraction—occasionally walk right into the house. An infuriated Hemingway had a brick wall six feet high built around the house.[4]

Stone ruled with an iron hand; as a New Deal social engineer, he was Hemingway's antithesis. On August 26, for example, under Stone's plan to make Key West a unique tourist experience, tipping was banned in Key West. There were fines for anyone who disobeyed. Signs were posted in all bars, restaurants, and hotels prior to Labor Day weekend.[5]

Through tourism, to Hemingway's great dismay, the inexorable climb out of decay and despondency had begun, and the place that he called the "St. Tropez of the Poor" started to see an influx of tourists—forty thousand would arrive by the end of 1935. Hemingway's anger at Stone was mitigated to a small degree by the Bonus Army vets who came down from the Upper Keys for recreation. Hemingway drank with them at Josie Russell's Bar, where they sat together and admired the great mural depicting General Custer and the Battle of Little Big Horn that adorned the bar.

Hemingway himself was a veteran. Turned down by the Army because of poor eyesight, eighteen-year-old Ernest had volunteered as a Red Cross ambulance driver. On July 8, 1918, while he was passing out chocolate candy, postcards, and cigarettes to Italian soldiers on the Italian front, an Austrian shell loaded with steel fragments and metal junk exploded a few feet away from Hemingway, killing one soldier, amputating the legs of another, wounding a third, and leaving Hemingway temporarily unconscious. Numerous pieces of metal had torn into his lower body, with the greatest damage to the right knee and foot. Despite the wounds, he dragged at least one of the wounded Italians to the trenches and was hit by a few machine-gun bullets along the way. In a letter to his parents he said that the bullets "felt like a sharp smack on the leg with an icy snow ball." At the hospital they tallied the number of fragments taken out of his body, and in another letter home he said, "My wounds were now hurting like 227 little devils driving nails into the raw."[6] There was talk of amputation, but Hemingway insisted instead on

A young Ernest Hemingway recovering from his wounds of July 8, 1918, in the Ospedale Croce Rossa Americana in Milano. This experience would not only help shape him as a writer but give him empathy for war veterans. (Hemingway Collection/ J. F. Kennedy Library)

removing all the fragments—*scaggia*—some of which he excised himself with the aid of a penknife and a swig of cognac, a procedure he would describe many times, often within earshot of reporters.[7]

He talked with the bonus vets about their shared war experiences and was inspired by them, turning them into characters who would end up in his Harry Morgan stories and in the novel *To Have and Have Not*. One day he came into the bar and was hailed by one of the vets who had a broken leg and had seated himself on a billiard table with a pair of crutches. The drunken vet's diversion for the day was to call a bar patron over, engage him in conversation, and then knock him out with a swift swing of a crutch. Three unsuspecting patrons had already fallen; Hemingway, forewarned, stayed clear of the crutch. This and scenes like it allowed Hemingway, in the words of his biographer, Carlos Baker, to "invent one of the most effective episodes in the novel."[8]

In early February 1935 the veterans in the Florida camps got paid for the first time in many weeks. Some vets drove to Key West and Miami in private automobiles. For those left in the camps, a small army of bootleggers showed up to sell illegal rotgut whiskey for $1.50 a pint, and a group of prostitutes arrived in the *Showboat*. The combination was deadly; in the words of the *Washington Post*'s Edward T. Folliard, a "booze rampage" began as the women, clutching "chunks of FERA cash," departed. The boozing, which lasted for about three days, was topped off by a wildcat strike in Camp 3 in Lower Matecumbe. "I have been in Port Said and that is supposed to be the toughest town on earth. I have been in the Bowery in New York and on West Madison Street in Chicago," said Bill Bevans, a veteran who arrived in the camp on the notorious payday and was Folliard's sole source for the story. "I have seen some pretty bad brawls, but man alive, I never saw anything like I saw down here." Folliard, who noted that 80 percent of the men in these "transplanted bonus camps" were expelled from Washington in 1932, said what they talked about "above all else" was the bonus.

Folliard's story, read with special interest in New Deal Washington, failed to report on the reality of the miserable camps and the fact that the men had serious grievances, as shown in a telegram, dated January 9, 1935, that landed on Louis Howe's desk: TWO HUNDRED VETERANS MEMBERS VETERANS REHABILITATION CAMP ONE, ISLAMORADA, FLORIDA WILL LEAVE FOR WASHINGTON UNLESS CONDITIONS ARE REMEDIED WITHIN OUR CAMP IMMEDIATELY. CONDITIONS DESPERATE. PETITION FOLLOWS WITH TWO HUNDRED SIGNATURES. SUGGEST DEPARTMENT OF JUSTICE INVESTIGATE.

The telegram was signed by four men in Camp 1. There is no record that it was answered. The strike that Folliard alluded to was called primarily to protest bad sanitary conditions, such as one water dipper in a camp for 425 men. The strike intensified when its leaders were driven out of camp for insubordination; it lasted for two weeks, and was quickly followed by another on February 22. Four new delegates were invited to meet with camp commanders to discuss sanitary conditions—and did not return. The vets believed their representatives had been arrested and "shanghaied" to Miami. On February 28 they presented a set of demands and told FERA to comply by 9:00 A.M. the next day, "or else." FERA took those two words to mean violence and sabotage. The National Guard was brought in immediately. Guardsmen cut off all communications between camps and between veterans and reporters. Stone blamed the strikes on "Reds" and agitators from Baltimore, two of whom he was holding in a Key West jail.[9] The men finally returned to work on March 4 after a weekend of leave.

When Stone called on FERA in Washington for help, officials sent him the agency's top troubleshooter, Captain William Hinchman, who improved sanitary conditions, got uniforms for the vets, created baseball and volleyball leagues, and allowed the vets to start their own newspaper—the *Key Veteran News,* the first issue of which lambasted the *Washington Post* for a garbled account of what really was going on in the camps.

. . .

Roosevelt, determined to block Patman's 1935 version of the bonus bill, began his lobbying against it a month before it landed on his desk. It was a foregone conclusion that both houses would pass the bill. Now it was up to Roosevelt to veto it, and for a host of reasons—ranging from the issue of consistency to the strain the bonus would put on the Treasury—he wanted the veto to stick. This would not be easy. The 1934 congressional elections had brought a new wave of pro-bonus legislators. Of 108 new members of the House, 91 were in favor of the bonus.[10]

An exchange of letters in mid-March between Democratic Representative E. W. Marland of Oklahoma and the president made it clear that Roosevelt had personal as well as fiscal reasons for opposing immediate payment. Marland argued that the bonus was a "long overdue debt" owed the men who had fought. During the war, he said, he had employed common laborers to dig ditches for $5 a day while providing them with food, lodging, and medical insurance. "Many of my employees enlisted, or were drafted, and went to France where they received only a fraction of the pay given common labor at home in less arduous and less hazardous occupations."

"You have given me a personal example," Roosevelt responded. "Here is mine to counterbalance it: from my own home county hundreds of men and women moved to munitions factory towns in 1917. They worked in these towns, in many cases, under terrible conditions—long hours, bad sanitation, poor food. Many of them died in the flu epidemic of 1918. Many of them had their health seriously undermined for the rest of their lives. Their government is doing nothing for them or for their widows or dependents. They were patriotic men and women and there were millions of them." Roosevelt then cited the 2.5 million vets who never went to France and lived a "healthy, disciplined outdoor life" at home, plus the 1 million who went to France but never got near the combat zones.[11]

Roosevelt's bonus position also encouraged the enmity of Huey Long, who had joined forces with Father Charles Coughlin, using the bonus as the key issue for Coughlin's fledgling political party, the National Union for Social Justice, and as a plank in the platform of Long's own Share the Wealth movement. The rhetoric of both men became more severe and their demands for the Patman legislation more uncompromising as the congressional vote and Roosevelt's promised veto neared. Coughlin called payment "the just wage which they earned ten times over."[12]

On Sunday, May 12, 1935, from the pulpit, Dr. Norman Vincent Peale, the highly influential pastor of the Marble Collegiate Reformed Church in Manhattan, "solemnly warned" America that "unless something is done to stop it, this country will become a dictatorship as sure as there is a law that lifts the tides. The dictator will be either Coughlin, or Long or a combination of the two." He called Coughlin "half mad with lust for power."[13]

Later that same Sunday, Coughlin held a gigantic rally in Detroit, calling for Roosevelt to sign the Patman bonus bill in the name of his growing number of followers—the "greatest lobby the people ever established." He said he would stage a mass meeting on May 22 in New York's Madison Square Garden.[14]

In early May, during a cruise on the presidential yacht *Sequoia*, Roosevelt asked Samuel Rosenman to help prepare the veto message for the bonus bill.[15] The two worked on the speech on the night of May 18.[16]

Roosevelt chose to deliver his veto message in person to a joint session of Congress on May 22, 1935. A personal veto to a joint session was unprecedented. The speech was nationally broadcast on the two major radio networks.

"Two days ago," Roosevelt said, launching into a speech fifty-five paragraphs long, "a number of gentlemen from the House of Representatives called upon me and with complete propriety presented their reasons for asking me to approve the House of Representatives bill providing for the immediate payment of adjusted service certificates. In the same spirit of courtesy I am returning this bill today to the House of Representatives."[17]

His main argument dealt with the veterans who were not disabled:

> *Some veterans are on the relief rolls, though relatively not nearly so many as is the case with non-veterans. Assume, however, that such a veteran served in the United States or overseas during the war; that he came through in fine physical shape as most of them did; that he received an honorable discharge; that he is today 38 years old and in full possession of his faculties and health; that like several million other Americans he is receiving from his Government relief and assistance in one of many forms. I hold that able-bodied citizen should be accorded no treatment different from that accorded to other citizens who did not wear a uniform during the World War. . . . The veteran who is disabled owes his condition to the war. The healthy veteran who is unemployed owes his troubles to the depression.*

Finally, he said that the complete failure of the Congress to provide additional taxes for an expenditure of this magnitude would in itself and by itself alone warrant disapproval of this measure.[18] FDR then put pen to paper and vetoed the bill on the spot.[19]

That evening, 23,000 howling, booing followers of Father Coughlin packed Madison Square Garden for an attack on Roosevelt cued to the veto. Coughlin called the veto "a money changers argument" from a man who at his inauguration had promised to "drive the money changers from the temple."[20] At Coughlin's side was James Van Zandt, national commander of the Veterans of Foreign Wars, who called for a barrage of telegrams and telephone calls to senators demanding that the veto be overturned.[21]

For the fifth time since 1922, the House overrode a bonus veto by an overwhelming majority of 322 to 98. The Senate, by a vote of 54 to 40—a margin of 8 votes—sustained the veto. The bonus was dead until the next session. It was a great disappointment, especially to the many vets who had stayed out of Washington, responding to pleas from the VFW and other bonus advocates.[22]

Some of Roosevelt's strongest supporters were disappointed, especially in the wake of his earlier actions on veterans' benefits. "My boy VOLUNTEERED for service in the world war when he was only 17 years old; was given intensive training in the aviation field, and hurried across and spent 18 months with the A.E.F. in France. We were so proud of him," wrote Robert L. Bell, a Presbyterian minister from Tuskegee, Alabama, after the veto. "But he came back a nervous wreck, and he was granted a small pension of $20 a month, and when you went into office, you stopped that, and now you refuse to give him the bonus." This from a man who, in the same letter, said that he had "the highest esteem and love for you."[23]

Among the people who admired him most for the veto were those with influence, power, and money. A note from polar explorer Admiral Richard Byrd commended him for his courage and added that his veto would "never be forgotten as long as the country lasts." James R. Atk, the president of Yale University, said, "History will permanently recall the superb courage and wisdom you displayed" in staving off one of the "most pernicious measures ever" offered in response to the pressure of a "shameless lobby."[24]

With the issue now dead, Patman and some others, including Van Zandt, tinkered with the wording of a new bill, planning to reintroduce it at the opening of the Seventy-fourth Congress in January 1936. The growing fear among New Deal stalwarts was that FDR's control over Congress was waning after the free ride of the First Hundred Days, of which it has been said, Congress "did not so much debate the bills . . . as salute them as they went sailing by."

Official Washington, convinced that the issue was dead for another year, was shocked to wake up on the morning of June 27 to find a thousand veterans under the leadership of Royal Robertson, the charismatic Californian, rallying in a vacant lot on Pennsylvania Avenue, at the site of the 1932 clash. "How the group slipped into Washington without attracting attention was something of a mystery," said the *New York Times* in an article headlined "New Bonus 'March' Surprises Capital." The *Wall Street Journal* said the men were in place "before any officials were aware that another bonus march was on."[25]

As early as January, in fact, Robertson had announced he was recruiting men for a new Bonus Army. He suggested that the vets avail themselves of the federal transient camps—now proliferating and well spaced along railroad lines—to house them on their way to Washington in June. Unlike other groups, this one, representing the poorest of the poor, wanted the bonus to be paid to veterans who were not paying income taxes. It called itself the Needy Veterans Bonus Association.[26] Since no "needy veteran" bonus bill was introduced in Congress, many of Robertson's followers drifted away.[27] Many chose to accept a free one-way ticket to the rehab camps in Florida or South Carolina.[28]

Then, three weeks later, on July 17, Representative Hamilton Fish Jr. of New York, who had just submitted a new bill to pay the bonus out of a recent $4 billion New Deal public works appropriation, invited Robertson and his remaining followers to a rally on the steps of the Capitol. They were denied a permit to demonstrate, so the two hundred or so bonus seekers went to a site near where Hushka and Carlson were killed. On July 28, the third anniversary of the 1932 expulsion, about two hundred old soldiers marched across the Potomac to Arlington National Cemetery to lay wreaths at the graves of their two slain comrades.

There would be much more wreath-laying in the weeks and months ahead.

A few days after the Arlington ceremony, the *New York Times* sent reporter Charles McLean to the South Carolina camps to write a serial exposé of the "war veterans' heaven" that the Roosevelt administration was alleged to have created in the fear that another "'Hoover bonus march' might descend on Washington." The articles, published over the course of the second week in August, said that the veterans were living in buildings that "surpass in comfort" the housing for the Regular Army. The men were "shell-shocked, whiskey-shocked and depression-shocked." A great proportion of the men—"perhaps 45 percent"—were "psychopathic cases and the local police report they have had to take a great number of them into custody."

Another article described how veterans in Blaney, South Carolina, were building "an old fashioned swimming hole" with all the trimmings. The last article, headlined "200 Veterans Build FERA Golf Course for Golfless Town," told of a project—"one of the strangest of New Deal undertakings"—using two hundred veterans to build a golf course for the town of Kingstree, which McLean described as a town of three thousand, "half of whom are negroes." Nothing in the article reflected the headline, except for the implication that the town's racial composition made golf there unlikely. This article also suggested that the men were disturbing the town and that twenty of them had wrecked the floor of a county jail after being arrested for drunkenness.[29]

Four days after the last article, the *Times* ran a headline, "Veterans' Camps to Be Abandoned," along with a line of self-congratulation: "The announcement as to the veterans' camps followed publication in the *New York Times* of a series of articles revealing their existence and describing conditions in them."[30]

The White House and FERA, in the person of Harry Hopkins, told the *Times* to announce to its readers that 3,500 people in veterans camps as well as 75,000 in the transient camps would be abandoned by the first of November, and the able-bodied would be sent to CCC camps or work-relief jobs. And what about the estimated 10 percent who would not accept the CCC or work-relief? the *Times* asked.

"They are not our funeral," Hopkins replied.

Just as the *Washington Post* report was refuted in the *Key Veteran News*, so the *Times* series was brought to task, this time by F. E. Simpson, representing all of the men in the Kingstree Camp. Simpson charged that McLean was so debauched on moonshine that he was not able to correctly report. The truth of this allegation will never be known, but it was clear that the rebuttal suggested that McLean had his eyes shut to the reality of the situation: the men working on the golf course were removing tree stumps by hand without the benefit of heavy equipment or dynamite (a point made in the *Key Veteran News* before the McLean article). Simpson invited McLean to return: "Come out to the golf course you wrote of but never saw. Grab a shovel and dig up a four-foot pine stump under a blazing South Carolina sun so you may learn how a veteran earns his dollar per day graft you spoke of. Then go home and write us a story—a story that will be inspired by your blistered hands and aching back."[31]

The August 26 issue of *Time* magazine called the camps "playgrounds for derelicts" and upped the percentage of psychopaths from the *Times*'s 45 percent to a full half. By then 4,274 veterans had been sent to southern camps, including 2,724 to Florida. Now, no matter what the vets said or did, their true story would not be heard in Washington. But Albert C. Keith, editor of the *Key Veteran News*, launched a counteroffensive. He sent ten copies of his newspaper and a letter to Eleanor Roosevelt, warning that the closing of the camps would be a "death sentence" for many of the men. To release them in November into winter, he said, would do nothing more than add to the relief rolls. He ended by inviting the First Lady to visit the Islamorada camps.[32]

Friday, August 30, 1935, was payday for the Keys veterans and the beginning of the long Labor Day weekend. Many took their money and headed for the watering holes of Key West, including Sloppy Joe's Bar, the Happy Days Club, and the Bermuda Café, all of which advertised in the *Key Veteran News*.[33] Others took off for Miami, where their baseball team would be playing its first road game on the Monday holiday.[34] This was also the day that the *Miami Herald* gave the public the first word of a tropical storm off the Bahama Islands, bringing warnings from the Weather Bureau. Northeast storm warnings were displayed from Miami to Fort Pierce as the storm moved closer.

Saturday afternoon, Ernest Hemingway finished working on a short story, mixed himself a drink, and gazed at the evening paper, the *Key West Citizen*. He saw that the storm, still called a "tropical disturbance," was now east of Long Island in the Bahamas and headed toward the Keys. He consulted a chart showing the paths of forty September hurricanes and concluded that this new storm could hit the Keys as early as Labor Day.

At 10:00 A.M. on Sunday, September 1, the Coast Guard station at Dinner Key near Miami received a weather forecast warning of "increasing N.E. winds probably reaching gale force over extreme south portion, and possibly of Hurricane force in the Florida Straits, tonight or Monday, with heavy Squalls in the Florida Straits." The Coast Guard put a seaplane in the air with message blocks—blocks of buoyant wood with a long colorful streamer, a warning message, and a reminder to "pass this information on to other vessels in your vicinity." The blocks were dropped near small boats without radio communications. The Coast Guard was also concerned about getting the warning to isolated Labor Day picnic parties on the Keys. The pilot made several trips, and when he ran out of blocks, he used paraffin-coated ice cream cartons with tape tails about two feet long. The pilot decided not to drop messages on the veterans' camps; he did not want to frighten the vets, and he assumed that those in charge had the situation under control. It was a faulty assumption.[35]

Hemingway, heeding the warnings, tied down his boat, the *Pilar*, on Sunday with a heavy hawser and then turned his attention to his home. By Monday morning he had nailed down the green shutters and cleared the yard of lawn furniture and loose objects. Like most year-round Floridians, Hemingway was extremely wary of hurricanes, especially because of two killer storms of the 1920s and the most recent devastating storm, which struck in September 1928. That storm created a lethal eight-foot wall of water from Lake Okeechobee in the Everglades, drowning 1,800 people, mostly poor black migrants brought in to harvest the local crops.[36]

When high winds finally hit Key West, Hemingway went out to check the *Pilar*, spent most of the night at the dock, and returned home as the winds abated. Having personally lost no more than a few trees and large branches, Hemingway was relieved; the worst of the hurricane had missed Key West.

The small hurricane, forty miles in diameter, with an eye only eight miles long, moved slowly, veering from a predicted course that would have taken it to Havana to one directed at the Florida Keys. In the forty hours it took it to travel from Andros Island in the Bahamas to its Matecumbe landfall, the winds had risen from 75 miles per hour to more than 200 miles per hour— the strongest recorded hurricane ever to hit the United States. The barometer

The southern end of Matecumbe Key, with the remains of the ferry that linked the forty-mile gap in the Key West Highway. Veterans' Camp 3 is at the top of the picture. (American Red Cross)

reading it produced, 26.35 inches, was the lowest ever recorded in the Western Hemisphere.[37] The gusts were estimated at speeds as high as 250 miles an hour—enough to turn granules of sand into tiny missiles that blasted flesh from human faces and sanded fingerprints from human hands.

At dawn on Labor Day, the vets remaining at Islamorada were looking forward to a day off. Many of them—perhaps 60 to 70 percent—were drunk before dusk. Some would still be drinking when the roof of the tavern blew off.[38]

Officials in charge of the camps knew the Keys were vulnerable to hurricanes, but as the storm strengthened, they ignored Coast Guard warnings. Because it was a holiday weekend, the work-camp trucks that might have carried the veterans north to safety were locked up. Instead of ordering a special train from Miami to evacuate the veterans early on, camp supervisors waited until they knew for certain that the hurricane would strike the Upper Keys. When Ray Shelton, assistant director of the camps and that weekend the man in charge, finally called for a train—a request passed through his superior, Fred Grant, in Jacksonville—it was too late. The train, ordered at around 2:00 P.M., was supposed to get to Matecumbe by 5:30. But a crew had to be mustered, so the train did not leave until 4:25. It reached Homestead, twenty-eight miles south of Miami, at 5:15. There it took fifteen minutes to switch the locomotive to the back of the train so that it could back south and go forward on its return trip through expected heavy weather. A thick cable that had fallen across the tracks ensnared the train for an hour and twenty minutes.

The full strength of the hurricane came ashore as the train arrived at Islamorada, shortly after 8:00 P.M. The wind and water was of such strength—two-hundred-mile-per-hour winds and an eighteen-foot storm surge—that it tossed all of the coaches and boxcars across the ground near the tracks like toys scattered by a petulant child. The only thing left standing was the locomotive, rendered useless when the surge reached five feet above the tracks and put out the fire in the firebox.

For every survivor there was a dramatic story. Local resident and store owner R. W. Craig and two friends watched as the store was leveled, then ran for cover, dug themselves in under railroad ties at a site fourteen feet above sea level, and hung on to the metal tracks as four tidal waves passed over them. The hours Craig spent alone—he could not see his two pals—turned into a "horrible, pain throbbing nightmare. Shivering there in the dark, holding on for dear life, alternatively praying and sobbing." He said he understood how people can lose their minds in killer storms. "And," he added, "as if such terror were not enough, hundreds of ugly crabs had descended upon us. While we clung fast to the vibrating steel, not daring to let go even momentarily to

First view of the relief train blown off the tracks by the Labor Day hurricane, September 2, 1935—photographed on Wednesday morning. (American Red Cross)

brush them off, the big-clawed creatures crawled over us from head to foot. They sought the protection of and warmth of our bodies, apparently, and the smaller ones worked their way inside our clothing, next to the skin."[39]

At first, the rest of the world knew nothing of the disaster. In Miami, by Monday evening, as the weather cleared, people congratulated one another: they were not going to get a hurricane after all. The day following the hurricane, the New York papers mentioned a "disturbance" in the vicinity of the Keys, while the *Washington Post* reported that the hurricane had caused only "minor damage" in Florida.

"When dawn broke," wrote a witness named Oliver Griswold, "crushed and dying survivors, some gibbering, some stern-faced and dumb-tongued, saw the incredible horror of bodies lying in windrows, bodies rolling midst sunken boats, bodies hanging from trees, bodies protruding from the sand. Some had no clothes, save belts and shoes, and no skin. They had been literally sand-blasted to death." Griswold's vision of horror would be repeated by those of many other survivors, the accounts differing in detail but not in intensity, in the days and weeks ahead.

In the hours following the disaster, the Keys were cut off from the rest of the nation. The tracks of the Florida East Coast Railroad were either destroyed or unusable. The winds were so high all day Tuesday that planes could not fly. Late in the day a few boats got through to evacuate the able-bodied and injured, who told their rescuers of the horrors they were leaving behind.

The White House, in retreat in Hyde Park, got the first word from the governor of Florida late on Tuesday that there had been a disaster in the Keys. The president fired back a notice at 10:45 that night: ARMY AND NAVY OR-DERED TO RENDER ALL POSSIBLE AID AND RED CROSS ALREADY AT WORK.[40]

On Wednesday morning, the first plane flew over the Upper Keys and came back with a report of the extent of the devastation and an idea of where boats should be dispatched to evacuate the living. By nightfall all the living, save for a few local residents who chose to stay, had been evacuated by an ad hoc armada of Coast Guard, pleasure, and fishing boats. On Thursday, crews including boys from a nearby CCC camp, FERA relief workers, Boy Scouts, and members of the Florida National Guard were sent in to remove the dead, and by Thursday night they had recovered 110 bodies, which were brought to Miami, where they would be placed into wooden coffins lined with metal. An additional 500 men were sent in Friday, so that 800 people were searching for bodies on Friday.

Outrage was growing over what had happened, particularly to the vets. On Wednesday the president received the first of many communications demand-

Graphic images, such as this widely circulated depiction of dead veterans being dragged behind a car, fueled the anger of veterans' groups. (Upper Keys Historical Society, Islamorada, Florida)

ing investigations. The first telegram was from the secretary of the Miami Chamber of Commerce, demanding to know why there was a delay in "attempting to take the veterans from the Keys."[41]*

Veterans in government charge had died horribly. Pressure was quickly building for some kind of explanation. Harry Hopkins, director of the Work Projects Administration, which encompassed FERA, and FDR's closest adviser, was the first to offer an explanation, stating to the Associated Press that advisories from the U.S. Weather Bureau had not been clear about the danger to the Keys. But, as Weather Bureau officials pointed out, the advisories had been accurate enough to allow others who took them seriously to safely avoid the hurricane. The retired chief of the Florida Weather Bureau sent President

---

*Another letter written the same day, but not received until a few days later, came from A. M. Coffin, who alleged that he actually talked with members of the president's staff when they accompanied the president on a fishing trip about the danger to the men in the camps if a fall hurricane hit the Keys. The man in question, a veteran who felt these men had been left to die like "rats in a trap," said he met with White House staffers at the Miami-Biltmore, where he was manning a tourist information bureau. Franklin D. Roosevelt Library, President's Official File #83, Disasters Box 2: Letter from A. M. Coffin, September 4, 1935

Roosevelt a telegram calling the Hopkins charge a "discreditable libel" on the bureau and asserted that the warnings were "timely, intelligent, definite."[42]

On Friday, Hopkins sent Aubrey W. Williams, his top assistant, to Florida to conduct an investigation. He told reporters that Williams was going to specifically find out why the train was not sent in time and why the men had not been evacuated to begin with. Accompanying him as deputy was Colonel George E. Ijams, assistant administrator of veterans' affairs in the Veterans Administration. The men immediately toured the disaster area by plane and then began a series of interviews. Aiding them was John J. Abt, assistant general counsel to the Works Progress Administration, assigned to FERA, who was brought as Williams's assistant. Abt had no illusions about why they were in Florida. "We were on a political mission to defend the administration against charges of negligence," he later wrote.[43]

Meanwhile, the president, who at first had wanted the men buried at Arlington National Cemetery with full military honors, became convinced on Thursday by those on the spot that decomposition was taking place at such an accelerated rate that this option was out of the question. An alternative plan was adopted: a mass burial in Miami on Sunday, September 8, of those bodies that had already been recovered and shipped to Miami, followed later in the day by a public ceremony with full military honors. The rest of the bodies still being found would either be cremated in Matecumbe or buried in plain pine boxes where they were found.[44]

Ernest Hemingway rushed to the ghastly scene by boat from his home in Key West on September 4 to find that the Long Key fishing camp was completely destroyed, as were all the settlements on both Upper and Lower Matecumbe. One of the first bodies he spotted was that of Joe Lowe, whom he identified as "the original of the Rummy in that story of mine 'One Trip Across.'"[45]

"Saw more dead than I'd seen in one place since the lower Piave in June of 1918," he later wrote in a letter to his editor, Maxwell Perkins: "Max, you can't imagine it, two women, naked, tossed up into trees by the water, swollen and stinking, their breasts as big as balloons, flies between their legs." He recognized them as the two women who ran a sandwich place and filling station three miles from the ferry. "We located sixty-nine bodies where no one had been able to get in. Indian Key absolutely swept clean, not a blade of grass, and over the high center of it were scattered live conchs that came in with the sea, craw fish, and dead morays. The whole bottom of the sea blew over it."

Hemingway then took aim at those he thought responsible.

"Harry Hopkins and Roosevelt who sent those poor bonus march guys down there to get rid of them got rid of them all right. Now they say they

The recovery of corpses at Islamorada. This image, hitherto unpublished, was taken by Ernest Hemingway and was discovered with a small collection of hurricane snapshots in the Hemingway holdings at the John F. Kennedy Presidential Library in Boston. (Hemingway Collection/ J. F. Kennedy Library)

should all be buried in Arlington and no bodies to be burned or buried on the spot which meant trying to carry stuff that came apart blown so tight that they burst when you lifted them, rotten, running, putrid, decomposed, absolutely impossible to embalm, carry them out six, eight miles to a boat, on the boat for ten to twenty more to put them into boxes and the whole thing stinking to make you vomit—enroute to Arlington."

When Hemingway returned to Key West on Thursday, a request was waiting for him from Joe North of the *New Masses*, an organ of American communism, to "do a piece for us." North said in his assignment telegram, "We had dispatches up North here several days before the storm broke that the vets were to be moved out in sufficient time. Next thing we read most of them were wiped out. And ironically, it was only a few weeks ago that some people were beefing about these vets living on Easy Street—they were being bribed to stay away from Washington, to keep out of a threatening Bonus March, which would hurt FDR's chance of re-election. [He was apparently referring to that suggestion, raised in one of Charles McLean's *Times* articles.] Well, the hurricane did the job as well as Herbie Hoover did at Anacostia Flats a few years ago."[46]

Hemingway agreed and wrote a tough, heavily emotional piece, filed a few days later. "Things were too bad to write about," he wrote to his friend Sara Murphy. "It was as bad as the war."[47]

Hemingway had left by the time serial cremations began. On Saturday, September 7, a priest, a rabbi, and a minister conducted back-to-back burial services on the banks of Snake Creek. After soldiers fired a volley and a Salvation Army trumpeter began playing taps, a man with a grimy face and callused hands stepped forward and set fire to the thirty-six pine boxes containing the remains of bloated, decomposing bodies. Elsewhere in the Upper Keys, other fires were set now and in the hours to come, so that at the end of the day all the recovered bodies that had not been shipped away for burial in Miami were reduced to ashes. New fires would be set for days, as more bodies were recovered. Reporters and cameramen leaving the disaster scene that night had to burn their clothes to get rid of the stench.

On Sunday, September 8, the remains of the 112 vets shipped out of Matecumbe were buried quietly and with no public participation, at Miami's Woodlawn Cemetery. Many of those being buried, and most of those burned in the previous twenty-four hours, were John Does, defying immediate identification because the sand had blasted away their fingerprints and other identifying characteristics.[48] There was neither enough time nor money to bury the men in coffins, so wooden crates were used. There was only one flag, used to momentarily drape each box.

At sundown 20,000 people gathered for the promised "ceremony with full military honors" in Miami's Riverfront Park, the site where an attempt had been made on Roosevelt's life three years earlier, to pay final tribute to the dead veterans—327 was the official number missing at this point. Navy planes flying overhead dropped rose petals. Representing Roosevelt was Colonel Ijams. The army detachment present was headed by Major General George Van Horn Moseley, whose private opinion of these men was that they were nothing more than "village bums." Abt wrote to his mother the morning after the service, despairing of the bickering among the Red Cross, VA, FERA, the governor, the sheriff, and the National Guard as to who was in charge of what. There was a fight between the American Legion and VFW as to who should go first in honoring the victims at the service. There were more "be-medaled generals, admirals, legionnaires, boy scouts, and other uniforms than were ever assembled on a battlefield." Two survivors tried to get into the services, but as Abt related it in a P.S. to his letter, they had "drowned the memory of the disaster in liquor" and were thrown out by the police.

While the ceremonies were taking place in Miami, Huey Long died from wounds received when he was gunned down as he walked into the capitol building in Baton Rouge for a special meeting of the state legislature. Among the many things on the evening's agenda was a bill to gerrymander the district of one of Long's political enemies, Judge Benjamin Pavy. Pavy's son-in-law, Dr. Carl Weiss, a Baton Rouge physician, shot Long once at close range in the abdomen. As he stumbled down the corridor, Weiss was killed by the senator's bodyguards in a hail of bullets. Long was rushed to Our Lady of the Lake Sanitarium, where he whispered, "I wonder why he shot me." Long died two days later.*[49]

The report of FERA assistant administrator Aubrey Williams was also given to the president on this eventful Sunday—a "preliminary report," created in a little more than twenty-four hours. Written by Abt, it exonerated FERA and thus the Roosevelt administration. Williams, sitting on a bed in a room he shared with Abt in the McAllister Hotel, called Hyde Park and read it to Roosevelt, then turned the report over to a stenographer. The report concluded that the disaster was beyond any "human factors" and that there was neither negligence nor mistaken judgment at work. The principal killer was said to be an unpredictable "tidal wave" estimated at eighteen feet.†

The conclusion, rendered after sixteen interviews—not one of which was with a surviving vet—determined that the weather advisories did not suggest an evacuation before 1:30 P.M. on Monday and that the men in charge "had a right to assume" that the train they ordered at 2:00 P.M. would arrive in ample time to pick up the men waiting at the Islamorada station. The last line of the fourteen-page report stated, "To our mind the catastrophe must be characterized 'as an act of God' and was by its very nature beyond the power of man or instruments at his disposal to foresee sufficiently far enough in advance to permit the taking of adequate precautions capable of preventing the death and desolation which occurred."[50]

But warnings had been given, and they had saved lives. A few days after the hurricane, twenty members of a picnic party on Indian Key, warned by a message block dropped in their midst, came to the Coast Guard Air Station to thank the men for saving their lives. All those on Indian Key had immediately

---

*Father Coughlin was told of Long's passing on his way to meet with Joseph P. Kennedy, head of the Securities and Exchange Commission. Terming it "the most regrettable thing in modern history," he said that a year earlier he had warned the senator of a plot to kill him in an ambush on the way from Baton Rouge to New Orleans. Long, said Coughlin, had planned to run for president in 1936 under the banner of Share Our Wealth.

†Though the term *tidal wave* has long been replaced by the more accurate *tidal surge*, this was the term used in 1932.

departed, with the exception of two men who refused to be alarmed by the message. The storm swept Indian Key bare of vegetation, and the two men were lost.

The full three-thousand-word "act of God" report was released officially to the press the next day; many newspapers carried the full text. From this point forward, the administration and its allies held steadfastly to this defense, no matter who suggested otherwise. To Abt's "amazement and chagrin," the report that he thought was intended for Roosevelt alone lost the qualifier "preliminary." It became the final word.[51]

The report itself created an immediate backlash, much of it stemming from its glib and quick dismissal of blame. The ministers of Miami may have been the first to react, alleging that the only people interviewed were the officials in charge of the camps and that the final report was "incomplete, misleading and untrue to facts."[52] Roosevelt's political advisers were becoming uneasier by the hour, as they read editorials, such as one in the *Virginian-Pilot* of Norfolk, which commented that "in the still unsettled question of why the evacuation of the veterans was delayed, there was the possibility of a national scandal." The *Miami Herald* predicted that the government's failure to protect the vets "may become a vital issue in next year's presidential election" and the *Akron Beacon Journal* titled its editorial on the morning after release of the Williams and Ijams report "Who Sent Them There?" The editorial said there were possible "political repercussions from the tragic experiment equal to those which blasted the Hoover campaign following the ghastly eviction of the bonus marchers from Pennsylvania Av. and Anacostia in 1932." The Akron editorial also said that demand was "sweeping the nation" for a real investigation.[53] The head of the VFW, James E. Van Zandt, called on Roosevelt to reject the report, labeling it "a whitewash as wide as the breadth of the combined white crosses that cover America's heroic dead buried in France."[54]

On September 10 came the first demand from Congress to the White House for an investigation. The demand produced a "joint" investigation by John Abt, representing FERA, and by the VA. The fieldwork was led by a crack investigator named David Kennamer who immediately contacted Abt. However, Abt said he was reluctant to work with Kennamer and insisted that it would be a "terrible mistake" to go back to the original witnesses for more information. The first man Kennamer interviewed was the Islamorada postmaster, John A. Russell, who said unequivocally that "those in charge of the camps" were responsible for the veterans' deaths because there was ample evidence that they should be moved out as early as Sunday.[55] At about this time

Abt returned to Florida to gather information for an exculpatory report, which would be used to defend the administration.

While Kennamer was developing his investigation, the September 17 issue of *New Masses* appeared with a scathing report on the disaster by Ernest Hemingway—an on-the-spot description of the hurricane horror that would become a classic in reporting history. Hemingway had titled the piece "Panic," but, unknown to him, it was retitled by North, the editor, "Who Killed the Vets?" On the eve of the article's publication, North wrote to Hemingway to tell him how thrilled he was with the final copy and noted the article's relevance: "Everybody still remembers Anacostia Flats, and it's near election time." North noted that reports were appearing that the bodies of the vets had been burned en masse, a development he saw as "chock full of dynamite, so symbolic of the plow-under program of Washington."* He understood that some of "the boys down Florida" were saying, "Hoover burned the vets out of Anacostia; Roosevelt drowns them."[56] North added that *New Masses* was trying to give the vets a hand in their fight for the bonus, and if we can "get them moving nationally as a result of the Key West exposure it will be a good thing."

Writing one of the angriest pieces he ever composed, Hemingway opened the article with these words: "Whom did they annoy and to whom was their possible presence a political danger? Who sent them down to the Florida Keys and left them there in hurricane months? Who is responsible for their deaths?"[57] He then noted that wealthy people, yachtsmen, "fishermen such as President Hoover and President Roosevelt, do not come to the Florida Keys in hurricane months. Hurricane months are August, September and October, and in those months you see no yachts along the Keys. You do not see them because yacht owners know there would be great danger, unescapable danger, to their property if a storm should come."[58]

While he did not accuse Roosevelt of killing the vets, that was his clear implication. "I hope he reads this," he wrote toward the end of the article, "—and how does he feel? He will die too, himself, perhaps even without a hurricane warning, but maybe it will be an easy death, that's the best you get, so that you don't have to hang onto something until you can't hang on, until your fingers won't hold on, and it is dark." His finale was pure rage: "I would like to make whoever sent them there carry one out through the mangroves, or turn one over that lay in the sun along the fill, or tie five together so they

---

*A reference to the New Deal's Agricultural Adjustment Act, which had encouraged farmers to plow under abundant crops to keep prices up.

won't float out, or smell that smell you thought you'd never smell again, with luck when rich bastards make a war. . . . Who left you there? And what's the punishment for manslaughter now?"[59]

For Hemingway, the *New Masses* article was a free pass from the Left and the reformers. Lincoln Steffens in the *Pacific Weekly* said that Hemingway now was writing for "the real people of the real publications."[60] The mainstream media, including *Time* and *Newsweek*, admired his indignation. The *New York Daily News*, on the other hand, was far less tolerant, calling Hemingway an unusually able writer who in their opinion had gone "nuts" in this instance: "Mr. Hemingway doesn't say so in so many words, but he leaves the clear inference that the democratic party in general and President Roosevelt and James A. Farley in particular murdered the veterans when the latest hurricane raked the Keys. This seems to us about the limit in the line of ridiculous accusations, but we haven't heard nothing yet." The *News* said that the gist of Hemingway's argument was that FDR was negligent in his inability to predict the landfall of a hurricane. "Hurricanes are twisty and erratic things. We do think the President ought to be excused exactly in advance: ought to be excused even by Reds who are sore because the President didn't leave a bunch of poor vets roosting outside Washington as raw material for the Reds to work on."[61]

North was pleased with the *News* editorial, which he saw as evidence of the beginning of a New Deal "whitewash." He sent it to Hemingway in a telegram asking for more on the subject. Hemingway, who had objected to the changed title of his *New Masses* article, fired back a message to North saying that the title "Who Murdered the Vets?" laid North open to the kind of editorial run by the *News*: HAVE NEVER ANSWERED ATTACKS ON ME WHETHER IN NEW MASSES, NEW REPUBLIC OR DAILY NEWS. STOP. MEN ARE DEAD NOW AND MORE WRITING BY ME WON'T BRING THEM ALIVE. STOP.

When the death toll was tallied, it was below an early estimate by Hemingway of 700 to 1,000; the toll would settle in at over 400 bodies found (408 is the number used to this day by the National Hurricane Service). Recovered veterans amounted to 259, with as many as 10 more who were never identified.[62] As late as 1965 construction workers dredging a rock quarry pulled in an automobile with 1935 plates and five skeletons inside.[63]

For his part, Hemingway revealed a rare side of himself when he wrote the *New Masses* piece. "It showed plainly that the Keys had become ingrained in his system," son and biographer Gregory H. Hemingway later observed. "He had become part of them literally and figuratively. The hurricane disaster made such an impression on him that, although he had become the acknowledged master of controlled prose, for once he dropped his literary guard."[64]

The questions posed by Hemingway were echoed elsewhere. A letter to FERA from West Palm Beach promised that the people of South Florida would not drop the issue "until the persons clearly guilty of criminal negligence or incompetency, or both, be brought to account before the bar of justice as well as held up to the public as the criminals they are."[65]

The anger was palpable at the Veterans of Foreign Wars convention in New Orleans on September 17, the issue date of the magazine containing Hemingway's article. One of the speakers, Smedley D. Butler told the VFW delegates to forget about the presidential race, which Roosevelt would win, but stick to the bonus and the truth of Florida deaths. Butler felt that Washington had decided that it was "a damned clever scheme" to gather the veterans every night from the streets of Washington to be sent to Florida to be drowned.

Butler, who shared the platform with Patman and Governor Eugene Talmadge of Georgia—the man bidding to wear Long's robes—demanded a full investigation of the Florida deaths: "Find out why they were sent down there; why they were not treated like civilians; why their bodies were burned."

The "Florida business," as Butler called it, helped embolden veterans to make themselves heard as loudly as possible on the bonus, which was now being paid to the wives and families of the men who perished in the hurricane. Patman followed with a prediction that the bonus would pass in January and the vets would have their money "in a short time thereafter."[66]

The next morning, eight more families became eligible for posthumous payment as eleven more bodies—eight veterans and three civilians—were retrieved from mudflats twenty-six miles north of Islamorada. One of the men found here had still been alive when washed ashore. It was not a good day. A group of about a hundred "negro workers," sent to help with the recovery of the dead by the Florida Emergency Relief Administration, were dismissed for staging a "mutiny" over complaints about mosquitoes that settled over them at night. The commander of the Florida National Guard appointed a panel to hold hearings on charges of general misconduct. Neither the mutiny nor the charges against the guardsmen amounted to anything. But the fact that they were made in the first place underscored the confusion, anger, and frustration that were rampant.[67]

The White House stood firm as leaders of the American Legion announced at its annual convention that it would conduct its own investigation, which began on October 12 in Key West under the direction of Major Quimby Melton, editor and publisher of the *Griffin (Ga.) Daily News*.

Washington was caught by surprise when individual veterans and smaller veterans' groups decided to launch their own investigations and then feed their findings to the American Legion team. On the first day of the Legion hearings, a survivor of Camp 3 from New York told about the trucks that sat idle when they could have been used to save lives. George D. Kennedy, a meteorologist-observer from Key West, said that he had called and warned the second in command of the camps, "It looks pretty bad," fifteen hours before the storm hit.[68]

On October 14, the American Legion panel, meeting in Miami, took the testimony of A. J. Wheeler, adjutant of the Miami Spanish-American War Veterans post. He said that he had conducted his own investigation and determined that "the officers deserted when the storm approached and left the men to their fate." He also said that the "lost" evacuation train "had steam up" on Sunday afternoon, the day before the storm, but had to wait a full day before official authority to move was granted. Paul Pugh, who was injured in the storm, testified from his hospital bed that Ray Shelton, the FERA official in charge of the three low-lying oceanfront camps, looked up from a card game on the night before the hurricane struck and said, "There is nothing to worry about."

Perhaps the most damaging testimony of this day came from Captain Ed Sheeran, an engineer with the Florida Highway Department and a survivor of a devastating 1926 Keys hurricane. He insisted that he had warned those in charge on Sunday that men would die unless they were evacuated. Sheeran asked for and got permission to give his full testimony in private.[69] Behind closed doors, he told the Legion that he was in charge of $400,000 worth of road-building machinery located on Matecumbe. Using the same weather forecasts that the government men had, on Sunday he decided to move all his equipment to a safe location and then to lash it down, a job he completed thirty-six hours before the hurricane hit. All of Sheeran's equipment was accounted for after the storm.[70]

None of the six men interviewed by the American Legion on these two dates had been interviewed by Williams and Ijams.[71] Before leaving Miami, the Legion investigators interviewed fifty people, including nine vets who had survived the hurricane but were still in the hospital. From Miami the panel members moved on to Tallahassee and then to Washington, where they talked with Ijams and others.

The final report was submitted to the National Executive Council of the American Legion on November 1, 1935, in Indianapolis, with a copy forwarded personally to President Roosevelt two days later by National Commander Ray Murphy. The report said that the tragedy was first and foremost "not an act of God" but rather a situation in which lives

> *could have and should have been saved. The vets were lost because of Inefficiency in the set up of the camps.*

Indifference of someone in charge as to the safety of the men.
Ignorance of the real danger from a tropical hurricane.
And these three "I's" can be added together and they spell "Murder at
   Matecumbe."[72]

The report suggested that the U.S. Army position a regiment of engineers in Miami for rescue work during future hurricane seasons, to erect temporary bridges, establish communications, and facilitate rescue operations. If such a unit had landed in Matecumbe on Tuesday, the report argued, "many lives" would have been saved. "Some witnesses told us that bodies discovered late in the week had been dead only 24 hours—according to physicians and undertakers." This meant that there were men still alive when Williams and Ijams were writing their rush-to-judgment report.

At one point in the report, the issue of the character of the men was addressed. During the course of their interviews with several authorities, the dead men were referred to as bums, drunkards, riffraff, and crazy men, and officials gave the impression that they "got what was coming to them." The American Legion report disputed this conclusion, saying if, indeed, the men were "subnormal," then it was incumbent on the government to take every precaution to protect them. "If they were incapable of caring for themselves then the government should have placed them in hospitals and not have sent them into the wilderness for rehabilitation."*

The American Legion report was read by the president—according to a letter of November 15 to American Legion commander Ray Murphy. Roosevelt told Murphy that the VA and FERA had concluded an investigation involving more than three hundred witnesses, "including the surviving veterans themselves," which he would soon share with Murphy for his "information and consideration."[73]

Neither the Kennamer VA report nor Abt's defensive FERA report ever

---

*Little was actually known about the veterans who died in the Labor Day hurricane, but some of the men from Camp 3 were profiled before their deaths in the *Key Veteran News*. They included veterans who seemed to be using the camps as a place to regroup and rise to the middle class from which they had descended. These were, of course, the stars of the camps and included Bill Hendren, a graduate of the University of North Carolina and a former high school principal; A. W. Mewshaw, a Duke graduate and a prosecuting attorney in Charlotte; and John T. McNulty, a former Broadway and movie actor, who was wounded and gassed during the war. He had lost his job as a stage manager with the Schuberts on Broadway but would go back on the stage as soon as someone would "sweep the cobwebs out of the Broadway theaters." At Camp 1 was boxer Jimmy Conway, once "close contender" for the light-heavyweight crown and winner of over $20,000 in three hundred fights. *Key Veteran News*, July 6 and August 10, from notes taken by author Willie Drye.

made it to Roosevelt's desk. There was no record of either in Roosevelt's papers, nor is there any evidence that either report was ever sent.

The American Legion report was published in the January 1936 issue of *American Legion Magazine* as an attachment to a report on the convention. Discussion of the report was sandwiched between a report on the operation of the American Legion Memorial Building in Paris and a discussion of a resolution on sound money. It seemed to create little, if any, stir in Washington or in the daily press, despite its conclusion of "Murder at Matecumbe."[74]

The Kennamer report, which landed on Hines's desk on September 30, filled three volumes with testimony, documentation, and a five-page conclusion: Ray Shelton, assistant director of the camps, Fred Ghent, director of veterans' camps for the state, and, to a somewhat lesser degree, Conrad Von Hyning, state FERA director, had not done what they should have to protect the men under their jurisdiction.

Kennamer held that the weather advisories "were not entirely accurate" but accurate enough to tell them of danger lurking off the coast, and sufficient to warn others. The warnings were strong enough to have put those responsible on notice to prepare an evacuation. The report held that the officials of the railroad started a train within a reasonable time after it had been ordered and that the road-building superintendent was to be commended for moving his bridge equipment to safety as early as Sunday. There were eight things that Shelton should have done, including asking the camp commanders to get their men ready to move. Shelton was also cited for having countermanded the order of an underling who had cut off the sale of beer and wine on Sunday in anticipation of the storm. Ghent, who was in Jacksonville at the time of the storm, was assigned a list of four failings, ranging from not having an evacuation plan to his delay in giving an order for a train after Shelton called him at 5:00 A.M. Sunday. Van Hyning was faulted for not making sure that an evacuation plan was in place with the railroad and for not communicating with Ghent from time to time after he had first heard of the hurricane.[75]

Kennamer stayed clear of larger issues—such as housing men in flimsy structures during hurricane season, just above the high-tide line—but he clearly saw ample evidence in the hours before the storm that there was plenty of blame to go around. FERA took aim at the Kennamer report, with Abt, Williams, and Hopkins working to rebut its major points. Ijams waded into the battle and sided with Kennamer, holding that, above all, arrangements should have been made for the train after the 10:00 A.M. Sunday advisory.[76]

There was an impasse, broken by Hines, who suggested that both reports be given to the president with a joint Kennamer-Abt statement. Kennamer agreed, provided it could contain his general comments, which restated the results of his investigation in stronger language. At this point, Aubrey Williams borrowed the VA's copy of the Abt report and the statement of facts agreed to by the two men. According to the records, Williams did not return either document, and apparently the president never saw them.

V Day for the Veterans

Nineteen thirty-five is gone, nineteen thirty-five is gone, in come nineteen and
*   thirty-six,*
I'm going to get the rest of my bonus money, Lord, and get my business fixed.
Men be careful, men be careful, who you give your money to,
Because as soon as you get broke, you know the whole round world is through
*   with you.*

—From "The Bonus Blues," Joe Pullium, 1936

THE SUCCESSFUL WHITE HOUSE blockade of the cash
bonus began to crack in late 1935 under the growing threat
of filibusters on legislation known to be especially close to President Roosevelt. A newly modified bill was scheduled for priority consideration as
James Van Zandt, head of the VFW, together with Ray Murphy, the new national commander of the American Legion, determined to solve the problem
once and for all.

To keep the National Economy League, a leading anti-bonus group, from
making countermoves, VFW and American Legion officers met privately on
November 10, 1935, to agree on tactics. The coalition was strengthened when
the Disabled American Veterans came aboard. For the first time since the end

of the war, the three largest veterans' groups were working in concert toward a common goal.[1]

On December 8, a Gallup poll was released that showed 55 percent of all Americans said yes when asked whether vets should get a bonus.[2] In his broadcast of January 5, 1936, Father Coughlin told the nation, "My friends, I have no fear of being a false prophet when I tell you that, without doubt, this so-called soldiers' bonus will be paid in the immediate future. Our long battle, in which I am happy to have played a part, is won! Victory is ours."[3] It was an open secret among his followers that there would be an attempt to defeat Roosevelt at the polls in November when he ran for his second term, thus picking up the standard dropped by the fallen Huey Long and his Share the Wealth movement.

The new bonus bill was swiftly reported out of committee and passed by the House on January 10, 1936, by a vote of 346 to 59. It reached the Senate on January 20 and went through 74 to 16. The new bill differed from that of Patman and his followers, including Father Coughlin, in that rather than being financed by expanding the currency—by simply printing new money—this bill called for the issuing of bonds in $50 denominations (immediately dubbed "baby bonds") that could be redeemed on June 15 or held at 3-percent interest to maturity in 1945. The government hoped at least some veterans would defer cashing them. The only suspense left at this point was whether Roosevelt would bother with another veto or simply approve the bill. The president actually had his press secretary prepare a press release for either contingency, then boasted that he had put one over on his staff.[4]

Roosevelt promptly and perfunctorily vetoed the bill, but this time without trying to rally support to sustain it. "The veto message itself," as summarized by Harold Ickes, "merely referred to the one on the previous bill and was totally lacking in vigor or argument of any sort."[5]

Back it went to the House on January 24 for a 325–61 override, then to the Senate on the following Monday, where the vote came as an anticlimax. This time, the issue was never in doubt: the senators destroyed Roosevelt's veto with a 76–19 vote, with all 95 members voting (the ninety-sixth seat, that of the late Huey Long, was still unfilled). Among those voting to override the veto was Senator Harry S. Truman, who had voted the straight New Deal line up to this point—and for this reason was known as "go-along, get along Harry." He felt compelled to break political ranks to support his wartime comrades.[6]

On January 27, 1936, the cash-now bonus finally became a reality, and Patman was able to tell the Speaker of the House, "Today . . . ends a seven-year fight that commenced May 28, 1929."[7] At 4:50 that same afternoon, Frank Hines handed the first printed application forms to a jubilant Van Zandt. Fifty minutes later, the forms were aboard DC-2s of the U.S. Air Mail Service and headed for veterans' organizations, local offices of the Veterans Bureau, and Hearst newspaper offices. The Hearst papers, longtime supporters of the bonus, announced a plan to set up a special Soldier's Bonus Bureau at each Hearst newspaper to distribute the forms.[8]

The government immediately put out an order for three thousand clerks to handle an estimated 45 million documents—applications, bonds, checks, and other forms—that would be needed to complete the job. In the old brick and steel Government Printing Office building, workers toiled around the clock to get ready. The next day's *Washington Post* headline read, "Soldier Bonus Becomes Law as Senate Crushes Veto, 76–19, Full Payment Sped for June 15."

Washington was abuzz with the political impact of the event. Roosevelt had lost, but the bill he had vetoed had also put money in the pockets of millions of voters in a presidential election year. Roosevelt was a winner even with a veto. And Patman had won, in that the bonus was assured. But he had also lost in the sense that it would be financed through the government's sale of Treasury bonds on the open market and not by printing new currency.

Roosevelt kept a close watch on the surge of cash into the economy. Postmaster General (and Democratic Party chairman) James A. Farley regularly sent the president a report on cashed-in bonus bonds. By July 31, Farley reported, payments totaled "slightly less than one billion one hundred million dollars."[9]

With an election nine months away, Roosevelt was one of the clear winners of the long bonus campaign. A week after his veto was overturned, a memo circulated between Louis Johnson, a lawyer and new national commander of the million-strong American Legion, and presidential press secretary Stephen Early, outlining FDR's record with veterans and contrasting it with Hoover's record. The memo, written for the vet vote, turned the veto into a political asset: "Every one knows that the President could have mustered enough votes in the Senate to sustain a veto; everyone knows that he did not. The President refused to compromise with his public conscience so far as his own duty was concerned; but with the same determination he permitted Congress to exercise its own judgment above his. His veto did the veterans no harm. If it hurt any one, that person was Franklin D. Roosevelt. We cannot condemn him for being honest—and courageous."[10]

The memo also gave a rendition of the New Deal's enduring appraisal of Hoover's behavior in the summer of 1932 when it said, "Hoover was afraid of the men who had saved the country in 1917 and 1918." From the moment Roosevelt had cut veterans' benefits in first few days of the New Deal, through the aftermath of the Labor Day hurricane, and through the saga of this second veto, nobody could ever accuse Roosevelt of being afraid of the vets—or, it would seem, of the press. A piece of campaign literature distributed by the Democrats, entitled "Veterans 1932 versus 1936," used photos of the expulsion, in contrast to the photos of vets working for the CCC and WPA, to show two different ways of reacting to the pleas of the needy. It credited the vets with bringing the realities of the Depression to the "doorstep of the Government."[11]

In mid-February an editor of the *Washington Herald* wrote to Stephen Early, asking about the state of the promised investigation into the deaths of the veterans in Florida. The editor said that the newspaper's inability to answer questions about the matter had lately caused embarrassment. Three days later Early replied, telling the editor that the White House had only the preliminary reports, and that it was impossible for him to say anything about any final reports. The final Veterans Administration report had in fact been completed on October 30, three days before the American Legion report was sent to the White House.

For six months there had been a relentless call for a congressional investigation into the Florida disaster, from the VFW, from the American Legion—and from Republicans. Some of them would use the death of the veterans for political advantage in the upcoming election, others were genuinely puzzled by the unswerving Roosevelt administration adherence to the verdict that the veterans had been killed by an act of God. The single loudest and most persistent force was that of Representative Edith Nourse Rogers, a Massachusetts Republican. As a leading advocate of more benefits and more VA hospitals, she had no peer as a champion for veterans.[12] After her husband died in 1925, she was elected to his seat in Congress and then was reelected in 1926. She immediately appointed herself the protector of disabled veterans and began proposing major legislation on their behalf. She became the first woman to ever have her name attached to successful legislation—a 1926 bill to expand the hospital system for veterans. The bill helped her gain a position on the House Committee on World War Veterans' Legislation.[13]

Rogers insisted repeatedly that the truth about the Florida deaths had been systematically withheld by the White House. At the end of February 1936, having demanded—and not gotten—an audience with President Roosevelt to obtain an official explanation of the Florida deaths, she claimed that there was a "reign of terror" at work in government agencies where, she charged, employees were "afraid to express themselves."*[14]

Rogers, at this point in her career, had become the epitome of toughness and determination. Her already solid reputation had begun to soar on December 13, 1932, when a deranged man entered the chamber of the House of Representatives with a loaded revolver and demanded the right to speak. While most Representatives rushed to the cloakrooms or dove underneath their desks, Rogers and Representative Melvin Maas of Minnesota calmly approached the man and got him to drop his gun. Police later found sticks of dynamite in his rented room. The two representatives were nominated for the Congressional Medal by those who ran for cover.[15]

Hearings on the Florida hurricane disaster were finally called on March 27, 1936, by the House Committee on World War Veterans' Legislation, convening under the guise of an effort to provide additional aid to widows and children of the victims and survivors. In reality, the committee's action amounted to an attempt by the Democratic majority to tidy up a mess that would not go away. The aid that the committee was supposed to be discussing was nothing more than a proposal to give the Florida vets and their families the same legal status as that already given to the younger men in the CCC and their dependents.

Chairing the committee was Mississippi Democrat John Elliott Rankin, a fifty-four-year-old veteran of the Great War, an economic liberal, and an ardent supporter of the New Deal who simultaneously and proudly championed states' rights and white supremacy. Though mild in appearance, Rankin had a reputation as a fire-eater and resembled Wright Patman, one of the fourteen Democrats on the committee, in his fierce determination never to give political ground without a fight. The minority chair was Rogers, one of six Republicans on the committee. Her strongest ally was the lone socialist Harry Sauthoff, a member of the Progressive Party from Wisconsin.

The hearings dragged on for more than six weeks. Twenty-three witnesses were called. Rogers, trying to show that the hearings were a "whitewash," hounded witnesses and tussled with Rankin and Patman—southern men not accustomed to tangling with a steel-willed, plainspoken Yankee Republican woman. As loyal Democrats, Rankin and Patman held steadily to the "act of

---

*When six Army pilots were killed within a week while carrying airmail, Rogers insisted that pilots were dying because they were not prepared for such work. When the practice was not stopped, she said the administration was guilty of murder and that more deaths "will be written in blood across the Record of this administration." She made this accusation four days before alleging the "reign of terror." *Boston Sunday Globe*, February 24, 1934.

God" position, often interrupting Rogers or invoking a "point of order" when she asked a question that deviated from the New Deal script. Their favorite trick was to answer for the witness whenever Rogers asked a tough question.

When Rogers tried to ask Ivan R. Tannehill, assistant chief of the Forecasting Service of the Weather Bureau at the time of the disaster, if, with his knowledge of hurricanes and the Keys, he would have selected Islamorada as a place to send the veterans for rehabilitation, Rankin invoked a point of order to stop the asking of "irrelevant questions." He also accused her of embarrassing the witness. "He looks like he is able to take care of himself," she replied.

Chairman Rankin said, "Yes, but the chairman of this committee is able to enforce the rules of the House. Confine yourself to the rules of the House."[16]

When Rogers really pressed on a matter of fact, as she did with Aubrey Williams, the author of the "act of God" claim, Rankin interrupted to say that while the Republicans drove these men out with bayonets in 1932, the Democrats came along and gave them jobs in Florida. Rogers did not fall for his baited hook, responding: "I am trying to get the information, and I think you are also, Mr. Chairman."[17]

At the very end of the hearings, Colonel John Thomas Taylor, the American Legion's chief lobbyist, attempted to present copies of its "Murder at Matecumbe" report and to have the report entered into the record. Rankin recoiled, saying, "We could not accept conclusions drawn from another investigation such as we have conducted here." Patman told Taylor to leave copies of the report for the committee to examine. Rankin quickly added, "Of course we are not saying that we will put it into the record." Realizing that the introduction of the damaging report was a lost cause, Rogers asked that some of the American Legion witnesses be called before the committee. Rankin told her that this would only postpone action on the compensation bill. When she moved to call an American Legion witness, Rankin refused to bring the motion to a vote. The hearings were closed.

A few weeks later, as the final report of the committee was made public, Rankin again insisted there was no blame to be assigned for the men's death. Rogers fired back with her own report, which asserted that "many blunders were made."

On June 1, 1936, the bill for relief for the hurricane victims came to a vote. Rogers rose to say that she was in favor of the bill, but that the men had died through "gross negligence." Rankin protested and asked all present to read the report of the committee. Rogers came back for one last round, saying that she would be delighted if the membership of the House read the hearings, because they had "whitewash" written all over them. She accused Rankin of refusing to call key witnesses and of keeping out of the record anything that suggested a contradiction of the administration's three-thousand-word "act of God" conclusion. Two members of the committee—Harry Sauthoff and Charles F. Risk, a Rhode Island Republican and veteran—supported Rogers. Risk noted that Rankin had shamelessly manipulated the rules to keep the record clean of anything he did not want to hear.

Rogers wanted to establish government culpability so that the victims of the hurricane would be treated as disabled veterans and awarded the status of service-connected disability. The government, she argued, realized that it was its responsibility to get the men out safely and in time. "These responsibilities were not carried out efficiently enough to save these men from death and others from an experience that will constantly affect already shattered nervous systems and bodies," she said. "To place them on the same basis as young boys in the C.C.C. camps is pitifully inadequate. It is ridiculous—it is a direct evasion of accepting responsibility—part of the whitewash so evident all through these hearings."[18]

The relief bill passed. Rogers finally got the Kennamer report a few days later, but the matter was, for all intents and purposes, closed. Questions of guilt or innocence would be left open. Material that could have answered these questions has either disappeared over the years or was not preserved to begin with.*

For reasons never made clear, neither the Abt nor the Kennamer report was ever "leaked" or read into the *Congressional Record*. Nor was the fact made public that the primary recommendation of the American Legion report was that a congressional investigation be ordered "to fix the blame, if any, on the party or parties responsible for the loss of life."

The man who knew the most about the matter was VA Investigator David W. Kennamer, who was brought on for a moment to verify the authenticity of a set of phone records but never identified as the author of the major study of the hurricane. Nor was his report alluded to during the hearings—but a copy was given to Rankin, who had exchanged several political favors with Roosevelt and was on FDR's reelection campaign committee. Rogers did not learn about the report until the hearings were almost over, when she demanded a

---

*The files containing the administrative records of the committee—letters, memos, and other documents—were sealed at the National Archives for fifty years. But the files were found empty, save for a copy of the bill itself, when we put in a request for them on February 21, 2002. What this means is that all of the collateral material collected by the committee and alluded to in the hearings—including a copy of the American Legion report and Abt's report—was destroyed or removed.

copy from VA Administrator Hines. Referred to Rankin, she was finally allowed to see a copy after the hearings were over.

What Rogers probably knew but could not say for fear of having the hearings closed by Rankin was that John Abt, who had been assigned to work with Rankin, was helping to engineer a whitewash based on his investigation, a secret that was not fully revealed until 1993, when Abt's autobiography was posthumously published. His report was written for and structured to meet Rankin's needs. Abt, a Communist, disliked Rankin and described him as one of the "worst reactionaries" in Congress. "But he was a Democrat with a political stake in the administration," Abt recalled, "so he and I teamed up as allies to exonerate the government, in an episode of my life I look back on without pride." He added that the best report filed on the hurricane was the one written by Ernest Hemingway.[19]

The original Abt report, which had disappeared without a trace, finally resurfaced in 2001 in papers held by Ray Shelton's daughter and was revealed to author Willie Drye after publication of the first edition of his book *Storm of the Century*.[20] The Kennamer report was kept from public view until sometime in the late 1980s, when it mysteriously surfaced after an earlier request by a writer was denied.

For a moment in the days before and just after payment, the press was given a holiday from the hard-luck stories of the Depression in favor of happier, more uplifting fare. For instance, three days before the bonus was paid, it was announced that the Washington Veterans Home at 2626 Pennsylvania Avenue in the District of Columbia would close its doors at the very moment of payment. The building was razed a few weeks later.

The home had been founded in an abandoned house in the winter of 1932 when J. J. Queally, an Episcopal minister working with the poor, stumbled on a pack of 150 homeless men living on food from garbage cans. They turned out to be veterans of the Bonus Army. In the four years since it was founded, the home had sheltered and fed more than 14,000 veterans. Under the stewardship of "Mother Steed"—Mrs. J. Nathaniel Steed, a woman who had run a canteen for soldiers in France during the Great War—and an elected board of five veterans, it provided a place where veterans could deal with poverty and depression without resorting to the streets and panhandling. Many of the men used the home as a base from which they operated until they found work. The home raised money and aided penniless veterans being discharged from veterans' hospitals, giving them a meal, a night's lodging, and a ticket home. For her part, Mother Steed fought with the Veterans Administration for money and went to court to defend any of her charges who got into trouble with the law.[21]

On June 12, as the Reverend Queally delivered a tearful farewell to a group of veterans, a dog named "Bonus" lolled by his feet. One of the vets had saved it from a nearby canal. Remarkably few Washingtonians knew of this mission, which had worked quietly and without publicity. In fact, its closing ceremony marked the first time its operation was described in the newspapers.[22]

Employees of the Veterans Administration, the Treasury Department, and the U.S. Postal Service worked overtime to prepare bonus packets for 3,518,000 veterans, with an ultimate cash value of more than $1.9 billion. Distribution of the packets to regional and local post offices began at the U.S. Post Office headquarters in Washington at midnight on June 15. Through announcements in newspapers and on radio, veterans were told to be at home on June 16 so that they would be able to sign for the registered mail handed to them by their postmen. Each vet got an application to be filled out and taken to the local post office, where "certification officers," after checking identification, handed over a receipt. This was converted into a U.S. Treasury check the vet could then cash at a bank or any other place that would take a government check.[23]

An army of postal workers leaving the main Manhattan post office at Eighth Avenue and Thirty-third Street with the first shipment of bonus bonds. (Authors' collection)

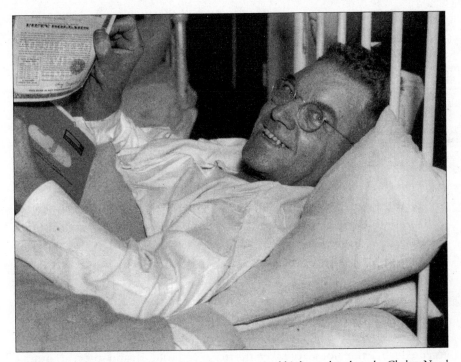

Veteran Alfred W. Hyadd of Allston, Massachusetts, received his bonus bonds at the Chelsea Naval Hospital on June 15, 1936, eighteen years after the end of the war. (Boston Traveler Collection/ Boston Public Library)

The process worked at amazing speed. Many vets who met the postman at the door on Tuesday, June 16, had cash in their hands by Thursday. "They're really DOUGHboys today!" the *Bridgeport Post* exulted on June 17, 1936, in its report on the postmen's delivery of nearly 3,500 bonus packets. Next day, the *Post* reported that the city's vets had cashed in $545,400 in checks. Like vets in other cities hard hit by the Depression, many Bridgeport bonus recipients said they would immediately spend the money to pay bills. Some said they would be buying clothes for their children. An oysterman said he would buy replacements for the tattered sails on his boat. Bridgeport banks reported scant increases in savings accounts; the cash bonus was going into cash registers. And a city official, echoing similar decisions by other cash-strapped cities and towns, said that relief aid would cease immediately for the families of bonus recipients.[24]

Throughout the nation, nearly half of the bonus bonds were cashed within two weeks after June 16. In a veteran's family with a typical Depression annual income of $1,400 to $1,600, the bonus meant an overnight 30 percent increase in income. For the nation, the two-week June infusion of cash equaled nearly 1 percent of the gross national product.[25]

The promised boost to local economies was huge—more than $40 million in the Washington, D.C., area alone—and merchants anticipated a boomlet of spending, a "bonus rush."[26] The process was not without ironies and provocative sidebars. In early February the *New York Times* carried a small piece entitled "Sing Sing Convicts to Get $50,000 from War Bonus."[27]

The payment of the bonus occasioned a moment of self-indulgence for some. "I've never had more than three suits of underwear in my life. Now I want twenty of 'em," an unidentified veteran told a reporter as he made a frontal attack on a haberdashery shop in southern California on bonus day.

Because so many of the veterans had borrowed against the value of the certificates, the average payment was $583, with a maximum of $1,585—but this was a lot for veterans who reported they could weather the next few years on as little as $30 a month.

One of the quirks of the payment was that any of the BEF men shipped home from Washington at government expense in 1932 were charged for their trips. On average, the lien was minimal—$15—but 5,160 were shown to have accepted a free ride home (or taken the ticket and sold it), and some, according to a VA source in Chicago, were taking the news of the deduction badly.[28] But they were in the minority. To the vast majority, the bonus was, as many called it, manna from heaven. Payment of the bonus produced, in the words of the *Literary Digest,* "varied episodes of comedy, pathos, adventure, romance and a smattering of tragedy." The *Digest* also said that the staff of a veterans' hospital in Chicago reported an overnight recovery of patients who got out of their sickbeds on payment day.[29]

It was a gaudy ending to the long battle for payment, and the newspapers and magazines stumbled over one another to find stories laced with irony and unintended consequences—men left their wives, while others bought engagement rings; some saved their bonus, and others lost it immediately to goldbrick schemes promising instant wealth. But for most the bonus was a moment of short-lived prosperity. John Alferi, the man who had accosted the president in 1935, drew $756.32—enough to buy three suits of clothing, two pairs of shoes, and several days of fishing and swimming in Long Beach, California. He also paid off a number of debts.[30]

John Taylor, senior archivist at the National Archives in College Park, Maryland, today remembers how excited his uncles were in anticipation of the bonus in 1936. "They were going to buy cars. Years later, I met someone who sold cars after the bonus was paid. He said he hadn't been able to sell any for a long time." Taylor remembered that one of his uncles bought a car for $12. "In those days five cents was hard to come by."[31] The Oliver twins who had boxed at Camp Marks recall that their father came home displaying $100 bills—they think there were eight of them—fanned out like a poker hand. It was more money than they or any of their friends had ever seen before.[32]

In the District of Columbia, the very men who had been forced to deal with the bonus marches of 1932–34 were in line for their own bonuses. More than a thousand public employees got paid, led by 222 members of the Metropolitan Police Force, a fact that went a long way toward explaining the respect that the vets and the police had for one another, dating back to the days of Pelham Glassford.[33]

The least reported story of the bonus payment in the mainstream press was its effect on black veterans who received substantial amounts of cash. The economic "disaster" predicted by Woodrow Wilson's secretary of the Treasury sixteen years earlier did not occur. And there was a boom in recorded blues songs—more than a dozen of them, including several cautionary songs, such as one by Amos Easton entitled "When I Get My Money (I Mean That Bonus)." The song opens as he hears that the veto has been overridden. Then it moves into the chorus:

> *When I get my bonus, I ain't gonna throw it away,*
> *I'm gonna save some to live on, workin' hard won't pay.*
> *Maybe I'll go to the tavern, and drink a little beer,*
> *I'm gonna buy Myrtle a souvineer.*
> *Ain't gonna pitch no parties, and pay the whole bill,*
> *Thought I'd buy me a V-8 Ford, don't believe I will.*[34]

Easton, who performed under the name of Bumble Bee Slim, was too young to be a veteran, but like a dozen other performers, he knew a good subject when he saw one. The Myrtle in the song is his pianist, Myrtle Jenkins, and the allusion to the Ford V-8 is to the car dealer who put an ad in the African-American newspaper *Chicago Defender* with photos of the Ford V-8 and the Lincoln Zephyr and the come-on: "Ex-soldiers! Special bonus blanks properly filled out by experts. Notary service free. Get your new Ford V-8."[35]

For those blacks and whites on the lower rungs of the economic ladder, the bonus offered the chance to move up a rung or two. For others, it was something as simple as a bus or train ticket. "My parents divorced when I was two years old and I never saw my father again until after the Veteran's bonus was given out in 1936," recalls Helen Barron Shupik of Bridgeport, Connecticut, today. "He sent the money to me for a trip to his home and, so, I took the bus from Fayettesville, Arkansas, to Lexington, Missouri. I will always have a fond spot in my heart for the Veteran's Bonus of 1936."[36]

In the months following payment, Father Coughlin and his National Union for Social Justice, now claiming to be 9 million in strength, made a run for the White House, as Coughlin intensified his attacks on the president, calling him "Franklin Double-Crossing Roosevelt" and a liar and betrayer. With Huey Long dead and the bonus paid, Coughlin decided not to run, even though he was the union's most popular leader. Instead he offered William Lemke, an obscure member of Congress from North Dakota, as its presidential candidate. The ticket garnered 2 percent of the popular vote. A week after the election Coughlin announced that the party was "thoroughly discredited" and that he was "withdrawing from all radio activity in the best interests of all people."[37]

At 9:00 A.M. on March 29, 1937, with the Matecumbe span rebuilt, the road connecting the Keys was finally opened. The railroad was never restored to service. The remains of the old bridge were sold to the State Highway Department, which used materials from the wreckage to extend Route 1 to Key West. Drivers riding on the road today are riding on the railbed. All that remains of the veterans' work are three finished bridge piers and several unfinished ones, which can be seen on the Gulf of Mexico side of the bridge. Jerry Wilkinson of the Upper Keys Historical Society says that it is easy to identify the three piers because they look "like three gray coffins setting on the bay water." Wilkinson also points to a small key near the piers, formed as the vets dumped rock and debris. Now covered with vegetation, it is called Veterans' Key.

The odyssey of the Bonus Army ended on November 14, 1937, with the dedication of a memorial crypt just off Route 1, in Islamorada. It contained bones and ashes of what was, by the best estimates at the time, 189 hurricane victims, 128 of them veterans not interred. Depicted in relief in native stone is the tidal surge that did so much damage and the crypt itself, designed and executed by artists of the Works Progress Administration. A WPA symphony orchestra was brought in to play the overture to Verdi's *Aïda*. A telegram from the president was read, and a nine-year-old survivor pulled the string to unveil the monument.[38]

A few days before, President Roosevelt had warned that a "state of international anarchy" had been unleashed upon the world. Japan had invaded China, and U.S. gunboats were evacuating American diplomats from Nanking. One of the gunboats, the *Panay*, would be sunk on December 12.

Adolf Hitler was already on the march. He had taken the Rhineland in defiance of the League of Nations. Italy had invaded Ethiopia. Another war was on the horizon. In that war, the memory of the long struggle of the Bonus Army would stir Americans, who wondered how the nation would treat a new generation of veterans. This time, those who marched off to war would come home to a new kind of bonus, won by a struggle they did not have to repeat.

The GI Bill

Legacy of the Bonus Army

THE 1936 BONUS had been paid only a few years before millions of Americans began to enter the military for a new world war. Initially, little thought was given to how the veterans of World War II would be treated when they returned to civilian life. But soon after the Japanese attack on Pearl Harbor and America's declaration of war, legislation was introduced in Congress to provide benefits for the men and women in the military. More proposed laws were offered with great regularity, commonly framed in terms of a cash payout or loans.

At the end of November 1943, with 11 million Americans in uniform, an advertisement sponsored by the *Milwaukee Journal* appeared in the *Washington Post*, fifteen other newspapers, and *Newsweek* magazine. It asked, "Is This His Reward?" and featured a picture of a sad-looking GI with a food tray from a soup kitchen. "This time," the text said, "let's not have any 'Soldier Boy' apple vendors . . . no more veterans' bread lines . . . no more bonus armies." At the bottom of the ad, in boldface, it proclaimed, "The power to act lies in Washington. It is up to you and your neighbors to create in your communities a demand for action."[1]

The article offered two free books—*They Can't Eat Medals* and *Wounded Soldiers Come Home . . . What Then?*—based on a long series of articles that began in the summer of 1943. These were written by a veteran reporter named

Frank Sinclair, a regimental sergeant major in World War I who had founded an AEF newspaper called the *Cro*. Sinclair filed story after story arguing for "wise and sympathetic treatment" for the veterans who would soon be coming home by the millions. The *Journal* took out ads in all the major newspapers, offering the free booklets and giving blanket permission to reprint Sinclair's articles. Copies of the books—there would be four in all—were sent to every member of Congress and anyone else in a position to make policy. Hundreds of thousands were mailed to citizens.

In July, when Sinclair filed his first article 21,828 American servicemen had been wounded and 16,696 killed, 31,579 were missing, and 21,541 were prisoners. Sinclair asked what was going to happen as those numbers climbed into the hundreds of thousands or millions. His first concern were the wounded, but he argued for college and vocational training for all veterans, Social Security credit for time in service, help in getting work, and unemployment insurance for those who could not get jobs. Sinclair warned that the nation faced gigantic problems when the war was won. Advances in medicine—such as penicillin and sulfa drugs, blood plasma and field x-ray machines—would mean more recoveries from wounds, but more powerful forms of destruction would mean that more men would be coming home with permanent disabilities.

For those needing rehabilitation, Sinclair reported that Washington had "unwound a new mess of red tape." It took months to determine if the veterans were deserving of such aid. A disability could qualify only if it was service-connected and "in the line of duty," despite an earlier promise that all men coming back would be given the treatment they needed. Under new rules uncovered by Sinclair, it would be the responsibility of the state to help those whose disabilities had not come "in the line of duty." The Veterans Administration was taking three to four months to make a judgment, months when veterans were out of work and without income.

Some of the returning vets, in desperation, grabbed at any job. Men with severe disabilities turned to public relief, the Red Cross, and other charities to survive. Between May 1 and July 31, 1943, in Milwaukee alone, of the 538 disabled men who returned, only 6 had unambiguous battle injuries (two had lost both legs). All the others had to have their cases adjudicated in Washington. Asked why the process was so slow, Fred Hines, still the head of the VA, said that it would take an additional ten thousand adjudicators to increase the speed.[2]

Sinclair backed up his numbers with real people, including those he met in a former exclusive girls' school in Forest Glen, Maryland, which had been converted to a hospital and rehab center for amputees. There he met Jimmy, a Coast Guardsman who had enlisted from a CCC camp. During the invasion of North Africa in November 1942, he had been shot and fallen overboard. He was taken prisoner, had his arm amputated at the shoulder, was repatriated, and was being fitted for a prosthetic arm at Forest Glen. He told Sinclair that all he needed now was a trade so that he could get work.

Sinclair probed the VA system and found it lacking. One-third of the doctors employed as civilians in VA hospitals had left to join the Army and the Navy, so there were not enough doctors for the two thousand new cases entering the system each month. Military hospitals were already so full that men still in need of rehabilitation were being transferred to the understaffed VA hospitals.

In the fall of 1943 Sinclair filed a story from Washington on early moves to create a World War II bonus—although most legislators were loath to use that term. Chairman Rankin of the House Committee on World War Veterans' Legislation had worked hard and successfully to get the base pay of servicemen and servicewomen raised so there would be no need to compensate them for the discrepancy with civilian pay, the source of discontent that had inspired the World War I bonus. Rankin wanted to prevent a repeat of history. "It took us thirteen years to get that award for the veterans of World War I," he told Sinclair. "That fight so hurt the veterans that no veteran of the last war had been president and very few of them have been governors."*[3]

Following the lead of Canada, Roosevelt and many members of Congress favored a flat separation fee for all those leaving service so that they would not have to rely on charity. The powerful National Association of Manufacturers, an opponent of the World War I bonus, favored a plan to give each veteran up to $550 in bonus money—called "separation pay"—in six monthly payments, plus allowances for family and $100 for civilian clothing. The American Legion advocated a hands-off policy in the matter of a bonus, leaving the issue up to the veterans themselves when the war was over.

But some legislators were already thinking that no kind of bonus would be enough. Representative Edith Nourse Rogers of the House Veterans Affairs Committee, who had been proposing rehabilitation bills since February 1942, argued for college training, for the disabled at least, and eventually for all who wanted it. At this point, all that Roosevelt was advocating was a year's free tuition.

Representative Lawrence H. Smith, a Wisconsin Republican, sponsored a bill to provide up to four years of free college or vocational education for all

---

*Harry S. Truman would prove him wrong when he became president on April 12, 1945.

veterans. Smith was spurred by his own experience: his college education had been interrupted by World War I; he went to France as a first lieutenant, was wounded, and returned as a disabled vet with a wife and child. "Had it not been for the state of Wisconsin, which paid my way through college as a veteran, I may never have been able to realize my life's ambition to become a lawyer," he told Sinclair.

Smith's vision was clear: a million veterans would pour into the colleges, keeping themselves out of the labor market for a year or more while the economy converted from war to peacetime. Many of the colleges would be overloaded, but former military bases could be converted to campuses. The cost would be enormous, but Smith said it would be regarded as an element of national defense—staving off depression and the need for massive public welfare while creating a new leadership class in America.[4]

At the end of 1943 there were 243 bills on veterans' legislation pending before Congress. They ranged from a proposal to give a flat $60 for everyone on discharge (exactly the same amount as in 1919) to schemes allowing vets to buy homes or farms at low interest rates. For his part President Roosevelt, in a Fireside Chat to the nation on July 28, 1943, cleared away any memories of his opposition to veterans' benefits. Veterans of this war, he said, "must not be demobilized into an environment of inflation and unemployment, to a place on a bread line or on a corner selling apples. . . . We must this time, have plans ready."

Beneath all of this was the very real fear that the nation would pay for lack of a comprehensive plan to help veterans by facing a much larger and more hostile version of the Bonus Army. Representative Hamilton Fish Jr., now a political foe of Roosevelt, agreed that veterans could not "come home and sell apples as they did after the last war, because if that is all they are offered, I believe we would have chaotic and revolutionary conditions in America." There was also fear for the economy. The Department of Labor forecast up to 15 million unemployed once the war ended, triggering the possibility that the nation might slide back into a depression.

Proposals were shuffled and sorted and finally refashioned by a group at the American Legion into what would become one of the most important—and most generous—pieces of social legislation in American history. The catalyst at work was a survey conducted by Commander Warren H. Atherton on the status of disabled men and women who had returned after two years of war. It showed a "highly unsatisfactory" pattern of neglect and bureaucratic red tape. He had collected the records of 1,536 disabled vets who had been forced to wait from three to eleven months before they could get care or compensation. Many had to rely on charity while they were being processed. Atherton warned of "the wrath of eleven million veterans after this war" if something was not done.[5]

The information from this survey was fed to a number of newspapers, and the Hearst chain picked up where Sinclair had left off, assigning three reporters to the job of reporting the stories of some of those 1,536 veterans. One of the vets was Marine Bill Smith, who in 1943 came back from Guadalcanal—the Japanese-held island invaded in August 1942—to a nation ill prepared to care for him. A Japanese grenade had destroyed part of his brain and left him partially paralyzed. Released from a military hospital and handed an honorable discharge, Smith suddenly was left without pay, and his mother had no monthly allotment check. At that time there was no mustering-out pay. There were benefits to be had—disability compensation of $100 a month, free hospitalization, and vocational training—but there was no one to help him through the maze of paperwork needed to get those benefits. When the paperwork was finally submitted, it took four months to process. While Smith and his mother waited, they lived on the charity of friends.[6]

A special committee of the American Legion met in Washington on December 15, 1943. In five weeks, a rough version of veterans' legislation was drafted by Henry Colmery, an Army Air Service flying instructor during World War I and the Legion's national commander in 1936. That draft, written in longhand by Colmery on Mayflower Hotel stationery, laid the groundwork for the eventual legislation, which provided six benefits: education and training; loan guaranty for a home, farm, or business; unemployment pay of $20 a week for up to fifty-two weeks; job-finding assistance; top priority for building materials for VA hospitals; military review of dishonorable discharges. First known as the American Legion Omnibus Bill, it quickly became known as the GI Bill of Rights.[7]

The legislation was opposed by leaders of America's educational elite because they feared that the hordes of former GIs would harm academia. Powerful southern politicians did not like the idea of several million African-American vets being given $20 a week as they made the transition from military to civilian life.

From the outset, Rankin treated certain provisions of the pending legislation as a frontal assault on white supremacy and the so-called two-tier economic system in Mississippi and in much of the old South. Under this system, black workers were paid the lowest possible wages and this, in turn, was used to keep the wages of the poor, white working class in check. So Rankin declared his own war on the equal unemployment provision of the bill, known as the "52-20 Club," which would give each veteran twenty dollars a week for a year while he was looking for work or applying to school. Rankin said it would create "tremendous inducement to certain elements to try to get unemployment compensation." It would, he insisted, encourage fifty thousand black servicemen from Mississippi to "remain unemployed for at least a year."

Edith Nourse Rogers immediately began hammering away at Rankin's intransigence, asking for a "moratorium on procrastination" and demanding that Congress "pass the GI bill now." By then, she noted, there were more than a million World War II veterans and for them "adequate assistance can mean the difference between a life of usefulness and one of misfortune and hopelessness."[8]

The Senate bill, S.1767, passed on March 24, 1944, by a 50 to 0 vote and was sent to the House, where Rankin continued to bottle it up in committee. When he finally allowed the bill to reach the House floor on May 18, it no longer contained the 52-20 provision, and passed 387 to 0.

Now the Senate and House versions needed to be reconciled on several levels by a joint Senate-House conference committee consisting of seven members from each body. Rankin, a member of the House group, termed the bill "explosive" and "half-baked." He declared that the conference committee was not going to be stampeded into getting it to the floor for a vote. The GI Bill stalled in committee once more.

Rankin was saddled with the label "G.I. Enemy No. 1" in *The Nation* magazine, which said that his "animosity toward the Negro is calculated to deprive all soldiers of unemployment protection and thus insure a large supply of labor at distress wages in the event of a post-war depression." Rankin's delay of the GI Bill on racial grounds, *The Nation* said, was "a rancorous expression of all that is most vicious in our national life."[9] The American Legion's national commander called a press conference to let Rankin know that his organization would fight him down to the level of "every voter in the country."

While Rankin had his roadblock in place, educators got a chance to express their doubts about the wisdom of putting these men and women, with their overwhelmingly working-class backgrounds, into the ivy-clad towers of academia. "No man can fight in a war without being changed by that experience," wrote Professor Willard Waller of Columbia University. "Veterans come home, but they come home angry."[10] Other objections from the educational community came from the heads of two of the nation's most prestigious universities, Harvard and the University of Chicago. James B. Conant, president of Harvard, lamented that the GI Bill failed "to distinguish between those who can profit most from advanced education and those who cannot." He said he feared that "we may find the least capable among the war generation . . . flooding the facilities for advanced education." Robert M. Hutchins, President of the University of Chicago, was also an opponent of the legislation, which he called a "threat to American education."

Conant, Hutchins, and others working to maintain the status quo at the elite schools, wanted a system by which the government gave money directly to the colleges and universities, which then would select a new elite based on their own criteria. (Conant, for example, referred to the brightest matriculating students as those who were there because of heredity and IQ.) After weeks of wrangling over the educational provision of the bill, what prevailed was a system of vouchers, which gave the individual the right to select his or her own education.

The bill seemed ready to be reported out of the seven-man House conference committee for final compromise with the Senate conferees, assuming a majority of House conferees agreed to do so. On June 1, Representative Margaret Chase Smith of Maine, a strong supporter of the veterans' legislation, told her constituents that by the time they read her message the bill would be "in the hands of the President." An ally of fellow Republican Edith Nourse Rogers, Smith was clear in asserting that the bill would "help our returning veterans adjust to civilian life again and ease as far as possible the sacrifices they have made for their war service."[11]*

Smith's optimism was unfounded, as she had not reckoned on Rankin's ability to sway other southerners on the conference committee. He managed to keep the bill from being sent to conference by a 4–3 vote. At the same time, Americans were totally absorbed by the invasion of Europe. Everything was on hold; even baseball games were canceled. As a result, the veterans' drama in Washington was being played offstage.[12]

Rage, however, was building against Rankin. On June 6, 1944—D-Day, when American troops were landing in Normandy—a resolution was passed by a local of the United Electrical Workers in Hartford, Connecticut, signed by its president, Ernest De Maio, and sent to the White House and to members of Congress. Its final paragraph said: "Resolved, that we condemn Congressman John E. Rankin, who is an open spokesman of race superiority and anti-Semitism in the House of Representatives, as well as an enemy of the interests of the soldiers, for his anti-labor record and especially for his stand on the G.I. Bill of Rights."[13]

---

*In 1945, Rogers and Smith were the first women authors of an equal rights amendment to the U.S. Constitution. As had seven previous attempts, their effort failed.

Days before a scheduled June 8 vote by the House committee conferees, one of their seven members, Frank Gibson of Georgia, decided to go home. He telegrammed his proxy to Rankin so that Rankin had the authority to cast Gibson's vote as he saw fit. However, on June 7 Gibson had a change of heart and instructed Rankin to send the bill to conference, for he now favored the full bill, including the 52-20 provision. Rankin balked and said that he would not honor this new proxy vote, thus effectively deadlocking the vote 3 to 3. At that point, it looked like the bill would have to be tabled until the next session of Congress in 1945, and six months of unrelenting work would be for naught.

Word of Rankin's refusal to honor Gibson's new proxy was passed by a former VFW commander in the House, Representative Pat Kearney of New York, to the American Legion's lobbyist. The two men decided Gibson had to be found and brought back to Washington to vote by 10 A.M. the next morning, June 8. All that was known was that he was traveling somewhere in his home state. The American Legion led the manhunt. Calls went out to radio stations asking for on-air pleas to locate him. The Georgia State Police sent search cars streaking down the highways and byways. At 11 P.M., Gibson pulled into his driveway and heard the telephone ringing inside his home. When he answered he was told that a car was on its way to whisk him to Waycross, Georgia, where an Army plane was waiting to take him to Washington. The plane, however, was found to be inoperative, and a new dash began to Jacksonville, Florida, two hundred miles away. There, a commercial Eastern Airlines DC-3 was being held for his arrival. A harrowing ride in the rain got him to the plane and he landed at Washington National Airport at 6:37 A.M. At 10 A.M. he burst into the House conference room and declared: "I'm here to lick anyone who tries to hold up the GI Bill of Rights. Americans are dying in Normandy—I'm going to expose anyone who doesn't vote for the GI Bill."[14]

Rankin and his two cohorts were forced to retreat, lest they be castigated as the only opponents of the GI Bill. The committee's vote was now unanimous. S.1767 headed for the floor and lightning approval with the 52-20 provision intact. On June 22, 1944, Franklin D. Roosevelt, putting aside his longstanding opposition to "privileges" for veterans in the face of a bill with massive popular support, attached his signature. The GI Bill of Rights became the law of the land. The event was recorded in a photograph showing Roosevelt flanked by an effervescent Rogers, and Rankin with his arms crossed.[15]

At that moment, Allied troops were liberating Europe under the command of General Dwight D. Eisenhower. One of his commanders, Lieutenant General George S. Patton, was leading his army toward the Seine. General Douglas MacArthur was planning the liberation of the Philippines. For the three generals, glory would come in World War II, and the Bonus March would be only an embarrassing, half-forgotten incident.

Because the nation's attention was fixed on the invasion of Europe, the passage of the GI Bill achieved only modest attention—except in the papers owned by William Randolph Hearst, the bill's biggest editorial backer. Many in the military were slow to learn about it, as word filtered out with only negligible fanfare. *Time* and *Newsweek* each ran an underwhelming piece of a few hundred words about passage of the bill.[16] As a result, historian Milton Greenberg, himself a beneficiary, notes, "To this day, World War II veterans cannot recall where, when or how they first heard of the GI Bill."[17]

Months after the GI Bill became law there were those who still saw the dark side of mass academic education. Writing in *Collier's* magazine in December 1944, Hutchins predicted, "Colleges and universities will find themselves converted into educational hobo jungles. [E]ducation is not a device for coping with mass unemployment." He warned that most Americans were not yet ready for "the education of a free man," and he denounced the

President Roosevelt signed the GI Bill on June 22, 1944, as Representative Edith Nourse Rogers looks over his shoulder. Behind the president stands Representative John Rankin with his arms crossed. (Veterans' Administration)

use of higher education "as a substitute for a dole or for a national program of public works."[18]

The response to Hutchins's dismissive words was quick and angry. A man who had been medically discharged after two years in the South Pacific and who was then at Notre Dame rebutted him in the pages of *Collier's*. He said Hutchins's argument was both "disillusioning and fallacious" and suggested that the colleges as well as the vets needed rehabilitation after the war.

In that same month, President Roosevelt received a disturbing report from the armed forces committee on post-war educational opportunities for service personnel. The committee fully endorsed the provisions of the GI Bill but worried that if too many veterans opted for education and then did not use that education to pursue productive and satisfying lives, a "terrible blight" would be put on academic institutions. The report pointed out that the forty to fifty thousand jobless university students in Germany between 1931 and 1935, along with the unemployed of the old German Imperial Army, spearheaded the rise of Hitler and the growth of the Nazi Party.[19]

The war ended a little more than a year later when Japan surrendered on September 2, 1945. At first it was not clear if the GI Joes and Janes actually understood the provisions of the GI Bill. An article entitled "GIs Reject Education" in the *Saturday Evening Post* concluded that as beneficial as the GI Bill seemed to be in theory, it had one conspicuous drawback: "The guys aren't buying it." But once veterans understood what the GI Bill had to offer, they began to take advantage of the opportunity to go to school. The GI Bill paid tuition of up to five hundred dollars a year—enough to get veterans into Conant's Harvard—along with textbooks and supplies and a stipend of fifty dollars a month; married vets got sixty-five dollars a month.

By 1948 Conant was converted, having discovered that "the mature student body that filled our colleges in 1946 and 1947 was a delight to all who were teaching undergraduates." Ten times more nonvets flunked out of universities than did veterans. "Vets didn't cut classes," James Brady, who went to school with many vets, wrote in 1996. "They did their homework, and many went home to their wives after school." And they worked to stay in school. "I knew one tough sailor," said Brady, "who got up at 4 every morning to clean a saloon's toilets. He'd swept and swabbed for Uncle Sam, and now he was doing it for a college degree."[20]

A number of state universities and colleges were so overwhelmed with eager vets that they quickly set up branches at deactivated military bases, like Fort Devens in Massachusetts and the Navy Pier in Chicago. Vets, who never in their wildest dreams envisioned a college education, gladly enrolled, willing to live once again in barracks and attend classes in makeshift classrooms. They were taught by dedicated professors and instructors—many of them vets themselves—who wanted to do their part for the ex-GIs.

The colleges were, in fact, revitalized, as were the men in the ivory towers who had doubted the vets. In an article in *Life* magazine, Conant admitted that, "for seriousness, perceptiveness, steadiness, and all other undergraduate virtues," the former soldiers and sailors were "the best in Harvard's history." At Columbia University in 1947, none of the 7,826 veterans in attendance was in serious academic difficulty. Such statistics were the norm on campuses across the country. Because of the GI Bill the doors of the colleges and universities were blown open for the middle and lower classes, setting the stage for the continued democratization of higher education. The number of conferred college degrees more than doubled between 1940 and 1950: the percentage of Americans with bachelor or advanced degrees grew from 4.6 percent in 1945 to 25 percent a half century later.

By the cutoff date of July 25, 1956 (which encompassed the Korean War), 2,232,000 veterans had enrolled in college using the GI Bill. The education produced 450,000 engineers, 238,000 teachers, 91,000 scientists, 67,000 doctors, 22,000 dentists, and more than a million other college-trained men and women. Nearly 8 million veterans took advantage of the GI Bill, some opting for a few weeks in the 52-20 Club, then college on the GI Bill, and then a VA loan to buy a first house.

Eleven million of the thirteen million houses built in the 1950s were financed with GI Bill loans. The GI Bill helped to create a well-educated, well-housed, new American middle class whose consumption patterns fueled the postwar economy. In *Post-Capitalist Society*, Peter Drucker wrote: "The GI Bill of Rights—and the enthusiastic response to it on the part of America's veterans—signaled the shift to the knowledge society. Future historians may consider it the most important event of the 20th century." Tom Brokaw, in his book *The Greatest Generation*, called it "a brilliant and enduring commitment to the nation's future."[21] Perhaps the most stunning conclusion was made by Michael J. Bennett, the primary historian of the GI Bill, who said, "After World War I, virtually every belligerent nation other than Britain and the United States had its government overthrown by its veterans. That didn't happen after World War II, largely because of the Marshall Plan, but there wouldn't have been such a plan if America's 16 million veterans—more than one fourth of the civilian work force—hadn't successfully readjusted to civilian life thanks to the GI Bill."

The enduring legacy of the Bonus Army goes well beyond the GI Bill. In the years following World War I, many Americans fearfully looked across the Atlantic at what happened when Russian and German veterans manned the barricades in revolutions of the Left and the Right. The veterans of the Bonus Army taught an American lesson to those who fretted over revolution: If you have a grievance, take it to Washington, and if you want to be heard, bring a lot of people with you.

John Henry Bartlett was there as a witness in 1932 and he saw the bonus marchers shrugging off the agitators who came from the Left and the Right, saw them peacefully petition their government—and then be driven from their capital by bayonets and tear gas. He looked beyond them and saw more: "Starvation, gaunt and hideous, was stalking over the land, and revolution was feared ready to break." In *The Bonus and the New Deal*, published in 1937 while the memories were still fresh, he observed that thanks to the Bonus Army "we may have been saved from a threatened insurrection."

By the time the GI Bill became a reality, America was looking at a new threat. In the mid-1940s and into the 1950s, communism became as feared as revolution was in the 1930s. Americans looked back and saw more Communists in the Bonus Army than had really been there. Ex-Reds, as they were called, came forth and exaggerated their influence over the Bonus Army. Ironically, their distorted, self-serving testimony did what their frustrated efforts in 1932 could not. Though they had been unsuccessful at infiltrating the real Bonus Army, they successfully infiltrated its memory.

American history is punctuated by moments and incidents that become prisms through which larger events are better understood—the Boston Tea Party, Nat Turner's Rebellion, the Alamo, John Brown's Raid. The march of the Bonus Army belongs in such company. But its significance has been obscured by time, even to its direct beneficiaries—the millions of later veterans whose bonus would be the GI Bill and the benefits that have followed to the present day. And, its legacy is everlasting. The First Amendment of the Constitution grants Americans the right "to petition the government for redress of grievances." Millions of Americans have since peacefully marched on Washington in support of various causes, their way paved by the veterans of 1932.

Acknowledgments

We wish to thank these people and institutions for the help they gave us.

Many of the pages of this book exist because they contain information discovered with the assistance of the skill, dedication, and wisdom of the people in that great American treasure, the Library of Congress. We wish to particularly thank the library's Dave Kelly, Tom Mann, and Abby Yochelson for their moral support. They were our chaplains. Thanks also to David Robinson of the Rare Books staff, for helping to sort out the three periodicals all named the *B.E.F. News*.

We were also given special guidance and assistance by the Historical Society of Washington, District of Columbia, and wish to especially thank Shireen L. Dodson, Barbara Franco, Susan Schreiber, Mychalene Giampaoli, Jill Connors Joyner, Gail Redmann, and Laura Schiavo.

Special thanks go to Gretchen Howard, of Garrett Park, Maryland, who helped let us know that we were on the right track. She heard about the project and said that she was already using the story of the Bonus Army in her classroom. The Great Depression had become a dull abstraction—margin calls, bank failures, and the ubiquitous photo of that man in a slouch hat selling apples for 5¢—and therefore hard to teach. The story of the Bonus Army, coupled with old newsreel footage from the summer of 1932, with its images of tanks and teargassed war veterans driven from the streets of Washington, brought the Depression alive and gave her a chance to talk about the government's obligation to those who serve.

Aaron D. Jaffe did extraordinary work during the summer of 2002 when he was assigned to us as an intern on loan from the Historical Society of Washington, D.C. He made many contributions, including his painstaking research into the precise location of the two dozen Bonus Army camps in Washington during the summer of 1932.

We thank Willie Drye, of Plymouth, North Carolina, author of the *The Storm of the Century*, for his generosity in sharing documentation of the Florida work camps, including the *Key Veteran News* and camp reports, and Jerry Wilkinson of the Upper Keys Historical Society, Islamorada, Florida, who gave up a day to show us where the tragic events of Labor Day, 1936, unfolded. Also thanks to Bill Mead for his generous contribution of books on the Florida hurricane, and Theodore F. Watts, for access to his remarkable collection of Coxey's Army and Bonus Army memorabilia and his knowledge of the era.

And thanks to these organizations and their people: the Association of the Oldest Inhabitants of D.C. (William N. Brown, Alex S. Coleves, the late Dr. Philip Ogilve, Sidney Hais, Nelson F. Rimensnyder, and Sherwood Smith); Boston Public Library (Aaron Schmidt); Bridgeport, Connecticut, Historical Society and Bridgeport Public Library (Mary K. Witkowski and Roseanne Mansfield); *Burns Times-Herald*, Burns, Oregon (Pauline Braymen, managing editor); Cleveland Public Library (Margaret Baughman, Amy Dawson); Federal Highway Administration (Richard Weingroff); Franklin D. Roosevelt Presidential Library (Raymond Teichman and Karen Anson); General Douglas MacArthur Foundation, Norfolk, Virginia (James W. Zobel, Edward J. Boone, Jr.); Helen Wadley Library, Islamorada Library, Florida (Jim Clupper); Herbert Hoover Presidential Library (Brad Bauer, Jim Detlefsen, Spencer Howard, Matt Schaefer, and Lynn Smith).

Historic Preservation Office, Government of the District of Columbia (Nancy Kassner); John F. Kennedy Presidential Library (Allan B. Goodrich, James B. Hill, and James Roth); Margaret Chase Smith Library, Skowhegan, Maine (Angela N. Stockwell); Martin Luther King Library, Washingtoniana Division (Faye Haskins, Susan Malbin); Massachusetts National Guard Military Museum and Archives (Colonel Leonid Kondratiuk, U.S. Army [Ret.]); Metropolitan Police Department, Washington, D.C. (Sergeant Nicholas Breul); National Archives (Larry MacDonald, Heather Saffer, Kate Snodgrass, John Taylor, John Vernon, and Mitchell Yockelson); National Park Service (Frank T. Faragasso and Mike Ryan); Portland, Oregon, Archives (Diana Banning, Brian Johnson); *Portland Tribune* (Joseph Gallivan).

279

Sinclair Lewis Society (Sally E. Perry); U.S. Army Armor School Research Library, Fort Knox, Kentucky (Lorraine M. Allen); Veterans Administration (Daniel C. Devine and Susan C. McHugh); Veteran's Administration Library (Cindy Rock, Joyce Zarrommahad); Wisconsin Historical Society (Nancy Mulhern); U.S. Military Academy, West Point, New York (Sheila Biles); University of California, Los Angeles, Department of Special Collections, Powell Library (Charlotte B. Brown and Dennis Bitterlich).

We would like to thank the following individuals who supported us in our attempts to get grants for the project. Not all of these attempts met with success, but it is with deepest appreciation that we name those who wrote recommendations on our behalf: William Allen of the *National Geographic Magazine*; former secretary of defense William S. Cohen; Donald M. Goldstein of the University of Pittsburgh; Dave Kelly of the Library of Congress; Joe Miller of the University of Virginia; Peter Gibbon of Harvard University and Boston University; Carol Schwalbe of Arizona State University; and John Vernon of the National Archives.

Scholars Lucy G. Barber of California State Archives, Jennifer D. Keene of the University of Redlands, and Donald Lisio of Coe College were most gracious in sharing their vast knowledge respectively of marches on Washington, of World War I, and of the Bonus Army. Joy Spalding put her scholarly knowledge of the history of Portland, Oregon, to work on our behalf. Sylvia Smith of the *Fort Wayne Journal-Gazette* combed the archives of her paper for coverage of the Bonus Army. Gail Wight of Stanford University, Edie Allen of Duke, and Jim Witte of Clemson unearthed key documents, including an elusive thesis that took months to locate. Betsy Barnett and Susan Beal contributed research time, and Andrew Dickson, who led us to their friend Cielo Marie Dorado Lutino, worked to unearth the Red files in Portland. We thank fellow writer Bob Skole for his help in sorting through the papers of Edith Nourse Rogers and Ernest Hemingway.

To tell this story, from the beginning we sought interviews with living eyewitnesses. We found them, too. "Slug Flyweights" Nick and Joe Oliver, brought to our attention by their sister Joan Hrutkay of Scenery Hill, Pennsylvania, were seven-year-old boys when they spent the summer of 1932 at the Bonus Army's major encampment in Anacostia.

James G. Banks and Charles P. Greene were young men living in Anacostia in 1932, with vivid memories of that summer so long ago, and we thank them for their time. Then there is Naaman Seigle, who was in the wrong place and still retains some of his original anger over being gassed. John Taylor recalled the impact of the bonus payment in 1936, as did Ned Dolan of Garrett Park, Maryland, and Mrs. Rudolph A. Shupik of Bridgeport, Connecticut.

One of our happiest finds was the diary of a man known as Steve Murray, whose remarkable account has been preserved as a previously unseen record. His daughter and son-in-law, Madeline and Bill Linebarrier of Asheboro, North Carolina, graciously invited us to their home, gave us a photocopy of Steve's diary, and told us about his life beyond the Bonus Army.

Book and memorabilia dealers who helped us locate treasures include Laurent Brocard, Craig Cassidy, Penny Daly, Jim Ludlum, Jim Mance, and Jack Waugamann.

Then there are the fellow writers and old and new friends who helped us in many ways, including their valuable suggestions for this book: Frank Dorsey, Paul Edlund, Joseph C. Goulden, Dana Hardacker, Charles D. Hartman, Bill Hickman, Jack Kujawski, Norman Polmar, Bob Shogan, Jim Srodes, Bob Stock, Joe Thompson, and Dan Moldea, who put the two of us together for this project at one of his writers' dinners. Members of both the Dickson and Allen families helped the cause in many ways, including bed-and-breakfast accommodations.

Finally we would like to give special thanks to Bob Uth and Glenn Marcus, for their belief that we could bring this story to the small screen; to Gail Ross, for making that deal happen; and to Cary Winfrey of the *Smithsonian* magazine, who gave us a platform to debut our version of the epic of Bonus Army. Our deep thanks to agent Jonathan Dolger, who has had faith in this book from the beginning, and to everybody at Walker & Company, starting with Jackie Johnson and George Gibson, and including Marlene Tungseth, copy editor Miranda Ottewell, and Linda Johns and Chris Converse for the Web site.

The first edition of *The Bonus Army*, published on February 1, 2005, immediately began rekindling memories that were passed on to us. In the process we have also been given greater insight into many characters in the book through relatives and associates of the dramatis personae. Walter W. Waters's great-grandson, Walter Leinoner, met us for breakfast in Seattle, where he lives today. The son of Herbert Benjamin, Ernst Benjamin, identified himself at a book signing and paid us the ultimate compliment: that we were among the few writers to get his father "right." Pelham Glassford's great-grandson, Bruce Christy, an artist and motorcyclist, and granddaughter, Lynne Glassford Christie, shared thoughts on his positive influence on the family both as an artist and a man whose legacy included unyielding commitment to racial tolerance.

A number of individuals, all elderly, told us of the effect of the bonus on themselves and their families. Aris Yanibas stood at the end of a lecture on the Bonus Army at the Pritzker Military Library in Chicago and told of his father being paid the bonus and having enough money to return to Greece and bring back a wife from his native village. Yanibas was born a year later—a true bonus baby. Jim McKenna told us over lunch at the National Press Club of his severe illness as a young child growing up in a blighted area of Pittsburgh. The bonus gave his parents the money for his medical treatment and a recuperation period in Florida.

Lois Holloway wrote to tell us that "the large man holding a club" in the photo on page 169 was her grandfather. "Standing on either side of my grandfather," she wrote, "are my then twelve-year-old father and his fourteen-year-old brother. My grandfather, grandmother, and their seven children were early members of 'Camp Camden.'"

The book, she said, "has particular meaning for my family" because it showed that the Bonus March had not been communist-inspired, a false accusation that had always plagued family memories. "One direct and somewhat ironic repercussion of the Bonus March," she said, "was that my grandfather marched my father into a Merchant Marine recruiting center when he turned seventeen, because he did not want Dad to serve in 'MacArthur's Army.' As a consequence, Dad did not benefit from the GI Bill of Rights."

Ronald Hinton, an emeritus member of the Stanford University faculty, knew Herbert Hoover and remembered how the expulsion of the Bonus Army had changed Hoover. He was "deeply embittered" and withdrawn because he "bore the brunt of the blame." *The Bonus Army*, Hinton said, showed that General Douglas MacArthur and George Patton were responsible for the rough handling of the marchers, not Hoover. But Hoover had to live with the blame. "When he became president," Hinton said, "Stanford had given him a great sendoff. When he returned to Stanford after his presidency, the general hatred pursued him. He was the butt of crude jokes. . . . Instead of passing his last years at his beloved Stanford, he withdrew to his family hometown" in Iowa. "I was appointed to the Stanford faculty in 1941, and I believe I am the last member of the Stanford community to have known him personally. His bitterness was evident."

The Long Shadow of
the Bonus Army

1932–Present: The Pet Rabbit, the White Stallion, and Other Myths

The Bonus March inspired many myths, which began to circulate immediately after the veterans' expulsion in 1932 and continue to this day. The earliest myth—"Two babies died of tear gas"—emerged from the shock of events on July 28. A baby did die that day, but not from tear gas. Some contemporary accounts of the July 28 events put the number of injured as high as 100—a figure that included all caught up in the melee: spectators, veterans, and their families. "More than 100 were killed, including two infants," stated a *New York Times* review of the book *Don't Know Much About History* in 1990.[1] That figure apparently became the basis for this summary published in a newspaper in 1992: "Before MacArthur's troops disengaged, more than 100 BEF campers had been injured or killed. Among them were two infants suffocated by gas and a 7-year-old boy who was stabbed by a bayonet while looking for his pet rabbit."[2] Then came "more than 100 casualties, including two babies who died of gas inhalation."[3]

The pet rabbit report was traced back to Johnstown, where veterans, still in shock, told their stories to Pennsylvania Health Department interviewers, who did not attempt to verify them. The interviewers were also told that two boys were fatally bayoneted.[4] There is no record showing that either of these reports is true. Nor is it true, as was often alleged, that General MacArthur rode a white stallion into the fray, although he may have posed with a horse to oblige photographers, according to one reporter. Rumors persisted of courts-martial for soldiers and Marines who refused to take part in the expulsion. There is no record of any such actions.

There is no eyewitness report of shots actually being fired by soldiers on July 28. But a version of that myth came to life in July 1949, when former First Lady Eleanor Roosevelt, writing in *McCall's* magazine, said: "I shall never forget my feeling of horror when I realized that the Army had actually been ordered to fire on the veterans." In her erroneous recollection, she did not say any shots were fired. But Secretary of War Patrick J. Hurley demanded an opportunity to respond, creating what historian Roger Daniels called "a key document in the conservative myth of the bonus march."[5]

Mrs. Roosevelt's statements, Hurley said, "do a grave injustice to former President Hoover and General MacArthur." He went on to say, "The Democratic National Committee, as well as the Soviet Comintern*
. . . declined to accept as true facts pertaining to the marchers' riot." Claiming that "Communists had gained control of the bonus marchers," he noted as proof that the biggest camp was named "Camp Marx,"

---

*The Comintern, or Communist International, was established by the Soviet Union in 1919, ostensibly to guide national Communist parties throughout the world toward common objectives. Secretly, it enlisted local Communists into espionage activities.

as if in homage to the author of *Das Kapital*. In fact it was named Camp Marks, in honor of a police officer who encouraged the vets to stay in Anacostia.[6]

1932–1935: At the Movies

Another form of myth came via the movies. One of them, the 1933 film *Gabriel Over the White House*, has lasted far beyond the 1930s. It was repeatedly screened in 2004 by both American Movie Classics and Turner Movie Classics, giving another generation a sense of how the Bonus Army touched American society.

Gabriel Over the White House, a fantasy based on the reality of the Depression, reveals Americans' undercurrent fear of revolution. In the film, newly elected President Judson Hammond, played by Walter Huston, at first dismisses widespread unemployment and racketeering as "local problems" (a phrase that President Hoover used). Then President Hammond, in a coma after an automobile accident, is miraculously revived. With what seems to be divine help (Angel Gabriel), he begins to lead America out of the Depression. Congress balks at his plans, so President Hammond dissolves Congress and becomes a dictator. When his secretary of war wants to send in troops to stop a protest march, Hammond refuses and, after visiting the marchers, announces the formation of a federal "army of construction" that amazingly presaged President Roosevelt's Civilian Conservation Corps. Dictator Hammond ends Prohibition and, in a crackdown on gangsters, has some executed by firing squads. To show his commitment to world disarmament, he blows up two battleships.

William Randolph Hearst, whose newspapers supported the bonus, was a major financial backer of Metro-Goldwyn-Mayer, the studio that produced the movie. Hearst, without screen credit, wrote some of President Hammond's speeches. A scene in which Hammond is shot at while in a car was changed because of the actual assassination attempt on President-elect Roosevelt on February 16, 1933.[7]

In this movie, and in others directly or indirectly mentioning the Bonus Army, some moviemakers used the veterans as a subject and Camp Marks as a set. In the film of *Washington Merry-Go-Round*, the burning of the camp at Anacostia is used as an element in the plot. On June 7, 1933, a movie opened nationwide entitled *Gold Diggers of 1933*, which featured Joan Blondell in a split skirt leaning against a lamppost singing Al Dubin's torchy "Remember My Forgotten Man" as an exultant parade of World War I soldiers was transformed into a despairing breadline:

> *Remember my forgotten man,*
> *You put a rifle in his hand.*
> *You sent him far away,*
> *You shouted hip hooray,*
> *But look at him today.*

The movie ends with a huge Busby Berkeley production number, vividly parading hundreds of "forgotten men" across the stage. The finale was, as Mordaunt Hall of the *New York Times* put it, "the World War Veteran."[8] At one point, as the ballad is sung, a cop begins to arrest a tramp sleeping on the sidewalk, only to leave him alone when he finds a war medal inside the lapel of his jacket.

The irony was hardly lost on a nation that had listened to its new president campaign, beginning on April 7, 1932, in a radio broadcast, on not losing sight of the "forgotten man at the bottom of the economic pyramid"—but to FDR the forgotten man was the farmer and the worker, not the veteran. The "forgotten man" speech set the tone and the course of Roosevelt's campaign; as one of his closest advisers put it, the speech "created a great deal of discussion at the time; in many quarters it evoked the epithet 'demagogue'— but it kept him in the front as the outstanding liberal fighter."[9]

Hollywood's censor, the Hays Office (named for former postmaster general Will H. Hays), developed a production code that is usually described as a reaction to explicit or suggestive sexual scenes in movies of the 1920s. But political commentary was also censored. There was, for example, concern over "dangerous material" in the *Gabriel Over the White House* script, such as the dismissal of Congress and the president becoming a dictator, and as a result some changes were made.[10]

Movies of despair, such as *I Am a Fugitive from a Chain Gang* (1932) and *Heroes for Sale* (1933), used veterans as central characters who marched off to war and found themselves desperate, discarded men of the Depression. In *Heroes for Sale*, a veteran tries to sell his Medal of Honor to pay for drugs to satisfy the addiction he has acquired from painkillers given to him for his war wounds. Such bitter stories were prohibited by 1934, with the imposition of political censorship by the Hays Office.[11]

The most notorious censorship of movies associated with fears of fascism involved Sinclair Lewis and his book *It Can't Happen Here*, published in 1935, five years after Lewis became the first American to receive the Nobel Prize for Literature. In the novel, a demagogic senator is elected president and declares himself dictator of America. Huey Long, who was believed to be the model for the president, was assassinated as Lewis wrote the novel, rushing to finish it in time for the 1936 presidential election. Another character, Bishop Peter Paul Prang, a radio preacher, was an obvious fictional version of Father Charles E. Coughlin. The book became a best-seller, its sales catapulted by the public's perception of the chilling possibility of revolution. Metro-Goldwyn-Mayer bought the movie rights. But as shooting was about to begin, MGM halted production because, Lewis said, the film dealt with political controversies that would result in boycotts by other countries—presumably dictator-ruled Germany and Italy. He blamed Hays and Samuel Goldwyn, who later denied this motivation for scrapping the film. Undaunted, Lewis arranged for the Federal Theater Project, part of the New Deal's Works Progress Administration, to put it on stage in eighteen cities in October 1936, in time to be seen by presidential voters.[12]

Fears of dictatorship from the Left or Right, a fallout from the Bonus Army experience, began to fade as the New Deal entered its second term. But modern film critics still turn to the Bonus Army to explain 1930s anxieties. One critic even found the vets in *King Kong* (1933), writing, "The defeat of the desire-driven ape by the military clearly comments on the 1932 dispersal by the U.S. Army of the Bonus Expeditionary Force."[13]

1935: The Veterans of Future Wars—Satire or Antiwar Movement?

As the twentieth century wore on and Americans looked back at the 1930s, the mood and nature of the college experience was commonly depicted by what was visually appealing in newsreel footage—stuffing phone booths with students, goldfish swallowing, and a general goofiness. The reality was often more political and to the point. The nation's youth in the middle to latter part of the Depression decade were often leery of authority and willing to challenge it in meaningful ways.

When, for example, Massachusetts mandated that all its teachers and professors take a loyalty oath—swearing to uphold the constitutions of the United States and the Commonwealth—students bristled. In November 1935 the issue came to a head when the chief of police in Williamstown herded the faculty of Williams College into the university chapel for a public swearing of allegiance in front of a notary public. Seeing this spectacle as an example of American fascism and academic cowardice, the students—including the grandson of an undisclosed U.S. president—mocked their timid elders with a display of swastikas, goose-stepping, and Nazi salutes.[14]

Hypocrisy was put on trial by these college boys and girls, who would later be known as members of "the Greatest Generation." Realizing that a war was in their future, they wanted, at least, to know what they would be fighting for. Would it be for acts of freedom—the Boston Tea Party, the Boston Massacre, Shea's Rebellion—or for acts of repression—Sacco and Vanzetti, book censorship by Boston's Watch and Ward Society, the Lawrence strike, and now the forced Williamstown oath?

Seeing future war as inevitable, why not treat it as a future folly? On the night of March 16, 1935, Lewis J. Gorin Jr. of Louisville, Kentucky, and seven friends at Princeton University's Terrace Club founded the Veterans of Future Wars and issued a manifesto that read in part:

> *Whereas it is inevitable that this country will be engaged in war within the next thirty years, and whereas it is by all accounts likely that every man of military age will have a part in this war, we therefore demand that the government make known its intention to pay an adjusted service compensation, sometimes called a bonus, of $1,000 to every male citizen between the ages of 18 and 36, said bonus to be payable the first of June 1965. Furthermore, we believe a study of history demonstrates that it is customary to pay all bonuses before they are due. Therefore, we demand immediate cash payment, plus 3 per cent interest compounded annually and retroactively from the first of June 1965, to the first of June 1935. It is but common right that this bonus be paid now, for many will be killed and wounded in the next war, and hence they, the most deserving, will not otherwise get the full benefit of their country's gratitude.[15]**

*In June 1965, the United States confirmed for the first time that Americans were being given combat assignments in South Vietnam.

That same night at all-female Vassar College, the Association of Gold Star Mothers of Veterans of Future Wars was chartered to gain support for sending young women to Europe to view the graves of their future sons—a parody on the practice of sending boatloads of real Gold Star mothers to Europe to visit the burial grounds of their fallen sons. The name was so offensive to so many that it was changed almost immediately to Home Fire Division of Veterans of Future Wars.

The Princeton-Vassar plan was to establish eight regional commanders for both groups and set up chapters on all American campuses. The idea spread swiftly, thanks to the well-connected Princeton boys, who among them harbored stringers for the *Philadelphia Inquirer,* the *New York Times,* and the Associated Press. Within ten days after this manifesto was released, the movement had swelled across the country, and by the end of March there were 120 college chapters from coast to coast, as well as many outside colleges, with a paid membership of over 6,000, including a number of faculty members and assorted politicians, one of them a former senator.[16]

Satellite groups—such as the Chaplains of Future Wars, organized among divinity students, and the Correspondents of Future Wars, among those aspiring to become journalists—were soon paying dues and giving the official salute of the Veterans of Future Wars: the right arm held out, palm up, beggar style. The Future Correspondents, founded at City College of New York, demanded training in "the writing of atrocity stories and garbled war dispatches for patriotic purposes." The CCNY group offered honorary membership to anyone who could come up with a motto for the next war as good as "Make the World Safe for Democracy."[17]

A like-minded group, the Future War Propagandists, formed at Rutgers, and there was a group of Future War Profiteers formed at Rensselaer Polytechnic Institute with the motto "Getting in on the Gravy Rather Than Being Made into Gravy." A distaff group, known as the Golddiggers of Future Wars, proposed to sit in the laps of the profiteers at champagne parties while "soldiers die for democracy" and there are "better and bigger profits for us." The motto of the Betsy Ross Sewing Circle for Mothers was "Making the World Safe for Hypocrisy." The Friends of the Veterans of Future Wars, initiated by a sympathetic librarian, contributed financially to the cause.

The fledgling chapters were not content to keep their demands to themselves but took them right to the top. OKLAHOMA CHAPTER MEMBERS VETERANS OF FUTURE WARS EARNESTLY SOLICIT YOUR SUPPORT INTRODUCING BILL TO CONGRESS DEMANDING PAYMENT OF $2,000 TO EACH PROSPECTIVE WAR VETERAN, read the telegram from Norman, Oklahoma, to President Roosevelt.[18]

A major force spurring this growth was the ire it provoked in its first days. A Texas Democrat, Representative William D. McFarlane, said the group "ought to be investigated," and the VFW put out a statement "wondering what Hobey Baker and Johnny Poe, as well as other alumni of Princeton who died in France, might say to this apparent insult to their service."[19] James E. Van Zandt, head of the VFW, said they were a bunch of monkeys "too yellow to go to war" and deserved a good spanking. Democratic Representative Charles A. Fuller of Arkansas said the group was "saturated with communism, foreign influence and a total disregard for American patriotism." The Red baiters and sputtering patriots had a field day, and the college boys loved it—Gorin insisted that Van Zandt was himself a Red and offered to debate him on national radio.[20]

One of the few voices of assent was that of Representative Maury Maverick of Texas, a wounded and decorated veteran, who had spent a year in hospitals after sustaining a spine injury from a German bullet, had lost parts of five vertebrae, and was rarely free from pain. He thought the scheme was "swell," saying that if we paid for our wars in advance, we wouldn't have any more wars, and this was fine with him. Maverick had recently introduced legislation that would take the martial "sex" out of ROTC by mandating the reading of antiwar material.[21]

Eleanor Roosevelt said, "I think it's just as funny as it can be! And—taken lightly, as it should be—a grand pricking of lots of bubbles." She thought the name of the Future Gold Star Mothers ill-advised, but believed that the idea of a women's auxiliary in itself was "very amusing."[22]

As this story played out and opposition grew, it was taken more and more seriously; the mood among students was increasingly antiwar, and the Veterans of Future Wars fit into that view. A poll of Columbia University seniors, published when the Veterans of Future Wars was only a few weeks old, said that a majority would refuse to fight in a war conducted outside the United States.[23]

Spring break occurred at the end of April for the Princetonians, and one of the original founders, Thomas Riggs Jr., son of the former governor of Alaska, returned to his home in Washington. On April Fool's Day he tried to register as a lobbyist, asking for $2.5 billion for his "pre-vets." Informed that he did not have to register, he met with a number of members of Congress and walked away with support from eight of them, including Maury Maverick,[24] who said he was willing to give them $10 billion "any old day."[25]

Suddenly the movement, now 20,000 strong, was becoming serious enough to inspire a countermovement of sorts. The American Legion opened a "first aid station and supply depot" in Washington in late April. Staffed by veterans of the Great War, it offered diapers and rubber pants and pretended to be staffed by members of the Gimme Bita Pi fraternity. The legion met its match in the students when they were invited to an open house at the mock first-aid station and sent back a telegram: APPRECIATE KIND INVITATION STOP . . . UNFORTUNATELY PRESSURE OF REAL BUSINESS PREVENTS ACCEPTANCE OF ANY PURELY SOCIAL ENGAGEMENTS STOP WHEN WE GET OUR BONUS WE CAN PLAY TOO.[26]

Less than a week later, Gorin's book *Patriotism Prepaid* was published, billed in a *New York Times* ad as the basis for "one of the most powerful youth movements America had ever witnessed!" The reviewers seemed split on whether this book, written in pure academic style, was satire or serious social criticism.[27] The *Times* thought it was satire, but the *Wall Street Journal* saw nothing less than "superb financial idealism" in Golin's argument that the next war would be so colossally expensive that "after adding the requisite sum to the amount necessary to pay veterans of past wars, there will be nothing left in the till."[28]

On May 31, with a membership of close to 50,000, the satire was pushed aside and the Veterans of Future Wars put forth a "peace without pacifism plan" that called for no declaration of war by the United States without a popular referendum.[29]

In April 1937, with graduation looming for its founders and without any advance notice, the Veterans of Future Wars was shut down and the charters of some 534 local posts revoked. The exercise was over, and Gorin and his pals announced that the group's bank account was $44 in debt at the closing (they had actually hoped to close with a positive balance of $56, but the bank had levied a service charge at the last minute).[30]

The Veterans of Future Wars was all but forgotten until November 30, 1941—eight days prior to the Japanese attack on Pearl Harbor—when the *Washington Post* carried a feature entitled " 'Veterans of Future Wars' Are Becoming Just That," by Edward T. Folliard. It opened with the question: "Where are they now, those droll college boys who, back in 1936 organized the Veterans of Future Wars and demanded a $1,000 bonus in advance?

"Answer: Some are in the Army and some are preparing to go into the Army—for the usual $21 a month without bonus." Folliard talked about Tommy Riggs Jr., who was registered and ready to go overseas with the army.[31]

By March 1944 six of the eight Princetonians were in uniform. Gorin, for example, was an artillery officer. A seventh was working in a key war industry. John C. Turner, the only one not in the war effort, had lost the use of both legs in an auto accident during his senior year and was working for CBS News.

The irony, observed as the war wore down, was that peace-loving American youth were as brave and determined as the enemy. Robert T. Oliver spoke for many when he wrote in the *Washington Post*, "While Hitler, Mussolini and the warlords of Japan were loudly teaching the glories and virtues of war, our youth were organizing peace demonstrations and mockingly joining the 'Veterans of Future Wars.' "[32]

The final irony was that a great number of the boys and some of the girls of the Veterans of Future Wars and its affiliates would soon be in line for a more generous bonus than the one they asked for in jest in 1936.[33]

Lewis Gorin went on to serve as an artillery captain in Italy, France, and Germany. He would later write *The Cannon's Mouth,* a history of field artillery in World War II, become an executive of Reynolds Metals, and run unsuccessfully for Congress in the 1950s. At his death on January 1, 1999, he was honored with an obituary by the late Robert McG. Thomas in the *New York Times.* According to his own obituary in *Editor and Publisher,* Thomas's obituaries, known to devotees as "McG's," were so good that he often got fan mail. Writing of Gorin, Thomas focused on his temporary stint as head of the Veterans of Future Wars, which for a moment made him the "most famous collegian in America who did not play football"; before he went on to a "long, respectable and thoroughly obscure career as a business executive."[34]

1949: Return of the Red Menace—the Bonus Army Meets the Cold War

Claims of Communist involvement in the Bonus Army persisted for decades. Benjamin Gitlow, Communist Party candidate for vice president in 1924 and 1928, claimed in a book published in 1949 that Soviet officials in Moscow "sharply criticized" U.S. Communists for their "failure to gain leadership and control" of the Bonus Army.[35] Despite such admissions of failure from the Communists themselves, both General MacArthur and President Hoover, in their memoirs, never wavered from their 1932 views of Communist involvement. MacArthur wrote, "The American Communist Party planned a riot of such proportions that it was hoped the United States Army, in its efforts to maintain peace, would have to fire on the marchers. In this way, the Communists hoped to incite revolutionary action. Red organizers infiltrated the veteran groups and presently took command from their unwitting leaders."[36]

Secretary of War Patrick J. Hurley went further. In his authorized biography, the author notes, "General MacArthur, having received information from Army Intelligence sources working among the bonus marchers that the Communists were in virtually complete control of the bonus army and that some elements within the camps were armed (they said several machine guns were found concealed in the camps), refused to merely move the rioters from the seized buildings back to their camps across the river and then keep his troops camped on the city side of the river overnight. He said bluntly, 'I will not permit my men to bivouac under the guns of traitors.'"[37] (No machine guns were found in the camps.)

Hoover, in his 1952 memoir, referred back to his attorney general's report on the marchers and estimated that nine hundred of the Bonus Marchers "were ex-convicts and Communists." He had wanted to "surround the camps and determine more accurately the number of Communists and ex-convicts among the marchers," but, as he tactfully put it, "Certain of my directions to the Secretary of War, however, were not carried out." Communism came up again when Hoover remarked upon "the activities of the Communists in opposing my election in 1932."[38]

The resurrection of the Communist-control claim can be traced to the earliest phase of the Cold War, when ex-Communists charged that a Red underground had infiltrated the federal government. John Pace, a leader of the Workers Ex-Servicemen's League, made headlines in the Hearst press with his claims of Communist infiltration, which he later presented in congressional testimony.

1963: Marching on Washington—Reincarnation of the Bonus Army

For years to come memories of the Bonus Army seemed to be stirred by any march on Washington. In 1963, when the nonviolent March on Washington was planned by A. Philip Randolph, longtime head of the Brotherhood of Sleeping Car Porters, it was compared to the Bonus Army. The *Wall Street Journal* used the failure of the Bonus Army to underscore its editorial belief that Randolph's proposed march amounted to a waste of time—"no marchers have ever stampeded Congress into action"—and some feared that the march could end the same way.[39] It did not. Instead, it became a signal moment in American history when the Reverend Martin Luther King Jr. gave his "I Have a Dream" speech.

When King and the Southern Christian Leadership Conference (SCLC) planned their Poor People's March in 1968, the Bonus Army's march was seen as a model for the nonviolent occupation of Washington. Stanley Levison,* a lawyer and businessman, initiated the idea, suggesting the Bonus Army model. (He was the only King adviser old enough to remember the 1932 event.) Levison's "idea of a camp of poor squatters illegally bivouacked on the Mall was a public relations gambit, proposed largely to attract press attention to the campaign in its early stages," according to Gerald D. McKnight in *The Last Crusade: Martin Luther King, Jr., the FBI, and the Poor People's Campaign.* On the eve of the Washington campaign, McKnight says, presidential assistant Matt Nimetz began circulating excerpts from *The Crisis of the Old Order,* by New Deal historian Arthur Schlesinger Jr., which described the eviction of the Bonus Army and its disastrous impact on the political future of Herbert Hoover. Drawing on that lesson, Nimetz urged that the White House "deal with the Poor People's Campaign in a civilized manner."[40]

King was assassinated on April 4, but the Poor People's March went on without him and was dedicated to him. When the first contingent of welfare mothers and clergymen arrived on April 22, they occupied one of the spots near the Capitol that bonus marchers had occupied thirty-six years earlier. Like the BEF, the 1968 marchers lobbied Congress and erected a tent city; theirs was on the National Mall and was called

---

*Levison, a Communist Party financial backer in the 1930s, was under FBI surveillance when he began advising King. Thus the FBI secretly obtained information about King. Notified by the Department of Justice that Levison was a Communist, King broke off contact with him.

Resurrection City. As tension rose in Washington about the encampment, and the population grew to upward of 15,000, the *New York Times,* in an editorial titled "'Shanty Town' on the Potomac," declared that some members of Congress and some members of the march were acting as if they wanted Washington to become the scene of an encounter "as dismaying" as the expulsion of the Bonus Army.[41] The House Rules Committee later approved (6–3) legislation calling for the forced closing of the encampment—over the objection of committee members who said a forced removal would be a repeat of the 1932 expulsion and bring on rioting.[42] Mindful of the violent eviction of the Bonus Army, the police and National Guard troops closed down the Poor People's tent city carefully and peacefully.[43]

The Bonus Army was also recalled when antiwar protesters began arriving in Washington in late April 1971. As thousands of protesters assembled on the National Mall, including an angry vet named John Kerry, Attorney General John Mitchell asked President Richard M. Nixon what should be done.

"Leave them there," Nixon said in one of his secretly recorded tapes. The verbatim transcript says: "I don't wanna, uh, like the Bonus March 'n' all that stuff. You recall poor old Hoover and MacArthur, you know."

Nixon, backed up by a memo from Pat Buchanan, asserted that Americans never forgave MacArthur for evicting the Bonus Army.[44] Ten days later, seven thousand Mayday protestors were arrested in a single day—the largest number of citizens arrested in a single action in American history. Critics faulted the government for not basing the mass arrests on any formal declaration; they noted that President Hoover had acted only after he had received a written request from the D.C. commissioners.[45]

Ron Kovic, a disabled Vietnam vet arrested in 1974 with three other vets for occupying the Washington Monument and a White House restroom, claimed he acted under the banner of the American Veterans Movement Bonus March Coalition.[46] Kovic had envisioned a "Nixonville," where ten thousand new bonus marchers would camp and demand veterans' benefits.[47]

There were other attempts to mobilize a new Bonus Army in 1992, 1994, and 1998, but none attracted more than momentary attention. One, though, did not lack poignancy: in 1994, after Veterans' Affairs secretary Jesse Brown announced that as many as 250,000 Vietnam vets were homeless, a group of them gathered across the street from the White House to demand government help.[48]

Appendix B
What Became of Them

JOHN J. ABT, who played a brief part in the Roosevelt administration's handling of the 1935 hurricane deaths of veterans in Florida, became the longtime chief counsel to the Communist Party of the United States, establishing precedents and making sure that being a Communist was not illegal. He was Sidney Hillman's counsel in the labor movement and a top aide in the 1948 presidential campaign of former vice president Henry Wallace. Abt seemed to have a Zelig-like ability to pop up at newsworthy moments. In 1924 he testified in the trial of two college fraternity brothers, Nathan Leopold and Dicky Loeb. In a famous trial the two young men were convicted of kidnapping and murdering fourteen-year-old Bobby Franks. Abt had been brought in to testify as to the "mental sickness" of the two men.[1]

John Abt was the man Lee Harvey Oswald tried unsuccessfully to contact between the time he was arrested for killing President Kennedy and shot by Jack Ruby in 1963. Abt, questioned by Lee J. Rankin, general counsel to the Warren Commission, told him that he had never heard Oswald's name before he heard it on the radio after the assassination.[2] In the days following the assassination, Abt turned over to J. Edgar Hoover his file on Oswald, including six handwritten letters from Oswald to the Communist Party in which he describes his activities in New Orleans and Dallas, requests a job on the *Daily Worker,* and solicits advice on his role in "the struggle for progress and freedom."[3] Abt died on August 10, 1991.

JOHN "MR. BONUS ARMY" ALFERI, as if trying to set a record, on January 3, 1937, arrived in Washington for the fifth consecutive year to declare that now that the bonus had been paid, he was on a new crusade: to secure a $60 per month pension for all veterans of the war. He would stay in Washington, he warned, until the pension was granted. He had a new slogan for this exercise in futility: "Give until it hurts, and soak the big guys who are drawing over ten grand every year." At this moment he faded into obscurity and, in terms of the national media that had helped create him as a character, was never heard from again.[4]

HERBERT BENJAMIN, the leader of the 1931 and 1932 hunger marches, was an avowed Communist and a leading organizer of dissent for two decades. He left the Communist Party in 1944 but, unlike others, did not denounce the party or renounce his beliefs. From 1953 to his retirement in 1978, he operated a crafts boutique, Pottery Fair, in Washington's exclusive Georgetown neighborhood. He died on May 10, 1983.

SMEDLEY DARLINGTON BUTLER, after going to Congress with his revelations about a plot against President Roosevelt, lectured frequently, donating half his fees to charity. Once he said "hell" during a radio broadcast and was cut off the air. In a small book, *War Is a Racket,* he looked back at his missions as a Marine officer in Latin America and wrote, "I spent most of my time being a high class muscle-man for Big Business, for Wall Street and for the Bankers. In short, I was a racketeer, a gangster for capitalism." From 1935 through 1937, he spoke for the left-wing League against War and Fascism, becoming increasingly anti-war at a time when America was preparing for war. He died on June 21, 1940, of what doctors called "an abdominal condition."

GEORGE L. CASSIDAY, the Man in the Green Hat, became a minor national celebrity with the publication of his syndicated newspaper memoirs in the fall of 1930. In the words of the *Washington Post,* he had "stolen first page notices right under the noses of men in the halls of Congress who would have given much to gain the front page space given to this remarkable character." After a series of unsuccessful appeals, he went to jail for eighteen months on April 30, 1931. Because he was well-connected and respected, however, he was allowed to serve his time during the day and go home at night. He went on to become the national commander of the Irish War Veterans. In that role he was one of those who put his hand in a glass bowl to select a number in the draft of July 18, 1941, a peacetime lottery "to make America strong" on the eve of America's entry into World War II. He died in 1967.

FATHER CHARLES E. COUGHLIN, the "radio priest," returned to the airwaves in the fall of 1937, but his broadcasts were discontinued for good in 1940. His periodical, *Social Justice*, was banned from the mails in 1941 by postal authorities because "it mirrored the Axis propaganda line." In 1966 he broke a self-imposed silence on the fiftieth anniversary of his becoming a priest. Despite his virulent attacks on Roosevelt in the later 1930s ("a great liar and betrayer"), he was now a much mellower person, saying he thought that "submission to authority was man's greatest virtue."[5] He died on October 27, 1979; his funeral was at the Shrine of the Little Flower in Royal Oak, Michigan, where he had served as pastor from 1926 until his retirement in 1966.

JACOB S. COXEY, the leader of Coxey's Army, later became an advocate of public works as a remedy for unemployment and ran for president as the Farmer-Labor Party candidate in 1932, earning a mere 7,309 popular votes. He was also an ardent proponent of free-silver monetary policy and an opponent of the gold standard. Although his march failed, Coxey's Army was a harbinger of an issue that would rise to prominence, as unemployment insurance became a key element in the future Social Security Act of 1935. On May 1, 1944, Coxey returned to Capitol Hill and completed the speech he had tried to deliver fifty years earlier. He died on May 18, 1951, at the age of ninety-seven.[6]

HERBERT H. CROSBY, the District commissioner who hired Pelham Glassford, began his Army career in 1893. He submitted his resignation as commissioner on April 9, 1933, but the newly inaugurated president, Franklin D. Roosevelt, asked him to stay until a new commissioner was named in the fall of 1933. Crosby then went to San Antonio, Texas, to become president of a bank. Illness cut short his new career, and he returned to Washington, where he died in January 1936 at the age of sixty-four, after a long illness from inflammatory rheumatism.[7]

VICE PRESIDENT CHARLES CURTIS was constantly chided for calling out the Marines during the remainder of the election year 1932. The day after the expulsion, he was in Las Vegas on his way to preside over the opening of the Olympic Games in California. When he was heckled about the bonus, he shouted back: "You cowards! I'm not afraid of any of you."

Curtis was the model for Vice President Alexander Throttlebottom in the hit Broadway musical *Of Thee I Sing*, book by George S. Kaufman, lyrics by Ira Gershwin, music by George Gershwin. In the musical, which opened on December 26, 1931, and ran for 441 performances, Throttlebottom is ordered to go into hiding because vice presidents are never to be seen. Curtis, found dead on February 8, 1936, was still listed on the rolls of the Interior Department as an Indian ward of the government as a member of the Kaw tribe.

VICE PRESIDENT CHARLES GATES DAWES won the Nobel Peace Prize for the Dawes Plan, the blueprint for German reparations after World War I. He was ambassador to Great Britain from 1929 to 1932. The song "It's All in the Game" was an adaptation of Dawes's composition without lyrics "Melody in A Minor." He died on October 27, 1979.

JOHN DOS PASSOS completed his epic *USA Trilogy* in 1936; it is regarded as his major work. He drew upon his experiences as an ambulance driver in World War I for *One Man's Initiation* (1920) and *Three Soldiers* (1921). Over time, he swung from the Left to the Right politically, although he would tell interviewers that his ideas had remained constant while the world itself changed. He wrote more than fifty novels and works of nonfiction. He died in October 1970.

DWIGHT D. EISENHOWER is quoted by a biographer, Carlo D'Este, as saying, "Probably no one had tougher fights with a senior man than I did with MacArthur. I told him time and time again: 'Why in the *hell* don't you *fire* me? Goddammit, you do things I don't agree with and you know damn well I don't.'

"That MacArthur could have ruined his career at the stroke of a pen does not seem to have bothered Eisenhower nor, he said, did it occur to him to worry about the possible consequences," D'Este continues.

"His stormy encounters with MacArthur undoubtedly toughened Eisenhower for the enormous pressures and demands that he would face during World War II. Nevertheless, their deteriorating relations took a heavy toll on Eisenhower who, at times, wished MacArthur had actually sacked him. MacArthur, however, was too shrewd to deprive himself of Eisenhower's services and ignored their differences."[8]

Eisenhower was appointed Supreme Commander, Allied Expeditionary Forces, in December 1943 and commanded the Allied forces that began the liberation of Europe with the Normandy invasion of June 6, 1944. He announced his candidacy for the Republican Party nomination for president on June 4, 1952. He was nominated at the Republican convention in 1952, and elected on November 4, 1952. During the campaign, the Democrats published a tabloid-style newspaper that linked him to the 1932 expulsion of the Bonus Army.[9] Eisenhower died on March 28, 1969, at Walter Reed Army Hospital in Washington, D.C.

HAMILTON FISH JR. remained a Republican member of Congress from New York until 1944 and was an eloquent critic of President Roosevelt. Until his death Fish was a stalwart backer of the American Legion. He was one of its earliest members.[10] He died on January 18, 1991, at the age of 102.

FLOYD GIBBONS went on to cover the war in Ethiopia, the Sino-Japanese War, and the Spanish Civil War. He died on September 24, 1939, at age fifty-two, having covered nine wars and revolutions. He was preparing to head overseas to cover the war in Europe when his heart gave out.

PELHAM D. GLASSFORD was appointed a federal conciliator in the strike of some fifteen thousand farmworkers in California's Imperial Valley in 1933. As in Washington in 1932, he found unwarranted claims of Communist influence. "After more than two months of observation and investigation," he was convinced "that a group of growers have exploited a communist hysteria for the advancement of their own interests . . . have welcomed labor agitation, which they could brand as 'Red,' as a means of sustaining supremacy by mob rule, thereby preserving what is so essential to their profits—cheap labor."[11]

In 1936, at the behest of a veterans' group, Glassford ran unsuccessfully for the House of Representatives from Arizona. On May 12, 1938, he predicted that there would be no presidential election in 1940; by then the nation would be in the hands of a dictator because the government and private industry had been unable to cope with the Depression. During World War II he returned to Washington, serving as internal security director for the army provost marshal general, whose duties included supervision of camps for prisoners of war and relocation camps (for Japanese and Japanese-Americans) in the United States. Glassford was awarded the Legion of Merit for his work in World War II.

Today if he is remembered at all, it is as an artist. He died on August 9, 1959. A few weeks after his death a letter was published in the *Washington Post* from an old friend named Gardner Jackson who recalled him with great fondness and respect: " 'Hap Glassford has remained for me since those days as a symbol of the ideal approach to the necessary, day-to-day social discipline exemplified by police forces. He was a West Point graduate who never acted like one, because he did not succumb to that academy's training and courses which discourage thinking except in military terms."[12]

ERNEST HEMINGWAY left Key West on the breakup of his marriage to Pauline Pfeifer. The remainder of his life is well documented elsewhere, but one footnote begs to be revealed. In declassified World War II OSS records, discovered while we were doing research in the Hemingway papers at the Kennedy Library in Boston, the intelligence service deals with his offer to work for his country: "Decided in the negative about Hemingway. We may be wrong, but feel that, although he undoubtedly has conspicuous abilities for this type of work, he would be too much of an individualist to work under military supervision."[13] Hemingway killed himself in Idaho on July 2, 1961.

FRANK T. HINES, who served in the Spanish-American War and was an Army general in World War I, remained administrator of Veterans' Affairs through World War II. A month after he resigned in 1945, President Truman appointed him ambassador to Panama, where he served for three years. Hines, who was usually referred to as General Hines, died in 1960 at the age of eighty-one.

J. EDGAR HOOVER treated the Bonus Army march as a milestone in his career-long search for Communists. His work under President Hoover continued under President Roosevelt, who in 1935 created the Federal Bureau of Investigation. Hoover's 1932 relationship with the Army's Military Intelligence Division

(MID) continued into the prewar years. During World War II, the FBI had jurisdiction for spy-hunting.*
Hoover ran the FBI until he died in his sleep on May 2, 1972, having led the FBI for forty-eight years.

HARRY HOPKINS was named secretary of commerce in 1938, a post he held until September 1940. During
World War II he became FDR's unofficial emissary to Winston Churchill and Josef Stalin. The administrator of the wartime Lend-Lease program, he also acted as the prime behind-the-scenes adviser to Roosevelt
at his Big Three conferences with Churchill and Stalin. Hopkins died in early 1946, succumbing to a long
and debilitating illness.

PATRICK J. HURLEY, who fought in World War I and rose in rank to lieutenant colonel, served as secretary of war until Franklin D. Roosevelt became president. When World War II began, he was called to active duty as a brigadier general and organized the secret transportation of supplies to MacArthur's troops
besieged in the Philippines. Later, he served as U.S. minister to New Zealand and Roosevelt's personal
representative, first to the Soviet Union and then as a fact-finder in Egypt, Saudi Arabia, Iran,
Afghanistan, India, Ceylon, and Burma. He was promoted to major general in February 1944 and left the
Army. In December 1944, Roosevelt appointed Hurley ambassador to China, plunging him into the sim-
mering civil war between Chinese Communists under Mao Tse-tung and China's pro-American ruler,
Chiang Kai-shek. When Mao seized power in 1949, a "Who lost China?" debate began in the United
States. Hurley resigned, charging that State Department career diplomats "continued to side with the
Communist armed party."[14] As an ardent anti-Communist, he unsuccessfully ran for the Senate in 1946
and 1948, blaming his defeats on "smears" that included his role in the Bonus Army episode in 1932 and in
China in 1944.[15] He remained a voluble anti-Communist for the rest of his life. Hurley died in Santa Fe,
New Mexico, on July 30, 1963.

GEORGE KLEINHOLZ, reminiscing about his leadership role in the Bonus Army, said in 1963 that he believed the Bonus March served useful purposes. "It got things for veterans they otherwise wouldn't have
gotten," he said. "And it took several years. There were political implications of long duration, too." He
added that he was sure that MacArthur failed to win a presidential nomination because 'he would never get
the veteran's vote.'"[16] When asked if he would do the Bonus March over, his wife broke in to say no, but he
said, "Well, yes, I think I would if I thought the cause was just."

As for the 1963 civil rights march, he thought it was "very foolish" but was quick to add, "Don't get me
wrong. I believe in their aims and I believe in civil rights for all, but I believe this march will have little effect on attaining those rights. I think the civil rights issue will be ironed out but I don't think that a march
of only one day is going to do any good."

FIORELLO LA GUARDIA became the very popular mayor of New York from 1933 through 1945. During
World War II he served as director of the Office of Civilian Defense. In 1946 he became director general of
the United Nations Relief and Rehabilitation Administration, which fed and gave shelter to millions of
Europeans displaced by World War II. He died on September 21, 1947.

JIMMY LAKE never stopped playing the role of Jimmy Lake as barkeep, burlesque impresario, and ring announcer. His most popular role came as the announcer for NBC's immensely popular Friday-night fights
in the early days of television. In his autobiography, published when he was seventy-eight years old, he proclaimed that "I've enjoyed every moment of my life, and that's all a man can ask."

Lake died on September 15, 1967, at age eighty-seven. His *Washington Post* obituary noted that Edward
R. Murrow had called him "one third Falstaff, one third Barry Fitzgerald and one third W. C. Fields."[17]

DOUGLAS MACARTHUR, to the surprise of many, was reappointed Army chief of staff in 1934 by Franklin D.
Roosevelt, beginning an often prickly relationship that would continue through the Depression and much of
World War II. When Roosevelt reappointed MacArthur in 1934, he let the general know how upset he was

*Several MID files from the years 1939 to 1941 were withdrawn from the National Archives by the FBI on June 27,
1980. They were still missing in 2003, when the authors submitted a Freedom of Information request for the documents. They showed that Bonus March veterans were still the subject of MID and FBI reports as late as 1940.
(There was no obvious reason for the withdrawal of the files in 1980.)

with the muckraking "Merry-Go-Round" column, which was highly critical of the New Deal. MacArthur took this as a hint and sued for $1.75 million, alleging that the columnists, Drew Pearson and Robert S. Allen, had subjected him to ridicule and contempt in a column written about him. A major element in the suit was the way Pearson and Allen had covered MacArthur and the events of July 28, when they depicted him as vain and cowardly.[18] The suit was quietly dropped and the general paid the legal fees for Allen and Pearson when it appeared that an unsavory detail might come out at the trial: Pearson had obtained the cooperation of a chorus girl, the daughter of a Chinese woman and a Scottish man living in Manila, who had given him a packet of highly embarrassing letters detailing her liaison with MacArthur. Pearson gave MacArthur the letters when the suit was dropped.[19]

MacArthur claimed that he dressed down Roosevelt in a discussion of the Army budget: "I spoke recklessly and said something to the general effect that when we lost the next war, and an American boy, lying in the mud with an enemy bayonet through his belly and an enemy foot on his dying throat, spat out his last curse, I wanted the name not to be MacArthur, but Roosevelt. The President grew livid. 'You must not talk that way to the President!' he roared. He was, of course, right, and . . . I told him he had my resignation as Chief of Staff. As I reached the door his voice came with that cool detachment which so reflected his extraordinary self-control, 'Don't be foolish, Douglas; you and the budget must get together on this.'"[20]

When the Japanese attacked Pearl Harbor on December 7, 1941, MacArthur was in the Philippines. As the Japanese drove MacArthur's troops down the Bataan Peninsula, Roosevelt ordered MacArthur to leave so he could fight elsewhere, and later awarded MacArthur the Medal of Honor. (MacArthur's father had received the Medal of Honor in the Civil War.) During the war, MacArthur essentially ran his own theater, as commander of the Southwest Pacific Area, while Admiral Chester Nimitz had the rest of the ocean as commander of the Central Pacific Area. He was so revered that when two men made disparaging remarks about him, the FBI arrested them and charged them with sedition; earlier, the California attorney general, future Supreme Court chief justice Earl Warren, had charged them with criminal libel.[21]

MacArthur's presidential ambitions flared briefly in 1944—he would have been a general running against his commander in chief—and became serious in 1948. Among the retired generals who endorsed MacArthur in 1948 was Pelham Glassford, who said of the expulsion of the bonus marchers, "MacArthur did a splendid job and there were no casualties. He had been put in charge because it was a sensitive situation which he was best qualified to handle."[22]

In June 1950, when the Korean War began, President Truman appointed MacArthur supreme commander of United Nations forces. After UN forces crossed the 38th Parallel—the border between North Korea and South Korea—MacArthur issued a statement indicating plans to expand the war into China by heading north toward the Yalu River, the boundary between China and North Korea. MacArthur was in contact with a Republican congressman sympathetic to his plans. Truman, bristling at MacArthur's insubordination, relieved him of command on April 11, 1951, a move that set off a political firestorm. Some of MacArthur's supporters saw a Communist plot and traced it back to 1932, when he attacked the Reds in the Bonus Army. (Then, he disobeyed his commander in chief by crossing a river; in 1951, he did not get a chance to do that again.) The ouster of MacArthur inspired an unsuccessful attempt to get him to run for the presidency in 1952. MacArthur died at Walter Reed Army Hospital in Washington on April 14, 1964, at the age of eighty-four.

EVALYN WALSH MCLEAN sold off her mansion, "Old Friendship," for the government to use as a housing project on the day after Pearl Harbor. During World War II she gave lavish parties for the members of the armed forces, For the women who attended, she would distribute some of her collection of rare jewels to be worn for the party and collected afterward.[23]

McLean died on April 26, 1947, still in possession of the Hope Diamond, which was bought by a jewelry dealer in 1958 and given to the Smithsonian Museum of Natural History, where it remains today. Wilma Waters, interviewed in her eighties, acknowledged that McLean not only paid for her trip to Washington but provided an apartment for the couple.

MAURY MAVERICK, who served and was wounded in World War I, was the county tax collector in 1932 when bonus marchers began appearing in San Antonio. He became the director of the War Veterans' Relief Camp, later renamed the Diga Colony (a backward anagram for Agricultural and Industrial Democracy). The camp faded away after Roosevelt's New Deal began providing direct federal relief. Maverick served in Congress from January 3, 1935, to January 3, 1939, and was mayor of San Antonio from 1939 to 1941. During World War II he served on the War Production Board and was chairman of the Smaller War Plants Corporation, a federal agency set up to help small businesses participate in war production. Writing about his experience in the *New York Times Magazine* on May 21, 1944, he complained about bureaucratic language, which he called "gobbledygook," inspired by the turkey, which is "always gobbledy gobbling and strutting with ludicrous pomposity." He thus joined his grandfather, Samuel A. Maverick, in contributing a word to the American language. Sam Maverick, a prominent rancher, had so many cattle that he did not brand them; cowboys began calling them "mavericks," and the word came to mean people who acted independently—which could certainly describe Maury Maverick. In Congress, while usually siding with Roosevelt, he sometimes opposed the leadership, leading a group of Democratic representatives who called themselves mavericks. He died in San Antonio, Texas, on June 7, 1954.[24]

His son, Maury Maverick Jr., was a legislator, lawyer, and freelance columnist for the *San Antonio Express-News* who represented conscientious objectors during the Vietnam War. "I would walk to a federal court with a boy who didn't want to kill or be killed in Vietnam," he wrote. "It was as if I had walked in with a mass murderer. People are frightened, including some judges, when you represent a political or religious dissenter." He died on January 28, 2003.

GASTON B. MEANS'S money from the Lindbergh swindle was never recovered. Means claimed that he had given it to Max Hassel, a New Jersey bootlegger, to be used for a liquor deal. Hassel was killed in gang warfare in 1933, and $213,487 was found in cash in his safe-deposit box. Means claimed that McLean's money was part of that sum, but it could not be proven, and Means was not known for telling the truth. He died in prison on December 12, 1938.[25]

HENRY O. MEISEL returned to Waukesha, where he became a motorcycle policeman. In 1934 he attempted to run for governor of Wisconsin as a Progressive, but conceded to Philip La Follete on the eve of the primary.[26]

ANDREW MELLON accepted the post of U.S. ambassador to Great Britain in February 1932, serving for one year and then retiring to private life in 1937, when he donated his art collection to the public, with funds for the erection of a building in Washington in which to house it. The building became the National Gallery of Art, which stands near the site of the eviction that led to the expulsion of the veterans on July 28, 1932. Mellon died on August 26, 1937, soon after construction of the National Gallery began.

STEVE MURRAY became a labor organizer in 1934 and was indicted and convicted of inciting to riot in what North Carolina newspapers called an "uprising" during a strike against textile mills in Kannapolis, "towel city of the nation." National Guard troops had been called out to quell the strike. Murray's two-year prison sentence was suspended providing he leave the state and not return for five years, but he did return and was jailed. He later became a contractor and continued playing music in religious string bands, not unlike the BEF band.

Murray died on June 3, 1978, in Asheboro, North Carolina. His daughter and son-in-law, Madeline and Bill Linebarrier, who gave us access to Murray's diary, live in Asheboro. The license plates on their car read "B.E.F. Band," and they now use the big iron cauldron that went to Washington with the band in 1932 as a planter.

JOHN T. PACE quit the Communist Party in 1935 and thereafter became a willing witness at hearings into Red subversion. In 1949, while living in Centerville, Tennessee, where he had become a farmer, a deputy sheriff, and a member of the American Legion, Pace told the Hearst newspapers that he had been instructed to foment rioting in the hopes that there would be bloodshed. Pace said that he was subject to the orders of Emanuel Levin, who kept a secret office in Washington.[27]

The Hearst series, published in the flagship *New York Journal-American* and other Hearst papers in 1949, began: "Hoping for bloodshed and violence, the Communist Party agents within the ranks of the bonus marchers used every Red Fascist trick to get President Hoover to call out the army in 1932." When Hoover and General MacArthur managed to keep blood from being shed, the story continued, "Red Fascist wrath was directed against these two great Americans—a raging 'smear' campaign that has lasted for almost two decades."[28] (Pace did not have firsthand information about the expulsion because he was in jail at the time.)

Pace had secretly testified before the House Un-American Activities Committee (HUAC) in 1938 and 1949, but, as historian Donald J. Lisio notes, the Hearst stories did not match Pace's testimony, which was "confused and contradictory." In 1938, for example, he told the committee that he had been "put on the pan" because his superiors felt that he and other Communist leaders had failed. In the 1949 testimony he said that the "Communist Party of the United States was severely criticized by the representative of the Comintern," a Moscow-trained official who said the party was "a swivel-chair organization."

In 1951, after President Truman fired MacArthur and Truman critics cried "smear," Pace was recalled before HUAC, but he added little more than congratulations to the committee for its work. He was congratulated in turn.

WRIGHT PATMAN was the author of one of the most popular publications ever published by the Government Printing Office, *Handbook for Servicemen and Servicewomen of World War II and Their Dependents, Including Rights and Benefits of Veterans of World War I and Their Dependents.* For a new generation of veterans his name was associated with getting them their due.

Patman spent forty-seven years in the House of Representatives, always playing the role of the maverick, the outsider fighting big banks, high interest rates, and the use of tax-free foundations as tax shelters. He was a declared foe of the Ku Klux Klan and, as a Texas legislator, pushed through legislation to curb the Texas Klan. In 1972 he was the first to call for an investigation of Watergate, a move that was initially blocked by the White House.

Patman died in 1976 at age eighty-two. His *Washington Post* obituary noted that during his long career he never mastered the simplest procedural motions that legislators must learn to make, "but he was probably the pricklest foe of central banking since Andrew Jackson abolished the Bank of the United States in 1836."

GEORGE S. PATTON JR., speaking to a group of officers in 1940, said, "War will be won by blood and guts alone." From then on, that was his nickname. His combat in World War II began with the North African invasion in November 1942, when he was in command of the Western Task Force that landed in Morocco. Promoted to lieutenant general and given command of the U.S. Seventh Army, he led it in the invasion of Sicily.

Twice in August 1943 Patton lost his temper when he encountered hospitalized soldiers who, while not physically wounded, were suffering from battle fatigue, which had been called "shell shock" in World War I. He accused both soldiers of cowardice, struck one across the mouth with his glove, and threatened to have the other shot. When doctors and hospital staff complained, General Dwight D. Eisenhower asked Patton for an explanation and directed him to apologize if reports of the incidents were true. Patton apologized to both men, the hospital staff, and his divisions, but when the incidents became public, there were loud cries for Patton's removal.

General Eisenhower accepted Patton's apologies and Patton went on to lead his troops to dramatic victories in France and Germany later in the war. His most spectacular maneuver was his race to save embattled Bastogne in December 1944. He died in defeated Germany on December 21, 1945, fatally injured in an automobile accident.

JOHN E. RANKIN remained in Congress until his attempted reelection in 1952, when he lost his seat. He was a virulent anti-Communist who fought long and hard to get the United States out of the United Nations. His greatest crusade was his attempt to preserve segregation. He once successfully defeated the idea of a special ballot to allow soldiers to vote from overseas because he felt it could lead to the end of the poll tax, a major force in blocking black voting rights. On the other side of the ledger, he introduced the bill that led to the Tennessee Valley Authority. He died in Tupelo, Mississippi, on November 26, 1960, and was interred in Greenwood Cemetery, West Point, Mississippi. His papers have been sealed from public view by order of his family.[29]

ROYAL W. ROBERTSON worked the lecture circuit for a short time after his appearance at the 1935 march, then dropped from public view.

He died on January 10, 1938, in Los Angeles at the age of forty-six. His obituary in the *Washington Daily News* underscored his rapid return to obscurity with the headline, "This Man Has Just Died; Do You Remember Him?" over his photograph. His obituary in the *Los Angeles Times* identified his group as "radicals," occasioning a letter from his father, which pointed out that the paper was confusing him with John Pace.[30]

EDITH NOURSE ROGERS was the first woman to have served as chairman (1950–52) of a major House committee, the Committee on Veterans' Affairs. In 1933 she was the first to speak out in Congress about Hitler's treatment of the Jews and his comments about American women; her life was threatened by Nazi sympathizers. In the fall of 1944 she was in London and Paris when the first V-2 rockets hit those cities.

Politically, Rogers supported the anticommunism of Senator Joe McCarthy (putting her at odds with Margaret Chase Smith); she opposed initial entry into the war in Vietnam because she felt America's real enemy was in Moscow. Fervent in her opposition to child labor, she fought for the forty-hour week and equal pay for women—but, as if to confound those who would turn her into a feminist icon, she embraced traditional views of womanhood. She never remarried. At age sixty-seven she was named in a contested divorce by the wife of a man on her staff, a charge that was later dropped.

Rogers never stopped fighting for vets and men and women in uniform, and she never seems to have bowed to pressure from the Pentagon or, for that matter, her own party. During the early days of the Korean War, outraged to find that Americans fighting in Korea were freezing to death or losing hands, feet, arms, and legs because of insufficient clothing, she charged the military with "tragic malfeasance of duty." She was doubly furious to find that men who died of cold were not considered "battle casualties." This led her to a campaign for a full and honest accounting of the human cost of war.[31]

Rogers died on September 10, 1960, in Boston after thirty-five years in the House of Representatives. During her career she introduced 1,242 bills, more than half of them dealing with veterans and the armed services. A veterans hospital in Bedford, Massachusetts, was renamed in her honor.

WILL ROGERS's biographer, Donald Day, wrote that the expulsion of the veterans in July 1932 "brought to Will's mind 'the trail of tears' over which his Cherokee ancestors had been herded by Federal troops."[32] Rogers died on August 15, 1935, in the crash of a plane in Alaska piloted by the famed Wiley Post, who was also killed. A nuclear-propelled submarine was named after Rogers in 1966.

SAMUEL I. ROSENMAN continued to be one of Roosevelt's closest advisers until the time of his death. In his memoir he claimed to have written FDR's first and last speech. Most of Rosenman's advising was done from his position as an associate justice of the New York Supreme Court, but he became a special counsel to the president from 1943 to 1945. Roosevelt, who had special nicknames for all those close to him, called Rosenman "Sammy the Rose." He died in 1973.

RAY SHELTON continued to work for the WPA for several years before starting his own construction company in West Palm Beach. He died in 1952 at the age of sixty-four.

W. BRUCE SHAFER JR., the "Father of the Bonus," continued plumping for veterans' rights for the rest of his life. He died in 1990.

GEORGE W. SHINAULT's murder had a long, difficult, and clouded solution. Many people harbored the belief that he had been assassinated in retaliation for the shooting of William Hushka. One prime suspect, William Bullock, was hunted down in various East Coast cities and captured and brought back to the district six times between 1933 and 1936. But each time he was released; in the words of the *Washington Post,* there had been "an error in classification of his fingerprints." Captured for the seventh time and brought back from Newark in April 1939, after "an error in his fingerprint classification had been rectified," he was arraigned and gave a confession, a fact that was reported in the newspapers. But three days later he pleaded not guilty and was brought to trial by jury on June 27. He was fingered as the killer by a friend who lived at the same address. Outside the hearing of the jury, Bullock insisted that he had signed the confession only because he was beaten and kicked by two investigating officers. Besides, he said, he did not know what he was signing because he could not read. The judge nonetheless admitted the confession, pointing out that he would present the jury with instructions as to what weight should be given to it. On March 13, 1940, Bullock was convicted of premeditated murder and was sentenced to die in the electric chair on July 8. The sentence was appealed, and on June 30, 1941, almost a year after he was slated to die, his conviction was overturned in the U.S. Court of Appeals by a judge who said that the "practice of extorting confessions from poor and ignorant men has been condemned by the Supreme Court," and that such a practice cannot be used to "send any man to his death." It was also determined that premeditation had not been proven. Bullock was reindicted in October 1941 on a new charge of killing a policeman while committing a felony, also a first-degree murder charge. A second trial was ordered, and this time he was sentenced to serve twenty years in jail.[33]

MARGARET CHASE SMITH, as a representative and a senator, developed a strong interest in military issues. During World War II, she secured a seat on the House Naval Affairs Committee, using the position to investigate congestion on the home front caused by the rapid war buildup. More important, she almost single-handedly won permanent status for women in the military. After four terms in the House, Smith was elected to the U.S. Senate in 1948, becoming the first woman elected to both houses of Congress. She came to national attention on June 1, 1950, as the first member of the Senate to denounce the tactics used by colleague Joseph McCarthy in his anti-Communist crusade. Following her "Declaration of Conscience" speech, some pundits speculated that she might be the vice presidential candidate on the 1952 Republican ticket. She died at her home on Memorial Day, May 29, 1995.

JULIUS F. STONE JR. returned to Harvard in 1937 (where he had previously earned a Ph.D in organic chemistry) for a law degree. Back in Key West, he became so deeply in debt and in such trouble with the Internal Revenue Service that he was forced to leave the country to escape prosecution. He found refuge in Cuba, but he and his self-appointed nemesis Ernest Hemingway fled after Fidel Castro came to power. Stone died in 1967 in New South Wales, Australia.[34]

HARRY S. TRUMAN made Key West his vacation home as president, helping to make the island one of America's most popular tourist destinations—fulfilling Julius Stone's dream and fueling the nightmares of tourist-loathing Ernest Hemingway. Truman's vote overthrowing President Roosevelt's veto of the bonus did not harm him politically. When he became president after Roosevelt's death in 1945, he oversaw the earliest impact of the GI Bill on American society. Harry S. Truman died on December 26, 1972.

LUCIAN K. TRUSCOTT wrote an eloquent memoir of life in Fort Myer (*The Twilight of the U.S. Cavalry: Life in the Old Army, 1917–1942*) and had a distinguished career in World War II. As a colonel he took part in a British commando raid and suggested that the U.S. Army emulate the British. From his suggestion came the U.S. Rangers. As a brigadier general he led a battle group in the November 1942 Allied invasion of North Africa. After serving as General Eisenhower's deputy, he took command of the 3rd Infantry Division for the invasion of Sicily and Italy. He became the commander of the 5th Army in December 1944 and succeeded General Patton as commander of the 3rd Army in Germany after Patton's death in September 1945. Truscott was the only general in the war to have successively commanded a regiment, a division, a corps, and a field army. He died on September 12, 1965, in Alexandria, Virginia.

WALTER W. WATERS returned to Washington in January 1935 to take a clerical job in the War Department, granted through the efforts of General Douglas MacArthur. Less than a month later, he resigned to form the National Soldier's Bonus League of America, in support of the Patman bill.[35] Waters later took a job as political adviser to Governor Harland of Oklahoma and lived there until the outbreak of World War II, when he joined the Navy. After the war he and Wilma moved to Nevada and then to Wenatachee, Washington, in the mid-1950s.

Waters died on April 22, 1959, at the age of sixty-one in the Walla Walla Veterans Hospital. In a 1992 interview with the *Wenatachee World*, Wilma Waters, then eighty-six, said, "Walt was an easy-going fellow. He had a respect for the service, was a modest man and was always writing poetry."[36]

ROY WILKINS became executive secretary of the NAACP in 1955; in 1965 the title of the position was changed to executive director, a position he held until 1977. In 1963 he helped organize the historic civil rights march on Washington, D.C. In the five minutes allotted to him at that event, he told the crowd that his old boss, W. E. B. DuBois, the man who had assigned him to cover the BEF, had died the night before in Ghana. The next speaker was Martin Luther King, who ran over his five minutes in what Roy Wilkins's nephew, Roger Wilkins, called "a Baptist sermon."[37] Wilkins died on September 9, 1981.

Prologue

1. Pelham D. Glassford Papers, University of California, Los Angeles Library Special Collections RG 679, box 14, folder 2. The date of Glassford's encounter is not given in his diary, but it is certainly sometime between May 20 and 22, with our best estimate being May 21. These notes were written by Glassford for an autobiography that was never completed.

2. Kenneth J. Heineman, *A Catholic New Deal: Religion and Reform in Depression Pittsburgh* (University Park: Pennsylvania State University Press, 1999), 23.

3. Talcott Powell, *Tattered Banners* (New York: Harcourt, Brace, 1933), 42–3.

4. In 1789, soon after ratification of the U.S. Constitution, Congress voted to continue the pension law passed by the Continental Congress in 1776. Veterans had to petition for their pensions, which had to be approved, first by federal judges and later by the secretary of war. Veterans of the War of 1812 were covered by laws that also gave half-pay pensions to their widows and orphans. More veterans began getting pensions after the Mexican-American War ended in 1846.

5. Only Union veterans were eligible. The Fourteenth Amendment barred Confederate veterans from receiving federal pensions. Congress in 1958 authorized payment to the last surviving Confederate. Amy W. Knight and Robert L. Worden, *The Veterans Benefits Administration: An Organizational History, 1776–1994.*

6. Arlen Specter, *Passion for Truth,* 10–11.

7. Cielo Marie Dorado Lutino, "Constructing Historical Memory: The Bonus March and the Great Depression," undergraduate thesis, Reed College, May 1994.

Chapter 1: Over There

1. Because Inauguration Day, March 4, fell on a Sunday in 1917, the inauguration of Woodrow Wilson to his second term was postponed to Monday. But Wilson, deciding that he must be inaugurated on the day stated in the Constitution, on Sunday morning went to an office in the Capitol and, in a private ceremony precisely at noon, was sworn in by the chief justice of the Supreme Court. Next day was the public inauguration.

2. Glenn D. Kittler, *Hail to the Chief* (Philadelphia: Chilton Books, 1965), 158–61. Inaugural text from the Avalon Project at Yale Law School, Documents in Law, History and Diplomacy.

3. Hanson W. Baldwin, *World War I* (New York: Harper & Row, 1962), 6, 16–18.

4. Ibid., 19, 47; Douglas V. Johnson II and Rolfe L. Hillman, *Soissons 1918* (College Station: Texas A&M University Press, 1999), 1–18; Henry W. Ruoff, *Book of the War* (Boston: Standard Publication Company, 1918).

5. Nancy Gentile Ford, *Americans All! Foreign-born Soldiers in World War I* (College Station: Texas A&M University Press, 2001), 17–19.

6. Barbara W. Tuchman, "How We Entered World War I," *New York Times Magazine,* March 5, 1967, 73.

7. Norman Polmar and Thomas B. Allen, *Spy Book: The Encyclopedia of Espionage* (New York: Random House, 1997), 616; Tuchman, "How We Entered World War I," 75.

8. Edmund W. Starling, *Starling of the White House,* 87.

9. *New York Times,* April 3, 1917.

10. Ibid.

11. *American Heritage History of World War I* (New York: Bonanza Books, 1982), 205; Byrun Farwell, *Over There* (pub), 35; *New York Times,* April 3, 1917.

12. One of the dissenting votes came from Jeannnette Rankin of Montana, the only woman in Congress. On December 8, 1941, she would cast the only vote against declaring war on Japan.

13. *New York Times,* April 4, 1917; Gene Smith, *The Shattered Dream,* 33–37. Hoover served without pay in both posts. Between 1914 and his death in 1964, if Hoover had to receive a salary, he gave the money to charity.

14. David H. Ewen, *Popular American Composers from Revolutionary Times to the Present: a Biographical and Critical Guide* (New York: H. W. Wilson Co., 1972), 43; *New York Times,* May 12, 1917.

15. John Toland, *No Man's Land* (Garden City: Doubleday, 1980), 204. There were also 80,446 National Guard officers and men already on the Mexican border, and about that many in state units. The U.S. Army general staff consisted of nineteen officers, too few even to plan an effective operation against Pancho Villa, the Mexican revolutionary turned outlaw.

16. *American Heritage History,* 207; Gary Mead, *The Doughboys: America and the First World War* (New York: Overlook Press, 2000), 4; Thomas B. Allen and Charles O. Hyman, *We Americans* (Washington, D.C.: National Geographic Society, 1999), 379.

17. Frank Freidel, *Over There: The Story of America's First Great Overseas Crusade* (Short Hills, N.J.: Burford Books, 2003), 50; Allen and Hyman, *We Americans,* 380.

18. Freidel, *Over There,* 50.

19. Ford, *Americans All!,* 3.

20. Mead, *Doughboys* (9), says 72 percent.

21. Odom, "Under the Gun," 100–105.

22. Ulysses Lee, *The Employment of Negro Troops* (Washington, D.C.: Center of Military History, United States Army, 1966), 4.

23. Robert H. Patton, *The Pattons,* 186–91. Pershing became romantically involved with a French artist commissioned to paint his portrait, and Nita eventually broke off the engagement.

24. Patton's military pedigree went back to an ancestor who was a general in George Washington's Continental Army.

25. The Hellfighters would serve 191 days in combat, including the Meuse-Argonne offensive. In the haze of battle for a while the Hellfighters advanced faster than the French troops on either flank, capturing the village of Sechault. For their work in the offensive the French awarded the regiment the Croix de Guerre, France's highest military honor.

In numerous bloody and uncelebrated clashes, enemies suddenly met while on patrol in no-man's-land. One night, a German patrol of about twenty men got so close to the Hellfighter trenches that Sergeant Henry Johnson could hear the sound of German snippers cutting through barbed wire. Then German grenades began exploding around Johnson and Private Needham Roberts, who fell, grievously wounded but still firing. Johnson, emptying his French rifle's three-shot magazine, killed several Germans. He clubbed some with his rifle butt and slashed others with a long knife the French called a sword-bayonet. As the German survivors vanished into the night, Johnson, legs and body riddled with twenty-one wounds, somehow dragged Roberts back to their trench. He was the first American soldier to receive the Croix de Guerre.

The commander of one of the regiment's machine-gun companies was Lieutenant James Reese Europe, who had been the leader of a celebrated New York City jazz band and a musical arranger for the dance stars Vernon and Irene Castle. Europe, as leader of the jazzed-up 369th Regimental Band, transformed one of his patrols into his ragtime song "On Patrol in No Man's Land." He wrote the lyrics in a French field hospital while recuperating from a poison-gas attack. He and his band toured France, introducing jazz to many French towns and giving the French the lasting image that would link jazz to black Americans.

26. John J. Pershing, *My Experiences in the World War,* vol. 2 (New York: Stokes, 1931), 244–55; Toland, *No Man's Land,* 414–25.

27. Frank B. Sibley, *With the Yankee Division in France* (Boston: Little, Brown, 1919).

28. *Columbia Encyclopedia,* sixth ed., 2003.

29. Martin Blumenson, *The Patton Papers, 1885–1940,* vol. 1 (Boston: Houghton Mifflin, 1972), 585–99.

30. Harry H. Semmes, *Portrait of Patton,* 51–52.

31. Toland, *No Man's Land*, 431.

32. Blumension, *Patton Papers*, 661; Martin Gilbert, *Atlas of the First World War* (London: Orion, 1994), 112.

33. Patton, *The Pattons*, 212–13.

34. Information courtesy of the 35th Division Association, PO Box 5004, Topeka, Kan. 66605.

35. Transcript of D. M. Giangreco, "The Soldier from Independence: Harry S. Truman and the Great War," U.S. Army Command and General Staff College, April 7, 2002, at the 69th Annual Meeting of the Society for Military History at the Frank Lloyd Wright Monona Terrace Convention Center, Madison, Wisconsin.

36. Dixon Wecter, *When Johnny Comes Marching Home* (Cambridge: Houghton Mifflin, 1944).

37. Oscar Theodore Barck Jr. and Manfred B. Nelson, *Since 1900: A History of the United States in Our Times* (New York: Macmillan, 1953), 270. Barck and Nelson call it "a great disappointment."

38. 67th Cong., 1st sess., S. Rep. 133.

39. A few months later there were twice as many illegal establishments operating inside the District as there had been legal ones before the act was passed. (The act was named for Texas senator Morris Sheppard, on whose farm an illegal 130-gallon still was discovered during Prohibition. The fact that the farm was in Jollyville, Texas, gave some the idea that the story was apocryphal, but it was true.) During Washington's three-year head start on the rest of the nation, local residents learned how to spot a speakeasy, connect with a reliable bootlegger, and brew beer or fabricate gin at home. To the average middle-class Washingtonian, the cocktail hour was infused with new meaning and celebrated as a point of honor. "Folks seemed to imagine that if they didn't serve cocktails, other folks would think they were obeying the law, and such a thought, to a liberty loving people, was naturally unbearable. So people served cocktails under prohibition who had never dreamed of serving them in their own homes before," the *Washington Herald* recalled of the early days of the Sheppard era. "The grand fiasco of the prohibition experiment was already becoming apparent" ("When and How Prohibition Came to Washington," *Washington Herald*, December 7, 1931). In 1931 there were more than two thousand illegal operations in the city.

40. George L. Cassiday, "Cassiday, Capitol Bootlegger, Got First Rum Order from Dry," *Washington Post*, October 25, 1930. Cassiday seems to have gotten along as well with those who voted "dry" as with those on the "wet" side.

41. " 'The Man in the Green Hat' Uncovers," *Literary Digest,* November 22, 1930, 10.

42. W. Bruce Shafer, interview by James Sweeney, February 16, 1977, Old Dominion University, 3–6. Available on the Old Dominion Web site: lib.odu.

43. The men in France knew of the concept even before the $60 bonus. "Why are the States going through all the expense of welcoming homecoming soldiers?" one man from the 33rd Division asked in a letter to *Stars and Stripes* (February 21, 1919). "Why not let the soldiers be discharged immediately upon their discharge in the United States and the States and Government give the soldiers who have done their bit, for democracy a bonus." He suggested that millions were being spent on these celebrations that would be better appreciated in cash. The term *bonus* was also one that the troops were familiar with because of the bonuses then being paid to baseball players, as in this *Stars and Stripes* headline of March 8, 1918: "Yanks and Athletics Still on Lookout for Material—Herzog after Bonus."

The earliest headline containing the word *bonus* that we could find was in the *Richmond (Virginia) Times-Dispatch* for February 1, 1919: "Bonus Agreed upon for Veterans of War." The headline is misleading because agreement was still weeks away. At this point the bonus was a mere $50.

44. *Congressional Record* 65, pt. 5: 4439.

45. R. C. Leffingwell, "The Soldier and His Bonus," *Saturday Evening Post*, May 15, 1930. Leffingwell was assistant secretary of the Treasury.

46. "Thousands March in Bonus Parade," *New York Times*, October 17, 1920; "Soldier Bonus Wins by 400,000 Here," *New York Times*, November 6, 1920.

47. Roger Daniels, *The Bonus March: An Episode of the Great Depression*, 22–23, points out that there was a faction in Congress that argued that the government had done enough, maintaining that it was up to private enterprise to provide a transition from war to peace by providing the vets with good jobs.

48. *World War Adjusted Compensation Act of 1924*, HR 14157, 66th Cong., 2nd sess., *Congressional Record* 63, daily ed. (May 29, 1920).

49. Here is the letter in its entirety with the "letter box" section of the newspaper:

Cleveland, Ohio
May 20, 1920

Editor The Advocate:—

For many months the bonus question has been see-sawing in our seat of government. It seems that the only opposition against it is the labor question—speaking more directly, Negro Labor. It has been argued pro and con that if bill is passed all the Negroes, especially those of the South, will leave their occupations.

It is said that their leaving would cause a great catastrophe in the present labor crisis. Why should the Negro cause such a breach in labor? When the war came the Negro was taken from the field and factory and placed in line to help fight for Democracy. Records show that he achieved success in that line. When the call for men was made the Negro responded nobly.

It is not the way of the Negro to get a few pennies ahead and then stop work. He is as much at home with five dollars as with fifty cents. He too had much to lose in giving himself to that great army whose one object was to elevate humanity. He would give himself more freely to labor if he were given a little money to start himself again on life's pathway.

If the bill should be passed approximately three million American soldiers not including Negroes, will be benefited.

Money will never pay for the agony, pain and sacrifice that these, our soldiers, suffered when they made the world safe for democracy.

SAMUEL V.PERRY
Pres. Y. M S. C.
2248 East 46th St.

50. Miller, *Pretty Bubbles*, 142; *New York Times*, July 28, 1919.
51. The Ohio Historical Society is the repository for the *Advocate* through its "African-American Experience in Ohio."
52. *Advocate*, January 17, 1920.
53. Ibid., May 8, 1920.
54. Leffingwell, "Soldier and His Bonus," 6, 60.
55. "Senate Prepares to Shelve Bonus," *Washington Post*, June 1, 1920.

Chapter 2: The Tombstone Bonus

1. Shafer interview, 6–7. McLean's drunkenness eventually drove him into such a state of madness that he ended his life in a mental hospital, convinced that he was a French secret service operative assigned to kill Ned McLean. Once elected, Harding spent time with McLean despite—or perhaps because of—his outrageous drunken behavior. In his book *Who Killed Society?* (New York: Harper, 1960), Cleveland Amory talks about the coolness of Mrs. Harding when McLean "urinated in the fireplace in the East Room (as well as down the leg of the Belgian Ambassador)."
2. Daniels, *Bonus March*, 36.
3. Will Rogers, *The Autobiography of Will Rogers*, ed. Donald Day (Boston: Houghton Mifflin, 1949), 88. He also wrote, "I think the best Insurance in the World against another War is to take care of the Boys who fought in the last one. YOU MAY WANT TO USE THEM AGAIN."
4. "Harding Says Bonus Now Would Imperil Country," *Wall Street Journal*, July 13, 1921.
5. Eugene P. Trani and David L. Wilson, *The Presidency of Warren G. Harding* (Lawrence: Regents Press of Kansas, 1977), 65.
6. "Edison at 75 Still a Two-Shift Man," *New York Times*, February 12, 1922; "Bonus Is Demanded by Veteran Throngs," *New York Times*, March 6, 1922.
7. "Votes Bonus, 333–70," *Washington Post*, March 24, 1922.
8. "Soldiers' Adjusted Compensation: Message of the President Returning without Approval the Bill H.R. 10874," 67th Cong., 2nd Sess., 1922.
9. Ibid., 5.

10. Daniels, *Bonus March,* 33.

11. National Industrial Conference Board, New York, Special Report no. 24, 46.

12. Barck and Nelson, *Since 1900,* 302.

13. "Bonus to Soldiers Paid in 19 States," *New York Times,* December 28, 1923. The New York State constitution had a provision prohibiting the borrowing of funds from the state for individuals, so the 1920 bonus law was declared unconstitutional. After a delay of four years a constitutional amendment allowing for the bonus was passed.

14. "Attacks on Bonus Resented at White House and Capitol," *Washington Post,* February 20, 1924.

15. "New Bonus Bill Based on Insurance Scheme," *Washington Post,* February 26, 1924.

16. "Veterans March in Bonus Parade," *New York Times,* March 2, 1924.

17. "Bonus Bill Passed by Senate 67–17," *New York Times,* April 24, 1934. A version offering immediate payment of the bonus in the Senate was defeated 47–38.

18. Donald R. McCoy, *Calvin Coolidge: The Quiet President* (New York: Macmillan, 1967), 233.

19. Arthur Mann, *La Guardia: A Fighter against His Times, 1882–1933.*

20. "Proceeding of Congress and Committees in Brief," *Washington Post,* May 20, 1924.

21. Frederick M. Kerby, in his widely distributed leaflet, *The Veterans' Bonus Law,* underscored the essential point of compensation: "The theory underlying the law is that men and women who served in the armed forces of the U. S. during the World War thereby sacrificed the opportunity of making more money during the period of their service, and that they should therefore receive an Adjusted Credit for the period of their service that will in some measure equalize what they would have made and what they actually received in Army or Navy pay."

22. William A. White, *A Puritan in Babylon,* 279. White calls Lodge's action a "political death warrant." As early as August 31, 1922, Lodge was on record as favoring the bonus when the *Wall Street Journal* reported that he thought that paying it would not adversely affect the nation's economy, as many of his fellow Republicans were saying.

23. "Comment of Today's Newspapers on the Senate Vote on Bonus Veto," *New York Times,* May 20, 1924.

24. Senate, *Veteran's Relief,* 72nd Cong., 2nd sess., 1932, 15–16; cited in Lawrence C. Jorgensen, "The Bonus Expeditionary Force, 1932" (master's thesis, University of Chicago, 1963). The bill provided for a few women, specifically: "Any woman who enlisted and served and was honorably discharged as yeoman in the Navy or Marine Corps."

25. The exact conditions were these: "If the veteran dies at any time after making application, or after receiving his policy and before the 20 years expire, the full amount of the policy is paid to the beneficiary he has named in his application. If no beneficiary has been named, or if the beneficiary named has died and no new beneficiary has been named, then, on the death of the veteran, the full amount of the policy is paid to his estate, and goes to his heirs at law. The veteran may name any person he desires as his beneficiary, without regard to relationship."

26. "Coolidge 'Exacted' Fee for Speech, Is Charge," *Washington Post,* October 27, 1924.

27. Hines to Garrard B. Winston, under secretary of the Treasury, October 21, 1924, Secretary's Correspondence, Soldiers' Bonus, RG 56, Box 114, National Archives.

28. Nancy Beck Young, *Wright Patman: Populism, Liberalism and the American Dream* (Dallas: Southern Methodist University Press, 2000), 15.

29. "National Affairs," *Time,* April 11, 1932, 10, 19.

30. Sherwood, Edwin Douglas, "Wright Patman and the Bonus Episode" (Master's thesis, Lamar University, 1988).

31. This was Patman's recollection at age seventy-seven as recorded in Joint Economic Committee, *The Federal Reserve System: A Study Conducted by Wright Patman* (Washington, D.C.: GPO, 1976), 86.

32. Hoover's optimism was unbridled: on the eve of the Crash, he said, "We in America today are nearer to the final triumph over poverty than ever before in the history of any land. The poor-house is vanishing from among us."

33. George L. Cassiday, "The Man in the Green Hat," five-part front-page series in the *Washington Post,* October 23, 1930–October 27, 1930. For his part, Cassiday played the game well as a savvy political handyman to his elected friends on the Hill. As a member in good standing in the Veterans of Foreign Wars, American Legion, and President's Garrison of the Army and Navy League, he helped marshal the

support of veterans for congressmen up for reelection. Once he traveled to the Midwest as an advance man for a dry Senator and unflinchingly defended his friend's support of the Eighteenth Amendment. He understood the importance of constituents and always found time to take them on an impromptu tour of the Capitol or find them a quart of their favorite scotch. His liquor was poured for many a constituent in congressional offices: "Some of them got a real thrill out of having a drink under the shadow of the Capitol Dome, it was something they could tell about when they got home."

34. Edward T. Folliard, "White House Hedge Hid Bootleg Gin," *Washington Post*, December 6, 1933.

35. Sarah Booth Conroy, interview with Frederick Drum Hunt, "Prohibition? Bottoms Up!" *Washington Post*, October 4, 1993.

36. Raymond Moley Jr., *The American Legion Story* (Westport, Conn.: Greenwood Press, 1975), 197; Donald J. Lisio, *The President and Protest*, 31–32.

37. Lisio, *President and Protest*, 31–32.

38. Ibid., 33.

39. Press conference statement, December 9, 1930, in William S. Myers, ed., *The State Papers and Other Public Writings of Herbert Hoover*, vol. I (New York: Doubleday), 459–60. Donald Lisio calls the December 9 statement "one of the most politically inept statements of his career," as Hoover clearly played into the hand of his political enemies. He adds, "Because he did not specifically denounce the bonus or direct his anger at the veteran's demands, some critics felt that Hoover had attacked all the needy who sought relief as well as the congressmen who were trying to help them." Lisio, *President and Protest*, 33–34.

40. "Parade to Capitol in Plea for Bonus," *New York Times*, April 9, 1932, 3.

41. House Committee on Ways and Means, *Payment of Adjusted-Compensation Certificates*, 72d Cong., 2d sess., January 1931. Rep. John Nance Garner makes the point (275) that this was the first time in ten years "that the leading financiers of the country have been called in to advise the committee concerning an economic problem. Heretofore we have generally looked to the Treasury Department and to Secretary Mellon to express that viewpoint. I do not know whether this procedure was occasioned because of loss of confidence in the Secretary of the Treasury, by the committee, or by the Congress, or by the country."

42. Ibid., 177. Mellon testified that the face value of the certificates outstanding totaled $3,409,304,122. To retire them at face value in 1931 would cost about $1,640,000,00 more than the actual present value, which was about $1,770,000,000.

43. Ibid., 382–83.

44. Ibid.

45. The final witness was Coxey.

46. Patton, *The Pattons*, 212. This is the headline that alerts the Pattons to the fact that Angelo is in Washington.

47. Ibid., 212. The primary source for Beatrice Patton's reaction is her personal journal, to which the author of that book, as George S. Patton's grandson, had sole access.

48. *Time*, March 9, 1931.

49. The presiding congressman chided Shafer on his "coarse language." John Nance Garner said there was nothing wrong with the language. The chair withdrew the objection, and the metaphor of the celluloid cat stood.

Chapter 3: A Petition in Boots

1. "Coxey Dies at 97; Led Army of the Idle," *New York Times*, May 19, 1951.

2. Ralph Thompson, "General Coxey's Hunger Marchers," *Current History*, January 1932, 550. For several generations "Coxey's Army"—as in "you look like Coxey's Army"—was a term of derogation, implying a general shabbiness and disorder. Coxey's men were celebrated as tramps in song and verse.

3. "Coxey Dies at 97"; also Gerald G. Eggert, "Coxey's March on Washington," *American History Illustrated*, October 1977, 23.

4. Ibid., 552.

5. John A. Garraty, ed., *Encyclopedia of American Biography* (New York: Da Capo, 1998), 235.

6. "On Their Weary March," *Washington Post*, May 5, 1894, p. 1.

7. Eggert, "Coxey's March," 31.

8. "Frye's Army Starved Out," *Washington Post*, July 1, 1894.

9. Dwight D. Eisenhower, *At Ease: Stories I Tell to Friends*, 155.

10. Paul Dickson and William D. Hickman, *Firestone: A Legend, a Century, a Celebration*, 74. In 1931, 993,000 miles were "surface" miles, a term that applies to unpaved roads. Some were dirt, some gravel, or other surfacings, but not paved as we know it today. As to whether these roads were "drivable" or not depends on a number of factors, such as weather.

11. Ada Rainey, "In the Realm of Art and Music," *Washington Post*, March 8, 1925. The critic suggested that if Glassford chose to leave the Army, he could be a successful artist.

12. The first time Glassford's name ever appeared in a feature article in the *Washington Post*, on March 8, 1925, it was not as a fighter but as a painter who had mounted a one-man show of decorative screens of his own design as well as others inspired by James McNeill Whistler and the fourteenth-century Chinese artist Wu Chen.

13. *Washington Post*, October 21, 1931.

14. "Politics Prevent Chiefs of Police from Enforcing Law, Says Glassford," *Evening Star*, unpaginated clipping, Bonus Army scrapbook, MLK Library.

15. David Rankin Barbee, "The Artist Who Became a 'Cop,'" *Washington Post*, November 15, 1931.

16. "Armistice of 1918 Recreated," *New York Times*, November 12, 1931; "Crowds Pack Auditorium For Gay Armistice Ball," *Washington Post*, November 12, 1931. If it were not for the fact that the money raised went to the "disabled and destitute" of the Great War, the evening would have had a deeper tinge of irony to it. For instance, at one station canteen "lassies" ladled soup from a faux soup kitchen.

17. The Army more than any other group in America knew the Bolsheviks because of the 15,000 American troops sent to northern Russia beginning in the fall of 1918, including, by chance, many from Michigan drafted only a few months before; they thought they were being shipped to France. They fought an unexpected guerrilla war in a Russian winter, with the temperature dropping to 55 degrees below zero. Officially, 353 died, but at least 127 were listed as dead when, in fact, their fate was unknown. Unofficially, many were believed to have died as prisoners in the hands of the Russians, and futile talks went on between the two countries into the 1920s, hampering U.S. recognition of the Soviet Union. Mead, *Doughboys*, 392–94; Meirion and Susie Harries, *Last Days of Innocence: America at War, 1917–1919* (New York: Random House, 1997), 299.

18. Edward Folliard, "When Reds Invaded Washington," *Washington Post*, December 2, 1956.

19. "Marchers Quit Washington in Trucks," *New York Times*, December 9, 1931.

20. "Military Intelligence Division Correspondence 1917–41," National Archives, Record Group 165, Box 2856, File 10110-2674.

21. "General Coxey Sympathizes with Hunger Marchers," *Washington Post*, December 3, 1931.

22. Edward T. Folliard, "Capitol Echoes," *Washington Post*, December 13, 1931.

23. Glassford's handling of the Hunger March, his general ability to come up with new ideas for modern policing, and his promise to make the Washington police the "finest of the fine" gave him wide, enthusiastic public support. "Writing of Movie Scenario, Glassford's Latest Work," said a headline in the *Washington Post*, December 26, 1931, alluding to his plan to make a movie teaching police how to be courteous in their dealings with citizens.

24. "Veterans Are Here to Plead for Cash," *Washington Post*, December 9, 1931. In reporting on the Seattle men, the *Washington Post* noted that another group of petitioners had arrived earlier from Portland, Oregon with signatures—the only mention of this group that could be found—suggesting that other petitioners may have been in the city. The Seattle group drew attention because they were arrested in Alexandria, Virginia, for trespassing on railroad property. They were given suspended sentences when the judge heard of their mission.

25. "Bonus Brigade Asks Permit for Parade," *Washington Post*, December 13, 1931.

26. "50 Veterans on Hike to Urge Full Bonus," *New York Times*, December 15, 1931.

27. William F. Elkins, "Wright Patman and the Veteran's Bonus Issue" (Master's thesis, University of Arizona, 1964), 26.

28. Joint Economic Committee, *Federal Reserve System*, 88.

29. "Veterans Leaders Cancel 1932 Parade," *Washington Post*, December 30, 1931.

30. Manchester, *The Glory and the Dream*, 48.

31. Historian Arthur Schlesinger Jr. noted that Hoover's name became "a prefix charged with hate"— the newspapers the homeless used to cover themselves were "Hoover blankets," farmers called jackrabbits

"Hoover hogs," and empty pockets pulled inside out were "Hoover flags." The origin of the term may have been a shantytown in Chicago which called itself Hooverville and had streets named Prosperity Road, Hard Times Avenue, and Easy Street. It came to national attention in 1930 ("Chicago Jobless Colonize," *New York Times,* November 12, 1930).

32. The 1932nd Psalm, by R. E. Jacobs, began with the lines

Hoover is my shepherd, and I am in want,
He maketh me to lie down on the park benches,
He leadeth me beside the still factories,
He leadeth me in the paths of destruction for his party's sake
Yea, though I walk through the valley of starvation
I do fear evil for he is against me.
His politics and the profiteers they frighten me.
He preparest a reduction of wages before me in the presence of mine enemies.
He anointest my income with taxes,
My expenses runneth over.
Surely poverty and unemployment will follow me all the days of the Hoover administration.

Powell, *Tattered Banners,* 245. Jacobs was active in the BEF. Another version of this appears in Robert S. McElvaine, *The Depression and New Deal: A History in Documents* (New York: Oxford University Press, 2000), 28.

33. Weaver, "Bonus March," 19.

34. Lisio, *President and Protest,* 44.

35. "Legion for Rum Vote as Cash Bonus Loses; Act Approved and Hit," *Washington Post,* September 25, 1931.

36. Kenneth J. Heineman, *A Catholic New Deal: Religion and Reform in Depression Pittsburgh* (University Park: Pennsylvania State University Press, 1999), 20.

37. Heineman, *Catholic New Deal,* 20–21. Al Capone, gangster boss of Chicago, was convicted on federal charges of tax evasion in 1931 and sentenced to 11 years in prison.

38. Leo Reed, letter to Herbert Hoover, December 31, 1931; Lawrence Richey, memorandum to White House staff, January 4, 1932. Heineman, *Catholic New Deal,* 23.

39. Ibid., 24.

40. An odd and rarely reported connection between Cox and the Mellons appears in Heineman, *A Catholic New Deal:* "The Republicans implied that either the Vatican, or Democratic supporters of Al Smith, had funded the entire operation. Hoover's well-publicized investigation of Cox backfired. He had been correct in one sense: a shadowy figure did provide assistance to the priest's caravan. Unfortunately, the figure in question was [Secretary of the Treasury] Andrew Mellon, who had quietly ordered his Gulf Oil service stations to dispense gasoline without charge" (27).

41. 72nd Cong., 1st sess., 1932, *Congressional Record,* 75, pt. 2:1400–1401.

42. *New York Times,* January 15, 1932.

43. Harvey O'Connor, *Mellon's Millions: The Biography of a Fortune; The Life and Times of Andrew W. Mellon,* 321. If there was any American public official most unlike Mellon, it was Charley Dawes. He had become absolutely fed up with his job—the excessive formality, the numbing politeness, the omnipresent aristocracy. Dawes, a forthright man given to forthright talk, tried to make the best of what he considered exile, spending his own money, for example, to hire American comedians to spill liquor down the necks of the British nobility. But even this could not make him happy. He quit on January 8, 1932, determined to return to the rough-and-tumble of American political life. Hoover now had a place where he could send Mellon that was not beneath the dignity of a former secretary of the Treasury. Dawes's odd nickname, "Hell and Maria," came from some words uttered before a congressional committee investigating charges of waste and extravagance in the conduct of the war. When a member of the committee asked Dawes if it was true that excessive prices were paid for mules in France, he shouted, "Helen Maria, I'd have paid horse prices for sheep if the sheep could have pulled artillery to the front!"

44. Mellon would serve for one year and then retire to private life. He served as secretary of the Treasury from March 4, 1921, to February 12, 1932, when he assumed his duties as ambassador to Great Britain.

45. Robert S. Gallagher, "Before the Colors Fade: The Radio Priest," *American Heritage,* October 1972, 38.

46. Donald Day, *Will Rogers: A Biography,* 285.

47. Edmund Starling, *Starling,* 289.

48. William Seale, *The President's House: A History,* vol. 2 (Washington, D.C.: White House Historical Association, 1986), 903.

49. "Turning Points in Detroit History," *Michigan History Magazine,* November/December 2000, 14.

50. Fraser M. Ottanelli, *The Communist Party of the United States* (New Brunswick, N.J.: Rutgers University Press, 1991), 33–34. At least fifty others were wounded. Calling this the Ford Massacre had a double edge. As Irving Bernstein points out in *The Lean Years: A History of the American Worker, 1933–1941* (Boston: Houghton Mifflin, 1960), "These policemen were hardly free agents. Clyde M. Ford, the mayor of Dearborn, was a distant cousin of Henry's and owned a Ford agency; Carl Brooks, the chief of police, was a former Ford detective" (433).

51. Allen and Hyman, eds., *We Americans,* 213–14.

52. Eugene H. Methvin, *The Riot Makers: Technology of Social Demolition,* 154.

53. John D. Hicks, *Republican Ascendancy,* 134. The legal name was Communist Party of the United States of America, but it was usually called the U.S. Communist Party.

54. U.S. Military Intelligence, *Surveillance of Radicals in the U.S., 1917–1941,* microfilm 86/236, reels 21 and 22, Library of Congress.

55. The school moved in 1932 from Fort Meade, Maryland. Students there included Dwight D. Eisenhower and George S. Patton Jr.

56. W. H. Jones Jr., "The Use of Tanks in Quelling Civil Disturbances," *Tank Studies* (US Army Tank School), 1932, 166–77. This is a truly difficult document to find. We obtained a copy through the lilbrary of the USA Armor School Research Library, Fort Knox, Kentucky, with the help of librarian Lorraine M. Allen and fellow Bonus Army researcher Dana Hardaker.

57. Tim Kirk and Anthony McElliott, eds., *Opposing Fascism* (New York: Cambridge University Press, 1999), 12–32.

58. The descriptions are unattributed, but they appear to come from reports of U.S. Army observers in Germany.

59. Thomas B. Allen, *War Games* (New York: McGraw-Hill, 1987), 121.

Chapter 4: Mobilizing a Bonus Army

1. Named after Sergeant Peter Weiser of the Lewis and Clark Expedition and the place where baseball Hall of Famer Walter Johnson was discovered by a scout and quickly shipped off to the Washington Senators.

2. "Idaho 2nd Infantry Expedition to Mexico, 1916," photographic collection, Utah State Universities Libraries, P0030, Special Collections and Archives.

3. T. Harry Williams, Richard N. Current, and Frank Freidel, *A History of the United States since 1865* (New York: Knopf, 1965), 383; Calvin L. Christman, ed., *America at War* (Annapolis, Md.: Naval Institute Press, 1995), 236.

4. Office of the Adjutant General, Major General C. H. Bridges, June 10, 1932; document provided to "10110" files of the Military Intelligence Division (10110-2669/455 to 10110-2723/32), National Archives. Villa was ambushed and assassinated on July 20, 1923; his assassins were never caught.

5. William L. Clements Library, University of Michigan, D. N. Diedrich World War I Collection.

6. Roger Daniels, *The Bonus March,* 77.

7. Maurice P. Sneller Jr., "The Bonus March of 1932: A Study of Depression Leadership and its Legacy," (Ph.D. dissertation, Corcoran Department of History, University of Virginia, 1960).

8. Waters's recollection of the beginning of the Bonus March appears in his ghostwritten memoir *B.E.F.* by W. W. Waters as told to William C. White. New York: AMS Press, 1970; reprinted from the original 1933 edition, p 14. In a 1992 interview, Mrs. Waters wondered whether copies of the book had been "bought up" to keep the story of the Bonus March from being known. The book was never suppressed; it can be found in many academic libraries and is routinely offered through used-book dealer groups on the Internet.

9. Nowhere in Waters's carefully parsed recollection was there any hint that there were others in Portland planning a bonus march. *Veterans on the March*, by Jack Douglas, the pseudonym of Izzie Zalph, a lifelong Communist, is described by Zalph's cousin, Larry Zolf, as the "official communist history" of the Bonus March. ("Reds under My Bed," *CBC News Viewpoint*, July 15, 2002.)

10. Waters, *B.E.F.*, p 11.

11. Daniels, *Bonus March*, 72; *Biographical Directory of the U.S. Congress*.

12. "Massed Veterans Present Congress With Bonus Plea," *Washington Star*, April 8, 1932, unpaginated clipping, Bonus Army scrapbook.

13. *New York Times*, April 9, 1932.

14. Robert V. Parker, "The Bonus March of 1932: A Unique Experience in North Carolina Political and Social Life," *North Carolina Historical Review*, January 1971, 64–89.

15. Committee on Ways and Means, 72nd Cong., 2nd session, April 11–29, 1932, 50–52.

16. *New York Times*, April 20, 1932.

17. *Morning Oregonian*, April 23, 1932.

18. *Fort Wayne Journal-Gazette*, May 6, 1932.

19. *Washington Star*, April 8, 1932, unpaginated clipping, Bonus Army scrapbook, MLK Library.

20. *Portland Oregonian*, December 1, 1974.

21. Waters, *B.E.F.*, 16; Daniels, *Bonus March*, 74.

22. Historian Roger Daniels, in *The Bonus March*, points out (73–74) that Oregon veterans, beneficiaries of a state bonus ($15 for every month of service after the first 60 days), were probably more aware of potential benefits than veterans from states that had not given bonuses.

23. Sneller, "Bonus March of 1932," 7.

24. *Portland Oregonian*, August 28, 1975.

25. A copy of the diary was given to the authors by Madeline and Bill Linebarrier of Asheboro, North Carolina. Through genealogical research on her family, Madeline Linebarrier had learned that the father she had known as "Steve Murray" was actually named Steve Mesker. Prior to joining the Bonus Army he had changed his name. He did this after his papers, including his bonus certificate and discharge, were found on the body of a dead railroad detective. Steve, in his daughter's words, had been "hoboing" nearby and had fled, taking on a new name, which he continued using for the rest of his life. We respect his Bonus Army nom de guerre. Steve Murray had fine handwriting and a fine grasp of the English language. When quoting from the diary, we have changed only punctuation, for clarity, and misspellings, which are rare.

26. Hazen, the original commander in chief of the march, would later claim he "organized the Bonus March," though he did not say how far he marched. H. B. Dewitz was his field marshal. As Waters tells it, without naming anyone, the commander in chief "was to travel ahead by automobile, arranging for food and transportation." Dewitz, also unnamed in Waters's memoir, had assistants, and one of them was Assistant Field Marshal Walter W. Waters. About 250 men (including about a dozen who had gone to Washington in the November 1931 march) signed up. Daniels, *Bonus March*, 76, 321.

27. "Survey of Transient Boys in the United States," *Monthly Labor Review*, January 1933, 92.

28. A. Waymen McMillen, "An Army of Boys on the Loose," *Survey*, September 1, 1932, 390.

29. "Homeless Wanderers Create a New Problem for America," *New York Times*, December 11, 1932; reprinted in David A. Shannon, ed., *The Great Depression* (New York: Prentice-Hall Spectrum, 1960), 55–58. The railroad information comes from a hearing in the U.S. Senate in 1933, an excerpt of which was published in *The Great Depression*, 58–61. Caroline Bird in *The Invisible Scar* says that in 1933 there were between 1 and 2 million on the road (66).

30. All Waters quotations are from his book unless otherwise credited.

31. Douglas, *Veterans on the March*, 28. Waters, always trying to keep a positive record for posterity, says, without naming Hazen, that the veterans "turned over to the police" a man who "had a gun in his possession."

32. Ibid.

33. Douglas, in *Veterans on the March*, 28, calls him "Taylor." The A. F. comes from the *Morning Oregonian*, July 8, which refers to "A. F. Taylor" as "camp commander of the Oregon unit."

34. Waters, *B.E.F.*, 33.

35. Murray seems not to have had discharge papers. He later said that all his identification papers were

found on the body of the railroad detective. At this point in the march, Waters did not seem to be scrupulous about seeing official discharge papers.

36. Richard Norton Smith, *An Uncommon Man*, 136.

37. Prime sources for the Portland–to–East Saint Louis leg: Waters, *B.E.F.*, 19–40; Douglas, *Veterans on the March*, 25–29. (Cheyenne elevation is 6,062 feet.)

38. *Clinton (Iowa) Herald*, May 18, 1924; Jorgensen, "Bonus Expeditionary Force."

39. Jacob Spolensky, *The Communist Trail in America* (New York: Macmillan, 1951), 44–45.

40. "Relief and Revolution," *Fortune*, August 1932, 74, 75.

41. Waters's version (*B.E.F.*, 34–38) differs slightly from Alman's, as reported in Douglas, *Veterans on the March*. Alman says the train got under way after officials in East Saint Louis sent a telegram saying, "Put on enough empties to carry that bunch of hoodlums" (29–30).

42. *Morning Oregonian*, May 19, 1932, 6; Jorgensen, "Bonus Expeditionary Force," 13.

43. Waters, *B.E.F.*, 40. Mention of the two-meal regime in *St. Louis Post-Dispatch*, May 20, 1932.

44. Waters, *B.E.F.*, 40–41.

45. Waters did not explain in his memoir how the B&O was able to serve an Illinois court order in Missouri. The information on Illinois comes from Alman, as quoted in Douglas, *Veterans on the March*, 30.

46. Rexford G. Tugwell, "Roosevelt and the Bonus Marchers of 1932," *Political Science* 87, no. 3 (1972): 363–376.

47. *St. Louis Post-Dispatch*, May 22, 1932.

48. *St. Louis Journal*, May 22, 1932.

49. Murray refers to the "Hoover line" several times.

50. This account of events in East St. Louis is based on Waters, *B.E.F.*, 41–56; *St. Louis Post-Dispatch* stories from May 20 to May 25, 1932; *New York Times*, May 23 and May 25; and Sneller, "Bonus March of 1932."

51. Waters, *B.E.F.*, 49–51.

52. A reference to the Workers' Council appears only in Douglas, *Veterans on the March*, 32–33. Alman gives a left-wing tone to his account, using "workers" and "rank and file," rather than "veterans," following the semantics of the Communist-backed Workers' Ex-Servicemen's League.

53. Sneller, "Bonus March of 1922."

54. *St. Louis Journal*, May 24, 1932.

55. *St. Louis Post-Dispatch*, May 24, 1932; an Associated Press dispatch in the *Evening Star* (Washington, D.C.), May 24, 1932, has a slightly different version of Munie's remarks.

56. Waters, *B.E.F.*, 54–55; Sneller, "Bonus March of 1932"; *New York Times,* May 25, 1932.

57. George Kleinholz, *The Battle of Washington: A National Disgrace* (New York: B. E. F. Press, 1932), 7.

58. "Loan of $25.5 to B&O Approved," *New York Times*, May 17, 1932. The B&O did get refinanced by the RFC in February 1933 by the lame-duck Hoover administration, according to the *Wall Street Journal:* " B&O Refinancing Plan in Operation," February 21, 1933.

59. Pelham D. Glassford Papers, University of California, Los Angeles Library Special Collections RG 679, box 14, folder 2; "Glassford Plans to House 'Army,'" *Washington Star*, May 25, 1932, Bonus Army scrapbook.

60. Glassford Papers, ibid.

61. The East Wing of the White House had not yet been built, and West Executive Avenue, not yet closed off by the Secret Service, was open to traffic.

62. Eisenhower, *At Ease*, 216: "In that administration, officers went to work in Washington in civilian clothes because a military appearance around the nation's capital was held to be undesirable."

63. Ibid., 213.

64. "One Soldier's Journey," unpublished memoir, George Van Horn Moseley Papers, Manuscript Division, Library of Congress, Washington, D.C. Moseley quotations are from the memoir, unless otherwise stated.

65. General George Van Horn Moseley to Herbert Corey, May 24, 1932, Moseley Papers; also quoted in Joseph W. Bendersky, *The "Jewish Threat": Anti-Semitic Politics of the U.S. Army* (New York: Basic Books, 2000), 202.

66. Lucian King Truscott, ed., *The Twilight of the U.S. Cavalry,* 9–17.

67. During the Great War, Miles, as a colonel, had commanded the 371st Regiment, an African-American unit that he ranked with "any regiment of any nation." Emmett J. Scott, *Scott's Official History of the American Negro in the World War* (Chicago: Homewood Press, 1919), chap. 16. The 371st, like the Harlem Hellfighters, served under the French flag.

68. Clayton D. Laurie and Ronald H. Cole, *The Role of Federal Military Forces in Domestic Disorders, 1877–1945,* 372.

69. Military Intelligence Division, file 10110-2661, "Estimate of the Subversive Situation," First Corps Area, January 2, 1932 (secret); National Archives.

70. The break-ins are described by Jeffery M. Dorwart in *Conflict of Duty* (Annapolis, Md.: Naval Institute Press, 1983), 1–3, 45–46. The operatives were Third Naval District Intelligence Officers Paul F. Foster and Glenn Howell. Strauss, who met Hoover in 1917 when Hoover was U.S. food administrator, served as an intelligence officer in World War II and later was chairman of the Atomic Energy Commission (AEC). Foster carried out confidential missions for President Roosevelt during World War II. He retired as a vice admiral and later became the general manager of the AEC. Nothing would be officially known about the ONI break-ins had not Howell kept a log (the source of the quotes). By ONI orders, no records were to be "supplied to the National Archives or any other agency to which the general public has access" (5). Howell, a swashbuckling counterspy, in a 1929 letter to the director of naval intelligence, became the first known officer to advocate the creation of a Central Intelligence Agency.

71. "Glassford Pleads for Bonus Vote to End Marches," *Washington Star,* May 26, 1932, Bonus Army scrapbook.

72. *Biographical Directory of the U.S. Congress.*

73. Lisio, *President and Protest,* 72.

74. *B.E.F. News,* June 1932.

75. Glassford Papers, RG 679, box 5, folder 16.

76. Crosby himself had been involved in controversy as a general turned civilian. A major general and chief of cavalry in 1926, Crosby was living in Washington and was interested in becoming the District commissioner in charge of a scandal-rocked police force. When he retired in 1930, opposition developed; District law called for commissioners to be civilians, and he was seen as more military than civilian. But President Hoover wanted a disciplinarian running the police force, and he appointed Crosby. The opposition died down and did not arise over the appointment of another general as chief of police.

77. "Glassford Named by Bonus Seekers," *Washington Star,* May 27, 1932.

78. Glassford Papers, RG 679, box 14, folder 2.

79. In the center of Judiciary Square is the National Law Enforcement Officers Memorial, dedicated to officers who died in the line of duty. See Douglas E. Evelyn and Paul Dickson, *On This Spot: Pinpointing the Past in Washington, D.C.* (Washington, D.C.: National Geographic Society, 1999), 108. One of the names on the memorial is George W. Shinault, a Washington police officer who figured in the Bonus March saga.

80. Glassford Papers, RG 679, box 14, folder 2.

81. *Washington (Ind.) Herald,* May 25, 1932. Salem had a sense of history as both the birthplace of William Jennings Bryan and the boyhood home of John T. Scopes, defendant in the famed 1925 "Monkey Trial" in which Bryan was the prosecutor.

82. *St. Louis Post-Dispatch,* May 25, 1932. Waters takes credit for arranging the escort, but the news account credits police initiative.

83. "State to Move 'Bonus Army,'" *Washington (Ind.) Herald,* May 25, 1932; quoted in Kleinholz, *Battle of Washington,* 7.

84. Douglas, *Veterans on the March,* 39.

85. *Portland Oregonian,* May 28, 1932.

86. *Mixer's Road Guide and Strip Maps* (1926), Wheeling, W.Va.–Uniontown, Pa.; Uniontown, Pa.–Cumberland, Md.

87. Wilbur E. Garrett, ed., *Historical Atlas of the United States* (Washington, D.C.: National Geographic Society, 1988), 187, 192–93; James Thomas Flexner, *Washington: The Indispensable Man* (Boston: Little, Brown, 1974), 24–26.

88. Waters, *B.E.F.*, 61.
89. *New York Times,* May 30, 1932.
90. Waters, *B.E.F.*, 66–63.

Chapter 5: An Army of Occupation

1. Waters, *B.E.F.*, 62.
2. Ibid., 63.
3. "Veterans' Army Is Due to Arrive in Capital Today," *Washington Post,* May 29, 1932.
4. Waters, *B.E.F.*, 63.
5. Daniels, *Bonus March,* 99.
6. U.S. Military Intelligence, *Surveillance of Radicals.*
7. Ibid., reel 21. Handwritten on the first page of this four-page report, which is stamped "Secret," is "Report from NY Police Dept." New York, like many large cities, had a Red Squad that kept known and suspected Communists under surveillance.
8. Daniels, *Bonus March,* 69.
9. Lisio, *President and Protest,* 55.
10. The report is attached to a letter, dated November 7, 1931, from Frank T. Hines, administrator of the Veterans Administration, to Theodore Joslin, a presidential secretary who dealt with the press. (Officially, there was no press secretary.)
11. Lisio, *President and Protest,* 58.
12. Starling, *Starling,* 296.
13. As quoted in Ottanelli, *Communist Party,* 18.
14. James G. Ryan, *Earl Browder: The Failure of American Communism* (Tuscaloosa: University of Alabama Press, 1997), 51.
15. Douglas, *Veterans on the March,* 120. Douglas also says Pace's family went back to colonial times, when a curve in the Duck River in Tennessee was named Pace's Bend.
16. *Washington Daily News,* June 3, 1932, Bonus Army scrapbook.
17. " 'Bonus Pilgrims' Reach Washington," *Fort Wayne (Ind.) Journal-Gazette,* May 30, 1932.
18. *New York Times,* June 6, 1932; cited in Matthew Stephen Simchak, "The Bonus March of 1932: The Failure of a Radical Alternative" (master's thesis, Trinity College, Hartford, Conn., 1969), 57.
19. May 25, 1932, papers of Irwin H. (Ike) Hoover, chief usher at the White House and no relative to President Hoover. Library of Congress. He kept a log of events, using it as the basis for *Forty-two Years in the White House.*
20. "President Hoover's Visit on Memorial Day, 30 May 1931," 13–17, Reed Collection, Valley Forge National Historic Park, National Park Service. Memorial Day was marked on May 30 from its inception in 1868 until 1971, when Congress declared Memorial Day a national holiday to be marked on the last Monday in May.
21. The *New York Times* and other newspapers made mention of Hoover's remaining in the White House on Memorial Day, 1932: "Homage to War Dead Will Be Paid Today Throughout Nation," *Times,* May 30, 1932; "25,000 in Washington at Massing of Colors," *Times,* May 30, 1932; "Hoover in Conferences over G.O.P. Platform," *Fort Wayne (Ind.) Journal-Gazette,* May 31, 1932.
22. Seale, *President's House,* vol. 2, 903.
23. Ibid.
24. Joel Boone Papers, Box 31, Folder Hoover 1930–1931, HH Notes—JTB 1930–33, 1959. Boone was a physician and career officer in the U.S. Navy. He was awarded the Medal of Honor for his courage as a medical officer in France in 1918, going after wounded Marines under machine-gun fire and "through a heavy mist of gas." During Coolidge's presidency, Boone served as medical officer for the Coolidge family on board the U.S.S. *Mayflower,* the presidential yacht, and was second in command to the White House physician, Dr. James F. Coupal. Coolidge preferred Boone to Coupal and saw him much more. Boone was also Mrs. Coolidge's personal physician; he was at the bedside of Calvin Coolidge Jr. when the boy died from blood poisoning in 1924. He also treated Herbert Hoover Jr., who had tuberculosis. When Boone began writing his autobiography in 1963, he used his notes, which were held with restricted access at the Li-

brary of Congress until they were opened to the public in 1995. Boone's son-in-law, Milton F. Heller Jr., wrote a short biography, *The President's Doctor*, which was published by Vantage Press (New York) in 2000.

25. Donald J. Lisio, in *The President and Protest* (73–74), says that President Hoover worked behind the scenes, secretly approving "the loan of hundreds of tents, cots, bedsacks, several field kitchens, the low-cost sale of Army rations and clothing to the veteran, and the use of federal property for quarters." Lisio notes that Glassford usually gets the credit for aiding the veterans, but "without Hoover's approval . . . the crucial supplies would not have been available."

26. Waters may have picked up the idea of passive resistance from the recent actions of Mohandas Gandhi, the Indian spiritual and political leader. In 1930, protesting the salt tax imposed by British rulers, he led a 320-mile march to the sea, where his followers could extract free salt. Waters's account of becoming commander is in *B.E.F.*, 65. Glassford's Information Notice appears in Daniels, *Bonus March*, 100.

27. Sneller, "Bonus March of 1932," 66.

28. Reichelderfer, Foulkrod, and Glassford testimony quoted from Senate Committee on District of Columbia, *Emergency Unemployed Relief and Care of Persons in Distress: Hearing on S. 4781*, 72nd Congr. 1st sess., June 1, 1932, 6, 9, 12, 17, 18, 20.

29. *Washington Times*, June 3, 1932.

30. The *Washington Daily News* on June 2, 1932, reported eight "bonus armies" en route to the nation's capital. Cities reporting veterans on the march included San Francisco, Oklahoma City, Denver, Chicago, Salt Lake City, San Antonio, Cleveland, Toledo, Albany, New York, and Camden.

31. Wide World photo, May 31, 1932.

32. *Washington Post*, June 1, 1932.

33. "Bonus Force Here Denies Red Backing," *Washington Post*, June 3, 1932.

34. *Washington Post*, June 1, 1932.

35. *New York Times*, June 1, 1932.

36. *Time* magazine, June 13, 1932.

37. "Federal Agents Probe Communist Bonus Activities," *Washington Star*, June 2, 1932.

38. Terkel, *Hard Times*, 28–29.

39. *Washington Star*, June 2, 1932.

40. "'The Bonus March of 1932: A Unique Experience in North Carolina and Political and Social Life," *North Carolina Historical Review*, January 1974, 76–78.

41. Sewilla LaMar, "I Marched with the Bonus Army," *Abbott's Monthly* 5 (September 1932): 3. *Abbott's* was a monthly newsmagazine published by Robert S. Abbott of the *Chicago Defender*. It is a remarkable historic source that is seldom cited in works about this period. We are indebted to Tom Mann of the Library of Congress for leading us to it.

42. Meisel recorded his trip and his days in Washington in *Bonus Expeditionary Forces: The True Facts, 1932* (Clintonville, Wis.: privately printed, 1932). He distributed it himself, selling it for 65 cents.

43. Waters, *B.E.F.*, 13.

44. "Bonus Plea Signed By 7 More in House," *Washington Post*, June 1, 1932.

45. Ibid. This appears in the same issue of the *Post* in which they were told to retreat and that their efforts were futile.

46. "Will Rogers' Dispatch," *Boston Globe*, July 30, 1932.

47. Walter Davenport, "But the Dead Don't Vote," *Collier's*, June 11, 1932, 89.

48. Arthur Leo Hennessy, "The Bonus Army: Its Roots, Growth, and Demise," 231, quoting an interview with Joseph Dwye, a local resident of the time.

49. *Fort Wayne Journal-Gazette*, June 2, 1932.

50. "Bonus Force Here Denies Red Backing," *Washington Post*, June 3, 1932.

51. "Federal Agents Probe Communist Bonus Activities," *Washington Star*, June 2, 1932, Bonus Army scrapbook.

52. Douglas, *Veterans on the March*, 120–21; *Toledo New-Bee*, June 2, 1932, June 3, 1932 (per Sneller, "Bonus March of 1932," 110).

53. *New York Times*, June 4, 1932.

54. Pace gave this version in congressional testimony in 1951: U.S. Congress, House Committee on Un-American Activities, "Communist Tactics Among Veterans Groups," 82nd Cong., 1st session, 1951.

55. *Washington Daily News,* June 3, 1932; cited in Sneller, "Bonus March of 1932."

56. *New York Times,* June 4, 1932.

57. *Cleveland Plain Dealer,* June 5, 1932; cited in Sneller.

58. Pace, in *HUAC 1951,* 1934–35, says that city officials faced "a pretty bad situation in Cleveland," noting the machine guns and the fact that so many police had been drawn from their regular beats that citizens feared an outbreak of crime and were uneasy, "which made us very gleeful."

59. Information about Carter comes from a one-page biography (which does not mention any railroad connection) in U.S. Military Intelligence, *Surveillance of Radicals.*

60. *Cleveland Plain Dealer,* June 6, 1932; *Pittsburgh Press,* June 9, 1932; both cited in Sneller, "Bonus March of 1932." Also, *Washington Star,* June 9, 1932, Bonus Army scrapbook.

61. "Federal Agents Probe."

62. "Federal Agents Probe."

63. The secret memo was not revealed until November 3, 1932; *Washington Post,* November 4, 1932.

64. "3000 In Bonus Army En Route Here; 3,200 Others Plan March," *Washington Daily News,* June 2, 1932, Bonus Army scrapbook. Glassford recalls setting up other smaller camps. He told the *B.E.F News,* July 2, 1932, that for one camp he selected a turnip patch in back of a frame shack occupied by an African-American family consisting of Mose Hawkins, his wife, and six kids. The turnip patch was overgrown. The grass was two feet high, so Glasssford got a horse-drawn power scythe and had the grass cut. The cuttings were used as stuffing for bed sacks that Glassford borrowed from the National Guard.

65. U.S. Grant III, grandson of the Civil War general and president, was the director of the agency. As historian Donald J. Lisio notes (*President and Protest,* 73), Grant was one of President Hoover's "almost anonymous, yet most trusted lieutenants." Lisio believes that Grant would not have granted permission for Anacostia without Hoover's approval.

66. "Federal Agents Probe."

67. "6000 More Veterans Are Expected Here; 100 Sleep in Open," *Washington Daily News,* June 3, 1932.

68. "This is Anacostia," *Washington Post,* May 8, 1965.

69. Interview with Charles T. Greene, May 2, 2002. Green, who was eighty-three when he was interviewed, is the former director of industrial safety for the District of Columbia.

70. Glassford Papers, RG 679, box 15, folder 5.

71. Hennessy, "The Bonus Army," 256–58.

72. "Bonus Plea Signed by Seven More in House," *Washington Post,* June 1, 1932.

73. Ibid.

74. Evalyn Walsh McLean, *Father Struck It Rich,* 303.

75. Ibid., 305.

76. Sneller, "Bonus March of 1932," 122.

77. "District to Truck Bonus Marchers Away from City on Next Thursday," *Washington Star,* June 4, 1932.

78. "Bonus Marchers Defiant as City Asks Leaders to Leave Thursday," *Washington Star,* June 5, 1932, Bonus Army scrapbook.

79. "Army Will Not Leave Capital," *Pittsburgh Post-Dispatch,* June 9, 1932.

80. "On to Washington," Literary Digest, June 11, 1932, 8.

81. "Bonus Marches Face Shrinking Hospitality," *Fort Wayne (Ind.) Journal-Gazette,* June 3, 1932, 1.

82. "'Bonus Army' Rallies for Parade Tonight," *New York Times,* June 7, 1932.

83. "Brooklyn March Planned," *New York Times,* June 5, 1932.

84. "Bonus Army Faces Misery in Capital," *Fort Wayne (Ind.) Journal-Gazette,* June 4, 1932, 1, 2.

85. "Bonus Army Here Ejects Six Reds," *Fort Wayne (Ind.) Journal-Gazette,* June 6, 1932.

86. "Dispatches as Bonus Army Mobilized on Wide Front," *Washington Post,* June 8, 1932.

87. Giblo, *Footlights, Fistfights and Femmes: The Jimmy Lake Story.* He took pride in the fact that Justice Oliver Wendell Holmes came to the Gayety each week and offered him the stock observation: "Is it good and dirty this week? If it's not, I'm not going to stay."

88. Ibid., 233–35.

89. *Washington Post,* June 8, 1932.

90. "100,000 View Parade of Bonus Army," *Washington Post,* June 8, 1932.

91. "Greatest Fistic Turn-Out Watches Slashing Battles for Bonus Army's Relief," *Washington Post,* June 9, 1932.

92. Waters, *B.E.F.,* 79.

Chapter 6: Hooverville, D.C.

Epigraph. Keene, *Doughboys,* 191.

1. *Washington Daily News,* June 9, 1932; cited in Sneller, "Bonus March of 1932." Named after Marks: Daniels, *Bonus March,* 110.

2. "Crosby Tells Glassford He May Lose His Job for Activities for Veterans," *Washington Star,* June 7, 1932, Bonus Army scrapbook.

3. *Washington Daily News,* June 10, 1932; cited in Hennessy. Waters (*B.E.F.,* 85) writes of $5,000 "in the treasury," but does not mention Coughlin.

4. "Bonus Army Asked to Leave Capital; Veterans Refuse," *New York Times,* June 9, 1932.

5. Ibid.

6. Douglas, *Veterans on the March,* 76, 77.

7. Glassford Papers for Marine information. Army field hospital: letter from Frank T. Hines, administrator of Veterans Affairs, to General MacArthur, August 18, 1932, Adjutant General Files, National Archives. Fort Hunt, originally part of George Washington's Mount Vernon estate, became a fort in the late nineteenth century, when the Army decided to increase defenses of the capital in anticipation of war with Spain. The guns of Fort Hunt, never fired in anger, were removed when the Great War began. The outpost became a place the Army did not know what to do with. In 1930 Congress authorized Secretary of War Hurley to hand Fort Hunt over to the Office of Public Buildings and Public Parks of the National Capital, then under control of retired major general Ulysses S. Grant III. He wanted the park as a recreational site along the George Washington Memorial Parkway, a new highway to Mount Vernon. A black ROTC corps had been given permission to bivouac at the camp during a summer training camp, but Hurley withdrew permission and placed the fort under the temporary control of Hines. He set up a hospital, which closed on August 12, 1932. (John Hammond Moore, "The Fort Hunt Saga: Guns, Bonus Marchers, U-BOATS, and Picnics," *Northern Virginia Heritage,* February 1980, 3–6, 20.

8. "Bonus Army Camp Called 'Frightful' by Health Officer," *Pittsburgh Post-Gazette,* June 10, 1932.

9. Waters, *B.E.F.,* 106.

10. "The Human Side of the Bonus Army,"*Literary Digest,* June 25, 1932, 113.

11. Waters, *Mass Violence,* 105.

12. Meisel, *Bonus Expeditionary Forces,* 9.

13. "Human Side of the Bonus Army."

14. "Veterans Dig in for Long Stay at Anacostia Camp," *Washington Daily News,* June 11, 1932.

15. "Human Side of the Bonus Army."

16. Meisel, *Bonus Expeditionary Forces,* 8.

17. "Human Side of the Bonus Army."

18. Douglas, *Veterans on the March,* 67.

19. Waters, *B.E.F.,* 68.

20. Douglas, *Veterans on the March,* 74.

21. Garner Jackson, "Unknown Soldier," *Survey* 58, no. 9 (August 1, 1932): 342.

22. Based on photographs.

23. "Sallies Big Help to Bonus Veterans," *Washington Post,* June 22, 1932, unpaginated clipping, Bonus Army scrapbooks, MLK Library.

24. Austin Kiplinger, "Growing Up in Washington I, An Inside-Outside View," *Washington History,* fall/winter 2000–2001, 11.

25. John Dos Passos, *The Best Times* (New York: New American Library, 1966), 70.

26. John Dos Passos, "The Veterans Come Home to Roost," *New Republic,* June 29, 1932, 177.

27. Thomas R. Henry, "Health Threat to 'Army' Grows," *Evening Star,* June 12, 1932, unpaginated clipping, Bonus Army scrapbooks.

28. Thomas R. Henry, "Bonus Camp Life Thrills Children," *Evening Star,* June 14, 1932, Bonus Army scrapbooks.

29. Charles Greene, interview by the authors, May 2, 2002. Greene was a director of industrial safety for the District of Columbia.

30. Joseph and Nick Oliver, interview by the authors, July 14, 2003.

31. Letter from Colevas to William Brown, March 8, 2003.

32. Meisel, *Bonus Expeditionary Forces,* 10.

33. The BEF and the police cooperated in the keeping a census. Here was the June 14 census, which uses the BEF's regimental system:

```
1st Reg. 8ths and I Sts. SE . . . . . . . . . . . . . . . . . . . . . . . . . . . . . 500
2nd Reg. 12th and D Sts SW . . . . . . . . . . . . . . . . . . . . . . . . . . . 450 (11 sick)
3rd, 4th, 5th , 6th Regiments at Camp Marks, Anacostia . . . . . . . . 13,650
7th Reg.
    3rd & Pennsylvania Ave NW  . . . . . . . . . . . . . . . . . . . . . . . . 2,350
    Camp Bartlett, 23rd and Alabama SE . . . . . . . . . . . . . . . . . . . 1,550
    Camp Meigs, 5th & Florida NE . . . . . . . . . . . . . . . . . . . . . . . 125
    202 A St. SE . . . . . . . . . . . . . . . . . . . . . . . . . . . . . . . . . . . . . 58
    Unattached . . . . . . . . . . . . . . . . . . . . . . . . . . . . . . . . . . . . . . 1,800

Grand Total  . . . . . . . . . . . . . . . . . . . . . . . . . . . . . . . . . . . . . . . 20,483
Men on sick call  . . . . . . . . . . . . . . . . . . . . . . . . . . . . . . . . . . . . 524
```

The police used a place-by-place census, conducted each day by on-the-spot inspections. By July 4, the police listed twenty-two locations besides Camp Marks, with a total of 20,876. Glassford Papers; U.S. Military Intelligence, *Surveillance of Radicals.*

34. James G. Banks, interview by the authors, April 30, 2002.

35. Frank A. Taylor, interview by the authors, April 28, 2002. In 1964 Taylor would become the founding director of the Smithsonian's Museum of History and Technology, now the National Museum of American History.

36. Dos Passos, "Veterans Come Home," 178.

37. Henry, "Health Threat."

38. John A. Garraty and Eric Foner, eds. "Lynching" entry, *Reader's Companion to American History* (New York: Houghton Mifflin, 1991).

39. *Cleveland Call and Post,* July 19, 1930.

40. James D. Calder, *The Origins and Development of Federal Crime Control Policy: Herbert Hoover's Initiatives* (Westport, Conn.: Praeger, 1993), 183. The first federal anti-lynching law was not passed until 1968, when the Civil Rights Act specifically made lynching a crime.

41. "The Secret City," *Crisis,* June 1932, 185–87.

42. "National Affairs," *Crisis,* July 1932, 222; "Schools," *Crisis,* August–July 1932, 272.

43. Banks, interview.

44. Green, interview. Green was not surprised at seeing blacks and whites together: "I was from California, and my sister and I were the only Negro kids in the schools I went to. My older sister was the only one in the high school."

45. Roy Wilkins, "Up in Harlem Down in the Delta," 119.

46. Roy Wilkins, "The Bonuseers Ban Jim Crow," *Crisis,* October 1932.

47. Jackson, "Unknown Soldier," 344. Not really the subject of this book, but this would appear to be a link between the NAACP and the concept of nonviolent resistance.

48. Constance McLaughlin Green, *The Secret City: A History of Race Relations in the Nation's Capitol,* 220.

49. *Crisis,* December 1932, 362.

50. From Wilkins, "Bonuseers Ban Jim Crow," 316.

51. Ibid., 124.

52. Truscott, *Twilight,* 124–126.

53. "Police Curb Students Opposed to M'Arthur," *New York Times,* June 9, 1932, 16. Many later accounts say that MacArthur (spelled *McArthur* in the *Times)* was "jeered" during the speech. But the police

detention of the three antiwar demonstrators was clearly taking place in another part of the campus. The demonstrators, two students and a former student, were later released without charges.

54. "Bonus 'Armies' Still on Move in This Area," *Pittsburgh Post-Gazette*, June 10, 1932.

55. "Record Senior Class at Pitt Given Degrees," *Pittsburgh Post-Gazette*, June 9, 1932; "'Army' of Veterans Rests in Camp at McKees Rocks," same issue.

56. Letter from Gilbert H. Grosvenor to Edwin A. Grosvenor, June 9, 1932. President Hoover did award the gold medal to Amelia Earhart Putnam on June 28 at Constitution Hall. Earlier that day Grosvenor and his wife had tea with the Hoovers and the Patmans and others. Decorations, as described in the official White House diary, were pink roses, pink larkspur, baby's breath, and ferns. Collection of Ike Hoover, White House usher, Library of Congress.

57. La Gorce to President Hoover, August 2, 1932, "World War Veterans—Bonus Correspondence," 1932, box 373; cited in Keene, *Doughboys*.

58. The *Washington Post* revealed the files on January 28, 1949, when the House Committee on Un-American Activities was investigating Communist subversion. The *Post* noted that the committee frequently consulted the files, as did federal investigative agencies.

59. Hurley to all area corps commanders, radiogram in secret code, June 10, 1932, Adjutant General's File, RG 94, Box 1181, National Archives. See also U.S. Military Intelligence, *Surveillance of Radicals*. The Army had a superb cryptography unit assigned to the Signal Corps. One of the major missions at the time was the cracking of sophisticated codes used by rumrunners. Elizabeth Friedman, an Army cryptanalyst, was pitted against a retired Royal Navy officer who ran the codes for a major rumrunning ring whose ships were tracked by the Prohibition fleet of the U.S. Coast Guard. She not only cracked the codes but testified at the trial that sent the rumrunners to jail. Elizabeth was the wife of William Friedman, the "father of American cryptology" and the developer of the unbreakable secret codes used by the Army in the 1930s and throughout World War II. National Security Agency's Center for Cryptologic History, "Cryptology, Elizabeth Friedman and the United States Coast Guard Thwart the Rumrunners."

60. Decoded reports from area corps officers, U.S. Military Intelligence, *Surveillance of Radicals*.

61. Communication from Commanding General, 3rd Corps Area, to the Adjutant General, July 5, 1932, AG 240 Bonus Section 1, RG 94, National Archives.

62. Joan M. Jensen, *Army Surveillance in America, 1775–1980* (New Haven, Conn.: Yale University Press, 1991), 203.

63. Memo of telephone call from G-2 2nd C.A. (Intelligence Officer, Second Corps Area) to Military Intelligence Division, Office of the Chief of Staff, June 3, 1932. U.S. Military Intelligence, *Surveillance of Radicals*.

64. J. Edgar Hoover to Colonel William H. Wilson, General Staff, Chief, Operative Branch, Military Intelligence Division, July 11, 1932. U.S. Military Intelligence, *Surveillance of Radicals*.

65. Report to Pelham Glassford from Private (patrolman) J. E. Bennett, June 20, 1932. U.S. Military Intelligence, *Surveillance of Radicals*.

66. District police reports area found in MID files; White House records, filed as Bonus March reports, contain copies of many of these police reports. Herbert Hoover Library; U.S. Military Intelligence, *Surveillance of Radicals*.

67. Jensen, *Army Surveillance*, 203.

68. Letter from Harry C. Lar to Major General George Van Horn Moseley, June 4, 1932. U.S. Military Intelligence, *Surveillance of Radicals*.

69. Glassford Papers.

70. Waters, *B.E.F.*, 95–96.

71. Douglas, *Veterans on the March*, 85–86.

72. Waters, *B.E.F.*, 95; *Washington Post*, June 7, 1932.

73. Glassford Papers.

74. Hennessy, "The Bonus Army," 252.

75. Ibid., 239–40.

76. "Bonus Army Asked to Leave Capital; Veterans Refuse," *New York Times*, June 9, 1932.

77. *Biographical Directory of the U.S. Congress*.

78. *Washington Post*, June 9, 1932; cited in Hennessy.

79. Sneller, "Bonus March of 1932," 131, 132; citing *Congressional Record,* 72nd cong., 1st sess., June 13, 1932, 12,910–12,935.

80. Hennessy, "The Bonus Army," 261.

81. "'America' Sung by Veterans at News of Defeat," *Washington Post,* June 18, 1932.

82. Daniels, *Bonus March,* 118.

83. Gore Vidal, *Screening History.*

84. Douglas, *Veterans on the March,* 152.

85. Daniels, *Bonus March,* citing *Congressional Record,* 72nd Cong., 1st sess., June 17, 1932, 1244.

86. Daniels, *Bonus March,* 120.

87. John D. Weaver, *Another Such Victory.*

88. "Vote on the Bill Is 62–18," *New York Times,* June 18, 1932; "Bonus Bill Loses in Senate," *Philadelphia Inquirer,* June 18, 1932.

89. Waters, *B.E.F.,* 149–50; "Glassford Makes Apology to B.E.F.," *Washington Star,* June 19, 1932, Bonus Army scrapbook. Chicken-blood incident recalled in Oliver twins interview.

90. Jorgenson, "Bonus Expeditionary Force," 58; Lisio, *President and Protest,* 113.

91. Waters, *B.E.F.,* 150.

92. Douglas, *Veterans on the March,* 156.

93. Lisio, *President and Protest,* 113.

94. "Glassford Makes Apology to B.E.F.," *Evening Star,* June 19, 1932, Bonus Army scrapbook.

Chapter 7: The Death March

1. *Washington Star,* June 19, 1932; *New York Times,* June 18, 1932.

2. District police undercover operatives kept Pace under surveillance and reported on speeches he and others made at Workers' Ex-Servicemen's League meetings. Most such confidential reports were filed in the District of Columbia's central files, as noted in Sneller, "The Bonus March of 1932," 146–48. Many others are filed under "Presidential Subject, World War Veterans—Bonus" in the Herbert Hoover Presidential Library. How the White House obtained the police files is not indicated.

3. "150,000 New Goal for Bonus Army: Many Start Home," *Philadelphia Inquirer,* June 19, 1932.

4. *New York Times,* June 19, 1932.

5. Waters, *B.E.F.,* 177.

6. In September 1914 General Joseph-Simon Gallieni, the military governor of Paris, needed troops to be transferred from a chaotic rail system to the front. When he found that the army was short of vehicles, he asked, "Why not use taxis?" Parisian taxi drivers picked up 4,000 soldiers from railroad cars and drove them to the battle that saved Paris. Georges Blond, *The Marne* (London: Prion, 2002).

7. "Troop Train Plan for Bonus Exodus Evolved at Capital," *New York Times,* June 20, 1932.

8. "German Veterans Bring Food to Camp Bartlett," *Washington Post,* June 20, 1932. Meisel, 12.

9. "Bonus Army Paper, with 25,000 First Run, Edited in Nook," *Washington Star,* July 13, 1932, Bonus Army scrapbook. The paper sold for 5 cents, of which the seller took 2 cents.

10. Waters said that his official roster of 28,540 bonus marchers—"perhaps half of the total who registered"—included men from forty-seven states (all but Nebraska), along with two men from Alaska, six from Canada, and one from the Philippines. Pennsylvania, with 4,796 men, had the most of any state. Waters, *B.E.F.,* 257–59.

11. "News Reels Receive Order to 'Go Easy' on Bonus Army," *Washington Daily News,* June 21, 1932.

12. These observations are made primarily from the large collection of news photos and postcards collected by the authors during the time of their research. One of the most interesting of the photographers was Royal A. Carlock, a veteran from Indiana who settled in Washington after the war. He created a livelihood for himself reproducing and selling photographs of what he called "the art & splendor of The City Beautiful." His black-and-white photographs were hand-colored in oils and sold in large number to tourists visiting the city during the post–World War I era. The most common subjects collectors will find are the Washington Monument and the Jefferson Memorial. His BEF photography was gritty and realistic, and he sold the pictures through the *B.E.F. News* at a price that allowed vets to resell them and make a profit.

13. Ryan, *Earl Browder,* 51. Browder's work as a Soviet agent did not become known publicly until the 1990s, when the National Security Agency released decrypted Soviet espionage messages, intercepted by U.S. intelligence agencies in the 1940s.

14. Report 14-41, July 1, 1932, to Crime Prevention Bureau from J. Apostolides and A. E. Fredette [undercover District police officers]. "Presidential Subject, World War Veterans—Bonus" in the Herbert Hoover Presidential Library.

15. Waters, *B.E.F.,* 154.

16. *Daily Worker,* June 27, 1932.

17. *Los Angeles Times,* June 30, 1932.

18. "Waters Acts to Drill Vets into Mobile Shock Troops," *Times-Herald,* June 30, 1932, Bonus Army scrapbooks.

19. "Gen. Glassford's Answer," *Washington Daily News,* July 1, 1932, Bonus Army scrapbooks. According to Green, *Secret City* (371), during this period Glassford spent close to $1,000 out of his own pocket.

20. *American Veteran,* July, 1932.

21. Lamar, "I Marched," 3.

22. "Bonus Men Find Congress Gone," *Evening Star,* July 2, 1932; "5,000 in Bonus Army Jam Capitol Steps," *New York Times,* July 3, 1932. Both the *Evening Star* and *New York Times* report Waters's claim that he had secured an interview with Roosevelt, but this was never mentioned again in the Washington papers, the *New York Times,* or the *B.E.F. News* and does not appear in his autobiography. The fact that Congress was planning to adjourn on Saturday of the Fourth of July weekend, which had appeared in the local papers and had been missed by Waters, suggests that this was not a man who had the ability to get an appointment with Roosevelt in the few hours between his nomination and his departure by plane for Chicago from Albany at 7:15 that morning. One can only imagine that Waters made this up to give a boost to morale on a bad day.

23. *New York Times,* October 19, 1932. This report refers back to the April statement in Pittsburgh. Governor Roosevelt sent Nels Anderson to New York contingent on June 12 and "offered to return them to New York State and give them jobs. They refused. . . . On the whole, they are all bonafide veterans of the World War." Letter, June 14, to Margaret A. Kerr, secretary-manager, Better America Federation, Los Angeles. Franklin D. Roosevelt Library, Presidential Correspondence, box 75, file 121.

24. Samuel I. Rosenman, *Working with Roosevelt* (New York: Harper & Brothers, 1969), 69.

25. Ibid., 70–71. Dorothy Rosenman recalled later that the vehicle that got the term launched the day after FDR first used it was a cartoon by Roland Kirby showing a plane flying from Albany to Chicago with "The New Deal" on its wings. Dorothy Rosenman's recollections appear in Katie Louchheim, *The Making of the New Deal: The Insiders Speak* (Cambridge, Mass.: Harvard University Press, 1983).

26. Blumenson, *Patton Papers,* 975, 982.

27. "Church Helps Find Grave for Son of Bonus Veteran," *Washington Post,* July 5, 1932.

28. "Two Veterans Held for Selling Food," *Washington Post,* July 4, 1932.

29. "Bonus Veterans Will Stage Mute Parade along Avenue," *Washington Post,* July 3, 1932.

30. William B. Mead and Paul Dickson, *Baseball: The President's Game* (Washington, D.C.: Farragut, 1993), 60. A sportswriter called the booing "a shocking manifestation of bad manners and lack of respect. . . . This must be the first time a president ever has been booed in public, and a ball game, of all places."

The booing by the vets was echoed in a sardonic letter that appeared in the July issue of *American Veteran:* "Why should you be concerned about food?" asked A. A. Van Orsdale of Houston. "Isn't the world's greatest food administrator, Mr. Herbert Hoover, there in Washington? Certainly, after having been able to feed Europe's starving millions, he ought to be able to feed a few thousand of our ex-servicemen."

31. Hoover's unpopularity with the vets was amplified by his long and steady support of Prohibition, which, according to a June poll of more than 10,000 Americans by *Literary Digest,* three out of four Americans now opposed. Despite its own support of Prohibition in the camps, the BEF was unequivocally for repeal, and vets had lobbied the Democrats for repeal. "Bonus Groups Favor Repeal in 'Platform,'" *Washington Post,* June 20, 1932.

32. Memo, July 5, 1932, Paul Killiam to Major Paschal, U.S. Military Intelligence, *Surveillance of Radicals.*

33. A story in the *Milwaukee Journal* (June 28, 1932) entitled "Bonus Chief's Wife to Hitchhike" reported that she was prepared to "start her journey clad in boots, hiking trousers and a man's blue shirt, carrying a red jacket and a small bundle of necessities."

34. McLean, *Father Struck It Rich*, 304–5.

35. Wilma Waters, interview by Sheila Graves, *Wenatachee World*, February 20, 1992, 9. Wilma also said that McLean gave money to pay for milk for the children of the BEF. Nowhere in this interview or elsewhere are there references to the two daughters whom Waters claimed he had in early interviews. This interview does say that the Waterses met in the cannery in Wenatachee, where they both worked and were married in 1930.

36. In an earlier secret message on "subversive activities," dated July 2, 1932, Lanza described Bundell as a recruiter who was signing up new BEF members in upstate New York. Lanza reported that Bundell and other speakers said that "the Bonus Army was in Washington to stay." Lanza added, "My general impression is that the Bonus Army is better organized than might be expected." U.S. Military Intelligence, *Surveillance of Radicals*.

37. NARA, AGO 240—June 10, 1932. Declassified in 1991, this memo was reproduced by authority of NARA on August 11, 2002, by the authors. The extraordinary nature of this item begs that it be reproduced here in its entirety as one of the "smoking guns" of the events leading up to the actions of July 28. The original shows that it was only seen by the Army and never got to the Navy, Congress, the Marines, or the White House. At one point in the memo it is stated that Camp Marks lies across "an unfordable stream" from Washington and that this would be a problem for the attackers but would be corrected:

> a. by defections from troops or Marines guarding bridges, thereby placing the bridges in possession of the Bonus Army. . . .
> b. by attacking with machine guns, stated to be already in the hands of the Bonus Army.

38. Military Intelligence Division, July 7, 1932, Report 14–28–13.

39. Pace later revealed that he had to call off several earlier parades of his followers because he feared attacks from the BEF—a fact confirmed by military intelligence reports. He also said that anytime he or other Communists tried to address the BEF, they needed police protection. House of Representatives, *Hearings Before a Special Committee on Un-American Activities*, 75th Cong., 3d sess., 1938, 2285–86. Pace also said that the party had been criticized as a "swivel-chair organization" for not exploiting the opportunity for revolution that the marchers presented. Pace also said that Browder and another high-ranking American Communist were later summoned to Moscow and dressed down for their failure in Anacostia.

40. Gene Smith, *The Shattered Dream*, 148.

41. Glassford Papers, RG 679, box, 15 folder 7. A copy of Walker's memo putting forward the scheme appears in Hoover papers.

42. "Hines Urges Speed in B.E.F. Rail Loans," *Washington Post*, July 11, 1932.

43. "Veteran 'Buried' Alive for Smokes, 'Exhumed.'" *Times-Herald*, July 11, 1932, unpaginated clipping, Bonus Army scrapbook, MLK Library.

44. *Washington Post*, July 12, 1932, unpaginated clipping, Bonus Army scrapbook, MLK Library.

45. *Los Angeles Times*, June 11, 1932.

46. Army intelligence reports include a detailed message from headquarters of the 1st Cavalry Division at Fort Bliss, Texas, to assistant chief of staff for G-2 (intelligence) in Fort Sam Houston, June 22, 1932; cited in Sneller, "Bonus March of 1932," 155–58.

47. "500 California Bonus Marchers at El Paso," *Washington Post*, June 21, 1932.

48. "700 Veterans Make Beds on Capitol Lawn," *Washington Post*, July 13, 1932.

49. Waters, *B.E.F.*, 165. There were variations on this line quoted elsewhere—"We didn't come here to eat soup and sleep in the jungle over at Anacostia" *(Time)*—but they all amounted to a brush-off.

50. *Los Angeles Times*, July 11, 1932.

51. Powell, *Tattered Banners*, 234–35. Powell notes in this 1933 book on veterans: "His bandaged head was merely a repetition of the 'soldier's maund' of Elizabethan days. The term was slang and it referred to self-inflicted wounds used by indigent veterans. Some poulticed their arms with a mixture of rust, soap and unslaked lime. When a blister appeared, they applied a linen cloth waiting until it stuck and then plucked it off. The result was a sore giving all the appearance of a gunshot wound" (39).

52. Ibid. Waters was not above a line or two of disparagement in his book, including quoting a California man who knew him: "Robertson? Hell I never saw him wearin' that brace when he was shootin' craps." Nothing else suggests that Robertson did not have serious spinal injury received while in the Navy, where he fell out of a shipboard hammock, and one must conclude that this amounts to a slur by Waters.

53. "A March of Death," *Evening Star,* July 14, 1932, unpaginated clipping, Bonus Army scrapbook, MLK Library.

54. "Extended Limit on B.E.F. Loans Granted by House," *Evening Star*, July 14, 1932, unpaginated clipping, Bonus Army scrapbook, MLK Library.

55. "Bonus Seekers in Night March around Capitol," *Washington Post,* July 14, 1932.

56. Daniels, *Bonus March,* 132.

57. "Marines Called, Leave Capitol; March Goes On,"*Washington Post,* July 15, 1932.

58. "The Curtis Blunder," *Washington Daily News,* July 16, 1932, unpaginated clipping, Bonus Army scrapbook, MLK Library.

59. According to the Office of the Architect, the architect of the capitol "is responsible to the United States Congress for the maintenance, operation, development, and preservation of the United States Capitol Complex, which includes the Capitol, the congressional office buildings, the Library of Congress buildings, the Supreme Court building, the U.S. Botanic Garden, the Capitol Power Plant, and other facilities." Reference to Richey, *Starling of the White House,* p. 283. Richey was appointed a Secret Service operative in 1901 at the age of sixteen, was briefly assigned to the Oyster Bay estate of President Theodore Roosevelt, and resigned in 1908, according to presidential physician Joel Boone, who quotes a *Washington Sunday Star* article of March 1929, headlined "President's Mystery Man." Boone Papers, chap. 22, Hoover Administration, 36–43.

60. Statement of Police Board of the Capitol, July 15, 1932. Glassford Papers, RG 679, box 15, folder 10.

61. Statement of Pelham Glassford, July 15, 1932, Glassford Papers, RG 679, box 15, folder 10.

62. Glassford Papers, box 15, file 7.

63. "Extended Limit on B.E.F. Loans Granted By House," *Evening Star,* July 14, 1932, unpaginated clipping, Bonus Army scrapbook, MLK Library.

64. Waters said the total number of veterans in Washington on July 16 was 22,574. Waters, *B.E.F.,* 174.

65. "Near Riot Threatens as Bonus Leader and Aides are Arrested," *Evening Star,* June 16, 1932.

66. Sneller, "Bonus March of 1932," 167.

67. Waters, *B.E.F.,* 168.

68. *New York Times,* July 17, 1932.

69. Bess Furman, *Washington By-Line,* 122–23.

70. Thomas R. Henry, "Lone Woman Saves Day," *Evening Star,* July 17, 1932, Bonus Army scrapbooks.

71. "Near Riot Threatens as Bonus Leader and Aides Are Arrested," *Evening Star,* June 16, 1932.

72. "Wide Area around Executive Mansion Blocked Off to Balk Picketing Plan," *Washington Post,* July 17, 1932.

73. *Washington Evening Star,* July 17, 1932.

74. Herbert Hoover Presidential Library, Boone Papers, 1112.

75. Sneller, "Bonus March of 1932," 174, quoting *New York Times,* July 17, 1932.

76. "B.E.F. Heads Agree to Drop Picket Idea," *Washington Post,* July 18, 1932, Bonus Army scrapbooks.

77. "460 Veterans More Request Return Funds," *Washington Post,* July 19, 1932.

78. Butler's Marine career began at the age of sixteen (he lied about his age with his mother's permission). He served in Cuba during the Spanish-American War and later in China, the Philippines, Honduras, Colombia, Panama, Nicaragua, Mexico, where his bravery won him a Medal of Honor, and Haiti, where he became one of the few heroes ever to be awarded a second Medal of Honor. His men—they called him "Old Gimlet Eye"—loved him, but most politicians did not. Given a leave of absence to become Philadelphia's commissioner of public safety, he smashed up speakeasies and tried to clean up a corrupt police force. But he had been given little real power. As a hero with a magnificent record and as the senior major general of the corps, after his resignation from the Marine Corps, he became interested in politics, a career move aided by the publicity he gained for his outspoken support of the Bonus Army. J. Robert Moskin, *The U.S. Marine Corps Story* (New York: McGraw-Hill, 1987), 208–9; *Marching to a Different Drummer: Unrecognized Heroes of American History* (Robin Kadison Berson, Westport, Conn.: Greenwood Press, 1994), 20.

79. "Butler Tells Bonus Vets to Stick it Out," *Times-Herald,* July 20, 1932, Bonus Army scrapbook. The first thesis that we were able to find on the Bonus Army was Stuart G. Cross's 1948 Stanford University master's thesis, "The Bonus Army in Washington, May 27–July 29, 1932."

80. *B.E.F. News*, July 23, 1932.
81. "B.E.F. Ignores Plea to Leave By Glassford," *Washington Post*, July 21, 1932.
82. Ibid.

Chapter 8: Tanks in the Streets

Epigraph. Douglas, *Veterans on the March*, 139.
1. Walt Whitman lived in a house in the 500 block of Pennsylvania Avenue; previously the house had been a gambling palace known as Pendleton's Palace of Fortune. (Evelyn and Dickson, *On This Spot*, 48.)
2. Meisel, *Bonus Expeditionary Forces*, 2. The June 14, 1932, report from National General Headquarters of the Bonus Army to the D.C. police puts the 7th Regiment strength at 2,300 (Glassford Papers). Meisel, describing the Pennsylvania Avenue camp around June 14, estimates its population at 2,000 to 3,000.
3. Jack Douglas, in *Veterans on the March*, identifies the veterans' leaders as George Alman, who had been deposed by Waters, and Edward Williams. Both men were left-wingers. Douglas's description of the encounter has the police captain saying, "We've been soft-pedaling but a change is coming," and Alman replying, "You're right, a change is coming. We're tired of it, too, and we're going to do something about it quicker than you may think." Douglas was not there, and Meisel was, so Meisel's eyewitness account is more reliable. Still, the Douglas version underscores the hostility growing between the left-led vets and the police. Meisel, *Bonus Expeditionary Forces*, 6; Douglas, *Veterans on the March*, 159. Alman was later deposed by Waters, supposedly because of this incident.
4. Mellon's personal contribution to the Federal Triangle would be the National Gallery of Art, built with his funds to house his extensive art collection. His son, Paul Mellon, was one of three trustees responsible for the building of the gallery. National Gallery of Art Web site; U.S. General Services Administration, "Historic Federal Buildings," GSA Web site.
5. Lisio, *President and Protest*, 78.
6. Cross, "Bonus Army," 27. Cross used as his source the Hoover Papers, then in the Hoover Library at Stanford University. These included the July 20, 1932, Heath letters. The papers were later reassembled and archived at the Herbert Hoover Presidential Library in West Branch, Iowa.
7. Sneller, "Bonus March of 1932," 184–86, using reports from the *Washington Evening Star* and *Washington Daily News*, July 20, 1932, and *New York Times*, July 21, 1932. The account essentially agrees with Douglas, *Veterans on the March*, 220–22.
8. Lisio, *President and Protest*, 144. Glassford's census of the area showed nine separate billets containing 824 by police count on July 26, including 150 WESL followers in one of the billets at 210 13th St. SW. (Glassford press statement, September 13, 1932.) The location of Pace's billet was described in *The Justice Department Investigation of the Bonus Army, September 10, 1932: Public Papers of the President of the United States/ Herbert Hoover, 1932–1933* (Washington, D.C.: GPO, 1956), 409–20.
9. Copy of commissioners' notice to Glassford, July 21, 1932. Glassford Papers, RG 679, box 15, folder 7.
10. "B.E.F. Ordered Off Camps by Noon August 4," *Washington Post*, July 22, 1932.
11. *Washington Daily News*, July 23, 1932.
12. "Washington Orders B.E.F. to Evacuate," *New York Times*, July 21, 1932.
13. "Veterans Get New Lease in Capital," *Baltimore Sun*, July 23, 1932.
14. Sneller, "Bonus March of 1932," 196–98; *Baltimore Sun*, July 23, 1932.
15. Handwritten notes transcribed, June 10, 1932, HH Notes-JTB 1930–1933, 1959. Boone Papers.
16. Laurie and Cole, *Role of Federal Military Forces*, 373. Lisio, *President and Protest*, 195, notes discussions of dispersion problems in Winship's "Memorandum for the Chief of Staff, Bonus Expeditionary Force," July 28, 1932. The memorandum looks back at discussions that occurred prior to July.
17. Secret letter, June 4, 1932, from Major General Samuel Hof, chief of ordnance, to commanding officer, Abderdeen Proving Ground, Maryland, Report of Operations against Bonus Marchers, AG 320.
18. Winship was the first judge advocate to receive the Distinguished Service Cross or the Silver Star. *Army Lawyer*, July 1997, 38.
19. Don Lohbeck, *Patrick J. Hurley* (Chicago: H. Regnery, 1956), 101.
20. Moseley reveals the proposed proclamations in an unpublished manuscript, "One Soldier's Journey," among the Moseley Papers. He gives no date for the first statement but gives June 14 for the second.
21. Laurie and Cole, *Role of Federal Military Forces*, 371.

22. The authors are indebted to Aaron Jaffe for his analysis of the relationship of Glassford and Waters.

23. The vet called himself Running Wolf, but his actual name was C. W. Taylor. Glassford testified as a character witness for Taylor in March 1933, when he was tried in Reading, Pennsylvania, for the murder of his estranged wife. "He went to the dairy to get milk for the children of the camp," Glassford testified. "He brought fuel from the municipal wood yard to use for cooking purposes and he kept me informed about particular cases in distress."

24. "Steam Shovels Ordered to Bonus Army Billets," *Baltimore Sun,* July 26, 1932.

25. Waters, in his account, does not mention this meeting. Lisio, *President and Protest,* 150–51, notes that Arthur Hennessy, "The Bonus Army," had interviewed Ward in December 1956.

26. Waters, *B.E.F.,* 192.

27. *B.E.F. News,* July 23, 1932. Glassford had told Bartlett that he personally would make sure the camp was run in military fashion. Glassford Papers, RG 679, box 15, folder 12.

28. Waters, *B.E.F.,* 198–200. Waters says he agreed to keep the meeting with MacArthur and Hurley secret. The *Washington Post* (July 27, 1932) mentions the meeting, and Waters, true to his word to Hurley, says they discussed the economic condition of the country.

29. Waters, *B.E.F.,* 203–4.

30. Carolyn Bartlett, "The Labor Day Hurricane of '35," *Islamorada Free Press,* August 31, 1988, 19–20. After his conversation with Glassford, Bartlett wrote a letter to Glassford with copies to Treasury Secretary Mills and local newspapers saying he would allow the veterans to occupy his land only if this were "agreeable to the Government and to the District." This stipulation, of course, wiped out the plan. But no one was aware of Bartlett's proviso when the fateful day began.

31. Sneller, "Bonus March of 1932," 208; Steve Murray diary.

32. Charles F. Mugge, of Hoboken, New Jersey, who commanded Camp Bartlett, said in an affidavit on September 10, 1932, that, after hearing of a call for men to come to Pennsylvania Avenue, he had suspicions and asked Waters, who denied it. Mugge rushed to Camp Marks to stop men from leaving, but "the damage had been done." Affidavit from Mugge, Glassford Papers, RG 679, box 14, folder 2.

33. References to Aldace Walker appear in the Glassford papers, but Glassford does not identify Walker or provide any background on him.

34. "Wrecking Crews to Oust Bonus Army This Morning," *Baltimore Sun,* July 27, 1932.

35. Wilford, commander of the 6th Regiment, later said that the man "had been planted there." Wilford said that the Texas contingent in that building had twice put him out that morning, but he had slipped back in. Wilford believed that government agents posing as veterans had tried to "provoke a riot to justify the calling out of the troops." Signed statement from Wilford, Glassford Papers, RG 679, box 14, folder 2.

36. "Two Play Pitch and Toss with Gas Grenade in Fight," *Philadelphia Public Ledger,* July 29, 1932.

37. Daniels, *Bonus March,* 147–49.

38. Patton's grand jury testimony, as published in ibid., 149. Waters, *B.E.F.,* 215, says two B.E.F. men "knocked the 'Red' down," picked up Glassford's badge, and handed it back to him. Glassford, in his accounts of July 28, does not mention the badge. Nor is the badge mentioned in Glassford's interview, on August 18, of McCoy and two other men. According to Glassford's handwritten notes, McCoy had served in the Navy and was discharged as a machinist mate first class. He was a member of the American Legion in Chicago and had been billeted on Missouri Avenue near Third Street. Glassford Papers, RG 679, box 14, folder 13.

39. Statement of Lieutenant Ira Keck, August 3, 1932; District of Columbia Records, Bonus Marchers (Veterans), 39–010, as cited in Hennessy, "The Bonus Army."

40. *Baltimore Evening Sun,* July 29, 1932.

41. "Bombs and Sabres Win Capital Battle," *New York Times,* July 29, 1932. This account, as do several others, says Scott had been awarded the Medal of Honor. But his name does not appear on the list of names maintained by the Congressional Medal of Honor Society. Glassford was quoted in some accounts as saying that Scott was a holder of the Distinguished Service Cross. Scott's skull was fractured, according to the casualty list prepared by the Associated Press, July 28, 1932.

42. Anderson, a reporter for the *St. Louis Post-Dispatch,* wrote this account for *The Nation,* August 17, 1932, 138–40.

43. Weaver, "Bonus March," 18–23, 92–97.

44. Bartlett, "Labor Day Hurricane," 101.

45. Waters, *B.E.F.,* 214. As Lisio, *President and Protest,* 178, points out, Patton "was the only police officer who claimed that Communists were at the eviction site. Glassford, who was equally familiar with the Communists, was convinced that none of them were involved in the brick battle." But Lisio (451) calls the group "a Communist delegation," and Weaver in "Bonus March," 93, calls them "radicals." Daniels, *Bonus March* (150), refers to the brick throwers as "the Communists."

46. Glassford notes on his interview of Olson that he had a Distinguished Service Cross, had been billeted at Camp Marks, and "claims he ran out to take flag out of the fight." Glassford Papers, RG 679, box 14, folder 13.

47. Sneller, "Bonus March of 1932," 211, based on Edwards's report in "Bonus March," 1932, Central Files, District of Columbia, which Sneller found in the Old District Building. These files may still exist, but workers at the D.C. Archives were unable to locate them.

48. "Bonus March Conditions," a 9½-page, single-spaced document apparently prepared for the White House. It bears a handwritten date, August 1, 1932, and notation, "Incidents & Criminal Components." The document contains reports on interviews of District commissioners and police officers (not including Glassford) by two of J. Edgar Hoover's assistants in the Justice Department's Bureau of Investigation. Herbert Hoover Presidential Library. Presidential Papers—World War Veterans, Bonus—Reports.

49. Lisio, *President and Protest,* 175.

50. Ibid.

51. Ibid., 183, quoting *Washington Evening Star* and *New York Times,* both July 28, 1932.

52. Statement of Officer Vernon West, August 3, 1932; District of Columbia Records, Bonus Marchers (Veterans), 39–010, as cited in Hennessy, "The Bonus Army."

53. Born in Lithuania, Hushka had come to America as a young man and started a butcher shop in Saint Louis. In 1917 he sold the shop, volunteered for the Army, and served in France. After his honorable discharge he drifted to Chicago, worked as a butcher, but never had a steady job. His wife divorced him and won custody of their daughter. By June 1932, when he heard about the B.E.F., he joined and headed for Washington. "I might as well starve there as here," he told his brother. Pals in the B.E.F. called him "Buddie Bill." He died almost instantly. A bullet through his heart had made him eligible for his $528 bonus, which went to his ex-wife. (*Time,* August 8, 1932; Bartlett, "Labor Day Hurricane," 7.)

54. *New York Times,* July 29, 193; Lisio, *President and Protest,* 186. Carlson died on August 2. As he died, Hushka was being buried at Arlington National Cemetery with full military honors. Waters and his staff, along with representatives from local American Legion and Veterans of Foreign War posts, were there. On the way to Arlington, the Hushka funeral procession circled the White House (*B.E.F. News,* August 6, 1932). Carlson was later buried at Arlington.

55. Bartlett, 32.

56. Raymond P. Brandt, interview by Jerry N. Hess, September 28, 1970, for the Harry S. Truman Presidential Library. "I told him the soldiers were coming and he couldn't believe it because he hadn't asked for them," Brandt said. Glassford's recollection: "Calling of Troops to Evict Bonus Army without Justification, Asserts Glassford," *New York American,* November 4, 1932. This was the seventh in a series of articles written by Glassford for Hearst newspapers.

57. Laurie and Cole, *Role of Federal Military Forces* (375), citing a July 28, 1932, memo from Winship to MacArthur, say that he "assigned" to MacArthur and Miles "direction over Chief Glassford and the District of Columbia police force, an assignment which was not authorized under any existing federal statue or Army regulation."

58. General Dwight D. Eisenhower, interview by Raymond Henle, July 13, 1967, Herbert Hoover Presidential Library oral history collection. Geoffrey Perret, in *Eisenhower* (New York: Random House, 1999), 113, doubts whether Eisenhower would have argued with his superior. "There is no mention of this famous rebuke to MacArthur in Ike's diary, a document so frank that much of it remained under wraps until 1998," Perret wrote.

59. John Eisenhower interview, National Press Club, November, 2003.

60. "Report of Operations against Bonus Marchers," from Brigadier General P. L. Miles to General Douglas MacArthur, August 4, 1932. Records of U.S. Army continental commands, 1920–1940, RG 394, National Archives.

61. "Summary of Events Troop 'F', July 28, 29, 1932," July 30, 1932. III Corps Area, District of Washington, National Archives.

62. Truscott, p. 127.

63. Blumenson, *Patton Papers,* vol. 2, 977.

64. *New York American,* November 4, 1932.

65. Glassford report in Hearst newspapers.

66. The units involved were a battalion of the 12th Infantry, a squadron of the 3rd Cavalry, a tank platoon (five tanks and men), and Headquarters Company from the 16th Brigade. ("Report of Operations against Bonus Marchers," Brigadier General Perry L. Miles to General Douglas MacArthur, August 4, 1932, U.S. Army Commands, RG 98, National Archives; cited in Sneller, "Bonus March of 1932," 230.) Backing up the active forces were nearly 800 men at Fort Myer. They had been sent there from Fort Meade, Fort Howard (near Baltimore), and Fort Humphreys (now Fort McNair) in northern Virginia. One company, about 160 men, was on call to be deployed at the White House but were not sent. Marine garrisons in Washington and Quantico, Virginia, were also placed on alert. (Laurie and Cole, *Role of Federal Military Forces,* 379.)

67. D'Este, *Eisenhower: A Soldier's Life,* 113. Davis would become General Eisenhower's adjutant general in World War II.

68. Glassford's account: "Calling of Troops to Evict Bonus Army without Justification, Asserts Glassford," *New York American,* November 4, 1932. Glassford wrote this as a series of articles for the Hearst newspapers. Bartlett quote: Bartlett, "Labor Day Hurricane," 32.

69. "Vet of the Bonus March," *New Orleans States-Item,* October 30, 1976.

70. MacArthur "joined me unexpectedly," Miles later wrote. MacArthur explained that he was there "at the suggestion of the President and the Secretary of War not to interfere in any way with my command but to furnish any additional orders which the situation might demand." [Brigadier General Percy L. Miles, *Fallen Leaves: Memories of an Old Soldier* (Berkeley, Calif.: Wureth Publishing, 1961, 307.)] There is no written record that the president made such a suggestion. It was clear throughout the day and long afterward that, while Miles was tactically running the operation, the true commanding officer was MacArthur.

71. Major General H. W. Blakeley, "When the Army Was Smeared," *U.S. Army Combat Forces Journal,* February 1952, 26–30. At the time of the Bonus March, Blakeley was a captain assigned to the 1st Battalion, 16th Field Artillery, stationed at Fort Myer.

72. "Capital Riots Like Great Movie Unroll before 'Grandstand' Seat," *Christian Science Monitor,* July 29, 1932. In 1971, covering a rally against the Vietnam War, Strout stood near on the site of the old Ford building, by then part of the Federal Triangle (*Christian Science Monitor,* April 24, 1971).

73. Reinhold Niebuhr, a professor at Union Theological Seminary in New York City, was working on his epic, *Moral Man and Immoral Society: A Study in Ethics and Politics,* when he read about the events in Washington. He had just written these words: "The fear of anarchy of American privileged groups and their self-appointment as the guardians of peace and order is significant only because it is so clearly expressed in a nation in which the classes have not become as distinct as in the older nations." Then he wrote this footnote: "As these lines are written, the American Government is using troops to disperse the 'bonus army' from Washington. Since the bonus army is merely a symptom of the unrest caused by the failure of the government to provide adequate relief for the unemployed, President Hoover's defense of the use of troops against the unemployed presents another perfect example of the superficiality of governments."

Responding to the fears of revolution then sweeping across America, Niebuhr went on to write: "Even when no anarchy is threatened and no violence is used by the classes which seek a more equal share in the processes of government and in the privileges of society, it is always possible for the privileged groups to predict anarchy on the score that the ambitious and advancing classes are unfit for the exercise of the rights which they desire."

74. Blakeley, "When the Army," 29.

75. "Troops Burn Anacostia," *Baltimore Sun,* July 29, 1932. Essary was runner-up for the Pulitzer Prize for his reporting on the events of July 28. Senator gassed: "Brevities of the Bonus Clash," *Evening Star,* July 29, 1932, Bonus Army scrapbooks.

76. Interview with Naaman Seigle, April 25, 2002.

Not everyone gassed was unwilling. "I was there," said Frank A. Taylor, ninety-nine, in an April 28, 2002, interview. "I had a buddy who liked to be in the middle of things. We were both officers. When the troops arrived from Fort Myer, he was a military nut and he was determined that he was going to be down there because the paper said they might use tear gas or something of the sort. He wanted to know what tear gas was like. He actually went down to expose himself to the tear gas and I went with him." Taylor was curator of the Smithsonian's Division of Engineering; his twenty years of advocacy led to the creation of the Museum of History and Technology, now the National Museum of American History, of which he was the first director.

77. Joseph C. Harsch, *At the Hinge of History* (Atlanta: University of Georgia Press, 1993), 12.

78. A. Everette McIntyre, interview by Studs Terkel, in *Hard Times* (1986), 17–18.

79. Descriptions and quotes: *Baltimore Evening Sun,* July 29, 1932.

80. Weaver, "Bonus March," 94.

81. Blumenson, *Patton Papers,* vol. 2, 978.

82. Wilfred Parsons, S.J., "The Rout of the Bonus Army," *America,* August 13, 1932, 445–47.

83. Weaver, "Bonus March," 94.

84. Sneller, "Bonus March of 1932," 238.

85. *Baltimore Evening Sun,* July 29, 1932.

86. Laurie and Cole, *Role of Federal Military Forces,* 381.

87. *Baltimore Sun,* July 29, 1932.

88. "Papers of Operation against Bonus Marchers," August 4, 1932, 6.

89. "Vet of the Bonus March," *New Orleans States-Item,* October 30, 1976.

90. I. S. David, "A Hero of 1917–1918; American of 1932: Holds Unsaluted Flag," *Washington Tribune,* August 5, 1932.

91. Brandt, interview.

92. Keck grand jury testimony, August 4, 1932; cited in Sneller, "Bonus March of 1932."

93. Sneller, "Bonus March of 1932," 243–44, quoting police officers' grand jury testimony.

94. Moseley unpublished biography, "Bonus March 1932" chapter. Moseley Papers, Library of Congress.

95. Eisenhower, in *At Ease,* writes that MacArthur said "he was too busy and did not want either himself or his staff bothered by people coming down and pretending to bring orders" (217). Miles, in *Fallen Leaves* (309), says that the message also included a warning about veterans in Anacostia having a machine gun. But MacArthur "sent word back that it was too late to abandon the operation, that the troops were committed, that we encountered no machine guns and that some of the troops had crossed the bridge already." (As Lisio, *President and Protest,* 212, points out, MacArthur had seen, corrected, and approved Miles's manuscript before publication.)

96. Miles, *Fallen Leaves,* 309–10.

97. Nick and Joe Oliver, interview.

98. Steve Murray diary.

99. Harsch, *At the Hinge,* 13.

100. "City of Hovels Is Wiped Out by Fire and Swords of Troops," *Evening Star,* July 29, 1932, Bonus Army scrapbook. For all of the reporters who crossed the bridge with the troops, one thing was beyond dispute, and that was that they had personally witnessed the torching of the camps. The list would include Essary, George Rothwell Brown, and Henry.

101. "Eye Witness Account of Bonus March Incident, Including the Burning of the Camp at Anacostia, 1932," RG 15, box 11, folder 7, "Purdy, Elbridge C," MacArthur Archives, Norfolk, Virginia.

102. War Department transcript of MacArthur press conference, July 29, 1932, Bonus March, Presidential File, Box 23, Herbert Hoover Presidential Library.

Some of the vets insisted that MacArthur was so saddened by what he was forced to do that he cried. The fact was that he had refused to don a gas mask and had himself been gassed.

103. *B.E.F. News,* August 6, 1932; "Father Lays Death of Ill Baby to Gas Used in B.E.F. Ejection," *New York Times,* August 9, 1932; letter from Major General H. L. Gilchrist, chief of Army Chemical Service, to Adjutant General, August 2, 1932, AG 240—Bonus, National Archives.

Chapter 9: The Long Morning After

1. *New Republic,* August 17, 1932.

2. Lawrence C. Jorgensen, "The Bonus Expeditionary Force, 1932" (Master's thesis, University of Chicago, August 1963), 97–98. Based on an interview by Jorgensen of McCloskey, April 30, 1962.

3. *New Republic*, August 17, 1932.

4. "Waters Urges All to Join New Force," *New York Times*, July 30, 1932.

5. *Evening Star*, July 29, 1932.

6. Lisio, *President and Protest*, 215, quotes Assistant Secretary of War F. Trubee Davison as saying that in a conversation sometime after July 28, 1932, Hoover told him that he had had "bawled MacArthur out" for crossing the bridge. But Hoover never publicly censured MacArthur or Hurley.

7. The changes are handwritten onto typewritten drafts. Hoover to Reichelderfer, July 29, 1932, "World War Veterans Bonus," Presidential Papers, Herbert Hoover Presidential Library.

8. Associated Press story out of Boston, August 2, 1932.

9. Hurley press release, August 3, 1932. Presidential Papers, Box 300, Herbert Hoover Presidential Library.

10. Hennessy, "The Bonus Army," 336–39. Cross, "Bonus Army," 45, points out that newsreel and newspaper photos showed soldiers setting the downtown fires. He gives an evenhanded assessment of the arson: "It seems probable that it was not originally intended to burn the shacks, but once the fires were started (either by accident, misunderstood orders or by the marchers themselves) the army saw no reason to stop them, except to try and save certain government property burned at Anacostia." That property included National Guard tents, most of which appear to have been set afire by the vets.

11. Carolin Giltinan (Mrs. Leo P. Haarlow), "An Eye-Witness on the Route of the B.E.F. in Washington," *Fortnightly Review* (St. Louis, Mo.), September 1932, 193–95.

12. Bartlett, "Labor Day Hurricane," 53.

13. "Bonus Seekers Ousted Here Rushed to West by Indiana," *Washington Post*, August 2, 1932.

14. "Troops Renew Gas Attack on Veterans," *Washington Evening Star*, July 29, 1932.

15. *Washington Post*, August 8, 1932.

16. "Girl Is Second Baby to Die," *New York Herald Tribune*, August 2, 1932.

17. White House, "Bonus March Conditions."

18. In 1952, when Miles wrote his memoirs, *Fallen Leaves*, key documents pertaining to July 28 were still classified. Miles's official report, like many other National Archives documents concerning U.S. Army involvement with the Bonus March, remained classified for many years. Yet he must have had access to some official documents, because he wrote a detailed account of July 28 actions, in which he puts the first phone call from MacArthur at "about 3 P.M." and the second one a few minutes later. As historian Donald J. Lisio points out (*President and Protest*), Miles sent MacArthur his manuscript for his approval. In a note accompanying the manuscript, Miles seems to endorse cross-the-river insubordination, for he wrote, "I have many times thought how unfortunate the country is that you were so restricted in advance by orders not to go beyond the Yahu in Korea."

In Hurley's typewritten War Department letter to MacArthur, as it appears in the National Archives, there is a handwritten "2:55 pm" under the July 28 date. Both the "2" and the second "5" appear to have been overwritten. At the bottom of the letter is a standard government time stamp. It shows that the letter was received by MacArthur at 2:15 *on July 29.*

Another version of the Hurley letter appears in the Douglas MacArthur Papers at the MacArthur Memorial in Norfolk, Virginia. That letter is handwritten, is not on a War Department letterhead, has the word "copy" written on the top, and with the date has a time: "2:55 PM." In the lower left-hand corner are the names "Walter W. Waters" and "John Pace." There is no record that either Waters or Pace ever received a copy of Hurley's letter. Nor is there any indication in the MacArthur archives why this handwritten document is there and not in the National Archives. The impression is that it is a personal copy provided to MacArthur by Hurley.

President Hoover did not officially designate a press secretary, but Theodore G. Joplin served as such. In *Hoover off the Record* he wrote what became the Hoover version of events on July 28: "The police were attacked as they began their work. . . . Under the personal command of General P. D. Glassford, the Superintendent of Police, who had played with the marchers throughout their stay, they resorted to their revolvers to defend themselves. One marcher was instantly killed and another fatally wounded within fifty feet of where General Glassford was standing.

"The rioting became so critical that the police could not cope with the situation. The District Commissioners so advised the White House by telephone, asking that troops be called out."

For the rest of his life, Glassford insisted that he had never requested federal troops. He believed that if the commissioners had let him order no more expulsions after the morning of July 28, he would be able to hold the situation steady and resume the next day, possibly with the evacuation to Camp Bartlett going on as planned.

19. *Evening Star*, July 29, 1932; *New York Times*, July 31, 1932. Newspaper stories about the arrest gave totals varying from twenty-six to thirty-six. The *Washington Herald*, on November 6, 1932, reported that "the thirty-five communists" who had been arrested were released in District Court for lack of evidence.

20. *Washington Daily News*, August 1, 1932.

21. "Army to Hold Rites for Bonus Marcher," *Washington Post*, August 2, 1932.

22. "Killing of Two in Riot Justified," *Washington Post*, August 3, 1932; "Jury Absolves 2 Policemen in Death of Vets," *Washington Herald*, August 3, 1932.

23. "Policeman Slayer of Bonus Veteran Is Shot to Death," *Washington Herald*, August 15, 1932.

24. Glassford later recommended that the three men not be prosecuted because they were combat veterans, had no connection with WESL or the Communist Party, and would be made into martyrs if punished (Glassford Papers). They seem never to have been put on trial.

25. *Washington Post*, July 31, 1932.

26. Mrs. Grace Hablitt to Hurley, August 4, 1932, Adjutant General's File, AGO-240, Box 1180, National Archives; cited in Hennessy, "The Bonus Army."

27. "A Cavalry Major Evicts Veteran Who Saved His Life in Battle," *New York Times*, July 30, 1932.

28. *Philadelphia Public Ledger*, July 30, 1932; *Washington Daily News* of the same date with headline "Army Major Forced to Throw Out Vet Who Saved His Life in the World War," Bonus Army scrapbook.

29. Truscott, *Twilight*, 129. In a 1924 letter to Patton, Angelo wrote, "We received your letter and sure thank you for your check as it helped us a lot. As it put us on our feet" (Blumenson, *Patton Papers*, vol. 2, 845). Robert Patton (*Pattons*, 212) writes that George Patton had recommended Angelo for the Medal of Honor; he also writes that Patton sent him $25 in 1939 after hearing, through another officer, that Angelo was in need.

30. *Washington Daily News*, July 30, 1932.

31. "Violence at Washington," *Boston Globe*, July 29, 1932.

32. "Bonus Army Ousts Reds at Johnstown; Waters Will Take Command Today; Food Shortage Becomes Serious," *Washington Post*, July 31, 1932; *New York Times*, August 5, 1932.

33. "Report on Bonus Expeditionary Force Emergency Camp Johnstown, Penna. Also Other Kindred Matters and Visits," Glassford Papers. The copy in Glassford's papers is frequently underlined, particularly in passages attesting to the veterans' character.

34. "Minutes of the Interstate Conference on Migrants," Harrisburg, Pennsylvania, August 11, 1932. Published as an appendix in Meisel, *Bonus Expeditionary Forces*, 48.

35. Jorgenson, "Bonus Expeditionary Force," 98; *Johnstown Tribune*, July 29, 1932; *Johnstown Democrat*, July 30, 1932.

36. "Johnstown Flood," National Park Service memorial, South Fork, Pennsylvania.

37. Ibid.

38. McCloskey, interview by Lawrence C. Jorgenson, April 30, 1962, in Jorgenson, "Bonus Expeditionary Force." McCloskey apparently endured the Bonus Army controversy because at the time of the interview he was a councilman.

39. *New York Times*, August 2, 1932; *Time*, August 15, 1932.

40. "Funeral Held for Shinault," *Washington Herald*, August 17, 1932.

Shinault was the seventh Washington policeman to die within a year. His murder occurred at a time of violence, much of which had profound racial ramifications. On Sunday, August 7, according to the *Herald*, a "gang of negroes" were alleged to have killed Park Policeman Milo J. Kennedy. On August 18, according to the same paper, an off-duty White House policeman named Ignatius Cole shot and killed Charles Young, an unarmed fifteen-year-old "colored prowler" in his neighborhood. The policeman and Young lived two blocks from each other. The next day, the coroner's jury rendered the same quick verdict it had handed to Shinault and Znamenacek—that Cole had acted in the "line of duty and in defense of his life." There was no investigation into any possible connection between the deaths of Hushka and Shinault. But, as Jack Douglas wrote in *Veterans on the March*, "The mysterious killing of Shinault . . . gave rise to stories that it was 'a put up job' because 'he knew too much.'" Douglas, whose book has been described as the official Communist history of the Bonus March, was not an objective historian. Yet his book, published soon after the events, reflected feelings some Washingtonians had at the time.

41. Statement of the Justice Department Investigation of the Bonus Army, September 10, 1932 (for publication on September 12); "Veterans Bonus," Hoover Library.

42. Daniels, *Bonus March*, 200.

43. Bill Linebarrier (Steve Murray's son-in-law) interview by authors, September 10, 2003.

44. Waters, *B.E.F.*, 257, said the roster sheets listed the names, addresses, and service numbers of 28,540 veterans—"perhaps half of the total who registered."

45. "Hurley Upholds Bonus Army Eviction," *New York Times*, September 13, 1932.

46. *Washington Herald*, September 15, 1932.

47. *Washington Herald*, September 18, 1931.

48. *New York Times*, September 13, 1932; Lisio, *President and Protest*, 254.

49. *Chicago Tribune*, October 21, 1932.

50. Starling, *Starling*, 300.

51. Hoover biographer David Burner agreed that the incident dealt a final blow to the incumbent: "In the minds of most analysts, whatever doubt had remained about the outcome of the presidential election was now gone: Hoover was going to lose. The Bonus Army was his final failure, his symbolic end." David Burner, *Herbert Hoover: A Public Life* (New York: Knopf, 1979), 312.

52. Memo from Hoover to Dodds, November 21, 1932. U.S. Military Intelligence, *Surveillance of Radicals*.

53. Ibid, reel 22. Date obscured.

54. "Troop Maneuvers Recall B.E.F. Rout," *Washington Post*, November 23, 1932.

55. *New York Times*, December 5, 1932.

56. *Time*, December 26, 1932.

57. Terkel, *Hard Times*, 31.

58. *New York Times*, December 12, 1932; Douglas, *Veterans on the March*, 278–280; undated, unlabeled clipping from MID 10110 files, Box 2855, which also contains clippings on plans for the 1933 Bonus March.

59. *Washington Star*, January 12, 1933.

60. Inauguration Day was changed by the Twentieth Amendment to the Constitution, which was passed by Congress on March 2, 1932, and ratified by the states on January 23, 1933. The amendment changed the date to January 20 and set the beginning of terms of senators and representatives to January 3.

61. Federal Bureau of Investigation documents pertaining to its investigation of the attempted assassination of President Franklin D. Roosevelt by Giuseppe Zangara on February 15, 1933, in Miami, Florida. Zangara was tried, convicted, and executed on March 20. According to the FBI documents, Zangara was cursing and railing against capitalists as he was put to death. The FBI report also noted that in August 1932, an operative of the Army's Military Intelligence Department (MID) reported seeing a suspicious character among the bonus diehards who were still on the streets of Washington. In February 1933 the operative discovered who the character was: Giuseppe Zangara, who later admitted that he had originally planned to kill Hoover.

62. Freidel, *Over There*, 85, 173.

63. *The Khaki Shirt*, undated publication of the Khaki Shirts, Chicago; Art J. Smith of Philadelphia to Paul Kenda, San Antonio, Texas, undated, Military Intelligence Division files 10110 266–45, National Archives.

64. Philip Jenkins, *Hoods and Shirts: The Extreme Right in Pennsylvania, 1925–1950* (Chapel Hill: University of North Carolina Press, 1997), 343. The Christian Front was associated with the German American Bund and Father Charles Coughlin. In January 1940 the Federal Bureau of Investigation arrested seventeen members of the Christian Front, charging that they planned assassinate "about a dozen Congressmen" and several prominent Americans of Jewish extraction. The FBI said its agents found several Christian Front arsenals containing weapons and explosives, including arms stolen from National Guard. The arrested Fronters hailed Coughlin as their leader. See Michael Sayers and Albert E. Kahn, *Sabotage! The Secret War against America* (New York: Harper & Brothers, 1942).

65. Douglas, *Veterans on the March*, 292–93.

66. U.S. Military Intelligence, *Surveillance of Radicals.*

67. Letter from John Alferi to Herbert Hoover, Palo Alto, California, May 8, 1933, Herbert Hoover Library.

68. *Washington Post,* April 28, 1933.

Chapter 10: The Return of the Bonus Army

Epigraph. From Roosevelt's Personal File, Roosevelt Presidential Library, Hyde Park, NY.

1. Biographical information on Fechner: *American National Biography* On Line; Quote from *Time,* February 6, 1936, 12.

2. Kelly McMichael Scott, "FDR, Lewis Douglas, and the Raw Deal," *Historian,* fall 2000.

3. Frank Freidel, *Franklin D. Roosevelt: Launching the New Deal* (Boston: Little, Brown, 1973), 247.

4. A founder of the America Legion, Johnson had immediately seen its political potential. His law firm, Steptoe and Johnson, was one of the most powerful firms in Washington because of his legion and Democratic connections. He served as the legion's national commander in 1932–33 and was rewarded for his loyalty to Roosevelt with his appointment as assistant secretary of war in 1937; he served in that post until 1940, later becoming the president's personal representative in India. Chief fund-raiser for President Truman's 1948 election campaign, Johnson became Truman's secretary of defense in 1949 and began a short, stormy career, presiding over the problems of military unification and the beginning of the Korean War. He resigned at Truman's request in September 1950.

5. Freidel, *Launching,* 449.

6. Scott, "FDR."

7. (Representative) Virginia E. Jenckes to Stephen Early, May 17, 1933, with enclosure of letter from Carl A. Sanderson, contact officer, Disabled American Veterans, Sebring, Ohio, May 15, 1993, Franklin D. Roosevelt Library.

8. *Washington Post,* July 1, 1933.

9. Samuel I. Rosenman, ed., *The Public Papers and Addresses of Franklin D. Roosevelt,* vol. 2, *The Year of Crisis* (New York: Russell & Russell, 1933), 99.

10. Clipping from unidentified newspaper, dated April 30, 1933, MID 10110 files, RG 165, Military Intelligence Division Correspondence 1917–1941, box 2855, declassified in 1974.

11. Doris Kearns Goodwin, *No Ordinary Time* (New York: Simon & Schuster, 1994.) 90; the incident is credited from Kenneth S. Davis, *Invincible Summer* (New York: Athenian, 1974), 107–8.

12. *New York Times,* April 28, 1932.

13. Arthur M. Schlesinger, Jr., *The Age of Roosevelt: The Coming of the New Deal,* 21. The quotation about revolution appears on page 5.

14. For Hoover, like Howe and Eleanor Roosevelt, the second bonus march was the occasion for a debut. Hoover had had an uneasy interregnum. Roosevelt had selected as attorney general—and Hoover's boss—Senator Thomas Walsh of Montana, who had said he would reorganize the Department of Justice "with an almost completely new personnel," presumably including J. Edgar Hoover. Walsh, a confirmed bachelor since the death of his wife in 1917, remarried five days before the Inauguration. On March 3, on a train taking him and his bride to the Inauguration, he died; the cause of death was listed as "unknown, possibly coronary thrombosis." Roosevelt chose Homer S. Cummings of Connecticut as attorney general, and Hoover immediately ingratiated himself with Cummings, deluging the White House with letters from supporters and working to win over Louis Howe, a fan of detective stories, by sending him inside information on Bureau of Investigation cases. On July 30, 1933, Cummings announced that Hoover had been appointed director of a "new Division of Investigation." Curt Gentry, *J. Edgar Hoover: The Man and the Secrets* (New York: Norton, 1991), 154–158.

15. J. Edgar Hoover, Memorandum for the Attorney General, April 28, 1933; FBI "Bonus March" files, released in August 2000.

16. J. Edgar Hoover to Ernest W. Brown, February 12 and February 20, 1932; FBI "Bonus March" files.

17. Douglas, *Veterans on the March,* 305–7.

18. Ibid., 309.

19. *Washington Post,* May 9, 1933.

20. *Washington Evening Star,* May 10, 1933.

21. *Washington Post,* May 9, 1933.

22. An indication of debate in the White House can be found in the Franklin D. Roosevelt Library's files for the period. While there was no memo about Howe's decision, there was a heavily underlined clipping of the *New York Times'* April 10 story about "Communists, loafers and tramps" coming to Washington. Among the underlined paragraphs was one quoting Doak Carter, who had been a BEF leader in 1932: "This movement can be killed off while it's young. But there is no time to lose."

23. *Washington Star,* May 5, 1933; *Washington Herald,* May 9, 1933.

24. Newspapers referred to Howe as "Colonel Howe," implying that he had been an Army officer. The "colonel" was an honorary title bestowed upon politicians and celebrities by the state of Kentucky.

25. *Washington Herald,* May 3, 1933.

26. *Washington Post,* May 2, 1933; *New York Times,* May 9, 1933; *Washington Star,* May 9, 1933.

27. *Washington Herald,* May 9, 1933; Douglas, *Veterans on the March,* 317; *Washington Post,* May 14, 1933.

28. *Washington Post,* May 11, 1933; *New York Times,* May 12, 1933.

29. *New York Times,* May 12, 1933.

30. Douglas, *Veterans on the March,* 303.

31. *Washington Star,* May 14, 1933, says "about 25 irreconcilables" refused to go to Fort Hunt; other sources put the number at fifty. By May 14 the total number of men at the fort was about 1,200.

32. *Washington Post,* May 31, 1933.

33. *Washington Post,* May 14, 1933; *Washington Herald,* May 13, 1933.

34. Henry O. Meisel, *The Second "Bonus Army,"* 1–12.

35. Ibid., 9.

36. The conversation is taken from Lela Stiles, *The Man behind Roosevelt: The Story of Louis McHenry Howe* (Cleveland: World Publishing, 1954), 264–65.

37. *New York Times,* May 17, 1933; Douglas, 324.

38. *Washington Post,* May 17, 1933; *Literary Digest,* June 3, 1933.

39. *Washington Daily News,* May 22, 1933.

40. *Washington Post,* May 31, 1933; June 4, 1933.

41. Jules Archer, *The Plot to Seize the White House* (New York: Hawthorn, 1973), 6–13.

42. Ibid., 176.

43. Garraty and Foner, *Reader's Companion.*

44. "Committee Calm Over Butler 'Plot,'" *New York Times,* November 26, 1934.

45. Walter Goodman, *The Committee* (New York: Farrar, Straus and Giroux, 1968), 10. As Goodman notes (19), Dickstein worked hard to back a proposal by Representative Martin Dies for the establishment of a House Un-American Activities Committee. John Rankin of Mississippi opposed the creation of what would be known as the Dies Committee and, later, HUAC, until he found "it would be headed by the Texan, Dies, and not by the Jew, Dickstein." Under Dies, HUAC shifted from looking for Nazis to looking for Communists. Dickstein was a Soviet spy who escaped detection. His secret life was not known until U.S. intelligence officials, in a program code-named Venona, decrypted intercepted messages between the United States and the Soviet Union in the 1940s. The Venona intercepts began to be officially released in 1995. Dickstein, who spied for money rather than ideology, was given the code name Crook by his Soviet intelligence handlers. According to *Spy Book,* Polmar and Allen, Dickstein spied from 1937 to 1940. He remained in Congress until 1945, when he became a New York State Supreme Court Justice. He remained on the bench until his death in 1954.

46. Records of Office of the Adjutant General, RG 407, Central Files 1926–39, Bonus 249 (3–4-36 to 5–28-32), box 1180.

47. Franklin D. Roosevelt to Rainey, February 26, 1934, FDR Library. In the file is also a letter chiding him for not saying "whom" and another saying his grammar was backed up by the Oxford Dictionary.

48. Telegram, March 10, 1934, from Van Zandt, FDR Library.

49. Daniels, *Bonus March,* 229.

50. Jeff Singleton, *The American Dole: Unemployment Relief and the Welfare State in the Great Depression* (Westport, Conn.: Greenwood Press, 2000), 146.

51. *Washington Post,* May 2, 1934.

52. Letter to the editor, *Washington Post,* April 27, 1934, 8.

53. Because of the camp's proximity to Washington, it became a show camp for such distinguished visitors as the king and queen of Great Britain. During World War II, the fort was a secret intelligence facility for the interrogation of selected German prisoners of war. Their cells were bugged. A declassified, translated transcript reveals that in one conversation a POW touched upon an issue that annoyed New Dealers: critics' comparison of CCC camps to Nazi Germany work camps. One officer tells another that he remembered Fort Hunt from happier days, when he used to bring his American girlfriends there. Then he adds: "It used to be a CCC camp." When his cellmate asks what the CCC is, the other replies: "It's something like the German Arbeitsdienst," the Nazi Work Service. The site is now Fort Hunt Park. National Park Service, "Fort Hunt—the Forgotten Story," published at http://www.nps.gov/gwmp/fohu/forgotten.htm.

54. Daniels, *Bonus March,* 232.

55. Carol L. M. Caton, *Homeless in America* (New York: Oxford University Press, 1990), 10.

56. *Richmond Times-Dispatch,* January 13, 1935.

57. *Norfolk Journal and Guide,* January 13, 1934.

58. Franklin D. Roosevelt to Robert Fechner, September 27, 1935, "CCC Negro Foremen," box 700, General Correspondence of the Director, Record Group 35, National Archives.

59. Robert Fechner to Robert J. Buckley, 4 June 1936; "CCC Negro Foremen," National Archives.

60. "Veterans Will Work on Road," *Florida Times-Union,* October 19, 1934; in Willie Drye scrapbook on the 1935 hurricane and events leading up to it, 97.

61. "'One-Man Bonus Army' Risked Death to Challenge Roosevelt," *Washington Star,* January 5, 1935.

62. Alferi had actually announced in a letter published in the *Washington Post* (November 18, 1934) that he was coming and that thousands of veterans were mobilizing for the trip.

63. "Text of President's Letter Regarding the Bonus." *New York Times,* January 1, 1935, Bonus Army scrapbook.

Chapter 11: Labor Day Hurricane

1. Drye scrapbook, 54.

2. *St. Augustine Evening Record,* July 5, 1934; Drye scrapbook, 53.

3. Michael Reynolds, *Hemingway: The Thirties,* 188–89.

4. Stuart B. McIver, *Hemingway's Key West* (Sarasota, Fla.: Pineapple Press, 1995), 66–67.

5. *Florida Times Union,* August 27, 1934; Drye scrapbook, 89.

6. Hemingway's wounds and experience were detailed in a series of clippings in a scrapbook kept by his grandparents in the Hemingway collection at the JFK Library in Boston, notably an article from the *Oak Parker,* October 5, 1918, entitled "Wounded 227 Times," containing a letter to his parents of August 18, and other *Oak Parker* articles, November 16, 1918, and February 1, 1919, when he comes back with two medals and much bravado, calling the war "great sport." This final article is written by a smitten reporter named Roselle Dean who calls him "handsome as Apollo" and ends her piece with this: "No story is quite complete without a thread of romance, and we are inclined to believe that somewhere in sunny Italy there is a dark-eyed, olive-skinned beauty, whose heart beats for one—and only one—'Americano' soldier."

The moment that Hemingway is wounded is replayed fictionally in *A Farewell to Arms* (New York: Scribner, 1995; original edition, 1929), 54: "I tried to breathe but my breath would not come and I felt myself rush bodily out of myself and out and out and out and all the time bodily in the wind. I went out swiftly, all of myself, and I knew I was dead and that it had all been a mistake to think you just died. Then I floated, and instead of going on I felt myself slide back. I breathed and I was back." There is another description that has gained a presence on the Internet, but it is always given without attribution and may be apocryphal: "'There was one of those big noises you sometimes hear at the front,' he later wrote. 'I died then. I felt my soul or something coming right out of my body, like you'd pull a silk handkerchief out of a pocket by one corner. It flew all around and then came back and went in again and I wasn't dead any more." The source of this may be an undocumented site called lostgeneration.com.

7. Carlos Baker, *Ernest Hemingway: A Life Story* (New York, Charles Scribner's Sons, 1969), 48–49.

8. Carlos Baker, *Hemingway: The Writer as Artist* (Princeton, N.J.: Princeton University Press, 1972), 207–8.

9. UP, "FERA Workers at Matecumbe Make Trouble," in Drye scrapbook, 83.

10. 74th Cong., 1st sess., 1935, *Congressional Record* 79, pt. 10:10649. There were those in Roosevelt's inner circle who saw a logic in the veto: "At Cabinet meeting this afternoon the Vice President said that the best thing that could happen on the pending bonus legislation would be for the Patman bill to go through, the President to veto this bill, and then to have the bill passed over the President's veto. He said that practically all of the Republicans in the House had voted for the Patman bill and that the Republicans in the Senate would do likewise. They would vote to pass it over the President's veto so that the President would have no responsibility for the legislation. If this should happen, the bonus would be taken out of next year's campaign." Harold Ickes, *The Secret Diary of Harold Ickes: The First Thousand Days, 1933–1935* (New York: Simon and Schuster, 1953), 356.

11. Franklin D. Roosevelt Library, President's personal file #95-C. The Marland letter was dated March 13, FDR's reply was dated March 15, and Marland replied in a letter dated March 17 that he still must vote for the bonus: "The very fact that you would trouble to write such a letter has 'sold me' more than anything else on the value of your leadership, and has convinced me of your sympathetic understanding of the bonus problem."

12. "Coughlin Rejects Third Party Move," *New York Times,* May 6, 1935.

13. "Dr. Peale Attacks Father Coughlin," *New York Times,* May 13, 1935.

14. "Coughlin's Bonus Plea," *New York Times,* May 13, 1935.

15. Ibid., 94.

16. "Roosevelt Cruises Leisurely on Sequoia; Will Fish a Bit Before Returning Tonight," *New York Times,* May 19, 1935.

17. FDR addresses the novelty of an in-person veto, "As to the right and propriety of the President in addressing the Congress in person, I am very certain that I have never in the past disagreed, and will never in the future disagree, with the Senate or the House of Representatives as to the constitutionality of the procedure. With your permission, I should like to continue from time to time to act as my own messenger."

18. *Public Papers of Roosevelt,* vol. 4, 182–93.

19. FDR, according to Ickes, *Secret Diary* (525), worked on the veto speech until early in the morning before its delivery. The president had asked his press secretary to prepare two press releases, one favoring the bill and the other vetoing it, and later told Ickes that he had "put it over" on his staff. Ickes was appalled by his "playful attitude on such an important measure."

20. "23,000 Here Cheer Coughlin Attack on the President," *New York Times,* May 23, 1935.

21. Ibid.

22. "Patmanites Fight New Bonus March," *New York Times,* May 16, 1935.

23. Bonus Veto B, FDR Library.

24. Bonus Veto B, Bonus Veto A, FDR Library.

25. "New Bonus 'March' Surprises Capital," *New York Times,* June 23, 1935; *Wall Street Journal,* June 30, 1935.

26. "'Chain Bulletins' to Raise Bonus Army to Be Launched," *Washington Star,* January 29, 1935, Bonus Army scrapbook. Ironically this item appears in the same issue of the *Star* as a photo and an announcement that Walter Waters was now working for the War Department in a job that had been obtained for him by General MacArthur.

27. "New Bonus 'March'," Bonus Army scrapbook.

28. Daniels, *Bonus March,* 240.

29. *New York Times,* August 11, 1935. Pictures run with the golfless article showed men in the camps playing checkers and reading in the camp library along with a picture of the camp itself. Over the pictures was the caption "Where Government Is Housing War Veterans to Keep Them from Capitol." The veterans' project evolved into the Swamp Fox Golf Course in Kingstree, North Carolina. Toby Welch, a golfer and unofficial historian of the course, told the authors that when the vets built it there were no golfers in Kingstree.

30. "Veteran's Camps to Be Abandoned," *New York Times,* August 16, 1935.

31. *Key Veteran News,* August 31, 1935. This will be the last issue of the newspaper. Copies of the *Key Veteran News* exist but are extremely rare. The xeroxed copies used for this work are from Willie Drye, who copied them from Jerry Wilkinson of the Upper Keys Historical Society. Wilkinson has spent many years assembling a full set.

32. Selected Records Relating to the 1935 Florida Hurricane, 55861, NARA, Record Group 69 006.1 Works Progress Administration.

33. House Committee on World War Veterans' Legislation, *Florida Hurricane Disaster* (Washington, D.C.: GPO, 1936).

34. Drye, *The Storm of the Century*, 71.

35. Drye, *Storm*, 102; Coast Guard report.

36. Drye, *Storm*, 72–3.

37. "Horrific Labor Day Storm of '35 Swept Away All but Memories," *USA Today*, June 8, 1999. The only other Category 5 was Camille, which went ashore in Mississippi and Louisiana in 1969, killing 256. Deadliest U.S. Hurricanes since 1900, according to the National Hurricane Center: (1) 1900, Galveston, Texas, Category 4, killed more than 8,000. (2) 1928, Lake Okeechobee, Florida, Category 4, killed at least 1,800. (3) 1919, Florida Keys, south Texas, Category 4, killed 600, mostly lost on ships at sea. (4) 1938, New England, Category 3, killed 600. (5) 1935, Florida Keys, Category 5, killed at least 408.

The official definition of a Category 5 storm is: "Winds greater than 155 mph. Complete roof failure on many residences and industrial buildings. Some complete building failures with small utility buildings blown over or away. Major damage to lower floors of all structures located less than 15 feet ASL and within 500 yards of the shoreline. Massive evacuation of residential areas on low ground within 5 to 10 miles of the shoreline may be required."

38. Testimony of Richard Lawrence Bow, an engineer working on the bridge at the time of the hurricane, September 1935, on file at the Islamorada Library.

39. R.W. Craig as told to George X. Sand, *Adventure Magazine*, November 1956, 51. This account of the hurricane and others like it can be found in the Monroe County Library, Helen Wadley Branch, Islamorada, Florida. The building is directly across the street from the memorial to the victims of the storm, and contains the best collection of records on the storm, including all of the reports of the investigations into the government response to the hurricane.

40. Memo from Stephen T. Early, September 3, 1935, FDR Library.

41. Telegram from B. R. Kessler to FDR, September 4, 1935, FDR Library.

42. Memo of September 6, 1936, from acting chief of Weather Bureau to FDR, FDR Library.

43. John Abt, *Advocate and Activist: Memoirs of an American Communist Lawyer*, 48.

44. Memorandum to president, September 6, 1935, FDR Library.

45. Ernest Hemingway, *Selected Letters, 1917–1961*, ed. Carlos Baker (New York: Charles Scribner's Sons, 1981), 423. "One Trip Across" appeared in *Cosmopolitan*, April 1934.

46. Joseph North to Ernest Hemingway, September 5, 1935; Hemingway Collection correspondence file, John F. Kennedy Library, Boston. To this day it is often assumed that Hemingway went to the *New Masses* because he had been turned down elsewhere. Even John Dos Passos, who tells him in a letter of September 20 that it was a damn fine piece in the *Daily Worker*, asks him: "Did Gingrich [editor at *Esquire*] fade out on the Hurricane piece?" Townsend Ludington, "The Fourteen Chronicle," *Gambit*, 1973, 482.

47. Honoria Murphy Donnelly, *Sara and Gerald*, with Richard N. Billings (New York: Times Books, 1982), 170.

48. Drye, *Storm*, 231.

49. "Coughlin Mourns Death of Senator," *New York Times*, September 11, 1935.

50. 74th Cong., Congressional Record, 437–41.

51. Abt, *Advocate and Activist*, 50.

52. Franklin D. Roosevelt Library, President's Official File #83, Disasters Box 2: Letter of September 10, 1935.

53. Franklin D. Roosevelt Library, President's Official File #83, Disasters Box 2: Letter enclosing the Akron editorial (September 9) from a Roosevelt partisan who was worried about "propaganda like this."

54. Drye, *Storm*, 232.

55. Record Group 69 006.1, WPA, *Selected Records Relating to the 1935 Florida Hurricane*. Statement of John A. Russell.

56. Joseph North to Hemingway, September 10, 1935; Hemingway Collection correspondence file.

57. Melver, *Hemingway's Key West*, 71.

58. Ernest Hemingway, "Who Murdered the Vets?" *New Masses*, September 17, 1935, 9.

59. Ibid., 10.

60. "Lincoln Steffens Speaking," *Pacific Weekly* (Carmel, Calif.), September 23, 1935.

61. Telegram from North to Hemingway, September 14, 1935; Hemingway Collection correspondence file.

> The News *seems to be on to the ways of the anti–New Dealers: "Every time a CCC boy out in Colorado is killed by a falling tree . . . we can expect to hear from the Communists and old dealers that Roosevelt was responsible."*

62. The estimate of 250–260 is based on Willie Drye's analysis after spending several years on *Storm.*

63. Carolyn Bartlett, "The Labor Day Hurricane of '35," *Islamorada Free Press,* August 31, 1988, 20. After the storm, Islamorada was a blank. One of the few structures that remained standing was a stone angel with a broken wing. During the hurricane, the angel was lifted from tiny Pioneer Cemetery, a final resting place for early residents of the Islamorada area, and dropped on the Old Highway that existed at the time. The angel can be seen today inside a fence on the grounds of Cheeca Lodge. Just beyond is a hurricane monument that marks a mass grave. A large stone features an impression of palm trees swaying with the wind, and beneath the tiled mosaic that forms the base of the monument are the ashes of many who died in the 1935 hurricane.

64. Gregory H. Hemingway, *Papa: A Personal Memoir* (Boston: Houghton Mifflin, 1976), 136–37.

65. Letter to FERA, October 15, 1935, FDR Library.

66. "New Bonus Drive Pledged by V.F.W.," *New York Times,* September 18, 1935.

67. *Miami Herald,* "Hurricane Survivors Recall Terror of '35," September 2, 1991.

68. Identical AP stories were filed in the *New York Times* and the *Washington Post* on October 13, 1935, with different headlines: "Florida Storm Toll Avoidable, Legion is Told" (*Post*) and "300 Storm Deaths Called Needless" (*Times*).

69. The front-page *New York Times* story on the American Legion hearings, October 15, 1935, was nothing less than sensational:

Men in Key Camps Called "Deserted,"
Witness at Legion Inquiry Says Officers Left Veterans "to Their Fate."
—WASHINGTON IS ACCUSED—
Declared to Have Delayed a Day
in Authorizing Florida Storm
Relief Train.

70. This appears in the final report of the American Legion.

71. Report to the President of the United States, September 8, 1936, 3–4, FDR Library.

72. Report of Special Investigation Committee, Florida Hurricane Disaster, to National Executive Committee, the American Legion, by Quimby Melton, Georgia, Chairman, FDR Library.

73. Letter from FDR to Murphy, November 15, 1935, FDR Library.

74. *American Legion Magazine,* January 1936, 5–7.

75. NARA Record Group 15, Sub-Group 5–3, Washington Records Group, Suitland, Maryland.

76. Ibid.

Chapter 12: V Day for the Veterans

1. Herbert M. Mason, "Battling for the Bonus," *VFW: Veterans of Foreign Wars Magazine,* May 1999, 18.

2. George Gallup, "America Speaks: Pay Cash Bonus, Say 55% in Weekly Poll," *Washington Post,* December 8, 1935.

3. Before that broadcast was over, Coughlin had a stunning announcement. His political party, the National Union for Social Justice, claimed it had just ended an initial period of twelve working days (December 13 to January 3) in which it had created a political organization for its "crusade." The results were stunning: 56,677 "units" of the party had been founded or were in the process of organizing. A unit contained a minimum of 100 members, allowing Coughlin to boast that in less than a month he had signed up 5,267,700 members. He closed by charging that the new Congress would deepen the nation's debt through more borrowing, creating "new bonuses for bankers." He added, "It is our business to organize so that the Seventy-fifth Congress of 1937 will be composed of Americans who restore America to its citizens." Reprint of his broadcast, "The Bonus and Neutrality," published by the Radio League of the Little Flower, Detroit.

4. Ickes, *Secret Diary,* 525. His entry for Friday, January 24, 1936: the president, speaking about the bonus bill, said "he had written it out in longhand and had worked on it until one o'clock Thursday morning. He had told neither [Marvin] McIntyre [a presidential secretary] nor [press secretary Steve] Early what he proposed to do on the bill, but he had instructed Early to prepare two press releases, one on the basis of a veto and one on that of an approval. . . . He chuckled as he spoke of how he had 'put it over' on McIntyre and Early. . . . I cannot see either the politics or the statesmanship in a course of this sort. . . . I do not like this playful attitude on such an important measure."

5. Ibid., 525.

6. David M. Kennedy, *Freedom from Fear: The American People in Depression and War, 1929–1945* (New York: Oxford University Press, 1999), 791, and David McCullough, *Truman* (New York: Simon & Schuster, 1992), 200.

7. 70th Cong. 2nd sess., 1936, Congressional Record 80, pt 1:1080.

8. *Washington Herald,* January 28, 1935.

9. Farley to Roosevelt, July 31, 1936, FDR Library.

10. Johnson to Early, FDR Library.

11. The pamphlet carries no further information as to its author or publisher. An interesting line in its foreword discusses the "Great Bonus March on Washington": "The Veterans declared that there are certain rights and privileges which belong to every citizen—the right to a decent life, and the right—implied rather than specified—to turn to your County for sympathetic help when you are in need."

12. "Vets' Bonus Hit by Mrs. Rogers," *Washington Times Herald,* January 4, 1931, Edith Nourse Rogers Papers, Schlesinger Library, Radcliffe Institute for Advanced Study, Harvard.

13. One final irony to the vote that passed the bonus was that Representative Edith Nourse Rogers, the one person in Congress in whom the veterans, by all accounts, had the most faith, voted against it, as she had with all the previous votes. She was given a free pass by the veterans on this issue because they respected her firm belief that the cost of redeeming the certificates would work against her efforts to obtain an omnibus hospitalization bill for all veterans who became ill. Rogers was now fighting to get broader health care coverage for all vets. She believed that the bonus certificate was the only insurance a veteran's family had. She did, however, support legislation to grant special relief for veterans in need. In June 1932, she had said the Bonus Army "represented maladjustments in the economic structure," which she felt should be fixed, but not by cashing in the veterans' sole item of value. "Bonus Army Analyzed by Congresswoman," *Times Herald,* June 12, 1932, Rogers Papers.

14. "Mrs. Rogers to Sift U.S. 'Terrorism,'" *Boston American,* February 28, 1936, Rogers Papers.

15. "Armed Man Terrorizes House," *Evening Star,* December 13, 1932; unpaginated scrapbook item, Rogers Papers. The scrapbook also yields a rare four-deck headline from the *Boston Post* of December 14:

CONGRESSMEN FLEE MADMAN WITH GUN

Mrs. Rogers of Bay State is Heroine When Crack Marksman Waves Loaded Weapon in House Gallery—Chamber Terrorized Before He is Disarmed—Intended to Make 20-Minute Speech and Shoot Any Interferer.—

Woman Member Calmly Tries to Quiet Him—Walks Toward Him Talking, Unafraid

Dynamite Found in Room He Occupied—Going to Blow Himself Up Afterward

16. Rankin and Patman carefully used the witness to establish the point that dangerous weather was to be found in all sectors of the country, and that the veterans in the Keys would have been in just as much jeopardy in New England or other parts of the South.

Mr. *Patman:* "So you can hardly go to an area in the United States where there is not the possibility of having your life taken by a flood or storm or hurricane or earthquake?"
Mr. *Tannehill:* "That is right."
Mr. *Patman:* "I think that is all."
Mrs. *Rogers:* "I have just one more question, Mr. Chairman. . . . Basing your opinion upon your scientific knowledge of storms, do you consider the area in Matecumbe a safe place to be in a hurricane?"
Mr. *Patman:* "In a hurricane?"
Mrs. *Rogers:* "Yes."

> *Mr. Patman:* "No place is safe. I will object to that question."
>
> *Mrs. Rogers:* "I am asking the witness."
>
> *Chairman Rankin:* "The Chair will take judicial notice of the fact that Matecumbe, Tupelo, Mississippi, Massachusetts, or anywhere else is unsafe in time of storm, and it is unnecessary to embarrass the witness."
>
> *Mrs. Rogers:* "I asked the question, Mr. Chairman."

She persisted, changing the phrase in her question to "during the storm season." When the witness was finally allowed to speak, he said it would be a safe place to live if the utmost precautions were taken.

> *Mrs. Rogers:* "You mean if they built houses that were suitable."
>
> *Mr. Tannehill:* "Or go somewhere else when the storm warning is posted."
>
> U.S. House of Representatives. Committee on World War Veterans Legislation, *Florida Hurricane Disaster,* 204–5.

17. Ibid., 450.

18. Box 13, folder 170, Rogers Papers.

19. Abt, *Advocate and Activist,* 50. Abt's memoir underscores the problem with the "act of God" report and the subsequent hearings in that these are the major "primary sources" available to researchers, of whom more than one has been led astray because of the effectiveness of the suppression of the Kennamer report and the fact that few know about the American Legion report.

20. Drye, *Storm,* paperback ed., 2003, 322–24. Drye got to see the carbon held by Shelton's only surviving child, Rae Shelton Cummings of Vero Beach, Florida, who has no idea how her father got the document, which is almost certainly the one extracted by Aubry Williams. Quoting directly from the postscript to the new edition of *Storm of the Century,* Drye, who has read the 56-page report, wrote, "In Abt's view, Shelton and his boss, Fred Ghent, handled the hurricane emergency exactly as they should have. They made no mistakes, nor were they guilty of even minor lapses of judgement." Abt acknowledged the fact that some witnesses gave testimony that blamed the three men cited by Kennamer but attributed this to the ordeal that he had lived through—"severe mental and physical strain."

21. "Veterans' Home Closing Leaves 'Mother' Steed without Boys," *Washington Star,* June 25, 1938, Bonus Army scrapbook.

22. "Fifty Veterans Here Say Farewell to Home the Bonus Will Close," *Washington Post,* June 13, 1936, Bonus Army scrapbook.

23. Associated Press report from Washington, June 13, 1936.

24. *Bridgeport Post,* June 14, 15, 16, 17, and 18, 1932.

25. Lester G. Telser, "The Veterans' Bonus of 1936 and the Abortive Recovery from the Great Depression" (Master's thesis, University of Chicago, 2000).

26. "Veterans in Washington Area to Get $40,000,000 Baby Bonds," *Washington Herald,* January 28, 1936; *Washington Times,* June 6, 1936, Bonus Army scrapbook.

27. *New York Times,* February 8, 1936.

28. *Chicago Tribune,* June 5, 1936.

29. "Bonus Joy and Woe: Dizzy Goings-On in No Man's Land of Sudden Wealth," *Literary Digest,* June 27, 1936, 7.

30. "'Box-Car' Alferi's 1-Track Mind Shunts from Bonus to Pension," *Washington Post,* October 17, 1936. Alferi's penultimate trip to Washington for the veteran's rights comes in October, when he returns—now beginning to plump for pensions—with $50 of his bonus money left. He promises to return in January of 1937 for the opening of Congress, where he will advance his new agenda.

31. Interview, September 24, 2002.

32. What did the bonus actually do for the economy? According to an analysis based on the work of Lester G. Telser from the University of Chicago by Aaron Jaffe, a student at Brandeis University working on this project as a researcher in the summer of 2002: "The bonds were most likely bought by wealthier members of society using funds that would not otherwise have been marked for consumption. One does not buy long-term government bonds if it would require any substantive change in spending patterns, so it is likely that the bonds were bought, and the bonuses issued, without taking any significant amount of money from the national system. Additionally, upon receipt of their bonuses the veterans spent about 80 percent of their face value in the first few months, leaving the remaining 20 percent untouched an entire

year so it could accumulate interest. (The relatively generous interest rate of 3 percent, which was a full half percent over the national maximum for savings accounts, could only be claimed if the bonus wasn't cashed out for a full year.) The net increase in the money supply during the time when the bonus was issued did not differ greatly from its normal pattern throughout the '30s, so any improvement could not be attributed to inflation. Yet the economy did jump shortly after the issuing of the bonus in '36 and again in '37 when most of the remaining 20 percent of bonus certificates were cashed. The amount of money did not increase drastically because the payment of the bonus was not funded by printing more money, the inflationist technique advocated by Wright Patman. The veterans needed all the money they could get for life's necessities, and since the interest rate on unclaimed bonuses was higher than that of a normal savings account, it was foolish to cash out more than was going to be spent. But, if the money supply wasn't increased, why did the economy improve so sharply shortly after the issuing of bonuses, and to a lesser extent, a year afterward? The reason is that Congress was willing to greatly increase its national debt. The government, in effect, borrowed money from wealthier Americans (in the form of secure and interest-bearing Treasury bonds) and gave it to a substantial minority of poorer Americans (the veterans of World War 1). The enlargement of the national debt actually helped, in the short term, to alleviate the pangs of the Depression."

33. "D.C. Rolls List 1,000 for Bonus," *Washington Star,* June 16, 1936, Bonus Army scrapbook.

34. Gudio van Rijn, *Roosevelt's Blues: African-American Blues and Gospel Songs on FDR* (Jackson: University Press of Mississippi), 122–23.

35. Ibid., 123n.18.

36. Letter to the authors, November 3, 2003.

37. Coughlin obituary, *Washington Post,* October 28, 1979.

38. Material supplied by Jerry Wilkinson, the Upper Keys Historical Society, and through the society's Web page, thefloridakeys.org. The monument accepted the ashes of survivors of the hurricane through the 1970s. In his book *Acts of God: The Unnatural History of Natural Disaster in America*, Theodore Steinberg considered the memorial and put the 1935 hurricane into context: "What little inclination existed to remember the catastrophe itself, however, was drowned out by an act of collective amnesia as buildings rose around the memorial. Homes and commercial buildings flew up just a few feet above high tide. Construction proceeded with little concern for wind resistance. The wake-up call came in 1960, when Hurricane Donna—nearly identical to the earlier system in terms of its path and a close rival in intensity—slammed into the Florida Keys. Although few lives were lost, financially, Donna was Florida's most destructive hurricane to date. 'In the 25 years between Keys disasters,' wrote Stephen Trumbull of the *Miami Herald,* 'the few feeble voices for restrictions have been shouted down by the builders of shoddy if sometimes showy houses—and the fillers of tidal mangrove swamps for sponge-like subdivisions barely above normal high tides'" (79).

Epilogue: The GI Bill—Legacy of the Bonus Army

1. *Washington Post,* November 24, 1943. The ad would run again at least once, on December 8, 1943, and in many other papers.

2. Frank Sinclair, *They Can't Eat Medals* (Milwaukee: Milwaukee Journal, 1943), 51–52.

3. Frank Sinclair, *America Faces a Challenge* (Milwaukee: Milwaukee Journal, 1943), 47.

4. Ibid., 49–50.

5. Moley, *American Legion Story,* 272.

6. Ibid. 273.

7. A search of the *New York Times,* the *Washington Post,* and the *Wall Street Journal* for the first mention of the term "G.I. Bill of Rights" discovered that it first appeared in the *Times* on March 9, 1944: "Formerly known as the American Legion omnibus bill, the bill now carries the endorsement of the Veterans of Foreign Wars." The coining of the name came from American Legion publicist Jack Cejnar, who first called it "a GI Bill of Rights," as it offered federal aid to help veterans adjust to civilian life in the areas of hospitalization, purchase of homes and businesses, and especially, education.

8. "Veterans Need Help Now," *Boston American,* February 28, 1944; Edith Norse Rogers Papers, Series XI news clippings, Schlesinger Library, Radcliffe Institute for Advanced Study, Harvard.

9. "G.I. Enemy No. 1." *Nation,* May 6, 1944, 527.

10. Michael D. Haydock , "The GI Bill," *American History,* September–October, 1999, 52–56, 68–70.

11. "Washington and You" column of June 1, 1944, Smith Library and Archives, scrapbook, vol. 448, 76.

12. It is hard to footnote a negative finding, but a search of the *Evening Star,* the most political of the Washington papers for the period May 25–June 10 did not yield a single article on the GI Bill or the Rankin Committee.

13. President's Official File 4675-R, Franklin D. Roosevelt Library.

14. Thomas A. Rumer, *The American Legion,* (New York: M.Evans and Co., 1990), 247–8.

15. Roosevelt had little to say about or do with the bill before it landed on his desk. Biographer Frank Freidel takes the position that the president was willing to let the veterans' groups and Congress move the bill. "Roosevelt husbanded his waning influence over Congress and did not spend any of it on this measure, so popular that it was not needed. His near silence was probably beneficial at making the bill less attractive as a conservative target." (Friedel, *Launching,* 503.)

16. Both articles are called "The G.I. Bill of Rights," *Newsweek,* May 29, 1944, 33; *Time,* April 3, 1944, 23. Time compared its easy passage in the Senate to a vote against man-eating sharks or the common cold. Neither magazine touched the Rankin racial issue or quoted the college presidents who were so strongly opposed to the bill.

17. Greenberg, *The GI Bill: The Law That Changed America,* (New York: Lickle Publishing, 1997), 18.

18. Robert Maynard Hutchins, "The Threat to American Education," *Collier's* December 30, 1944, 20–21; Milton Greenberg, *The GI Bill: The Law That Changed America,* 39.

19. President's Official File 83, 4675-R, Franklin D. Roosevelt Library.

20. James Brady, "In Appreciation, the GI Bill," *Parade,* August 4, 1996, 4–5.

21. Peter F. Drucker, *Post-Capitalist Society,* (New York: HarperBusiness, 1993), 3. Drucker wrote that 1945, the year when GIs began to take advantage of the bill, marked a divide in world history comparable to 1776, the year the American Revolution began, and also the year James Watt perfected the steam engine and Adam Smith published *The Wealth of Nations.* He also wrote, We are clearly in the middle of this transformation; indeed, if history is any guide, it will not be completed until 2010 or 2020. But already it has changed the political, economic and moral landscape of the world"; Tom Brokaw, *The Greatest Generation* (New York: Random House, 1998), 372.

Appendix A: Long Shadow of the Bonus Army

1. Kenneth C. Davis is the author of *Don't Know Much about History.* In *Newsday,* September 21, 1995 ("Our 'Real History' Is Seldom Tidy"), he wrote that "hundreds" were injured and "two infants died, suffocated by Army tear gas."

2. Weston Kosova, "Bringing the War Home, Gen. MacArthur's Anacostia Campaign," *City Paper* (Washington, D.C.), January 2, 1992.

3. "Bonus Marchers Besiege Washington," *Roll Call,* April 23, 1999 (an edition that included the section "Congress in the 20th Century").

4. "Report on Bonus Expeditionary Force Emergency Camp Johnstown, Penna. Also Other Kindred Matters and Visits," Glassford Papers, UCLA Library Department of Special Collections.

5. Daniels, *Bonus March,* p. 257.

6. Patrick J. Hurley, "The Facts about the Bonus March," *McCall's,* November 1949, 142–43.

7. *Gabriel over the White House, American Film Institute Catalog.*

8. Review of the film *Gold Diggers of 1933, New York Times,* June 8, 1933.

9. Rosenman, *Working with Roosevelt,* 61.

10. Letters to Hays and others are quoted in the *American Film Institute Catalog* entry on *Gabriel over the White House.* The catalog also notes that Louis B. Mayer, a Republican, was appalled by the anti-Hoover tone of the movie and held up release of the film until after the 1932 presidential election.

11. Thomas Doherty, *Pre-Code Hollywood: Sex, Immorality, and Insurrection in American Cinema, 1930–1934* (New York: Columbia University Press, 1999).

12. "Lewis Says Hays Bans Film of Book," *New York Times,* February 16, 1936; "Hays Denies Order to Ban Lewis Film," *New York Times,* February 18, 1936; "Will Hays Bans New Lewis Book As a Movie Play," *Washington Post,* February 16, 1936; "Lewis to Get $1,050 Weekly From WPA for Rights to Play," *Washington Post,* October 30, 1936.

13. Robert Torry, "'You Can't Look Away': Spectacle and Transgressiom in *King Kong*," *Arizona Quarterly* 49, no. 4 (1993): 61–77.

14. "Future War 'Vets' Use Barbed Satire to Take a Dig at War," *Washington Post*, March 22, 1936. The Manifesto was first published in the *Daily Princetonian* of March 14, 1936. Their spoof continued to be one of Princeton's best-known and most fondly remembered jokes, and the papers of the group are housed in the archives at Princeton. The Veterans of Future Wars is also documented by *Time* magazine's film series entitled *March of Time* (vol. 2, no. 4).

15. Gary Dean Best, *The Nickel and Dime Decade: American Popular Culture during the 1930s* (Westport, Conn.: Praeger, 1993), 146.

16. "Future Veterans Said to Total 6,000," *New York Times*, March 24, 1936. The senator was David A. Reed of Pennsylvania.

17. "Future Veterans Bow to Criticism," *New York Times*, March 21, 1936.

18. March 17, 1936, OFO5-OF 95C, FDR Library.

19. "Future Wars Bonus Drive Called 'Crazy,'" *Washington Post*, March 18, 1936.

20. "House Hears Future Veterans Denounced for Unpatriotism," *Washington Post*, April 2, 1936.

21. Oswald Garrison Villiard, "Issues and Men," *Nation*, April 18, 1936, 450.

22. "Future Veterans Amuse First Lady," *Washington Post*, April 3, 1936.

23. "Columbia Seniors Cool to New Deal," *New York Times*, March 25, 1936.

24. "Lobbies for Bonus in College Recess," *New York Times*, April 2, 1936.

25. "Future War 'Vets,'" *Washington Post*, March 22, 1936.

26. "Legion's Depot for Veterans of Future Smacks of Nursery," *Washington Post*, April 25, 1936. The vets got on the radio with the grand opening of the first-aid station and sang the ditty:

Let's be wise, let's be prudent
Sings the modern college student
We will never fight the foe
Unless we're paid before we go

27. The *New York Times* was especially troubled as to how to characterize the Veterans of Future Wars, finally creating the term *serio-satirical* to describe it. "Youth Asks a Program," *New York Times*, June 28, 1936.

28. "The Financial Bookshelf," *Wall Street Journal*, May 4, 1936. Gorin's book was also presented as his senior thesis at Princeton.

29. "New Peace Plan Urged," *New York Times*, June 1, 1936.

30. "Future Veterans Give Up Trenches," *New York Times*, April 4, 1937. The Veterans of Future Wars was brought back for a brief moment on the Princeton campus at the beginning of the Korean War in 1950, according to an item in the October 25, 1950, *Wall Street Journal*. Considered by many a "stale joke," it miscarried almost immediately, marking the organization's final decline.

31. "'Veterans of Future Wars' Are Becoming Just That," *Washington Post*, November 30, 1941.

32. "When Pacificists Decide to Fight," *Washington Post*, January 23, 1944.

33. In 1949, claims of Communist control of the Bonus Army were lavishly publicized by the Hearst press, which ran a series entitled "Inside Story of Plot against Hoover." The series was based on extensive interviews of John Pace, an ex-Communist in 1932 and a Tennessee deputy sheriff when he talked to Hearst reporter Howard Rushmore in 1949. (Pace was elaborating on testimony he had given to a congressional committee.) One of the stories in the Hearst series, published on August 29, 1949, begins: "Hoping for bloodshed and violence, the Communist Party agents within the ranks of the bonus marchers used every Red Fascist trick to get President Hoover to call out the army in 1932." When Hoover and General MacArthur managed to keep blood from being shed, the story continues, "Red Fascist wrath was directed against these two great Americans—a raging 'smear' campaign that has lasted for almost two decades." Pace's story was taken up in the December 1951 *Reader's Digest* as "The Story of a Smear," which aired Pace's claim that the rioting was touched off by "a flying communist wedge carrying an American flag" and that it was a Communist who ripped the badge from Glassford's shirt. In February 1952, the *U.S. Army Combat Forces Journal* carried an article, "When the Army Was Smeared," by Major General. H. W. Blakeley. The subhead: "The Communists turned the bonus march of 1932 intro a vicious slander of the Army." Blakeley quotes from the *Digest* piece and goes on to say, "The Army has been the chief victim, of this smear to

which many newspapers and magazines have been continuing contributors." A new Army view comes in "The Bonus March: A Forgotten Stain," *Military Review,* March–April 2000, in which Bryon Greenwald writes, "In reality, hardly any criminals or communists were" in the Bonus Army. "Ninety-four percent were bonafide veterans and few had ever committed a crime of consequence."

34. *Editor and Publisher,* January 24, 2000, 37.

35. Benjamin Gitlow, *I Confess: The Truth about American Communism* (New York: E. P. Dutton, 1940), 328.

36. Douglas MacArthur, *Reminiscences* (New York: McGraw-Hill, 1964).

37. Lohbeck, *Hurley,* 112.

38. Herbert Hoover, *The Memoirs of Herbert Hoover: The Great Depression, 1929–1941* (New York: Macmillan, 1952), 225. There was more direct Communist opposition in 1932, in the form of Communist Party candidates for president and vice president. William Z. Foster, the Communist candidate, got 103,253 votes; by comparison, Norman Thomas, the Socialist Party, got 884,649 votes.

39. Chalmers M. Roberts, "Aug. 28 'March' Could Prove Negro's Vindication," *Washington Post,* July 21, 1963; "Past Offers Little Encouragement to Negroes Marching on Capitol," *Wall Street Journal,* August 27, 1963.

40. Gerald D. McKnight, *The Last Crusade: Martin Luther King, Jr., the FBI, and the Poor People's Campaign* (Boulder, Colo.: Westview Press, 1998), 22–23.

41. "'Shanty Town' on the Potomac," *New York Times,* May 9, 1968.

42. "Hill Delegation Visits Resurrection City, Promises Hearings," *Washington Post,* June 6, 1968.

43. Paul Hodge, "When the Vets Got a Bruising Sendoff," *Washington Post,* April 25, 1971.

44. Transcript of Oval Office conversation between 4:18 and 4:31 P.M., April 21, 1971, Conversation 485–4, number 1, Nixon Tapes, NARA.

45. Sanford J. Unger, "Mayday Poses Legal Questions," *Washington Post,* May 16, 1971.

46. "Veterans Demand to See Nixon," *New York Times,* July 19, 1974.

47. "Two Viet Vets Plan 'Nixonville' in U.S. Capital," *Chicago Tribune,* June 23, 1974.

48. Jim Abrams, "In the Home of the Brave, Vets Live on the Streets," *Buffalo News,* February 24, 1994.

Appendix B: What Became of Them

1. "State Accuses Girl of Lying for Loeb," *New York Times,* August 8, 1924, p1.

2. Warren Commission report and hearings [microform]. Report of the President's Commission on the Assassination of President John F. Kennedy, Glen Rock, N.J.: Microfilming Corp. of America; Ann Arbor; University Microfilms International [distributor], 1992.

3. From fellow writer and friend Joseph C. Goulden: Abt was identified in Venona cables of April 29, 1944, and May 13, 1944. (Venona was the code name for Soviet intelligence messages intercepted and decrypted by U.S. code breakers.) The New York *rezidentura* (resident spymaster) Akhmerov sent a cable to Moscow discussing a "group in Washington" of which Abt was a member. (He was identified by the code name "Amt.") The cables dealt with the decision that Abt should conceal his Communist membership and continue working covertly to maintain his usefulness. A précis of what Abt did is contained in John Earl Haynes and Harvey Klehr, *Venona: Decoding Soviet Espionage in America* (New Haven, Mass.: Yale University Press, 1999). Abt admitted his Communist membership in his posthumously published autobiography, *Advocate and Activist.*

4. "One-Man Bonus Army Returns to Capital," *Washington Post,* January 4, 1937.

5. "Father Coughlin Breaks Silence," *New York Times,* May 27, 1966.

6. Obituary, *New York Times,* May 19, 1951.

7. "Hourglass," *Washington Post,* January 19, 1936.

8. Carlo D'Este, "Dwight D. Eisenhower: Douglas MacArthur's Whipping Boy," *Military History Quarterly,* winter 2003.

9. "Eisenhower Scored on '32 Bonus 'War,'" *New York Times,* October 25, 1952.

10. The American Legion was founded in March 1919 in Paris. Among the founders were Theodore Roosevelt Jr. and Medal of Honor winner William J. Donovan, who in World War II would lead the Office of Strategic Services, origin of the Central Intelligence Agency. Other early legionnaires were veterans

Ogden Mills, who succeeded Andrew Mellon as secretary of the Treasury in the Hoover administration, and Harold C. Ross, who became editor of *American Legion Weekly* and later founded the *New Yorker.* During his tenure as editor of the *American Legion Weekly,* Ross said, he was told to ignore the bonus issue: "At convention after convention the membership would unanimously vote in favor of the bonus, but the leadership would have none of it. . . . I was given to understand that we on the magazine were suppose to 'kiss it to death.'"

11. Walter J. Stein, *California and the Dust Bowl Migration* (Westport, Conn.: Greenwood Press, 1973), 225.

12. "Memories of a Chief," *Washington Post,* August 20, 1959.

13. Document dated May 1, 1944, RG 226, E 99, Records of the OSS, box 53, folder 3, National Archives.

14. Lohbeck, *Hurley,* 430.

15. Ibid., 454.

16. Oregon Journal, August 28, 1963.

17. *Washington Post,* September 17, 1967.

18. "MacArthur v. Pearson (D.C. Supreme Court, 1934)," *New York Times,* May 17, 1934. Pearson, who had reported firsthand on the eviction for the *Baltimore Sun,* and Allen published a book that contained a sardonic portrayal of MacArthur during the eviction. At one point they had photographers pose MacArthur beside his horse.

19. Oliver Pilat, *Drew Pearson: An Unauthorized Biography* (New York: Harper's Magazine Press, 1973), 141–46.

20. Douglas MacArthur, *Reminiscences,* 110–11.

21. "F.B.I. Jails Noble and Jones after Slur on Gen. MacArthur," *Los Angeles Times,* April 1, 1942.

22. "Two Ex-Generals Term MacArthur Best U.S. Leader in Peace or War," *Los Angeles Times,* April 3, 1948.

23. "Mrs. Evalyn Walsh McLean, Capital Society Leader Dies," *Washington Post,* April 27, 1947.

24. L. Patrick Hughes, "Beyond Denial: Glimpses of Depression-era San Antonio," Austin Community College; published at http://www.austin.cc.tx.us/lpatrick/denial.htm; "Maury Maverick Dies at 58; Former Congressman, Mayor," *Washington Post,* June 8, 1954.

25. Julie P. Means, "My Life With Gaston B. Means," *Washington Times-Herald,* October 15, 1939.

26. "Wisconsin Primary: A Third Party Test," *New York Times,* September 18, 1934.

27. Howard Rushmore, "Ex-Red Tells How 'Smear' of Hoover and MacArthur Started," *New York Journal-American,* August 30, 1939.

28. "Moscow Ordered Riots in 1932 Bonus March," *New York Herald-American,* August 28, 29, and 30, 1949. The articles were reprinted in the *Congressional Record.*

29. Obituary, *Washington Post,* November 28, 1960.

30. Letter to the editor, *Los Angeles Times,* January 19, 1938.

31. Rogers Papers. Marked Korea speech, box 13, folder 170.

32. Day, *Will Rogers,* 291.

33. "D.C. Officer's Alleged Killer Under Arrest," *Washington Post,* May 29, 1935; "D.C. Returning Suspect in Killing of Policeman," April 29, 1939; "Suspect Pleads Not Guilty of Killing Officer," *Washington Post,* May 4, 1939; "Police Say Man Admits Killing Shinault," *Washington Post,* May 1, 1939; "Bullock on Trial Monday in Policeman's Death," *Washington Post,* June 24, 1939; "Willie Bullock Goes on Trial in Shinault Death," *Washington Post,* June 27, 1939; "Bullock's Friend Testifies He Saw Officer Killed," June 28, 1939; "Judge Admits 'Confession' at Bullock Trial," *Washington Post,* June 29, 1939; "Policeman's Slayer Gets Death in Chair," *Times-Herald,* March 13, 1940; "Court Asked to Review Reversal in Murder Case," July 19, 1941; "Bullock Retrial Move Brings Jeopardy Plea," *Washington Post,* November 15, 1941; "Bullock to Face New Murder Trial," *Washington Post,* December 3, 1941; "D.C. Policeman's Slayer Sentenced to 20 Years," *Washington Post,* June 26, 1943; "Death Takes Slayer of Policeman," November 10, 1950.

We asked Sergeant Nick Breul, a homicide detective with the District's Metropolitan Police Department and its unofficial historian, to look over this case, based on a pile of newspaper clippings. "I found the news reports of Shinault's death very interesting, particularly the inconsistencies in location of the incident, where he was shot, and even some speculative journalism regarding whether or not Shinault saw his killer," Breul says. "I would assume that whatever was located at 39 F Street NW or 73 G Street NW is a high-rise now. What is curious to me is why he got so far ahead of his partner, but then died next to the scout car. As a policeman, you would not enter a building, or leap out of a car presumably because you see something, without communicating it to your partner. Most of the reports say he was shot in the front yard, or while entering the residence, and his partner was so far away that he did not see who fired the shot. I don't think the position of 'Emergency Man' [the designation of Shinault's passenger-seat position] means you go and handle the call by yourself. If for a moment I were to put on my Oliver Stone cap, I could see a crafted scenario in which a 'fight call' comes over the radio, they have conveniently switched positions in the car, and Edwards is slow to get out of the car 'looking for his flashlight.'(What time in the night was this? The sun doesn't set until 8:30 or 9 in August.) This delayed Edwards from getting to the house, where the reported disturbance was. This gave enough time to let Shinault get enough separation to be shot—and for Edwards to have plausible deniability, letting the man loose in a maze of alleys. Sounds a little like *Serpico*.

"However, there was at least one eyewitness who testified that it was Bullock who shot Shinault, and he was convicted. I have some faith in the system. While the case is puzzling and so close to the Bonus Army shootings to certainly raise eyebrows, without the full case file, it would be impossible to say they are connected. And it certainly seems reasonable that this was just a 'killin.'"

Bullock died in Lorton Prison of a stroke in 1950. His obituary in the *Washington Post* said, "Police at first believed Shinault had been shot in retaliation for killing William Hushka in line of duty during the bonus army uprising of July, 1932. Then they learned Bullock's identity and began a nationwide search for him."

34. McIver, *Hemingway's Key West*, 67.
35. "Chamber Is Urged to Fight the Bonus," *New York Times*, February 13, 1935.
36. Sheila Graves, "Reflecting on Desperate Times," *Wenatachee World*, February 20, 1992.
37. Roger Wilkins, *A Man's Life* (New York: Simon and Schuster, 1982), 177.

Bibliography

§§§ = Eyewitness accounts of expulsion
^^^ = Eyewitness accounts of trek to Washington and camp life
◉ = Unpublished academic thesis

Abt, John, and Michael Myerson. *Advocate and Activist: Memoirs of an American Communist Lawyer.* Urbana: University of Illinois Press, 1993.

Adams, David. "Internal Military Intervention in the United States." *Journal of Peace and Research* 32, no. 2 (1995): 197–211.

Adams, Samuel Hopkins. *Incredible Era: The Life and Times of Warren Gamaliel Harding.* Boston: Houghton Mifflin, 1939.

Adjutant General of the Army. *American Decorations.* Washington, D.C.: GPO, 1937.

Adkins, Robinson E. *Medical Care of Veterans.* Report prepared for the Committee on Veterans' Affairs. 90th Cong., 1st sess., 1967. Committee Print 4.

Albright, Robert C. "New Deal Estimate of Jobless Well under A.F. of L. Figure; Lone Debate Stirs Calm of Capital Leaders Try to 'Deceive' Public as to Cost, Hastings Says." *Washington Post,* February 26, 1935.

Allen, Anne Beiser, and Jon L. Wakelyn. *An Independent Woman: The Life of Lou Henry Hoover.* Westport, Conn.: Greenwood Press, 2000.

Allen, Frederick Lewis. *Since Yesterday: The Nineteen-thirties in America.* New York: Harper & Brothers, 1939.

Ambrose, Stephen E. *Americans at War.* Jackson: University Press of Mississippi, 1997.

American Automobile Association, *Official Northeastern Tour Book.* Washington, D.C.: American Automobile Association, 1932.

Anderson, Edward. *Hungry Men.* Garden City, N.Y.: Doubleday, 1935.

Anderson, Paul Y. "Tear Gas, Bayonets and Votes." *Nation,* August 17, 1932.

Anderson, Sherwood. *Memoirs.* New York: Harcourt, Brace, 1942.

Archer, Jules. *The Plot to Seize the White House.* New York: Hawthorn, 1973.

Atwell, Edward F. *Washington, the Battle Ground: The Truth about the "Bonus Riots."* Washington, D.C.: Patriotic Publishing Society, 1933.

Baker, Carlos. *Ernest Hemingway: A Life Story.* New York: Scribners, 1969.

Ballads of the B.E.F. New York: Coventry House, 1933.

Barbee, David Rankin. "The Artist Who Became a 'Cop.'" *Washington Post,* November 15, 1931.

Barber, Lucy Grace. *Marching on Washington.* Berkeley: University of California Press, 2002.

Barck, Oscar Theodore Jr. and Manfred B. Nelson. *Since 1900: A History of the United States in Our Times.* New York: Macmillan, 1953.

Bartlett, Carolyn. "The Labor Day Hurricane of '35." *Islamorada Free Press,* August 31, 1988.

Bartlett, John Henry. *The Bonus March and the New Deal.* Chicago: M. A. Donohue, 1937.

Baxter, Jeff. "Bonus Marchers Besiege Washington." *Roll Call,* April 22, 1999.

Beare, Nikki. *Pirates, Pineapples, and People.* Miami: Hurricane House, 1969.

Bendersky, Joseph W. *The "Jewish Threat": Anti-Semitic Politics of the U.S. Army.* New York: Basic Books, 2000.

Bennett, Michael J., *When Dreams Came True: The GI Bill and the Making of Modern America.* Washington, D.C.: Brassey's, 1996.

Bernstein, Irving. *The Lean Years: A History of the American Worker, 1933–1941.* Boston: Houghton Mifflin, 1960.

Berton, Pierre. *The Great Depression, 1929–1939*. Toronto: McClelland & Stewart, 1990.

Best, Gary Dean. *FDR and the Bonus Marchers, 1933–1935*. Westport, Conn.: Praeger, 1992.

———. *The Nickel and Dime Decade: Popular Culture during the 1930s*. Westport, Conn.: Praeger, 1993.

Biles, Roger. *A New Deal for the American People*. DeKalb: Northern Illinois University Press, 1991.

Bird, Caroline. *The Invisible Scar*. New York: Longman, 1966.

§§§ Blakeley, H. W. "When the Army Was Smeared." *Combat Forces Journal*, February 1952.

Blumenson, Martin. *Patton: The Man behind the Legend*. New York: Berkeley, 1985.

———. *The Patton Papers, 1885–1940*. Boston: Houghton Mifflin, 1972.

Boller, Paul F. Jr. *Presidential Campaigns*. New York: Oxford University Press, 1996.

Boothe, Clare. "MacArthur of the Far East: If War Should Come He Leads the Army That Will Fight Japan." *Life*, December 8, 1941.

Brokaw, Tom. *The Greatest Generation*. New York: Random House, 1998.

Brown, E. Francis. "The Bonus Army Marches to Defeat." *Current History* (New York) 36, no. 6 (1932): 684.

Bruner, Felix. "City Planner Designed Large Blocks That Bred Slums.; Fugitive from South Also Helped Build Hidden Hovels." *Washington Post*, January 10, 1934.

Burlingame, Roger. "The Impossible Next War." *Scribner's Magazine*, April, 1936.

Burnett, Gene M. *Florida's Past: People and Events That Shaped the State*. Sarasota, Fla.: Pineapple Press, 1988.

Butler, Smedley D. *War Is a Racket*. Los Angeles: Feral House, 2003 (reprint of original 1935 edition).

Calder, James D. *The Origins and Development of Federal Crime Control Policy: Herbert Hoover's Initiatives*. Westport, Conn.: Praeger, 1993.

Carr, Virginia Spencer. *Dos Passos: A Life*. New York: Doubleday, 1984.

Cassiday, George L. "The Man in the Green Hat." 5-part front-page series. *Washington Post*, October 23, 1930–October 27, 1930.

"Cavalry Major Evicts Veteran Who Saved His Life in Battle." *New York Times*, July 30, 1932.

Chamber of Commerce of the United States of America. *Request to the President of the United States to Veto the Soldier Bonus Bill; Presented by the Chamber of Commerce of the United States*. Washington, D.C.: GPO, [1922].

Chambers, Clarke A. *The New Deal at Home and Abroad, 1929–1945*. New York: Free Press, 1965.

Clausen, John. *American Lives: Looking Back at the Children of the Great Depression*. New York: Maxwell Macmillan International, 1993.

Clayton, James. *The Years of MacArthur. Vol. 1, 1880–1941*. Boston: Houghton Mifflin, 1970.

Coit, Margaret L. *Mr. Baruch: The Man, the Myth, the Eighty Years*. Boston: Houghton Mifflin, 1957.

Congdon, Don. *The '30s: A Time to Remember*. New York: Simon & Schuster, 1962.

Conklin, Paul K. *The New Deal*. 2d ed. Arlington Heights, Ill.: Harlan Davidson, 1975.

§§§ Considine, Bob. *It's All News to Me: A Reporter's Deposition*. New York: Duell, Sloan and Pearce, 1951.

§§§ Cowley, Malcolm. "The Flight of the Bonus Army." *New Republic*, August 17, 1932. Appears in Don Congdon, *The '30s: A Time to Remember*.

◼ Cross, Stuart G. *The Bonus Army in Washington, May 27–July 29, 1932*. Master's thesis, Stanford University, 1948.

Daniels, Roger. *The Bonus March: An Episode of the Great Depression*. Westport, Conn.: Greenwood, 1971.

Davis, Kenneth S. *Soldier of Democracy: A Biography of Dwight Eisenhower*. Garden City, N.Y.: Doubleday, 1945.

Day, Donald. *Will Rogers: A Biography*. New York: David McKay, 1962.

D'Este, Carlo. *Eisenhower: A Soldier's Life*. New York: Henry Holt, 2002.

Dickson, Paul, and William D. Hickman. *Firestone: A Legend. A Century. A Celebration*. New York: Forbes, 2000.

Donnelly, Honoria Murphy. *Sara and Gerald*. With Richard N. Billings. New York: Times Books, 1982.

Douglas, Jack. *Veterans on the March*. New York: Workers Library, 1934.

Douglas, Marjorie Stonernan. *Hurricane*. New York: Rhinehart, 1958.

Drye, Willie. *The Storm of the Century*. Washington, D.C.: National Geographic Books, 2002.

Eckley, Wilton. *Herbert Hoover*. Boston: Twayne, 1980.

Edens, John A. *Eleanor Roosevelt: A Comprehensive Bibliography*. Westport, Conn.: Greenwood Press, 1984.

Eisenhower, Dwight D. *At Ease: Stories I Tell to Friends*. Garden City, N.Y.: Doubleday, 1967.

————. *Eisenhower: The Prewar Diaries and Selected Papers, 1905–1941.* Baltimore: Johns Hopkins University Press, 1988.

Eliot, Thomas H. *Recollections of the New Deal: When the People Mattered.* Edited by John Kenneth Galbraith. Boston: Northeastern University Press, 1992.

◉ Elkins, William F. "Wright Patman and the Veterans' Bonus Issue, 1930–1936." Master's thesis, University of Arizona, 1964.

Ellis, Edward Robb. *A Nation in Torment: The Great American Depression, 1929–1939.* New York: Kodansha Globe, 1995.

Ewy, Marvin. *Charles Curtis of Kansas, Vice President of the United States, 1929–1933.* Emporia: Kansas State Teachers College, Graduate Division, 1961.

Fausold, Martin L. *The Presidency of Herbert C. Hoover.* Lawrence: University of Kansas, 1985.

Federal Writers' Project, Works Progress Administration. *Washington, City and Capital.* Washington, D.C.: GPO, 1937.

Folliard, Edward T. "'Veterans of Future Wars' Are Becoming Just That." *Washington Post,* November 30, 1941.

————. "What a Party the Veterans Had at Their 'Paradise' in Key West; But Let Bill Tell You about It, for He's an Authority; Peace Returns as Men Hail Patman Bonus Bill's Advance." *Washington Post,* March 24, 1935.

Folsom, Franklin. *Impatient Armies of the Poor: The Story of Collective Action of the Unemployed, 1808–1942.* Niwot: University Press of Colorado, 1991.

Foner, Eric and John A. Garraty. *A Reader's Companion to American History.* New York: Houghton Mifflin, 1991.

Freidel, Frank. *Launching the New Deal.* Boston: Little, Brown, 1973.

ᴧᴧᴧ Furman, Bess. *Washington By-line: The Personal History of a Newspaper Woman.* New York: Knopf, 1949.

Galbraith, J. K. *The Great Crash.* 3d ed. Boston: Houghton Mifflin, 1972.

Gallagher, Robert S. "Before the Colors Fade: The Radio Priest." *American Heritage,* October 1972.

Gallico, Paul A. "Drop Ring, Mat License Fees, McCloskey's Clean-up Goal." *Washington Post,* February 28, 1935.

Gerson, Simon W. *Pete: The Story of Peter V. Cacchione, New York's First Communist Councilman.* New York: International Publishers, 1976.

Giblo, Helen. *Footlights, Fistfights and Femmes: The Jimmy Lake Story.* New York: Vantage Press, 1957.

§§§ Giltinan, Caroline. "An Eye-Witness on the Rout of the B.E.F. in Washington." *Fortnightly Review,* September 1932.

Glad, Paul W. *The Dissonance of Change, 1929 to the Present.* New York: Random House, 1970.

Goodrich, David L. "The Day They Gassed the Bonus Army." *Cavalier,* November 1961.

Gosoroski, David M. "'Brotherhood of the Damned' Doughboys Return from the World War." *VFW Magazine,* September 1997.

Graves, Sheila. "Reflecting on Desperate Times." *Wenatchee World,* February 28, 1992.

Green, Constance McLaughlin. *The Secret City: A History of Race Relations in the Nation's Capitol.* Princeton, N.J.: Princeton University Press, 1967.

————. *Washington: A History of the Capital, 1800–1955,* vol. II. Princeton, N.J.: Princeton University Press, 1962.

Green, Harvey. *The Uncertainty of Everyday Life, 1915–1945.* New York: HarperCollins, 1992.

Greenberg, Milton. *The GI Bill: The Law That Changed America.* New York: Lickle, 1997.

Greenwald, Bryon. "The Bonus March: A Forgotten Stain." *Military Review,* March/April 2000.

Griswold, Oliver. *The Florida Keys and the Coral Reef.* Miami: Greywood Press, 1965.

Gunther, John. *The Riddle of MacArthur.* New York: Harper, 1950.

Hallgren, Mauritz A. "The Bonus Army Scares Mr. Hoover." *Nation,* July 27, 1932.

Hardacker, Dana M. "U.S. Veterans and the Bonus Expeditionary Force of 1932." *Historicom: The Illustrated History Journal.*

Harrison, S. L. "Hemingway as Negligent Reporter." *American Journalism,* Vol. II, No. 1, winter 1994, 11–19.

ᴧᴧᴧ Harsch, Joseph C. *At the Hinge of History.* Athens: University of Georgia Press, 1993.

Heaps, Willard A. *Riots, U.S.A., 1765–1965.* New York: The Seabury Press, 1966.

Hearn, Charles. *The American Dream in the Great Depression.* Westport, Conn.: Greenwood Press, 1977.

Heineman, Kenneth J. *A Catholic New Deal: Religion and Reform in Depression Pittsburgh.* University Park: Pennsylvania State University Press, 1999.

Hemingway, Ernest. *Selected Letters, 1917–1961.* Edited by Carlos Baker. New York: Charles Scribner's Sons, 1981.

———. *To Have and Have Not.* New York: Scribners, 1937.

———. "Who Murdered the Vets?" *New Masses,* September 17, 1935.

◼ Hennessy, Arthur Leo. "The Bonus Army: Its Roots, Growth, and Demise." Doctoral thesis, Georgetown University, 1957.

Hicks, John D. *Republican Ascendancy, 1921–1933.* New York: Harper and Row, 1960.

Hines, Frank T. *Veterans' Relief: Statement on Veterans' Relief Looking to the Adoption of a National Policy.* U.S. Senate, 72d Cong., 2d sess., 1932.

Hinshaw, David. *Herbert Hoover: American Quaker.* New York: Farrar, 1950.

Hodge, Paul. "When the Vets Got a Bruising Sendoff." *Washington Post,* April 25, 1971.

Hogan, Bill. "The Battle of Anacostia Flats." *Regardie's,* August/September, 1982.

Hoover, Herbert. *The Memoirs of Herbert Hoover: Years of Adventure, 1874–1920.* New York: Macmillan, 1951.

———. *The Memoirs of Herbert Hoover: The Great Depression, 1929–1941.* New York: Macmillan, 1952.

———. *The Memoirs of Herbert Hoover: The Cabinet and the Presidency, 1920–1933.* New York: Macmillan, 1952.

———. "Text of Hoover's Statement on Calling for Troops to Put an End to Bonus Rioting in the Capital." *New York Times.* July 29, 1932.

"Hoover Says Bonus Undermines Credit." *New York Times,* March 30, 1932.

"Hoover Outlines Economy Program; Demands Congress set up Joint Board: Legion Head Backs President on Bonus." *New York Times,* April 6, 1932.

Hoover, Irwin H. (Ike). *Forty-two Years in the White House.* Boston: Houghton Mifflin, 1934.

Hunt, Frazier. *The Untold Story of Douglas MacArthur.* New York: Devin-Adair, 1954.

Hurley, Patrick J. "The Facts about the Bonus Match." *McCall's,* November 1949, 2, 142–43.

Ickes, Harold L. *The Secret Diary of Harold L. Ickes: The First Thousand Days, 1933–1936.* New York: Simon and Schuster, 1953.

Jackson, Gardner. "Unknown Soldiers." *Survey,* August 1, 1932.

James, D. C. *The Years of MacArthur, 1880–1941.* Boston: Houghton Mifflin, 1964.

Jenkins, Philip. *Hoods and Shirts: The Extreme Right in Pennsylvania, 1925–1950.* Chapel Hill: University of North Carolina Press, 1977.

Johnson, Gerald W. "The Bonus That Was Earned." *Harpers Magazine,* September 1936.

Johnson, Walter. *1600 Pennsylvania Avenue: Presidents and the People, 1929–59.* Boston: Little, Brown, 1960.

Jones, W. H. Jr. "The Use of Tanks in Quelling Civil Disturbances." *Tank Studies,* U.S. Army Tank School (1932): 165–77.

◼ Jorgensen, Lawrence C. "The Bonus Expeditionary Force, 1932." Master's thesis, University of Chicago, 1963.

Joslin, Theodore G. *Hoover off the Record.* Garden City, N.Y.: Doubleday, 1934.

Kaltenborn, H. V. *It Seems Like Yesterday.* New York: G. P. Putnam's Sons, 1956.

Keene, Jennifer D. *Doughboys, the Great War, and the Remaking of America.* Baltimore: Johns Hopkins University Press, 2001.

Kelley, Frank, and Cornelius Ryan. *MacArthur: Man of Action.* Garden City, N.Y.: Doubleday, 1950.

Kennedy, David M. *Freedom from Fear: The American People in Depression and War, 1929–1945.* New York: Oxford University Press, 1999.

Killigrew, John W. "The Army and the Bonus Incident." *Military Affairs,* summer 1962.

Kiplinger, Austin. "Growing Up in Washington, I: An Inside-Outside View," *Washington History,* fall/winter 2000–2001.

Kleinberg, Howard. "Storm Killed 256 War Veterans." *Miami News,* July 31, 1982.

Kleinholz, George. *The Battle of Washington: A National Disgrace.* New York: B. E. F. Press, 1932.

Knight, Amy W. and Robert L. Worden. *Veterans Benefits Administration: An Organizational History, 1776–1994.* Collingdale, Pa.: Diane, 1995.

Kohn, Richard H. "Out of Control: The Crisis in Civil Military Relations," *National Interest*, spring, 1994.

Kosova, Weston. "Bringing the War Home." *City Paper*, Washington, D.C., December 20, 1991.

Lamar, Sewilla. "I Marched with the Bonus Army." *Abbott's Monthly*, September 1932.

Laurie, Clayton D., and Ronald H. Cole. *The Role of Federal Military Forces in Domestic Disorders, 1877–1945*. Washington, D.C.: GPO, 1997.

Lee, Clark, and Richard Henschel. *Douglas MacArthur*. New York: Henry Holt, 1952.

Leffingwell, R.C. "The Soldier and His Bonus." *Saturday Evening Post*, May 15, 1920.

Leuchtenburg, William Edward. *Franklin D. Roosevelt and the New Deal, 1932–1940*. New York: Harper and Row, 1963.

Liebovich, Louis. *Press Reaction to the Bonus March of 1932: A Re-evaluation of the Impact of an American Tragedy*, Columbia, S.C.: Association for Education in Journalism and Mass Communication, 1990.

Lisio, Donald J. *The President and Protest: Hoover, Conspiracy, and the Bonus Riot*. Columbia: University of Missouri, 1974.

———. *The President and Protest: Hoover, MacArthur, and the Bonus Riot*. New York: Fordham University Press, 1994.

Lohbeck, Don. *Patrick J. Hurley*. Chicago: Regnery, 1956.

Long, Gavin. *MacArthur as Military Commander*. Conshohocken, Pa.: Combined Publishing, 1998.

Louchheim, Katie. *The Making of the New Deal: The Insiders Speak*. Cambridge, Mass.: Harvard University Press, 1983.

Lovin, Clifford R. "Herbert Hoover, Internationalist, 1919–1923." *Prologue* 20, no. 4 (Winter 1988).

Ludington, Townsend, ed. *The Fourteenth Chronicle: Letters and Diaries of John Dos Passos*. Boston: Gambit, 1973.

———. *John Dos Passos: A Twentieth Century Odyssey*. New York: E. P. Dutton, 1980.

◾ Lutino, Cielo Marie Dorado. "Constructing Historical Memory: The Bonus March and the Great Depression." Undergraduate thesis, Reed College, May 1994.

Lyons, Eugene. *Our Unknown Ex-President*. Garden City, N.Y.: Doubleday, 1948.

MacArthur, Douglas. *Reminiscences*. New York: McGraw-Hill, 1964.

^^^ Maher, Daniel B. "One Slain, 60 Hurt as Troops Rout B.E.F. with Gas Bombs and Flames; Anacostia Huts Fired; Men Are Denied Right to Return to Capital." *Washington Post*, July 29, 1932.

Maloney, John W. "Science Battles Death and Disease in Wake of the Great Hurricane; Workers with Masks in Stricken Region Seek to Avert Pestilence." *Washington Post*, September 8, 1935.

Manchester, William. *American Caesar: Douglas MacArthur, 1880–1940*. Boston: Little, Brown, 1976.

———. *The Glory and the Dream*. Boston: Little, Brown, 1974.

———. Letter to the Editor. *New York Times*, November 4, 1990.

———. "Rock Bottom in America." *New York Magazine*. undated, early 1976.

Mann, Arthur. *La Guardia: A Fighter against His Times, 1882–1933*. Chicago: University of Chicago Press, 1959.

Marcus, Sheldon. *Father Coughlin: The Tumultuous Life of the Priest of the Little Flower*. Boston: Little, Brown, 1973.

Marsh, Benjamin C. *Lobbyist for the People: A Record of Fifty Years*. Washington, D.C.: Public Affairs Press, 1953.

Mason, Herbert M. Jr. "Battling for the Bonus." *Veterans of Foreign Wars Magazine*, May 1999.

McDonald, W. F. "The Hurricane of August 31 to September 6, 1935." *Mon. Weather Review* 63 (1935): 269–71.

McElvaine, Robert S. *The Depression and New Deal: A History in Documents*. New York : Oxford University Press, 2000.

———. *Down and Out in the Great Depression: Letters from the "Forgotten Man."* Chapel Hill: University of North Carolina Press, 1983.

McGee, Dorothy Horton. *Herbert Hoover: Engineer, Humanitarian, Statesman*. Rev. ed. New York: Dodd, Mead, 1965.

McGoff, Kevin. "The Bonus Army." *American History Illustrated* 12, no. 10 (1978), 28–37.

McIver, Stuart B. *Hemingway's Key West*. Sarasota, Fla.: Pineapple Press, 1993.

M'Kee, Oliver Jr. "The Bonus Battle." *Washington Post*, September 27, 1932.

McLean, Evalyn Walsh. *Father Struck It Rich*. With Boyden Sparkes. Boston: Little, Brown, 1936.

§§§ Meisel, Henry Otto. *Bonus Expeditionary Forces: The True Facts, 1932.* Clintonville, Wis.: privately printed, 1932.

———. *The Second "Bonus Army."* Clintonville, Wis.: privately printed, 1933.

Methvin, Eugene H. *The Riot Makers: The Technology of Social Demolition.* New Rochelle, N.Y.: Arlington House, 1970.

Mettler, Suzanne. "Bringing the State Back in to Civic Engagement: Policy Feedback Effects of the G.I. Bill for World War II Veterans." *American Political Science Review,* June 2002.

Moley, Raymond. *The American Legion Story.* Westport, Conn.: Greenwood Press, 1966.

§§§ Monk, Edmund G. "The Day the Bonus Army Was Defeated." *Sunday Star,* Washington, D.C., July 27, 1957.

Morrow, Felix. *Bonus March.* New York: International, 1932.

National Industrial Conference Board. *The Soldiers' Bonus.* New York: NICB, 1923.

O'Connor, Harvey. *Mellon's Millions: The Biography of a Fortune; the Life and Times of Andrew W. Mellon.* New York: John Day, 1933.

Ottanelli, Fraser M. *The Communist Party of the United States.* New Brunswick, N.J.: Rutgers University Press, 1991.

Parker, Robert V. "The Bonus March of 1932: A Unique Experience in North Carolina Political and Social Life." *North Carolina Historical Review,* January (1971): 64–89.

Parks, Lillian Rogers. *My Thirty Years Backstairs at the White House.* New York: Fleet, 1961.

Parks, Pat. *The Railroad That Died at Sea: The Florida East Coast's Key West Extension.* Brattleboro, Vt.: Stephen Greene Press, 1968.

Parsons, Wilfred S. J. "The Rout of the Bonus Army." *America,* August 13, 1932.

Patman, Wright. *Handbook for Servicemen and Servicewomen of World War II and Their Dependents, Including Rights and Benefits of Veterans of World War II and Their Dependents.* Washington, D.C.: GPO, 1942.

———. *Handbook for Servicemen and Servicewomen of World War Ii and Their Dependents, Including Rights and Benefits of Veterans of World War I and Their Dependents.* Washington, D.C.: GPO, 1945.

Patton, George S. Jr. "Federal Troops in Domestic Disturbances." *Military Essays and Articles by George S. Patton, Jr.,* edited by Charles M. Province. George S. Patton, Jr. Historical Society, San Diego, Calif., 2002.

Patton, Robert H. *The Pattons: A Personal History of an American Family.* New York: Crown, 1994.

Pilat, Oliver. *Drew Pearson: An Unauthorized Biography.* New York: Harper's Magazine Press, 1973.

Perkins, Dexter. *The New Age of Franklin Roosevelt, 1932–1945.* Chicago: University of Chicago Press, 1957.

Perret, Geoffrey. *Eisenhower.* New York: Random House, 1999.

———. "MacArthur and the Marchers." *MHQ: The Quarterly Journal of Military History* 8 (winter 1996): 74–79.

———. *Old Soliders Never Die: The Life of Douglas MacArthur.* New York: Random House, 1996.

Phillips, Cabell. *1929–1939: From the Crash to the Blitz.* New York: Macmillan, 1969.

———. *The 1940s: Decade of Triumph and Trouble.* New York: Macmillan, 1975.

Powell, Talcott. *Tattered Banners.* New York: Harcourt, Brace, 1933.

Powers, Richard Gid. *The Life of J. Edgar Hoover: Secrecy and Power.* New York: Free Press, 1987.

Price, John W. "The Army Evicts the Bonus Marchers." *Military Review* 21 (May 1971): 56–65.

Principe, Anthony J. "Meeting America's Promise." *Officer,* August 2001.

§§§ Purdy, Elbridge C. "Eyewitness Account of Bonus March Incident Including the Burning of the Camp at Anacostia, 1932." Transcript of testimony on file, MacArthur Archives, Norfolk, Va.

Putnam, Carl M. "The CCC Experience." *Military Review* 53, no. 9 (1973): 49–62.

Rasch, Bradley W. "Consequence: A Forgotten Concept." *Phi Beta Kappan,* July 1997.

Rauch, Basil. *The History of the New Deal.* New York: Creative Age Press, 1944.

Raymond, Harry. "The Siege of the Capital." *New Masses,* July 1932.

Reese, Phillip. "Soldier's Diary Draws Interest of NPR, Shows Steve Murray Marched with the So-Called Bonus Army in 1932, Demanding Payments Promised to Soldiers by the US Government." *Greensboro (N.C.) News Record,* June 24, 2000.

Resch, John. *Suffering Soldiers: Revolutionary War Veterans, Moral Sentiment, and Political Culture in the Early Republic.* Amherst: University of Massachusetts Press, 1999.

Reynolds, Michael. *Hemingway: The Thirties.* New York: Norton, 1997.

Rich, Bennett Milton. *The Presidents and Civil Disorder.* Washington, D.C.: Brookings Institution, 1941.

Rogers, Will. *The Autobiography of Will Rogers.* Edited by Donald Day. Boston: Houghton Mifflin, 1949.

Roosevelt, Eleanor. *This I Remember.* New York: Harper and Brothers, 1949.

Roosevelt, Franklin D. "The Forgotten Man." Speech, April 7, 1932, from *The Public Papers and Addresses of Franklin D. Roosevelt,* vol 1, *1928–32* (New York City: Random House, 1938), 624.

Rosenman, Samuel I. "Working with Roosevelt." New York: Harper and Brothers, 1952.

Ross, Davis R. B. *Preparing for Ulysses: Politics and Veterans during World War II.* New York: Columbia University Press, 1969.

Rudeen, Marlys, ed. *The Civilian Conservation Corps Camp Papers: A Guide.* Chicago: Center for Research Libraries, 1991.

Schlesinger, Arthur M. Jr. *The Age of Roosevelt.* Vol. 2, *The Coming of the New Deal.* Boston: Houghton, 1959.

Schmidt, Hans. *Maverick Marine : General Smedley D. Butler and the Contradictions of American Military History.* Lexington: University Press of Kentucky, 1987.

Schnapper, M. B. *American Labor: A Bicentennial History.* Washington, D.C.: Public Affairs Press, 1975.

Schorr, Daniel. "Roll Back to the Days before F.D.R.? No Way." *Christian Science Monitor,* April 21, 1985.

Seldes, Gilbert. *The Years of the Locust.* Boston: Little, Brown, 1933.

Severo, Richard, and Lewis Milford. *The Wages of War: When America's Soldiers Came Home—From Valley Forge to Vietnam.* New York: Simon and Schuster, 1989.

Semmes, Harry H. *Portrait of Patton.* New York: Paperback Library, 1955.

Sexton, Patricia Cayo. *The War on Labor and the Left.* Boulder, Colo.: Westview Press, 1992.

◉ Sherwood, Edwin Douglas. "Wright Patman and the Bonus Episode." Master's thesis, Lamar University, 1988.

◉ Simchak, Matthew Stephen. "The Bonus March of 1932: The Failure of a Radical Alternative." Master's thesis, Trinity College, Hartford, Conn., 1969.

Sinclair, Frank. *America Faces a Challenge.* Milwaukee: Milwaukee Journal, 1943.

———. *They Can't Eat Medals.* Milwaukee: Milwaukee Journal, 1943.

Smith, Gene. *The Shattered Dream: Herbert Hoover and the Great Depression.* New York: William Morrow, 1970.

Smith, Page. *Redeeming the Time: A People's History of the 1920s amd the New Deal.* New York: Penguin Books, 1987.

Smith, Richard Norton. *An Uncommon Man: The Triumph of Herbert Hoover.* New York: Simon and Schuster, 1984.

———. *Wounded Soldiers Come Home . . . What Then?.* Milwaukee: Milwaukee Journal, 1943.

◉ Sneller, Maurice P. Jr. "The Bonus March of 1932: A Study of Depression Leadership and Its Legacy." Master's thesis, University of Virginia, Charlottesville, Va., 1960.

Snoman, Daniel. *America Since 1920.* New York: Harper and Row, 1968.

Snyder, Louis L. *A Treasury of Great Reporting.* New York: Simon and Schuster, 1949.

Solomon, Mark. *The Cry Was Unity: Communists and African Americans, 1917–36.* Jackson: University Press of Mississippi, 1998.

Specter, Arlen. *Passion for Truth.* New York: William Morrow, 2000.

Standiford, Les. *Last Train to Paradise: Henry Flagler and the Spectacular Rise and Fall of the Railroad That Crossed an Ocean.* New York: Three Rivers Press, 2002.

Starling, Colonel Edmund W. and Thomas Sugrue. *Starling of the White House: The Story of the Man Whose Secret Service Detail Guarded Five Presidents from Woodrow Wilson to Franklin D. Roosevelt.* New York: Simon & Schuster, 1946.

Stiles, Lela. *The Man behind Roosevelt: The Story of Louis McHenry Howe.* Cleveland, Ohio: World Publishing, 1954.

§§§ Strout, Richard L. "Capitol Riots Like Great Movie Unroll before 'Grandstand' Seat," *Christian Science Monitor,* July 29, 1932.

———. "Vet Protests—1932, 1971." *Christian Science Monitor,* April 24, 1971.

Sullivan, Lawrence. "B.E.F. Hid Explosives Here, Johnson Says; Representative Declares U.S. Will Prove Reds Inspired Men." *Washington Post,* August 16, 1932.

◉ Telser, Lester G. "The Veterans' Bonus of 1936 and the Abortive Recovery from the Great Depression." Master's thesis, University of Chicago, 2000.

Terkel, Studs. *Hard Times: An Oral History of the Great Depression.* New York: Pantheon, 1970.

Thomas, Lowell. *Old Gimlet Eye: The Adventures of Smedley D. Butler as Told to Lowell Thomas.* Illustrated by Paul Brown. New York: Farrar & Rinehart, 1933.

Thurston, Elliott. "First Reel of Rooseveltian National Drama Draws to Exciting Close; Swift Action Keeps Climax Still Vague." *Washington Post,* February 25, 1934.

"Future Veterans." *Time,* March 30, 1936.

Time Capsule: 1933. New York: Time Incorporated, 1967.

Torry, Robert. "'You Can't Look Away': Spectacle and Transgression in King Kong." *Arizona Quarterly* 49, no. 4 (1993): 61–77.

Trout, Steven. "Where Do We Go from Here? Ernest Hemingway's 'Soldier's Home' and American Veterans of World War I (2)." *Hemingway Review,* January 2000.

§§§ Truscott, Lucian King. *The Twilight of the U.S. Cavalry: Life in the Old Army, 1917–1942.* Edited by Lucian K. Truscott III. Lawrence: University Press of Kansas, 1989.

Tugwell, Rexford G. "Roosevelt and the Bonus Marchers of 1932." *Political Science Quarterly* 87, no. 3 (1972): 363–76.

U.S. Congress. Joint Committee on Veterans' Affairs. *Veterans' Affairs* vol. 4. 72d Cong., 2d sess., February 1933.

U.S. House of Representatives. *Appropriation for Veterans Temporarily Quartered in District of Columbia.* 72d Cong, 1st sess., 1931.

U.S. House of Representatives. Committee on Un-American Activities. *Communist Tactics Among Veterans' Groups.* 82d Cong., 1st sess., 1951.

U.S. House of Representatives. Committee on Ways and Means. *Payment of Adjusted-Compensation Certificates.* 72d Cong., 2d sess., January 1931.

U.S. House of Representatives. Committee on World War Veterans' Legislation, *Florida Hurricane Disaster.* Washington, D.C.: GPO, 1936.

U.S. Military Intelligence Reports. *Surveillance of Radicals in the U.S., 1917–1941.* Edited by Randolph Boehm. Frederick, Md.: University Publications of America, 1984. Microfilm reels containing extensive files on the Bonus Army (reels 21 and 22).

United States. Pension Office. *Annual Report of the Bureau of Pensions,* September 25, 1930.

Unofficial Observer. "Mrs. Roosevelt a Driving Force in New Deal; First Lady's Life Crowded with Action She's Given Credit for First Leading F.D.R. into Politics. Energy, Wide Interests Unprecedented among Presidents' Wives." *Washington Post,* March 4, 1934.

^^^ Vidal, Gore. *Screening History.* Cambridge, Mass.: Harvard University Press, 1992.

Villiard, Oswald Garrison. "Issues and Men." *Nation,* April 8, 1936, 450.

Walch, Timothy. *Eisenhower: The Prewar Diaries and Selected Papers, 1905–1941.* Baltimore: Johns Hopkins University Press, 1988.

Waldrop, Frank C. "General MacArthur, the True Soldier, Leaves the Army." *Washington Herald-Times,* October 17, 1937.

Walter, Edward. *The Rise and Fall of Leftist Radicalism in America.* Westport, Conn.: Praeger, 1992.

Warren, Harris G. *Herbert Hoover and the Great Depression.* Westport, Conn.: Greenwood Publishing Group, 1959.

Waters, Walter W. *B.E.F., the Whole Story of the Bonus Army.* With William C. White. New York: AMS Press, 1970 (reprinted from 1933 edition).

Watkins, Tom H. *The Hungry Years: A Narrative History of the Great Depression in America.* New York: Henry Holt, 1999.

———. *The Great Depression: America in the 1930's.* Boston: Little, Brown, 1993.

Weaver, John D. *Another Such Victory.* New York: Viking Press, 1948.

———. "Bonus March." *American Heritage* 14, no. 4 (1963): 18–23, 92–97.

Webb, Robert N. *The Bonus March on Washington, D.C.: May–June 1932.* New York: Franklin Watts, 1969.

Wechsler, James. "Treason among the Future Veterans." *Nation,* May 27, 1936.

Wecter, Dixon. *The Age of the Great Depression, 1929–1941.* New York: Macmillan, 1948.

Weigley, Russell F. "The American Military and the Principle of Civilian Control from McClellan to Powell." *Journal of Military History* 57, no. 5 (October 1993).

White, Owen P. "General Glassford's Story." *Collier's,* October 29, 1932.

White, William A. *A Puritan in Babylon.* New York: Macmillan, 1938.

————. "The Story of a Smear." *Reader's Digest,* December 1951.

Wilkins, Roy. "The Bonuseers Ban Jim Crow." *Crisis,* October 1932.

————. *Standing Fast: The Autobiography of Roy Wilkins.* With Tom Mathews. New York: Viking Press, 1982.

Winslow, Susan. *Brother, Can You Spare a Dime: America from the Wall Street Crash to Pearl Harbor.* New York: Paddington Press, 1976.

Zinn, Howard. *LaGuardia in Congress.* Westport, Conn.: Greenwood Press, 1972.

Zipser, Arthur. *Workingclass Giant: The Life of William Z. Foster.* New York: International Publishers, 1981.

The following publications were those most frequently consulted for reference.

Baltimore Sun, B.E.F. News, Chicago Tribune,, Christian Century, Christian Science Monitor, Cleveland Advocate, Los Angeles Times, The Nation, The New Republic, Newsweek, New York Times, The Oregonian, The Oregon Journal, Philadelphia Inquirer, Philadelphia Public Ledger, Stars and Stripes*, Time, The Wall Street Journal, The Washington Daily News, The Washington Post, and *The Washington Tribune*

*The full World War I run of this Paris-based newspaper is on-line through the Library of Congress American Memory.

Page numbers in *italics* refer to illustrations and maps.
Page numbers from 301 refer to endnotes.